Competition
and Controls
in Banking

Competition and Controls in Banking

A STUDY OF THE REGULATION
OF BANK COMPETITION IN
ITALY, FRANCE, AND ENGLAND

David A. Alhadeff

PUBLICATIONS OF THE INSTITUTE OF
BUSINESS AND ECONOMIC RESEARCH
UNIVERSITY OF CALIFORNIA

UNIVERSITY OF CALIFORNIA PRESS
Berkeley and Los Angeles, 1968

University of California Press
Berkeley and Los Angeles, California

Cambridge University Press
London, England

Library of Congress Catalog Card Number: 68–26063
Printed in the United States of America

To Charlotte

To Charlotte

Preface

The regulation of bank competition has been a highly controversial topic in the U. S. for several years, and during the past few years this question has come increasingly to the fore in many European countries as well. Much of the controversy centers on the indirect controls (e.g., merger or entry regulations) and direct controls (e.g., various rate regulations) that governments can use to regulate bank competition. Indirect controls can affect bank behavior by their impact on the market structure of banking markets; direct controls can have a direct impact on bank behavior. An analysis of the possible market effects of regulating bank competition must consider not only the particular kinds and forms but also the particular combinations of the controls. It is the purpose of this volume to explore the complex relationships in this largely uncharted area. While this study deals with a critical concern of public policy, its emphasis is entirely on analysis, not prescription.

This study of the regulation of bank competition is based on the legal and institutional frameworks of three countries: Italy, France, England. In each case, I have examined the major kinds, forms, and combinations of controls that affect bank competition and have analyzed their effects in terms of the market structure of banking markets, the operations of banking markets, and the efficacy of monetary policy. I have also drawn upon the experience in these three countries to test a hypothesis about a particularly important aspect of the interrelation of the regulations on banking structure and those on the conditions of bank competition. According to a widely held view (so much taken for granted that it is almost never examined), governments which make, or are willing to make, extensive use of direct (especially rate) controls on bank competition can afford to ignore the nature of the market structure in banking markets on the grounds that direct controls per se can attain the desired market results. This hypothesis (which is probably based on an implicit analogy with government regulation of public utilities) has been tested against the experience in Italy, France, and England where the authorities, acting either directly or through government-approved bank ententes, have made extensive use of direct controls on bank competition.

ix

To my knowledge, the present study is unique in its attempt to present a detailed and systematic analysis of the regulation of bank competition in terms of the interrelation of the regulation of banking structure and the regulation of the conditions of bank competition. In order to show how different regulatory frameworks have affected the structure and performance of banking markets, and the efficacy of monetary policy, I was also obliged to develop (as far as existing data allowed) my own analysis of the market structure of banking markets in each of the countries included in this study. Thus, as a by-product of its major objective, this study has helped to fill a serious gap in the literature on European banking, which is still overwhelmingly institutional and descriptive. I hope that others with a deeper and more intimate knowledge of those banking systems will be enticed to carry further the examination that has been opened in these pages.

A number of important changes in the banking structures and competitive rules occurred during the course of this study. In France in particular, the authorities began in 1965 to make drastic changes in the rules which govern the structure and conditions of bank competition. I have included a discussion of the major reforms that were announced through the first half of 1967, but I have not slighted the prereform period. Indeed, in a volume whose main purpose is to study the regulation of bank competition, the analysis of the prereform period of heavy regulation is more interesting and can shed more light on the major questions raised in this inquiry than a study of the more recent moves to dismantle the regulatory framework. The analysis of the prereform period also provides an excellent background for assessing the market significance of the recent reforms and of the additional reforms that are sure to follow.

It is a pleasure to acknowledge my many debts in connection with this study and to express my appreciation to all those who have contributed to it. This study was launched during a sabbatical leave in Europe in the spring semester, 1963. I am grateful to friends on the staff of the Federal Reserve Board who provided me with letters of introduction for a number of interviews in Italy, France, and England. I remember with gratitude and pleasure the many hours of stimulating conversation with European bankers, government officials, economists, and others.

I am particularly indebted to Dr. Gian Franco Calabresi, Director of the Associazione Bancaria Italiana, and to Dr. André Boccon-Gibod, Inspector General of the Bank of France; both were kind enough to read some of the chapters in this study and to give me their comments. In thanking them, I wish also to relieve them from responsibility for any views and conclusions I have expressed.

I am also highly indebted to the Ford Foundation for a fellowship that made it possible for me to devote full time to this project during the academic year 1964–1965. Throughout the duration of this study, I have benefited from the devoted assistance and counsel of my wife, Charlotte P. Alhadeff. The accuracy of this volume, especially in the statistical information, has been improved by her skill and diligence in tracking down, filling gaps in, and resolving ambiguities in the source materials.

Chapter XI is substantially similar to an article on "The Abolition of the Official Minimum Loan Rate in France," which was published in the Banca Nazionale del Lavoro, *Quarterly Review*, September, 1967; and I am grateful to the editor, Dr. Luigi Ceriani, for permission to reprint much of that article in the present volume.

Finally, I wish to express my appreciation for the clerical assistance provided by the Institute of Business and Economic Research at the University of California, Berkeley. The manuscript was ably typed by Miss Adrienne Demarest, assisted by Miss Lillian Demarest.

David A. Alhadeff

August, 1967

Contents

Part Four: INTERNATIONAL COMPARISONS

Introduction

In all modern economies, the banking system plays a central role in the economic functions of mobilizing the country's savings, supplying a chief means of payment, and allocating economic resources. In an attempt to ensure that the banking system will perform these vital functions in an optimal manner, governments establish rules which banks must observe. This study is about two sets of rules that affect bank competition: rules about banking structure, and rules about the conditions of bank competition. Rules about banking structures are concerned with mergers, entry, branching, and so forth; rules about the conditions of bank competition are concerned with actual or limit rates in loan and deposit markets, geographic zones of activity, and so forth. As modern governments have typically chosen to regulate on both counts, they have also had to determine the precise kind and extent of regulation to establish in each set. The rules about the banking structure may be aimed at achieving a competitive structure, a monopolistic structure, or some intermediate form of market organization. The rules about the conditions of bank competition may provide for intensive regulation of bank behavior, for little or no regulation, or for some intermediate amount. It is the purpose of this study to examine the regulations about banking structure and the conditions of banking competition: their variety and extent, their effects on the structure and operations of banking markets, and their role as adjuncts of monetary and economic control.

This study has been divided into four parts. Parts One, Two, and Three deal with the regulation of bank competition in Italy, France, and England respectively. There are six chapters on each country, and a broadly similar format has been employed to examine the nature and impact of the competitive controls in the three countries. The first chapter in each part provides a brief introduction to the banking system of the country—the major banks, the diversity of the banking structure, the rationale for including some banks and not others—and some of the historical circumstances of the banking evolution and development in each country that have left their mark on the outlook of the present-day banks.

1

The second chapter deals with the regulation of bank concentration in each country. This includes a discussion of the present levels of bank concentration and how they came about, as well as the rules which each government has prescribed to influence the banking structure and bank concentration.

The third chapter discusses the regulations on the conditions of bank competition, especially the regulations about deposit rates, loan rates, and geographic zones of activity: How and why did the direct controls on competition originate? What purpose (or purposes) were they originally intended to serve? Has that purpose changed over time? What are the exact forms of the controls in each country? It will be shown that the forms of the direct controls on bank competition have often remained unchanged in spite of drastic changes in the objectives of competitive regulation. This raises the further question (to be examined at a later point) of whether the forms of the controls are still appropriate for the ends they are now intended to serve.

The next two chapters examine how each country's particular combination of regulations on bank concentration and on the conditions of bank competition has affected the structure and operations of its banking markets. The banking markets included in this study—counterparts of the important economic functions (mentioned above) performed by banks in each country—are the markets for transactions deposits, short-term savings deposits, and short-term business loans. Because a given set of rules can have quite different results on different banking markets, the relation between the market behavior of those markets and the rules on banking structure and conditions of competition is particularly complex. In this part of the analysis, it will also be possible to observe the relation between the level of competition which the regulatory authorities may have intended to preserve (when they initiated or sanctioned the restraints on competition) and the level which has in fact been attained. A number of other important aspects of the regulation of bank competition are also examined in these chapters: How have the controls on bank competition been affected by competition from other kinds of financial institutions? Are the direct controls on bank competition widely violated or scrupulously observed? Have the control systems been sufficiently flexible to meet changing credit conditions, or have they imparted rigidity to both the structure and the level of rates? What have been the consequences of the controls for banks? For bank customers? How have the control systems dealt with depositors and borrowers? Has one group been systematically favored over the other? Has the balance between them been sought by deliberate policy or has it been an unintended by-product of the control systems? Do the controls bear evenly on all banks, especially on large and small banks? Under a system of controls to restrain bank competition, do some borrowers and depositors enjoy the benefits of greater bank competition than other borrowers and depositors? If so, are these differences related to size? More generally, do large and small borrowers have different bargaining power in systems where cartels can restrict competition with government sanction and, in some cases, enforcement? Have the control systems conferred monopoly advantages on the banks at the expense of borrowers or depositors? How, if at all, have the governments sought to prevent this result of restraining competition? Have they been successful?

The last chapter in each of the first three parts of the study shows how the regulations on bank competition have been used to increase the efficacy of monetary controls. Exactly how has this been done in each country? How do the competitive controls that have been employed as monetary controls fit into the framework of the traditional instruments of monetary control? Has this use of the competitive-control apparatus significantly increased the ability of the monetary authorities to implement their credit policies?

Part Four draws upon the institutional and analytical framework in Parts One, Two, and Three to present some international comparisons of important aspects of the regulation of bank competition and to highlight some of the key interrelations of the regulation of banking structure and the regulation of the conditions of bank competition.

Part One
Italy

Part One.
July

I
Banking Structure in Italy

The financial institutions which compose the banking population of modern Italy are a heterogeneous group, but they have important elements in common. The Italian Banking Law of 1936 (and subsequent administrative regulations) sought to make a clear distinction between credit institutions which collect short-term savings and supply short-term credit (called *aziende di credito*) and those which specialize in medium- and long-term savings and credit.[1] This distinction is widely but not universally observed. For example, savings banks are classified as short-term credit institutions but they are limited neither to short-term savings nor to short-term credits. Although such discrepancies blur the image of the aziende di credito as a clear-cut grouping of institutions with an exclusively short-term emphasis, they do not negate the usefulness of this category in a first approximation identification of the short-term credit institutions.

At the end of 1965, 1,287 banks were classified as aziende di credito (Table 1). Owing in many cases to their different origins and different historical development, these banks differ widely in size, in geographical location, and in some of their activities. The conventional classification of these banks—often reflecting their historical differences—is as follows: (1) *public law banks (istituti di credito di diritto pubblico)*, (2) *banks of national interest (banche di interesse nazionale)*, (3) *ordinary credit banks (banche di credito ordinario)*, (4) *people's cooperative banks (banche popolari cooperative)*, (5) *savings banks (casse di risparmio; monti di credito su pegno di 1ᵃ categoria)*, and (6) *other credit organizations (altre aziende di credito)*. This conventional classification groups banks according to certain broad characteristics, but the categories are by no means homogeneous.

The six public law banks (in order of their deposit size in 1965) are the Banca Nazionale del Lavoro, Banco di Napoli, Istituto Bancario San Paolo di Torino, Monte dei Paschi di Siena, Banco di Sicilia, and

---

[1] The authorities made this distinction to ensure that the maturity of assets would be matched to the maturity of liabilities. Cf. Banco di Roma, *The Italian Banking System* (Rome, 1960), p. 54.

Banco di Sardegna.[2] The Banca Nazionale del Lavoro differs from the
others in a number of ways. First, it is a comparatively young bank,
created by the state in 1913 and reorganized in approximately its present
form in 1929. Other public law banks are among the world's oldest
banks, and one of them (the Banco di Napoli, founded in 1539) may
be the oldest existing bank. Second, the Banca Nazionale del Lavoro
is owned by the government; the others are not. This is just a technical
difference, however—the government, while respecting certain traditional considerations, appoints the directors of the other public law
banks—and is due to the fact that the other public law banks have no
outstanding share capital. Their origins are mostly philanthropic or
charitable and their capital funds have grown by donations and contri-
butions as well as by the accumulation over the centuries of that part of
their earnings which was not allocated for public assistance and charity.
Third, the Banca Nazionale del Lavoro is preeminently a commercial
bank and places particular emphasis on lending to large business firms.
The other public law banks also conduct a commercial banking business but with significantly less emphasis on large business loans.[3] Fourth,
the Banca Nazionale del Lavoro operates all over Italy, whereas the
other public law banks tend to be concentrated in the particular regions
with which they are historically associated. As their names suggest, the

TABLE 1

Distribution of Banks, Branches, and Deposits
in aziende di credito, end of 1965

Category	Number of banks	Number of branches	Deposits (million lire)
Public law banks	6	1,480	4,613,918
Banks of national interest	3	786	3,725,461
Ordinary credit banks[a]	188	2,405	4,608,643
People's cooperative banks	210	1,679	2,421,524
Savings banks[b]	91	2,878	5,274,184
Other credit organizations	789	857	336,159
Totals	1,287	10,085	20,979,889

a This is a combination of two categories shown separately in the *Bollettino*, viz.,
"Societa per azioni e in accomandita per azioni" and "Ditte Bancarie"; see p. 154.
b Including First-Class pawn banks.
SOURCE: Banca d'Italia, *Bollettino*.

[2] The Banco di Sardegna, now a public law bank, was classified before 1961
with the group of ordinary credit banks.

[3] The public law banks also perform other credit operations (such as real
estate loans) through separate and ostensibly autonomous departments, but
credit operations of a noncommercial, non-short-term character are outside the
scope of this study.

Banco di Napoli is dominant in the areas formerly covered by the old Kingdom of Naples; the Banco di Sicilia, in Sicily; the Monte dei Paschi di Siena, in Tuscany; and the Istituto San Paolo di Torino, in Piedmont.

The three banks of national interest (ranked by their size in 1964) are the Banca Commerciale Italiana (head office in Milan), the Credito Italiano (head office in Milan), and the Banco di Roma (head office in Rome). The three banks of national interest, established between 1880 and 1895, are newcomers on the Italian banking scene as compared with the typical public law bank. Despite their comparatively recent origins, they are among the largest banks in Italy, and like the Banca Nazionale del Lavoro (which in many ways resembles the banks of national interest more than the public law banks), their operations are nationwide. Indeed, their widespread geographical coverage is an essential part of the legal basis for their classification—the 1936 Banking Law designated as banks of national interest only banks with branches in at least thirty of Italy's ninety-four provinces.[4]

Virtually from their founding, the banks of national interest were important suppliers of credit to Italian business and especially to large business, and this has continued to the present. The banking reform legislation of the 1930's severed the pattern of mixed banking in which all three banks had been heavily involved. As an unintended consequence of the separation of the banks' commercial lending operations from their equity investments in various industries, these banks became in effect nationalized banks. In 1933, when the Italian government established IRI (Istituto per la Ricostruzione Industriale) to take over the equity holdings of the mixed banks, IRI also acquired almost all of the share capital of these three banks.

The banks of national interest have been included with the private banks in the later analysis of the competitive characteristics of the Italian banking structure because, in spite of their nationalization, they retain substantial independence from government interference in their daily operations. Indeed, the government appears to support their determination to be independent. As a matter of policy, IRI (the common shareholder) permits each national interest bank to conduct its affairs as if it had no connection or common interest with the others.[5] In the same spirit, the government treats them like private banks. For

---

[4] There were 94 provinces in 1936; there are now 91.

[5] According to Gerbi, ". . . IRI, far from moderating or co-ordinating the action of the several banks under its control, actually stimulates rivalry among them, restricting its control to internal administration, as if these banks were independent subsidiaries operating in different countries." Antonello Gerbi, "Italy," in *Banking Systems* ed. Benjamin H. Beckhart (New York, 1954), pp. 437–438.

one thing, the government makes it a point not to favor the nationalized banks by giving them more advantageous competitive terms than the private banks; for example, the restraints imposed on the conditions of bank competition apply as fully to the nationalized banks as to the private banks. Similarly, to generate uniformity of labor costs and, to this extent, to put private and public banks on an equal competitive footing, the government permits the public banks to do business with the same labor unions as the private banks.[6]

The ordinary credit banks are a rather mixed lot. Most are private banks, but some are owned by IRI. Some (like the Banco di Santo Spirito, founded in 1605 by Pope Paul V) are very old, but most were formed within the last hundred years. The period after the First World War was a particularly active period in the establishment and growth of the banks in this group. Most ordinary credit banks are small and tend to be concentrated in the northern part of the country; a few (like the Banca Nazionale dell'Agricoltura, the Banca d'America e d'Italia, the Banco Ambrosiano, and the Banco di Santo Spirito) are moderately large.[7] The small banks are essentially provincial or even local banks; some of the larger banks have expanded outside of local and regional boundaries, with fairly widespread branches throughout the country. The ordinary credit banks generally conduct a short-term commercial banking business, though some are authorized to engage in certain other business as well.

The people's cooperative banks originated as part of the cooperative movement of the mid-nineteenth century. At the outset, these banks were mutual organizations, operated for the benefit of members and based on the capital subscribed by the members. In due course, they developed into regular deposit banks. A few (like the Banca Popolare di Novara, and the Banca Popolare di Milano) are very large, but most are small and confine their operations to their local areas. Because of their origins and small size, they tend to concentrate their credit operations with small business firms, and they are quite active in that area.

The miscellaneous category of other credit organizations includes the *rural and artisan banks* (*casse rurali e artigiane*), small organizations which are located in rural areas that do not have branches of the larger banks. They collect the tiny savings of rural workers and make small loans at favorable terms to their rural members. Although these banks

---

[6] Cf. Camera dei deputati, *Commissione d'inchiesta sui limiti posti alla concorrenza nel campo economico*, seduta del 22 novembre 1962 (resoconti stenografici di interrogatorio del Dottor Guido Carli), p. 4.

[7] At the end of 1959, these four banks held about 30 percent of the net deposits of their group. Cf. Luigi Ceriani, "The Commercial Banks and Financial Institutions," in *Banking in Western Europe*, ed. R. S. Sayers (Oxford, 1962), pp. 134–135. There were 156 banks in this group in 1962.

perform a useful service in their local areas, they are an insignificant part of the Italian banking structure (Table 1).

In Italian banking literature, *banca* refers to any banking institution in the five bank categories described above; *aziende di credito* is a broader term which includes the savings banks as well as the *banche*.[8] The basis for this distinction is that the banche, while differing in many ways, tend to be predominantly commercial banks, that is, those emphasizing short-term commercial lending and (especially among the large banks) demand-deposit operations. By contrast, the savings banks are authorized to handle medium- and long-term as well as short-term credits, and their savings deposits are much more important than their demand deposits. In spite of these differences, the savings banks are included in this study because they are important alternative suppliers of current accounts, savings accounts, and short-term commercial credit (Table 2). This accords with the official view that "Commercial banks and savings banks may be conveniently treated together since the asset and liabilities structure of the two groups is less dissimilar in Italy than in most foreign countries."[9]

TABLE 2

Distribution of Deposits and Loans, end of 1965
(million lire)

Bank category[a]	Savings deposits	Current accounts	Short-term Loans	Medium-term and Long-term Loans
Banche				
Public law banks	1,898,367	2,715,551	3,581,699	227,870
Banks of national interest	1,136,461	2,589,000	3,290,588	—
Ordinary credit banks	2,382,233	2,153,901	3,197,632	123,342
People's cooperative banks	1,503,742	824,765	1,506,955	84,478
Totals	6,920,803	8,283,217	11,576,874	435,690
Savings banks (and first-class pawn banks)	3,904,000	1,370,184	1,793,635	1,317,722

a These figures are based on 365 firms which held (at end of 1965) almost 98 percent of all bank deposits. For a breakdown of the composition of this total, cf. *Bollettino*, March–April, 1966, p. 123.
SOURCE: Banca d'Italia, *Bollettino*.

---

[8] Cf. Gian Franco Calabresi, "Credit and the Banking System in the Post-War Period," in Banco di Roma, *Ten Years of Italian Economy, 1947–1956* (Rome, 1956), p. 252, n. 1. Hereafter, unless otherwise noted, *banks* will refer to this broader grouping.

[9] Banca d'Italia, *Abridged Version of the Report for the Year 1956* (presented to the ordinary general meeting of the stockholders), p. 51, note. Hereafter, this will be called Bank of Italy, *Annual Report*.

The Italian savings banks date from the first half of the nineteenth century, and the first six savings banks were opened in Venetia in 1822.[10] A major objective of the savings banks was to encourage the poor to save by providing them with a secure repository and attractive yields. The bulk of savings bank funds have always been invested in mortgages, but as the savings banks grew, they expanded their operations (especially during the last two decades) to include most of the credit operations conducted by commercial banks. They have nevertheless remained true to their historic origins, and much more than the other bank categories, they continue to deal with small savers and small borrowers. The savings (and pawn) banks have established a thick network of branches, mostly in northern Italy. They range in size from very small, entirely local institutions to the Cassa di Risparmio delle Provincie Lombarde (headquarters in Milan), one of the largest banking institutions in Italy and the largest savings bank in Europe.[11]

Finally, the list of banking institutions should be supplemented by adding the Post Office Savings. Funds placed with the Post Office Savings do not compete with the short-term credit operations of the banks, because the postal savings are loaned (by Cassa Depositi e Prestiti, an agency of the Treasury) in a variety of medium- and long-term credits (which are outside the scope of this study). The Post Office does, however, compete with banks in collecting deposits. Since the Post Office Savings has an outlet in each of the 15,000 post offices in Italy, the Post Office bank has a far more extensive system of branches in all parts of the country than all of the commercial and savings banks combined. In 1965, Post Office deposits amounted to 5,000 billion lire,[12] as compared with 21,000 billion lire deposits in the banking system.

---

[10] Banco di Roma, *Review of Economic Conditions in Italy*, July, 1948, p. 234.

[11] Cf. Cassa di Risparmio delle Provincie Lombarde, *Italia economica, 1961* (Milano), p. 284.

[12] Cf. Banca d'Italia, *Bollettino*, March–April, 1966, p. 119.

II

Regulation of Bank Concentration

CONTROLS OVER MERGERS AND ENTRY

The Bank of Italy exercises indirect control over the extent of potential competition within given areas by its authority to regulate the banking structure. Under the Banking Act of 1936, the Bank of Italy has full power to approve or to disapprove bank mergers[1] and to control the opening of new banks or branches.[2] A bank cannot even shift the location of a branch within the same *commune* without prior authorization from the authorities.[3] The Bank of Italy also has authority to order the closing of a particular branch because of "faulty working" or to achieve "a better territorial distribution of credit concerns. . . ."[4]

Although the Bank of Italy retains the ultimate authority to grant or withhold branch permits, it has twice in recent years (end of 1958 and early 1961) asked the Associazione Bancaria Italiana (ABI) to prepare recommendations as a basis for the Bank of Italy's decisions on branch applications. In carrying out this responsibility, the ABI tried to reconcile the views of its bank members with the Bank of Italy's broad policy on entry matters. In recent years, the Bank of Italy has tried to "ensure a balanced distribution of various categories of banking institutions, such as to make room for the coexistence of decision centers at different removes from government power and thereby to *avoid the drawbacks of excessive concentration.*"[5] Similarly, the government has tried to encourage and facilitate the opening of branches

---

[1] Cf. Associazione Bancaria Italiana, *Raccolta di testi legislativi e normativi in materia creditizia, La legge bancaria*, V edizione (Roma, 1962), Articles 47, 48, and 53, on pp. 57, 58, and 61.

[2] Cf. *ibid.*, Article 28, pp. 37–38.

[3] Cf. "Trasferimenti di sportelli bancari," in *La legge bancaria, op. cit.*, p. 95.

[4] Cf. Article 34, *La legge bancaria, op. cit.*, p. 41.

[5] Governor Guido Carli, Bank of Italy, *Annual Report for 1961*, p. 97 (my italics).

in southern Italy as part of its program to stimulate the economic development of that region.[6] Under this policy, applications for branches in the south (especially in Sicily) have been favored over applications in the rest of the country.[7]

The allocation of new branches among competing applicants was one of the severest problems faced by the ABI. The process involved much stiff bargaining, and many factors were taken into account.[8] One of the most important was the area's potential. If the area could support another bank or branch, the ABI was inclined to authorize the new entry even when it prejudiced an existing bank. Another consideration was the branch status of the applicant. For example, if two banks wanted to open a branch in the same area, and one already had a branch in that area, the ABI was inclined to give the other bank a chance in order to avoid the presence of only one bank in a single place. The ABI also considered whether either bank had submitted other branch applications for other areas. If one bank had applied for only one branch permit and another had applied for (say) three, the ABI was inclined to favor the single-branch applicant and tried to satisfy the other bank on some of its other applications. The size of the applicant was also an important consideration. If one applicant was a large bank and the other was small, the ABI considered whether the area was already represented primarily by large or small banks, and then made its allocation so as to redress the balance. The nature of the business demand in the community and the comparative ability of each of the applicant banks to satisfy this demand was also taken into account.

The ABI attributed its success in reconciling competitive applications to the "reciprocal sacrifices" made by the banks,[9] but it also had a big club to wield: it could threaten to return the matter of branch applications entirely to the Bank of Italy. This was neither an idle threat nor an attractive alternative, for the governor of the Bank of Italy had made it clear that "should the banks, by ill fortune, fail to come to an agreement, we shall again not shirk our responsibilities, and the choices we shall be called upon to make will obviously not be uninfluenced by our judgment of the individual banks' willingness to tow [sic] the line."[10]

---

[6] Cf. "L'intervento dell'Avv. Siglienti ai lavori della Commissione d'inchiesta sui limiti alla concorrenza," in Associazione Bancaria Italiana, *Bancaria*, February, 1963, p. 216.

[7] *Ibid.* Cf. also testimony of Governor Carli in Camera dei deputati, *Commissione d'inchiesta sui limiti posti alla concorrenza nel campo economico*, seduta del 22 novembre 1962 (Resoconti stenografici di interrogatorio del Dottor Guido Carli), p. 18.

[8] This information is based on the author's interviews.

[9] Siglienti testimony (see n. 6 above), p. 217.

[10] Governor Carli in Bank of Italy, *Annual Report for 1961*, p. 97.

Even if there had been no threat of punitive action against unco-operative banks, the banks apparently would have preferred a system of "self-administration" to direct government control. In part, this preference reflected a belief that the ABI was *less* subject to political pressure than the Bank of Italy; that is, the bankers apparently believed that the ABI was more likely than the government to base its recommendations on "objective" (i.e., nonpolitical) considerations.

After the ABI's 1961 branch recommendations had been carried out, the authorities deemed it advisable to call a halt to new branch openings, except in special cases, such as communities left without a bank, or communities which clearly need a new bank because of a shift of economic activity, or in connection with the salvage of banks in financial difficulties.[11] In view of the new policy, the Bank of Italy decided to handle these "exceptional authorizations" entirely on its own.

CHANGING PATTERNS OF BANK CONCENTRATION

It is pertinent to examine the historical trend of banking concentration, not only to gain perspective on the present level of banking concentration in Italy but also to observe the impact of government policy on the changing pattern of bank concentration. Many new banks were formed after the First World War, but this trend was stopped and even reversed by the Banking Law of 1926, which inaugurated a government policy of fostering concentration. Under the new policy, consolidations and closings during the ensuing decade cut the number of banks in half and the number of branches by a third (Table 3). The Banking Law of 1936 gave another boost to the process of concentration; and, by the end of the Second World War, there were only 1,432 banks and 6,889 branches as compared with approximately 4,000 banks and almost 12,000 branches in 1926.

The government's policy of fostering greater concentration of banking affected the distribution as well as the total number of banks and branches. Between 1938 and 1945, the total number of banking offices fell from 7,384 to 6,889. This net reduction was borne entirely by the ordinary credit banks, the cooperative peoples' banks, and especially by the small banks which comprise the "other banks" category (Table 4). In spite of a decline in the total number of banking offices, the public law banks, the banks of national interest, and the savings banks actually increased their branches. Thus, except for some of the savings banks, the policy of increasing bank concentration was put into effect by

---

[11] For a further discussion of entry policy with respect to new branches, cf. Associazione Bancaria Italiana, Serie Tecnica, Circolare n. 111, "Appertura di nuovi sportelli bancari," (Rome, September 6, 1965).

branch expansion in the large banks with regional and even national
branch systems, and by branch reduction in categories where the banks
are typically medium-size or small banks.

In the postwar period, the number of banks continued to fall more
or less continuously to a low point of 1,234 banks in 1957 (Table 3).
At its meeting of October 31, 1957, and again on August 8, 1962, the
Interministerial Committee reaffirmed its policy (which had been in
effect since the immediate postwar period) of opposition to the open-

TABLE 3
Number of Banks and Banking Offices, 1926–1965

Year	Number of banks	Number of branches
1926	3,977	11,837
1936	2,070	7,726
1938	1,849	7,384
1939	1,725	7,061
1940	1,651	6,879
1941	1,566	6,887
1942	1,491	6,872
1943	1,467	6,855
1944	1,461	6,848
1945	1,432	6,889
1946	1,393	7,237
1947	1,360	7,508
1948	1,294	7,403
1949	1,278	7,592
1950	1,261	7,773
1951	1,240	7,826
1952	1,243	7,842
1953	1,236	7,874
1954	1,237	7,910
1955	1,243	7,964
1956	1,237	8,269
1957	1,234	8,631
1958	1,247	8,651
1959	1,266	8,713
1960	1,263	9,211
1961	1,261	9,258
1962	1,258	9,838
1963	1,287	9,953
1964	1,298	10,005
1965	1,287	10,085

SOURCES: For 1926 and 1936, First International Credit Conference, Vol. II, p. 289.
For 1938, Gian Franco Calabresi in Banco di Roma, *Ten Years of Italian Economy*
(Rome, 1956), p. 239. For 1939–1948, see *Annuario delle aziende di credito e
finanziarie, 1941–1949* (Rome, 1949) p. 7. For 1949–1965, Banca d'Italia, *Bollettino*.

TABLE 4

Net Change in Total Banking Offices, 1938–1945

Kind of bank	Number	Percent of 1938 total
Public law	97	10.2
National interest	25	4.4
Ordinary credit	−232	−13.2
People's cooperative	−194	−16.8
Savings	129	8.0
Other	−320	−23.6

SOURCE: Computed from figures in Calabresi, *Ten Years of Italian Economy* (see Table 3), p. 239.

ing of new banks except for cooperative banks and then only in cases of proven need.[12] The number of exceptions proved to be rather large, and the number of banks increased to a postwar high of 1,298 by the end of 1964 (but fell back to 1,287 in 1965).

In contrast to their prewar policy of reducing the number of branches, the authorities in the postwar period authorized an increase in the number of branches in every year except 1948. By the end of 1965, the number of branches had reached 10,085. Thus, between 1947 and 1965, the authorities had authorized a net increase (after allowing for liquidations or mergers) of 2,577 branches. The postwar policy on concentration was reflected in the allocation as well as in the number of new branches. In sharp contrast to the prewar pattern, the public law banks and the banks of national interest increased their branches far less than the people's cooperative banks, the savings banks, or the ordinary credit banks (Table 5). Under the government's postwar policy on entry, the authorities granted one-third of the net increase in banking offices to the savings banks, one-half to the people's cooperative and ordinary credit banks, but only about one-sixth of the new offices to the public law banks and the banks of national interest. In part, this distribution was due to the government's views on bank concentration, but it was also influenced by the government's program for economic development. In connection with the latter, the government (especially in recent years) has encouraged the opening of banks and branches in backward areas, rural areas, and other areas which could potentially support a banking office but did not have one. By contrast, the postwar policy of the largest banks in Italy has been to establish branches in provincial capitals and other important centers, but they have shown

[12] Cf. Associazione Bancaria Italiana, Serie Tecnica, Circolare n. 161, "Legislazione bancaria costituzione di nuove aziende di credito" (Rome, December 27, 1966).

no great interest in opening branches in those areas where government policy has favored branch applications.[13]

Table 6 shows how the government's changing views on bank concentration influenced the distribution of banking offices between 1938 and 1965. As a result of the policy between 1938 and 1945 to increase concentration by favoring the big banks at the expense of the smaller banks, the percentage of total banking offices held by the large public law and national interest banks increased, and the percentage held by

TABLE 5
Net Change in Total Banking Offices, 1947–1965

Kind of bank	Number	Percent of 1947 total	Net change in each category / Net change for all categories (%)
Public law	+323	+27.9	+12.5
National interest	+136	+20.9	+ 5.3
Ordinary credit	+588	+32.4	+22.8
People's cooperative	+615	+57.8	+23.9
Savings	+916	+46.7	+35.5
Other	− 1	− .1	(a)

aLess than .05 percent.
SOURCE: Computed from data in Banca d'Italia, *Bollettino*.

TABLE 6
Distribution of Banking Offices, 1938, 1945, 1965

	Percent of total			Net change		
Kind of Bank	1938 (1)	1945 (2)	1965 (3)	1938–1945 col. 2 minus col. 1 (4)	1945–1965 col. 3 minus col. 2 (5)	1938–1965 col. 3 minus col. 1 (6)
Public law	12.9	15.2	14.7	+2.3	−0.5	+1.8
National interest	7.7	8.6	7.8	+0.9	−0.8	+0.1
Ordinary credit	23.7	22.1	23.8	−1.6	+1.7	+0.1
People's cooperative	15.6	13.9	16.6	−1.7	+2.7	+1.0
Savings	21.7	25.2	28.5	+3.5	+3.3	+6.8
Other	18.3	15.0	8.5	−3.3	−6.5	−9.8

SOURCE: Figures for 1938 and 1945 were calculated from Calabresi, *Ten Years of Italian Economy* (see Table 3), p. 239. Figures for 1965 were calculated from Banca d'Italia, *Bollettino*.

---

[13] Cf. Siglienti testimony (see n. 6 above), p. 217.

the other bank categories decreased (with the conspicuous exception of the savings bank category). The discontinuance of that policy during the postwar period led to a reduction in the percentage of total banking offices held by the large-bank categories and an increase for the smaller-bank categories (except for the tiny banks which comprise the "other banks" category). Thus there was a tendency for the latter policy to counteract the effects on the distribution of banking offices of the pre-war policy. For the twenty-seven-year period as a whole, the significant changes were the increase in the percentage of total offices held by the savings banks and the fall in the percentage held by "other banks."

CURRENT POLICY ON BANK CONCENTRATION

In recent years, it has been government policy to maintain approximately the existing levels of bank concentration. As the president of the Italian Bankers Association stated to the Parliamentary Inquiry on Competition: "We and the authorities responsible for this sector believe that the size achieved by the four or five large banks represents the *optimum* in relation to the needs of our country."[14]

The size-distribution of banks in 1962 (when the preceding statement was made) is shown in Table 7; and the bank concentration[15] implicit in that distribution is shown explicitly (in terms of loans as well as deposits) in Table 8. Bank concentration is somewhat higher when measured in terms of loans rather than deposits because the large banks tend to have higher loan-to-deposit ratios than the smaller banks. For example, the loan-to-deposit ratio in the top three banks was 85.8 percent, 75.2 percent in the next three banks, and 77.6 percent in the seventh to the twelfth largest banks, but it was only 55.3 to 59.0 percent for the 734 banks in the three smallest-size classes.[16] The general pattern of concentration is quite similar whether measured in terms of deposits or loans. The three largest banks controlled more than a fifth of the banking system's resources, the top dozen more than one-half, and the forty-two largest controlled more than three-fourths. This concentration is quite moderate by European standards[17] (specifically, as

---

[14] *Ibid.* (italics in original).

[15] The reader is reminded that bank concentration is not synonymous with market concentration. As will be shown later, the extent of bank concentration can, however, have an important influence on the character and extent of possible bank rivalry in various banking markets. It can also influence the nature and effectiveness of the government's efforts to regulate the conditions of bank competition.

[16] Carli Testimony to Parliamentary Inquiry, *op. cit.*, (see n. 7 above), Prospetto No. 4, p. 28.

[17] Cf. Siglienti testimony, *op. cit.* (see n. 6 above), pp. 211–212.

will be shown later, in comparison with the levels in France and England).[18]

The present pattern of bank concentration in Italy, while not deemed perfect in all details, has widespread support on a number of grounds. First, the banking structure influences the allocation of credit in Italy— there is a long-established tendency for large banks to do business with large business firms, and for medium and small banks to accommodate the credit demands of medium-size and small customers.[19] Thus, if the medium-size and small banks were eliminated by mergers, the large business firms would probably get more credit but at the expense of the medium-size and small customers. The authorities have been opposed

TABLE 7

Size Classification of Italian Banks, by Deposits and Loans, June 30, 1962

Size class (lire)	Number of banks	Loans (billion lire)	Deposits (billion lire)
100 million and under	355	9	16
100–250 million	234	22	39
250–500 million	145	30	51
500–750 million	77	31	47
750–1.0 billion	53	28	46
1.0–2.5 billion	130	130	201
2.5–5.0 billion	62	142	221
5.0–7.5 billion	40	170	251
7.5–10.0 billion	23	154	201
10–25 billion	61	680	1,060
25–50 billion	29	619	1,005
50–75 billion	12	460	697
75–100 billion	5	256	422
100–250 billion	13	1,263	1,877
250–500 billion	6	1,566	2,018
500–750 billion	3	1,425	1,896
750 billion and over	3	2,397	2,794
Totals	1,251	9,382	12,842

SOURCE: Testimony of Governor Carli in Camera dei deputati, *Commissione d'inchiesta sui limiti posti alla concorrenza nel campo economico*, seduta del 22 novembre 1962 (Resoconti stenografici di interrogatorio del Dottor Guido Carli), Prospetto No. 4, p. 28.

[18] It is not low by American standards. In the United States in 1960, it took ten banks, not three, to control 20 percent of the system's deposits; and more than 100 banks, not a dozen, to control half of the system's deposits. Cf. David A. Alhadeff, "Bank Mergers: Competition Versus Banking Factors," *Southern Economic Journal*, January, 1963, p. 222.

[19] Cf. Giuseppe Lanzarone, *Il sistema bancario italiano*, ed. Giulio Einaudi (Torino, 1948), pp. 414–415.

to that outcome for a number of reasons, but especially because it would raise concentration in the business sector.

Second, the authorities believe that "the present structure of the banking system, with decision-making centers which are autonomous from each other and to a certain extent from the public powers, sufficiently guarantees that independence which is a condition of impartial behavior in this sector."[20] This is important to the authorities who, while continuing to approve of mergers in individual cases, stress that "this implies no departure from the objectives of having our credit system based on a large number of mutually independent decision centres."[21]

Third, many approve of the present level of concentration in the belief that it strikes a reasonable balance between some of the positive and negative aspects of concentration. Thus, one authority on Italian banking, writing in 1948, noted with approval the reduction of banks from more than 4,000 before 1926 to 1,393 by 1946, but expressed strong doubts about the desirability of any further increase in concentration, given the particular characteristics of the Italian economy.[22]

TABLE 8

Concentration of Italian Banks, by Deposits and Loans, June 30, 1962

Number of banks	Percent of total number of banks	Percent of total loans	Percent of total deposits
Top 3	.2	25.6	21.8
Top 6	.4	40.8	36.5
Top 12	.9	57.5	52.2
Top 25	1.9	71.0	66.8
Top 30	2.3	73.7	70.1
42	3.3	78.6	75.5
71	5.6	85.2	83.3
132	10.5	92.5	91.6
155	12.3	94.1	93.2
195	15.5	95.9	95.2
257	20.5	97.4	96.9
387	30.9	98.8	98.4
440	35.1	99.1	98.8
517	41.3	99.4	99.2
662	52.9	99.7	99.6
896	71.6	99.9	99.9
1,251	100.0	100.0	100.0

SOURCE: Same as Table 7.

[20] Testimony of Governor Carli (see n. 7 above), p. 10.
[21] Governor Carli in Bank of Italy, *Annual Report for 1964*, p. 134.
[22] Lanzarone, *op. cit.*, pp. 513–514.

In this view, the positive aspect of concentration was that it permitted risks to be distributed over a wider geographical area and reduced the liquidity requirements of the banking system. Its negative aspect was that the bureaucratization which is associated with concentration might reduce the bankers' sense of responsibility and spirit of initiative. In addition, concentration placed great power in a few hands, and this power could be used against the public interest.

Fourth, the present level of bank concentration commends itself to the authorities on the grounds of banking efficiency. Some believe that the efficiency of the banking system could be improved if some of the smallest banks were eliminated by merger,[23] but few, if any, believe that the overall costs of the four or five largest banks would be reduced by mergers among them.[24] On the other hand, they fear that, if present barriers to entry were relaxed to reduce concentration, the resulting multiplication of banking offices might raise the cost of credit.[25]

Fifth, the authorities oppose a further increase in bank concentration lest the elimination of many medium-size and small banks hamper the government's plans for economic development in less developed areas. According to this view, the government's concentration policy after 1926 was responsible, at least in part, for the present distribution of banking offices in Italy that is "not always uniformly adequate to the development and possibilities of the single regions."[26] As noted earlier, the large banks have not been too interested in establishing branches outside of the major centers. The authorities are concerned, therefore, that without the medium-size and smaller banks to fill this gap, the

---

[23] In 1965, the Bank of Italy conducted a special survey of profit and loss accounts of banking firms which showed that there was a sharp break between the costs (as a percent of total supply of funds) of the smallest banks and those in the next-higher-size class. This difference has been ascribed to the fact that the small banks deal in smaller average amounts and with a different type of client. However, in view of the sharpness of the break in costs between the two categories, it is also presumed that a "contributing factor may be the lower degree of capacity utilization because of an insufficient volume of business." Cf. Bank of Italy, *Annual Report for 1965*, pp. 106–108. It is presumably this finding which led the Bank of Italy to conclude that, in the interests of efficiency, some change in the size of small banking firms may be demanded. Cf. *ibid.*, p. 130.

[24] Cf. Siglienti testimony (see n. 6 above), p. 217. Cf. also Lanzarone's view that the bureaucratization which accompanied the growth of concentration led to wastes which significantly increased the expenses of administration. Cf. Lanzarone, *op. cit.*, pp. 516–518.

[25] Cf. Carli testimony (see n. 7 above), p. 19. According to Carli, this happened in Germany after free entry into banking was permitted.

[26] Glauco della Porta, "The Italian Banking System," in Banco di Roma, *Review of Economic Conditions in Italy*, July, 1960, p. 419.

development of the rural and backward areas would suffer, owing to a lack of adequate banking facilities and bank credit.

Finally, the authorities have been reluctant to permit any further increase in concentration, especially by a merger of the present large banks, because it might eliminate competition among them.[27] Although the authorities approve of restraints on bank competition, they do not want to eliminate competition entirely. It is the official view that, given the regulatory framework within which the banks must operate, "the system has a sufficient degree of competition to stimulate progress."[28]

[27] Siglienti testimony, *op. cit.* (see n. 6 above), p. 217.
[28] Governor Carli in Bank of Italy, *Annual Report for 1962*, p. 123.

III

Regulation of the Conditions of Bank Competition

BACKGROUND OF RESTRAINTS ON COMPETITION IN BANKING

Bank competition in Italy is now regulated by an Interbank Agreement, drawn up by the bank cartel and sanctioned by the regulatory authorities; but cartels and cartel types of restraints are not new in Italian banking. Even before the first bank cartels were formally organized after the First World War, a "profound feeling of solidarity" existed among some of the banks with a similar structure (e.g., the people's banks and savings banks) and "save in a very few cases, there was no competition among members in the respective districts."[1] In July, 1918, four large banks had achieved sufficient collaboration in the granting of credit that "it did no good to shop around from one to the other."[2] In 1919, some of the bigger banks organized a cartel for the purpose of "disciplining the competition among the banks . . . to avoid the costly cornering of the clients at the risk of subsequent bank crises."[3]

The early cartels were private, voluntary, limited to agreements on loan rates and some commissions[4]—and not entirely satisfactory to their sponsors. In part, their effectiveness was limited because they were voluntary. In addition, they had no power to regulate entry, and since

---

[1] Banco di Roma, "The Italian Bankers Association (A.B.I.)," *Review of Economic Conditions in Italy*, September, 1950, p. 387.

[2] Shepard B. Clough, *Economic History of Modern Italy* (New York and London, 1964), p. 205.

[3] Banco di Roma, "The Italian Banking System after the War," *Review of Economic Conditions in Italy*, May, 1954, p. 254.

[4] Cf. Associazione Bancaria Italiana, "La Structure du système bancaire italien au point de vue de la liquidité," in Associazione Bancaria Italiana, *Papers and Proceedings of the First International Credit Conference* (Rome, 1953), II, 290.

332.1 Aℓ39c
c. 1

the state imposed no entry barriers, many new banks were opened during a few years after the First World War. Between 1919 and 1926, 143 ordinary credit banks (75 joint-stock banks and 68 private banks) and numerous branches were opened;[5] and by 1926 there were 3,977 banks and 11,837 branches.[6]

The Banking Law of 1926 abruptly terminated the period of free entry into Italian banking. This act, a major landmark in Italian banking legislation, was intended to reform the banking structure and to improve the safeguards on deposits.[7] The important reforms included the following: the Bank of Italy was given a monopoly of note-issue (instead of having to share the note-issue with the Banco di Napoli and Banco di Sicilia), minimum capital requirements were established for banks, and a compulsory safety reserve was established. For the purposes of this study, the most interesting reforms were the requirements that banks be listed on a special register and that new banks or branches be approved by the Ministry of Finance in consultation with the Bank of Italy. It was widely believed that the failure to regulate bank entry in the period following the First World War had led to excessive entry; the Banking Law of 1926 not only halted entry but also encouraged mergers and consolidations.

The controls established over the banks by the 1926 law were a prelude to the much broader range of controls authorized by the Banking Law of 1936. The 1926 law had regulated the collection of savings to protect depositors. The 1936 law went further and declared that "The collection of savings from the public in whatever form and the exercise of credit activities are functions of public interest. . ."[8] To implement this view, a comprehensive system of bank controls was established. The new act reaffirmed the entry and merger provisions of the earlier legislation and vested those controls in an "inspectorate for the defense of savings and the regulation of credit." The inspectorate was also authorized to issue instructions (in accordance with the decisions of the Committee of Ministers) about maximum deposit rates of

---

[5] Cf. Banco di Roma, "The Italian Banking System," *Review of Economic Conditions in Italy*, March, 1948, p. 89.

[6] Four banks, however, controlled 50 percent of commercial bank deposits in 1926. Cf. S. R. Cope, "Italy," in A. M. Allen *et al.*, *Commercial Banking Legislation and Control* (London, 1938), p. 257.

[7] Cf. Guido Carli, "Relations Between The Central Banks Of Italy, Switzerland And Austria And The Commercial Banks In Those Countries," in *Relations Between The Central Banks And Commercial Banks*, lectures delivered at the Tenth International Banking Summer School, Garmisch-Partenkirchen, September, 1957, pp. 45–57.

[8] Article 1, Royal Decree Law, March 12, 1936, n. 375 in Associazione Bancaria Italiana, *Raccolta di testi legislativi e normativi in materia creditizia, La legge bancaria*, V edizione (Rome, 1962), p. 21.

interest, the conditions for savings and current accounts, minimum loan
rates, commissions on services rendered by banks, and other terms and
conditions of the banking business.[9]

The 1936 legislation was designed to increase the scope of administrative control and to reduce the emphasis on competition, in line with
the Fascist philosophy of the corporate state.[10] In establishing an inspectorate with wide-ranging powers, the act of 1936 provided a powerful
controlling organization which "if used fully, would make the
Italian banking system a state organization in all but name."[11] Bank
competition was also regulated in the belief that excessive competition
would impair bank soundness and lead to bank losses. During the
banking crisis of the 1930's, many Italian banks experienced severe
liquidity problems, and the Italian government had been obliged to
rescue some of the banks in order to protect depositors.

Notwithstanding the government's view that there were too many
banks, the serious liquidity problems of the banks during the '30's
appear to have been due not to "overbanking" and "excessive competition" but to the regime of mixed banking (which was subsequently
explicitly prohibited by the Banking Law of 1936). Mixed banking,
which permitted the same institution to conduct both a commercial and
an investment banking business, was an outgrowth of the Italian desire
to industrialize rapidly combined with an inadequate capital market
to finance long-term investment. These circumstances led many Italian
banks to make long-term loans to business firms, and even to establish
new enterprises with their own funds. Mixed banking led to abuses
that threatened both the liquidity and the solvency of the banks—for
example, an improper allocation of bank funds due to the interlocking
interests of the banks' commercial and investment banking operations.

During the depressed business conditions of the '30's, three of the
country's largest banks (Banca Commerciale Italiana, Credito Italiano,
and Banco di Roma) faced a severe liquidity problem because of a
drastic decline in the value of some of their industrial securities.[12]
The banks established affiliates to relieve them of their industrial securities, but their efforts were too slow and unavailing for the magni-

---

[9] Cf. Article 32, *ibid.*, p. 40. This discussion of this important piece of banking legislation is limited to those parts of the 1936 act which bear directly on
bank competition.

[10] In his budget speech of May, 1933, the Minister of Finance noted the
movement toward a more "disciplined" banking organization and commented
that "In the conception of the Fascist Government this result could only be
achieved through unity of direction, closed organization, hierarchical gradua-
tion and discipline." Cited in S. R. Cope, *op. cit.*, p. 260.

[11] This is how the 1936 act struck an observer, writing in 1938. Cf. Cope,
p. 275.

[12] Cf. Clough, *op. cit.* (see n. 2 above), p. 249.

tude of the job they faced. Accordingly, on January 23, 1933, the government took action to salvage the situation by creating a new institution, the Istituto per la Ricostruzione Industriale (IRI), using state funds. To pump funds into the illiquid banks, IRI acquired some industrial securities held by the banks and also some of the stock of the banks. IRI originally intended to sell those securities to private groups, but many of the securities were not marketable because the companies were not sound,[13] and, in the case of banks and public services, the government decided that it would be desirable to retain control. IRI thus became a permanent holder of important bank and industrial shares.

The 1936 legislation also brought to a head the pressures which had been accumulating to strengthen the competitive controls. The original cartel agreement had been eased somewhat in 1929,[14] and though the cartel set the terms on which bank services were supplied, it did not control the rates on other bank operations. In 1932, the Bank of Italy began to exert pressure for a stronger cartel. In response to this official prodding, the ABI (which had been established as a bank trade organization by the ordinary credit banks in 1919) promoted a new cartel to reinforce and extend the controls of the earlier cartel. To strengthen the cartel (membership continued to be voluntary in spite of the official encouragement for the new cartel) the Banking Act of 1936 put the power of the state behind the cartel's decrees.

During the prewar years, the ABI gradually assumed greater importance as an instrumentality through which the banks could organize their cartel activities. During this period, too, its activities on behalf of the cartel acquired an increasingly official aura owing to behind-the-scenes encouragement from the regulatory authorities. The activities of the ABI were curtailed during the war period. In 1945, after the collapse of the corporate state, a new bankers' association was established which retained the name of the old association and inherited much of its authority, prestige, and activities.

Although the government which came to power after the Second World War was philosophically opposed to many of the controls established by its totalitarian predecessor, it was not disposed to do away with all of the former controls on bank competition. Some officials (like Luigi Einaudi, then governor of the Bank of Italy) favored less controls and more competition, but others (like Donato Menichella, then

---

[13] For a discussion of IRI's activities, including its salvage operations with the banks, cf. Pasquale Saraceno, "Twenty-five Years of Activity of the Istituto per la Ricostruzione Industriale," in *Review of Economic Conditions in Italy*, January, 1959, pp. 5–29.

[14] Cf. Antonello Gerbi, "Italy," in *Banking Systems*, ed. Benjamin H. Beckhart (New York, 1954), p. 454.

director-general and later governor of the Bank of Italy) wanted even
stronger controls to increase the safety of the system. The upshot of
these divergent views in government circles was that the preexisting
controls on banks were largely continued. The control powers over
deposit and loan rates and other conditions of bank competition (formerly exercised by the Credit Inspectorate and the Committee of
Ministers) were vested in an Interministerial Committee for Credit
and Savings,[15] which has continued to exercise those controls, operating
through the bank cartel.

The authorities eventually withdrew their support from the cartel,
not because of a changed view about the need or desirability of controls,
but because of the cartel's failures. In spite of changes from time to
time, the cartel rates established by the Interministerial Committee
had become increasingly unrelated to the underlying market realities,
and this led to widespread violations of the cartel, especially the cartel's
maximum deposit rates. In the face of the widespread violations, the
authorities abandoned their efforts to enforce the existing rate schedules and encouraged the banking fraternity to agree voluntarily on a
new set of rates and banking terms. On February 1, 1954, after a pro-
longed period of negotiation among the banks, a new Interbank Agreement, containing the terms voluntarily agreed upon, was signed by
banks representing 98 percent of total bank deposits.[16] Although the
bank of Italy did not officially approve the new cartel agreement, no
one doubted that its tacit acquiescence was intended as approval.[17]

The system of controls that was developed during the postwar years
has continued to the present. Moreover, in lieu of the tacit approval
of earlier years, the authorities now explicitly sanction the Interbank
Agreement: on January 28, 1963, the Credit Committee formally declared the Interbank Agreement to be in the public interest.[18] This
action completed the process of transformation which was under way
for four decades, and a cartel that began as a voluntary organization
among a few private banks has ended as a virtually compulsory organi-

---

[15] By a law of July 17, 1947, the direct supervision of credit was delegated
to the Bank of Italy. Cf. Banco di Roma, *The Italian Banking System* (Rome,
1960), p. 5.

[16] Cf. Gerbi, *op. cit.*, p. 447.

[17] The Bank of Italy's willingness to go along with the new cartel may have
been due in part to official indecision stemming from the conflict of views
about competition versus controls. In addition, even those officials who were
opposed to controls on principle may have felt that the time was not propitious
for pressing antimonopoly action. The war and the aftermath of inflation
had seriously undermined the capital position of the banks, and there was a
widespread disposition to permit the banks to enjoy a sheltered position until
their fundamental soundness had been assured.

[18] Cf. Bank of Italy, *Annual Report for 1962*, p. 69.

zation, embracing virtually all banks and performing an important role as an instrument of the government's monetary and economic policy.

CONTROLS ON THE CONDITIONS OF BANK COMPETITION

Controls on Interest Rates and Commissions

The controls on the conditions of bank competition include interest rates (on loans and deposits), commissions (on bank service), and other restrictions on bank activities.[19] The Banking Law of 1936 and subsequent amendments empowered the Bank of Italy to set maximum deposit rates, minimum loan rates, the conditions for deposit- and current-account operations, and the commissions for various banking services. In practice, as noted earlier, the Bank of Italy delegates this authority to the banking cartel, which in turn prescribes the approved rate structure as part of an interbank agreement.

The Italian Bankers Association (ABI) is responsible for working out the agreement to regulate bank competition. At the annual members' meeting, the president of the ABI presents his views on the most important policy questions facing the banks. Since the meeting is attended by the secretaries of the economic ministries, the governor of the Bank of Italy, and other important officials, the president's policy pronouncements are accorded the status of a quasi-official report. The speeches and reports presented at this meeting serve as a point of reference for the technical committees of the ABI, which arrange the details of a common approach on matters of banking policy. One of the technical committees prepares the detailed draft of the interbank agreement on rates and other matters. This particular committee, consisting of from twenty to twenty-five people, is supposed to represent all the bank members. Although the ABI's membership is composed of banks from well-defined bank categories (public law banks, banks of national interest, ordinary credit banks, people's cooperative banks, savings banks, and rural banks), the members are not officially represented on ABI committees by representatives from each bank category. This is supposed to emphasize the common interest of all banks and, by minimizing the opportunity for banks in each category to concentrate on their narrow self-interest, to make common agreement less difficult.

---

[19] These are by no means the only controls available to the authorities to regulate the operations and conduct of the banking system. Like the banks in most countries, those in Italy are regulated on numerous technical matters designed to ensure the liquidity and solvency as well as to make them responsive to the central bank's monetary policy. Those other controls will be ignored in this discussion unless they also happen to be used to regulate competition among banks.

The fact remains, however, that the interests of different bank groups frequently do differ. On the matter of defining fixed conditions for bank services, for example, the interests of banks with widespread networks of branches are frequently different from those of banks located exclusively (or overwhelmingly) in large cities.[20] When the technical committee is unable to agree on a point to be included in the Interbank Agreement, the matter is referred to a second committee composed of representatives of each of the six bank categories. Each bank group has three representatives on the committee, but each group has only one vote. If this second committee also is unable to agree, the matter is referred to the president of the ABI. If the issue is particularly sensitive, the president of the ABI will informally seek the advice of the governor of the Bank of Italy.

The above is the normal procedure for working out the routine agreements which do not make great changes in the Interbank Agreement—a state of affairs that may continue for years on end. If major changes were contemplated, a larger group of bank representatives would be convened. This was last done for the Interbank Agreement of 1954, which established the basic structure of the cartel rates that (with some modifications)[21] has been in force to the present. Under the 1954 agreement, the cartel stipulates the commissions for a wide variety of bank services, the minimum loan rates, and the maximum deposit rates.

The cartel's minimum loan rates (which are tied to Bank Rate) depend on whether the loan is secured or unsecured, the kind of collateral (for secured loans), the maturity of the loan, and even the particular form of the loan (bill, overdraft, advance, etc.). A representative sample of these rates is shown in Table 9. The volume of current-account overdrafts is far greater than bill discounts (the second most important form of bank lending) even though overdraft rates are higher than rates on promissory notes or discounts. In part, borrowers prefer overdrafts because there are fiscal charges made on bills.[22] In addition, the cost of overdrafts (even after allowing for the compulsory commission of 0.125 percent of the maximum amount of the overdraft outstanding per quarter or any fraction thereof) is not always higher than the discount rate, because the interest on overdrafts is paid only on the amount of credit actually used by the borrower.

The cartel sets the minimum loan rates for all lire loans, but it did not have an agreement about foreign currency loans until 1960, when

[20] Cf. "Italian Bankers Association," *Review of Economic Conditions in Italy*, September, 1950, p. 393.

[21] Cf. chapter V for a discussion of the loan and deposit rate changes made after the 1954 Agreement.

[22] Cf. Bank of Italy, *Annual Report for 1961*, p. 55.

they had become a more important part of the banks' activity. The agreements establish minimum rates for loans in dollars, sterling, and ten other foreign currencies,[23] and the minimum rates are related (by a system of stated margins) to the interest rates on those currencies in London and other foreign markets. There are two kinds of agreements: one is among the large commercial banks and is revised weekly; another includes a much larger number of banks and is revised infrequently.[24]

The cartel also stipulates the maximum rates on the large number of deposit categories in Italian banking. The distinction between demand-deposit and time-deposit accounts is not sharply drawn in all

TABLE 9
Cartel Minimum Loan Rates, 1966

Item	Rate (percent)
Blank (unsecured) credits	
Current-account overdrafts	7.00 + .125[a]
Promissory notes	5.75
Financial discounts	5.50
Discounting of commercial paper (depending on maturity of the bill)	5.00 − 5.75
Credits guaranteed by government securities	
Overdrafts	4.25
Promissory notes	4.00
Credits guaranteed by quoted shares, goods	
Overdrafts	6.50
Promissory notes	5.50[b]
	5.75[c]
Credits guaranteed by unquoted shares	
Overdrafts	6.75
Promissory notes	5.75

a Per quarter-year.
b Guaranteed by shares.
c Guaranteed by goods.
SOURCE: Prepared for the author by the ABI.

[23] Cf. G. Carroll Martenson, *The Euro-Dollar Market* (Boston, 1964), p. 43. The cartel agreements on foreign currency loans are less rigid and extensive than on lira loans. (Cf. Francesco Masera, "International Movements of Bank Funds and Monetary Policy in Italy," Banca Nazionale del Lavoro, *Quarterly Review*, December, 1966, p. 324.

[24] Cf. Oscar L. Altman, "Recent Developments in Foreign Markets for Dollars and Other Currencies," Joint Economic Committee, *Factors Affecting the United States Balance of Payments* (Washington, 1962), p. 506.

cases. The basic division for deposit accounts is between current accounts (*conti correnti*) and savings accounts (*depositi a risparmio*). The sums on deposit in "free" current accounts (*c/c liberi*) can be withdrawn on demand; the "tied" *(vincolati)* current accounts must be left in the bank for a fixed period or, alternatively, for an indeterminate period but with advance notification required before withdrawal.[25] The free accounts are further subdivided into "ordinary" current accounts (*c/c ordinari*) and "correspondence" current accounts (*c/c di corrispondenza*). The former are usually small, personal accounts which in theory can be withdrawn only by check; the latter are typically business accounts which the customer can also withdraw by instructions contained in a letter.[26]

The distinction between demand and time accounts is also blurred in the case of savings accounts (depositi a risparmio). Some savings accounts (the *depositi a risparmio liberi*) can be withdrawn by check (but deposits must be made at the bank); others are "tied."[27] The "free" savings accounts are further divided into "ordinary" accounts, savings books, and small savings books. There is no limit on the amounts in the ordinary savings accounts, which are demand deposits and can be withdrawn by check. The limit on savings book accounts is 100 million lire per account; and withdrawals are limited to 100,000 lire at sight, 200,000 lire after one day's notice, 500,000 lire after three days' notice, and more than 500,000 lire after ten days' notice. The limit on small savings-book accounts is 1,000,000 lire; and withdrawals are limited to 50,000 lire at sight, and ten days' notice for any larger withdrawal.[28]

The basic structure of maximum rates for all of these deposit categories has not been changed much since it was established by the 1954 Interbank Agreement. The cartel allows a higher maximum rate on large current accounts than on small accounts (Table 10). Before the 1954 agreement, maximum rates were stipulated for an even finer breakdown by size of demand account. After the 1954 agreement, these rates were set at a uniform ceiling of 2½ percent for all accounts with an average balance of more than 5 million lire, in order to "remove the drawbacks which the previous scale of rates had imposed on medium-size Banks."[29] The effect of the change was to raise the rate on accounts

---

[25] Cf. Pasquale Saraceno, *Le operazione bancarie* (Milan, 1957), p. 122.

[26] Cf. Bank of Italy, *Annual Report for 1954*, p. 49.

[27] In general, a deposit maturity of eighteen months (one year, before January, 1963) is the dividing line between short- and longer-term financial institutions.

[28] Cf. Joint Economic Committee, *A Description and Analysis of Certain European Capital Markets*, 88th Congress, 2d Session (Washington, 1964), pp. 180–181.

[29] Bank of Italy, *Annual Report for 1954*, p. 48.

between 5 and 50 million lire by one percent but to reduce the rate on the large accounts of 100 million lire and more by one-half percent. At present, a particularly favorable rate is allowed on public-agency accounts which exceed 500 million lire.

The cartel also allows different rates for small banks. Banks with less than 500 million lire deposits can pay as much as one-quarter percent more, and the rural and second-class pawn banks can pay as much as one-half percent more than the other banks. These differential

TABLE 10
Cartel Maximum Deposit Rates, 1966

Current accounts (conti correnti)	Percent
C/c di corrispondenza	
Free accounts (liberi)	
With a yearly average balance less than 5 million lire	0.50
With a yearly average balance more than 5 million lire	2.00
Tied accounts (vincolati)	
Less than 100 million lire	
3 – 6 months	2.25
6 – 12 months	3.00
12 – 18 months	3.75
More than 100 million lire	
3 – 6 months	2.75
6 – 12 months	3.50
12 – 18 months	4.25

Savings accounts and certificates (depositi a risparmio)	Percent
Free (liberi)	
Free (ordinary)	0.50[a]
Savings books	1.25[a]
Small savings books	1.50[a] (maximum deposit: 1 million lire)
Tied (vincolati)	
3 – 6 months	2.25[a]
6 – 12 months	3.00[a]
12 – 18 months	3.75[a]

[a] Rural and second-class pawn banks can increase the rate by .50 percent; banks with less than 500 million lire deposits can increase the rate by .25 percent.
SOURCE: Prepared for the author by the ABI.

rates are allowed as a matter of public policy: the banks with the higher ceiling rates tend to be located in the rural and less developed parts of the country where the public's savings are often held in cash ("under the mattress"), and higher rates are permitted in those areas to entice the savings into banks. The cartel also allows different maximum deposit rates according to maturity and size of account—higher ceiling rates for longer maturity or larger size. The size distinction is based on "the lower cost of handling larger deposits, and the better opportunity they offer for alternate investments."[30]

Enforcement of the Rate Agreements

The cartel agreements on rates and commissions have the approval of the Bank of Italy, but they are not formally promulgated as an official edict of the central bank. The Interbank Agreement on rates is thus technically a "voluntary" agreement among the banks, and violations of the cartel's rate agreement do not bring into play the full range of punitive measures at the disposal of the Bank of Italy. To enforce its decisions, the cartel relies on the punitive arrangements which the banks "voluntarily" accept when they join the ABI. The ultimate sanction, exclusion from the cartel with loss of certain privileges and benefits which accrue to members, is a last resort and is invoked only after repeated violations. The more usual penalty for violating the rate agreement[31] is a fine (which can be as much as one hundred times the amount of the infringement of the limits set by the cartel on deposit and loan rates). The monetary penalty is less a deterrent on its own terms than an expression of the moral pressure which is brought to bear on the offending bank. Until recently, the moral pressure of the ABI was the primary instrument for enforcing the Interbank Agreement on rates. To increase the effectiveness of this pressure, the ABI requires that the Interbank Agreement be signed personally by the administrators and the president of each member bank. "With this action," the president of the ABI stated, "we have done all that we can do."[32] In recent years, the governor of the Bank of Italy has added his immense moral authority to the Interbank Agreement.[33] The governor has not gone beyond exhortation, but he has left no doubt that he would resort to more formal measures if they should become necessary.

---

[30] Bank of Italy, *Annual Report for 1953*, p. 61.

[31] Under ABI rules, one bank can charge another bank with violating the agreement, and a hearing is held to examine the charge.

[32] "L'intervento dell'Avv. Siglienti ai lavori della Commissione d'inchiesta sui limiti alla concorrenza," in Associazione Bancaria Italiana, *Bancaria*, February, 1963, p. 214.

[33] Cf. Guido Carli, "Verso un assetto piu efficente del mercato monetario e finanziario," *Bancaria*, November, 1962, pp. 1273–1279.

Other Controls on the Conditions of Competition

Interbank competition is restrained by controls (other than on loan and deposit rates) which set well-defined limits on the form and scope of bank competition. For example, the cartel controls banking hours strictly and rigidly. If exceptions are allowed, the business that can be transacted under the terms of the exception is strictly regulated. Thus, banks or branches that cater to a particular clientele (e.g., banks located near markets, railway stations, airports, and so forth) are sometimes authorized to provide banking services outside of regular hours, but they must limit such business strictly to the special clientele for which the exception was granted, and they are expressly forbidden to transact any other business during the irregular hours.[34]

Competition is also regulated with respect to the manner of soliciting customers. The regulation on this point is brief but pointed: "Banks (*aziende di credito*) are absolutely forbidden to solicit new clients with methods which are not in keeping with the dignity of the banking function. Such a prohibition, which applies especially to visits to residences to solicit *new* clients, particularly if these are already receiving credit from other banks, also includes the gratuitous supply of printed matter or other such items, sending propaganda circulars, and especially granting credit without a specific request by the interested party."[35] Two parts of this prohibition are particularly worth stressing: the restraints on competition for the business of clients who are already doing business with another bank, and the prohibition against offering a loan as a device to attract customers.

A particularly important restriction on the scope of competition is the "territorial competence" rule. This regulation restricts the mobility of both banks and borrowers—but not of depositors.[36] It restricts the mobility of banks by designating a "zone of competence" for each bank (and branch) and requiring that each bank (and branch) confine its operations to its prescribed zone. It restricts the mobility of borrowers in a similar way. For purposes of territorial competence, individuals are classified by their place of residence, and the regulation makes no concession for a business firm which has branches, factories, or offices outside of the zone in which it is legally domiciled.[37]

The authorities can make exceptions to territorial competence restrictions in special cases, such as inadequate local credit facilities. In

---

[34] Cf. *La legge bancaria, op. cit.* (see n. 8 above) p. 172.

[35] *Ibid.*, p. 159 (italics in original).

[36] The regulation strictly forbids a bank to solicit deposits outside of its area, but it does not prohibit a bank from receiving deposits from customers who are outside of its zone of competence. Cf. *idem.*

[37] Cf. *ibid.*, p. 158.

granting exceptions, the Bank of Italy considers two additional factors: (1) whether the customer conducts at least part of his activity in that area, and whether the amount of credit he gets from banks in the area is in relation and proportional to his local business; and (2) whether an exception would prejudice the conditions of sound competition— that is, would local banks be injured by permitting outside banks to lend in that area.[38]

To obtain an exception to the territorial competence rule, a bank had to provide the Bank of Italy with the following information: name and description of the client and description of his business; nature of the bank's relationship with the customer (e.g., discount, rediscount, current account, advance on securities or merchandise, banking services, etc.); and a summary of geographical information including the prospective client's residence and "statistical data of a demographic, economic and banking character."[39]

The territorial competence restriction was introduced after the passage of the Banking Law of 1936, and until the reform of mid-1966, the authorities did not permit a large number of exceptions.[40] The purpose of the original territorial competence regulation was twofold: (1) "to combat one of the most insidious and troublesome forms of banking competition . . ."[41] and (2) to induce banks to confine their relationships to customers in their own zones where banks could excercize better control. In keeping with these purposes, the original regulation had stipulated that a bank (or branch) outside of a provincial capital had to restrict its operations to the territorial boundaries of its *commune*. A bank (or branch) in a provincial capital could operate anywhere within the province, but a small bank of a local character had to limit its operations to the town or towns in which it was located, even if that town was the provincial capital.

At its meeting of July 8, 1966, the Interministerial Committee on Credit and Savings modified the territorial competence restrictions to take account of economic changes that had been accumulating over a thirty-year period.[42] As far as the first goal was concerned, the committee stated that the original regulation had stressed the possible injury to small banks from the competition of large banks located outside of the district but had ignored the advantages (wider range and more efficient services as well as better terms) that the best economic operators

---

[38] Banca d'Italia, *Assemblea generale ordinaria dei partecipanti*, 1952, p. 429.

[39] *La legge bancaria, op. cit.* (see n. 8 above), p. 158.

[40] Cf. Vera Lutz, "The Central Bank and the System of Credit Control," in *Banking in Western Europe*, ed. R. S. Sayers (Oxford, 1962), p. 158.

[41] *La legge bancaria, op. cit.*, p. 157.

[42] This discussion of the new regulation is based on Associazione Bancaria Italiana, Serie Tecnica, Circolare n. 166, "Competenza territoriale delle aziende di credito" (Rome, December 29, 1966).

of the zone could secure from large banks. In the committee's view, those advantages had become more important than the disadvantages in the country's present stage of economic development, and especially in the less developed regions or provinces. Significantly, the committee decided that it would be better to secure those advantages by enlarging the territorial competence of the large banks instead of authorizing them to establish branches in provincial capitals (where they had no offices). Not only would this hold down the operating costs of banks (and therefore improve the possibility that banks could offer better terms to their customers) but it would also mean that the competition from the more powerful banks would have a lesser impact on the small banks.

The committee stated that changing economic circumstances had also altered the efficacy of the territorial competence restriction in securing the second goal. When the regulation was introduced, the provincial capitals were also the economic and banking centers in each province. As a result of improvements in communications and in transportation (especially by automobile), the economic and banking centers frequently extend into adjacent provinces as well. Similarly, many municipalities that are administratively autonomous have been incorporated into larger urban agglomerations.

In view of these developments, the committee framed a new territorial competence regulation, based on the concept of a "zone of economic influence." Pending a full and detailed inquiry into the boundaries of these zones, the committee ordered the following changes to be put into effect on an experimental basis: Large banks (i.e., those with total deposits in excess of 300 billion lire) with headquarters or a branch in the principal city of an economic region can now make loans anywhere in the region, and large banks that are located outside of the principal city can operate anywhere in the province.[43] Similarly, small banks of a clearly local character can now be authorized (if they are deemed worthy by virtue of their size and efficient organizational structure) to ignore the limits of their particular commune and to lend within the larger urban agglomeration of which they are a part.

CHANGING VIEWS ABOUT THE ROLE OF CONTROLS ON COMPETITION

Over the years, the restraints imposed on bank competition have been justified in different ways. In the 1919 cartel, competitive restrictions

---

[43] As a result of these changes, four large banks (Banca Nazionale del Lavoro, Banca Commerciale Italiana, Credito Italiano, Banco di Roma) can operate anywhere in Italy. Cf. *idem*.

were imposed "to regulate . . . a competition that might have been detrimental,"[44] that is, to ensure that banks did not endanger their capital and the safety of their deposits by carrying their rivalry for customers "to the limit of imprudence." The view that competition must be restrained to prevent "a disorderly action and an increase in costs, damage and risk for the operation of credit and for the very stability of the credit and monetary system of the country"[45] is perhaps the most enduring reason for restraining bank competition.

After the First World War, the absence of controls on entry was blamed for an overbanked situation and excessive bank competition. This was an important consideration behind those provisions of the banking legislation of 1926 and 1936 that increased concentration. Once accomplished, however, the concentration that the state encouraged in order to prevent too much bank competition became in turn an independent reason for preserving and extending the controls on bank competition. As one writer put it, bank controls and even direct government intervention became essential, owing "to the formation of banks of such size that it was impossible for the State not to take an interest in their credit policies and in the protection of the depositors who entrusted their savings to them."[46]

The growth of bank concentration led to controls on the conditions of bank competition for another reason. As one writer explained, bank competition in the classical sense of perfect competition is not possible in Italy because "one of the fundamental factors of this situation is lacking, that is to say the existence of banks of almost equal size and importance, in which case none of them would exert any considerable influence on the price of services rendered and received, the result being that prices would be fixed by the market and each bank compelled to accept them."[47] Under a concentrated banking structure, bank rivalry is oligopolistic rivalry, with a danger of cutthroat price competition; hence, "the 'cartel' among banks . . . is justified . . . by the advisability of preventing the delicate mechanism of credit to be upset."[48]

Bank competition has also been restricted in order to preserve a particular banking structure. Whereas it was argued in an earlier period that the number of banks had to be held down to prevent undue bank competition, it has been argued more recently (by Governor Carli in

---

[44] Banco di Roma, "The Italian Banking System," *Review of Economic Conditions in Italy*, November, 1951, p. 496.

[45] *Ibid.*, November, 1960, p. 645.

[46] "The Italian Banking System," July, 1947, p. 214.

[47] C. Bresciani-Turroni, "Interest Rates in Italy," *Review of Economic Conditions in Italy*, January, 1949, p. 16.

[48] *Idem.* He also recognized, however, the danger that the agreements could "deteriorate into an actual monopoly detrimental to the country."

testimony before a parliamentary inquiry on the state of competition in the Italian economy) that bank competition had to be controlled to preserve the existing number of banks. The Italian banking system now consists of a few large banks that operate on a national basis and numerous medium-size and small banks with a regional or local scope. In Governor Carli's view, bank competition must be restrained to protect the medium-size and small banks from the competition of the large nationwide branch banks. As the latter can transfer funds to any part of the country "without any cost except the cost of a telephone call," they can at any time concentrate sufficient resources at any point in the country to exclude all of the existing banks and to force out all marginal banks.[49] Hence, controls to restrict competition are needed to preserve a structure in which small banks, operating at regional or local levels, can coexist with large nationwide branch banks.[50] As noted earlier, the authorities consider it important to preserve the existing banking structure, with decision-making authority distributed among a number of different-sized banks, to ensure an "impartial" allocation of credit among business firms. In short, bank competition is restricted to prevent an increase in industrial concentration, for if the small firms were deprived of necessary credit, they would be forced to merge with the large firms.[51]

Finally, the controls on bank competition have received their most recent and emphatic support from the monetary authorities, who regard the competitive controls as important instruments of monetary policy and, indeed, of the government's broader economic policy.[52]

---

[49] Cf. testimony of Governor Carli in Camera dei deputati, *Commissione d'inchiesta sui limiti posti alla concorrenza nel campo economico*, seduta del 22 Novembre 1962 (Resoconti stenografici de interrogatorio del Dottor Guido Carli), p. 11. The testimony does not spell out the underlying assumptions of the process by which the local banks would be forced out. Thus, it is not clear whether the small banks are assumed to be inherently less efficient than the large banks (and thus unable to match the large bank's terms) or whether, regardless of comparative efficiency, they would be vulnerable (in the absence of controls) to cutthroat competition by a larger bank determined to eliminate a smaller rival in order to establish a local monopoly.

[50] Governor Carli has also stated that it is against the public interest to permit competition to eliminate banks by bankruptcy. Cf. *ibid.*, pp. 10–11.

[51] In recent years, the government's concern about the impairment of competition in industry led to a parliamentary inquiry. Cf. "Testo del disegno di legge per la tutela della liberta della concorrenza—Relazione ministeriale e parere del CNEL," *Rivista internazionale di scienze sociali*, January–February, 1960, pp. 85–105.

[52] This is discussed in Chapter VI.

IV
Competitive Regulations and Market Structures

The market structure of banking markets is related to the level of bank concentration, but the relationship is neither simple nor unique. One reason is that bank concentration is typically calculated on a nationwide basis, and many banking markets are not nationwide. In Italian banking markets, the analysis of the relation between bank and market concentration is further complicated by the territorial competence rule which fragments some but not all banking markets. Since territorial competence rules place limitations on a nationwide loan market but not on a nationwide deposit market (except for the restriction on soliciting deposits), it is convenient to examine separately the factors which affect the market structure of loan and deposit markets.

MARKET SEGMENTATION AND MARKET STRUCTURE IN LOAN MARKETS

Under the territorial competence regulation, each business firm must restrict its bank borrowings to the area where it has its legal headquarters. However, equal treatment under the territorial competence rule does not ensure equal effects, and in spite of the Procrustean adjustment which confines all borrowers to "local" markets, they do not all face equal market conditions. The major reasons are differences in borrower mobility, lender preferences, bank concentration in local markets, and nonbank alternatives.

Territorial Competence and Borrower Mobility

One reason that equal treatment under the territorial competence rule can have unequal effects is that borrowers are inherently unequal in terms of mobility. The inherent differences in borrower mobility are highly associated with borrower size. Most large business firms have excellent credit ratings, and bankers in any part of the country can easily secure information about the credit standing of major firms. By contrast, most small borrowers do not have prime credit ratings; even if they had, it would be more difficult or costly for a distant than for a local banker to appraise their credit position. As the Bank of Italy once observed, "Credit to small and medium-sized businesses is . . . inevitably based on the personal qualities of the owners . . . and only bank managers who keep in close contact with these people can follow changes in such management with the necessary continuity and attention."[1]

On the basis of their usually superior credit ratings[2] (including the ease of securing information about them), large borrowers would normally enjoy a much greater mobility than small borrowers. Other things being equal, territorial competence per se would tend to neutralize this inherent superiority and, to this extent, would bear more heavily on the large (and medium-size) than on the small borrowers. Because of inherent limitations on their mobility, most small borrowers would be restricted to their local areas even if territorial competence restrictions did not exist, whereas in the absence of artificial restraints, the larger business borrower could typically command access to bank suppliers over a wider geographical area and, at least for the largest borrowers, over the entire country.

Credit ratings and other pertinent characteristics which affect a borrower's inherent mobility are not the same for all medium-size or small borrowers; hence, all borrowers within a particular size-group will not be equally affected by territorial competence restrictions. Territorial competence rules may have little or no effect on the weakest borrowers in each size category because their inherent mobility may be more limiting than the legal restrictions. Bankers commonly require an exhaustive credit investigation before lending for the first time to a small borrower, and the expense and bother of such an investigation will not seem worthwhile in many cases. As a result, some small borrowers are confined to a single bank even when they are located in a major city with a large number of banks. By contrast, the strongest (i.e., with the best credit ratings and other pertinent characteristics) of the medium-size and small borrowers could be affected by territorial competence restrictions if, in the absence of those restrictions, they would have been able to secure access to banks in adjacent zones. Thus, the

---

[1] Bank of Italy, *Annual Report for 1958*, p. 116.

[2] In this connection, cf. Governor Carli's statement that "Credits of small and medium amount are those scrutinized most closely. Banks seem to think that such credits involve heavier risks because the firms to which they are extended might go bankrupt, whereas credits to large firms, especially those in the public sector, are thought to be immune from this particular risk" (Bank of Italy, *Annual Report for 1964*, p. 136).

territorial competence rule per se would restrict (but not, of course, to the same degree) the mobility of the strongest medium-size and small borrowers as well as of the large borrowers.

In sum, as a result of inherent differences in mobility, different-sized borrowers may face quite different banking alternatives in spite of being located in the same territorial zone. This is confirmed by surveys which show that large firms, in contrast to small firms, can borrow at the same time from several banks.[3] The "fractionalization" of loans to large borrowers has been ascribed to a number of factors, including "the banks' own practices of *risk evaluation*, competition among banks, the legal ceiling on credits, and the *greater wealth of information available* on this class of credit users."[4]

Lender Preferences

Aside from inherent differences in mobility, all borrowers in a given zone do not have equal access to all of the banks in that area because of restrictions, self-imposed by banks, which limit banker mobility. These self-imposed restrictions reflect different banker preferences which most commonly lead large banks to deal with large borrowers, and small banks to deal with small borrowers.[5] These different preference patterns are not necessarily related to the differences in borrower credit ratings. In many cases, they go back to the historical origins and early development of banks in the different bank categories. Thus, virtually from their inception, the banks of national interest were important suppliers to large business. Their emphasis on large borrowers contrasts strikingly with the behavior of other bank categories. At the end of 1965, for example, the banks of national interest and the ordinary credit banks handled about the same volume of loans, but the latter banks had more than four times as many borrowers as the former (Table 11). There is also a disproportion between the volume of loans and the number of customers at the national interest banks and the public law banks. As noted earlier, the most important public law bank, the Banca Nazionale del Lavoro, closely resembles the banks of national interest and places great emphasis on its dealing with large firms. This is less true in the other public law banks, and the category as a whole resembles the ordinary credit banks rather than the national

---

[3] Cf. *ibid.*

[4] Bank of Italy, *Annual Report for 1964*, p. 110 (my italics). It is interesting to note that small as well as large banks participate in loans to large borrowers. Cf. *ibid.*, p. 137.

[5] These lender preferences are frequently matched by corresponding borrower preferences.

TABLE 11

Total Loans and Number of Borrowers, by Kind of Bank,
December 31, 1965

Bank category	Borrowers		Loans	
	Number	Percent	Amount (million lire)	Percent
Public law	848,031	18.8	3,809,569	25.2
National interest	146,133	3.2	3,290,588	21.8
Ordinary credit	696,497	15.5	3,320,974	22.0
People's cooperative	485,219	10.8	1,591,433	10.5
Savings and first-class pawn	2,326,088	51.7	3,111,357	20.6
Totals	4,501,968	100.0	15,123,921	100.1

SOURCE: Banca d'Italia, *Bollettino.*

interest banks. At the opposite extreme, the savings and first-class pawn banks accounted for only about 20 percent of total bank loans, but they dealt with half of the total bank borrowers—dramatic evidence of their tendency to deal with medium-size and small borrowers.

The tendency for banks in different categories to deal with borrowers in particular size-groups appears to be due to differences in banker preferences based on size of borrower and not to any tendency to concentrate their loans in those sectors where a particular size of borrower happens to predominate. Table 12 (mean loan size in different sectors, by kind of bank) reveals a very high consistency in the rank order of the bank categories in each sector: national interest banks (invariably first), public law, ordinary credit, people's cooperative, savings, and first-class pawn banks. As this bank tendency (to concentrate their lending in particular borrower size-groups) limits the effective alternatives available to different borrowers in the same zone of competence, it cannot be ignored in any attempt to determine the effective concentration facing any particular borrower.

Bank Concentration in Local Areas

Another reason why all borrowers are not affected equally by the territorial competence restrictions which confine them all to their "local" areas is that bank concentration differs widely in different areas and this, in turn, is associated with different levels of local market concentrations. There are no suitable figures on the extent of local market concentration in local markets in different parts of the country, but the existence of differences is strongly suggested by the wide regional differences in bank concentration (as measured by the distribution of

TABLE 12

Mean Loan Size in Different Sectors, by Kind of Bank,
December 31, 1965
(million lire)

Bank category	Non-commercial and financial	Public works and services	Agricultural and food	Industrial and commercial (non-food)	All industries
Public law	1.6	18.9	4.3	15.7	4.5
National interest	9.4	25.6	19.8	27.9	22.5
Ordinary credit	2.1	9.2	3.4	9.4	4.8
People's cooperative	1.6	6.5	2.0	6.3	3.3
Savings and first-class pawn	.8	5.3	2.2	3.4	1.3
All banks	1.2	9.7	3.6	10.1	3.4

SOURCE: Calculated from data in Banca d'Italia, Bollettino. A certain amount of medium- and long-term loans are included in these figures, but they are not very important (except for the savings and pawn banks in which medium- and long-term loans were 42 percent of total loans).

bank loans among different-sized banks—Table 13). Thus, loans made by "three big banks" (the banks of national interest) as a percentage of total bank loans in each region ranged from a low of 3.4 percent in Basilicata to a high of 33.7 percent in Puglia. At the other extreme, the loan share of the "other banks"—essentially regional branch banks and small local banks—was 88.8 percent in Valle d'Aosta, 38.1 percent in Sicilia, and 25.5 percent in Campania. The low figures for "other banks" in Sicily and in other southern regions is due to the weight of the Banco di Sicilia and the Banco di Napoli (both included in the "six big banks" figure). Indeed, as these two banks are particularly well entrenched in the south, the loan concentration in the south and the islands is even higher than is suggested by the three-bank or six-bank figures. To repeat, these figures on bank concentration do not describe the extent of local market concentration in different regions, but in view of the magnitude of the differences, they do lend support to the probability of wide differences in the market concentration of "local" markets in different parts of the country.

TABLE 13

Regional Distribution of Bank Loans, June 30, 1962

(percent)

Region	Three big banks[a]	Six big banks[b]	Other banks
Piemonte	23.7	34.8	65.2
Valle d'Aosta	11.2	11.2	88.8
Lombardia	22.4	34.3	65.7
Liguria	32.5	54.5	45.5
Trentino–Alto Adige	13.5	21.6	78.4
Veneto	20.6	33.5	66.5
Friuli-Venezia Giulia	25.4	43.3	56.7
Emilia-Romagna	17.9	28.8	71.2
Toscana	17.2	28.4	71.6
Umbria	15.6	26.0	74.0
Marche	11.3	27.0	73.0
Lazio	23.4	54.3	45.7
Abruzzi e Molise	14.6	45.8	54.2
Campania	29.8	74.5	25.5
Puglia	33.7	60.8	39.2
Basilicata	3.4	21.9	78.1
Calabria	20.1	46.1	53.9
Sicilia	15.7	61.9	38.1
Sardegna	22.5	47.9	52.1

a Banca Commerciale Italiana, Credito Italiano, Banco di Roma.

b Banca Nazionale del Lavoro, Banca Commerciale Italiana, Credito Italiano, Banco di Roma, Banco di Napoli, Banco di Sicilia.

SOURCE: Governor Carli's testimony in Camera dei deputati, *Commissione d'inchiesta sui limiti posti alla concorrenza nel campo economico*, Seduta del 22 novembre 1962 (Resoconti stenografici di interrogatorio del Dottor Guido Carli), pp. 37 and 34.

Although all borrowers are confined to their "local" areas by territorial competence regulations, large borrowers have an advantage over other borrowers. First, they have access to all major banks—large borrowers are typically located in major cities, and all large branch banks have offices in all major cities. Second, as a result of branch banking, the large borrowers in any one major city are not limited to the resources which each large bank can raise in that particular city.[6] Thus, in spite of the territorial competence restriction on large-borrower mobility, the bank-concentration figures for the country as a whole can provide a better (but not perfect) index of the bank concentration facing large borrowers in a particular major city than the apparent banking concentration within that city. In other words, the presence of large branch systems tends to equalize the effective concentration faced by large borrowers in widely separated zones of competence and thus helps to counteract the concentration-increasing effects which territorial competence restrictions might otherwise have on large-borrower markets.[7]

The equalizing tendencies which operate in large-borrower markets are far less effective in the medium-size- or small-borrower markets. In part, this is because the large branch banks, although they have offices in all major cities, are less important suppliers to small and medium-size borrowers than to large borrowers. In addition, the large branch banks do not all have offices in many local areas outside of major cities.

The latest liberalizations of the territorial competence restrictions can overcome this lack to some degree, but (as the Interministerial Committee has acknowledged) the extension of a bank's territorial competence is not a complete substitute for local offices. Because of inherent limitations on their mobility, most small borrowers could not overcome the differences in local market concentration even in the absence of territorial competence restrictions. This is less true for the medium-size borrowers, and it seems likely, therefore, that the territorial competence restrictions bear most heavily on the borrowers in this size-group.

Alternative Sources of Funds

Finally, all borrowers in a particular zone of competence do not face equal market-structure conditions because they do not have equal access

[6] In a country with extensive branch banking, banking resources can be shifted easily and quickly to any part of the country by interbranch transfer of funds. For this reason, it is not possible to derive an unambiguous measure of bank (loan) concentration in many Italian cities. In any attempt to calculate bank concentration in major cities (where the banking structure consists of a number of local banks and of branches of many regional and all large national banks), the only unambiguous figures pertain to the local banks.

[7] On the other hand, the presence of large branch systems also makes for a higher level of market concentration in the large-borrower markets than would otherwise exist.

to alternative sources of funds. In this case, too, the differences are largely related to size of borrower. Large firms have an advantage over medium-size and small firms with respect to three alternative sources of funds. First, by virtue of their large size, large firms can secure funds from the capital market, and those funds can sometimes substitute for bank loans. Second, large firms have been able to secure a much larger volume of funds from internal sources than medium-size or small business firms.[8] Third, at least some large firms have an advantageous position with respect to the market for foreign currency loans. In the usual case, the Italian authorities have decreed that, in order to discourage excessive borrowing of Euro-dollars, "non-banks can only borrow through the intermediary of banks in Italy."[9] This is an important restriction because the domestic bank suppliers of foreign currency loans operate in a rather highly concentrated segment of the loan market. In 1962, for example, three large banks supplied 42.4 percent of foreign currency loans in Italy, and six large banks supplied 68.6 percent (Table 14). On the other hand, at least some large borrowers in the foreign currency loan market are not limited to domestic suppliers—for example, leading corporations which are members of, or associated with, international groups, especially in sectors such as oil.[10] By their ability to tap suppliers in foreign countries, such large borrowers operate in a less concentrated market for foreign currency loans than other borrowers. Moreover, because of substitutability character-

TABLE 14

Foreign Currency Loans, by Kind of Bank, June 30, 1962

Bank category	Amount (billion lire)	Percent of total
3 large banks[a]	318.2	42.4
6 large banks[b]	514.2	68.6
50 principal banks	717.2	95.6
365 banks[c]	749.9	100.0

a The three banks of national interest.
b See Table 13 on p. 45, n. b.
c See Table 2 on p. 11, n. a.
SOURCE: Testimony of Governor Carli, *op. cit.* (see Table 13), Table 6, p. 30.

---

[8] In recent years, this has become a less important source of business financing than in previous years. Cf. Bank of Italy, *Annual Report for 1965*, p. 22. Between 1959 and 1961, self-financing accounted for 60 percent of gross investment; between 1962 and 1964, the figure had fallen to 39 percent. *Ibid.*, pp. 138–39.
[9] Paul Einzig, *The Euro-Dollar System*, 2d ed. (London, 1965), p. 123.
[10] Cf. Paolo Baffi, "Monetary Developments in Italy from 1961 to 1965," Banca Nazionale del Lavoro, *Quarterly Review*, March, 1966, p. 26.

istics between lira loans and foreign currency loans,[11] a large borrower
who can tap a supplier in a foreign country may affect the terms he
secures in the lira loan market as well.[12]

Medium-size and small firms have one important advantage over
large firms in terms of alternative sources of funds. As a matter of
national policy, the government encouraged the growth of medium-
size and small firms, in part by government subsidies for medium-
and long-term credit. Under the terms of Law No. 623, medium-size
and small firms in northern and central Italy can secure credit up to
a maximum of ten years at a preferential rate of 5 percent. The terms
are even more liberal in the south: a preferential rate of 3 percent
on loans with a maximum maturity of fifteen years.[13] The volume
of privileged credits (i.e., eligible for government subsidies under Law
No. 623) has been rising in recent years. Between 1961 and 1965, the
volume of privileged credits outstanding rose by 1,300 billion lire.[14]
These medium- and long-term sources are at least partial alternatives
to bank credit because, in practice, the distinction between the short-
and longer-term credits granted by Italian banks is sometimes blurred.
During the postwar period in particular, "probably some part of
what were formally short-term loans, or 'callable' loans, were in reality
being used to finance permanent investments in stocks and in plant and
equipment, unaccompanied by any pre-established plans for refinancing
at long-term."[15]

In spite of this government assistance, the medium-size and small
business firms depend far more than the large firms on bank credit.
In large firms, the ratio of bank debt to sales is strikingly lower than
in medium-size and small firms—only one-half of one percent for the

---

[11] According to Einzig, "Originally Euro-dollar facilities lent for commercial
purposes served almost exclusively the requirements of foreign trade, but
gradually they came to be used extensively also to meet domestic requirements" (*The Euro-Dollar System*, p. 40).

[12] In the absence of official prohibitions (or other obstacles) to borrowing
abroad, a large borrower's ability to tap a supplier in another country can
alter his market-structure position by increasing the total number of his
possible suppliers, whereas a foreign currency loan secured from a domestic
bank (whether native- or foreign-owned) would not alter the number (although
it may have some marginal effect on the concentration) of his alternative
sources. On the other hand, even in the absence of any market-structure effects, foreign currency loans supplied by domestic banks can exert a rate-
reducing influence on domestic loan markets if they constitute a net increase
in the country's supply of loanable funds.

[13] Cf. Interrogatorio del Dottor Guido Carli, in Camera dei deputati, *Commissione d'inchiesta sui limiti posti alla concorrenza nel campo economico*,
seduta del 22 Novembre 1962, Table 15, p. 39.

[14] Cf. Bank of Italy, *Annual Report for 1965*, p. 83.

[15] Cf. Luigi Ceriani, "The Commercial Banks and Financial Institutions,"
in *Banking in Western Europe*, ed. R. S. Sayers (Oxford, 1962), p. 131.

largest firms as compared with a high of 18.5 percent for the smallest firms (Table 15). Moreover, the funds that medium-size and small firms secure from industrial credit institutions[16] are probably not a net addition to their bank lines. In 1962, for example, when the medium-credit institutions supplied a larger volume of funds to medium-size and small firms, the banks did just the reverse. This was due in part to the growing pressure for funds in that year,[17] but it may also have been due to the fact that the collateral requirements of the medium-credit institutions left the medium- and small-size firms without adequate collateral to secure bank loans.[18]

To summarize some of these observations about banking markets, it seems clear (in spite of the crude figures) that market concentration is relatively low in the large-borrower markets. Large borrowers have other alternatives in addition to bank loans, but market concentration in the large-borrower markets would be low (cf. Table 8)[19] if it were

TABLE 15

Sales and Bank Loans of Selected Firms, by Size of Firm, 1960

Sales volume (billion lire)	Number of firms	Sales (billion lire)	Bank debt (billion lire)	Bank debt/Sales (percent)
3 – 5	42	170.3	31.4	18.5
5 – 15	87	778.2	90.2	11.6
15 – 25	28	537.3	71.9	13.4
25 – 50	16	559.8	64.7	11.6
50 – 100	4	253.7	22.9	9.0
100 – 200	4	591.8	23.1	3.9
More than 200	1	508.4	2.6	0.5

SOURCE: Testimony of Governor Carli, *op. cit.* (see Table 13), Table 18, p. 43. The figures do not apply to all firms in the indicated categories but only to those firms for which the indicated information was available.

[16] These include the Istituto di Credito per il finanziamento a medio termine alla media e piccola industrie in Piedmont, Lombardy, Venetia, Emilia, Liguria, Tuscany, Umbria, the Marches, Latium, etc.; the Istituto per lo Sviluppo Economico per l'Italia Meridionale (ISVEIMER); the Istituto per lo Sviluppo della Sicilia (IRFIS), which operates in Sicily; and Credito Industriale Sardo (CIS) for Sardinia. These institutions derive their funds both from the government and from private sources. In addition, these institutions can secure rediscounts, advances, and various subsidies from Mediocredito, a central institution.

[17] Bank of Italy, *Annual Report for 1962*, p. 107.

[18] Vera Lutz, *A Study in Economic Development* (London, 1962), p. 115. In addition, a larger liability on medium-term credits would affect a firm's credit-worthiness in terms of a bank loan.

[19] While the classifications are obviously not directly relevant, it is suggestive to compare the grouping of American manufacturing industries according to seller concentration. Cf. Joe Bain, *Industrial Organization* (New York, 1959), pp. 124–133.

calculated entirely in terms of banking concentration (and assuming that overall bank concentration can be accepted as a rough index of bank concentration in the major large-borrower markets). Even when they are located in the same local areas, medium-size and small borrowers face more limited alternatives than large borrowers. They depend far more than large firms on bank financing, and they are also more limited in terms of strictly banking alternatives. Because of a combination of inherent limitations on small-borrower mobility, and self-imposed restrictions on lender mobility, the weakest small borrowers may be restricted to a single bank even in major cities with a large number of banks. Others are less narrowly restricted; but when they are located in areas where the level of local bank concentration is higher than the national level, they (unlike large borrowers) cannot count on the equalizing tendencies of branch banking to overcome the market effects of the higher bank concentration.

THE DIVERSITY OF DEPOSIT MARKETS

From a legal point of view, a basic distinction is made between current accounts and savings accounts, but from the cartel's point of view (in regulating the rate structure on deposits), a more important division (which cuts across both the current account and the savings account categories) is between "free" accounts (including the *conti correnti ordinari*) and "tied" accounts. In the 1954 Interbank Agreement, the cartel set a uniformly low maximum rate of one-half percent for conti correnti ordinari and free ordinary savings accounts, whereas the lowest maximum rate for the tied accounts, of both the current and savings account varieties, was 2.50 percent. Broadly speaking, the free accounts are demand-deposit accounts (with some reservations in the case of *depositi a risparmio liberi*); the correspondence current accounts, which include the greater part of the available funds of business firms, are also demand accounts, and their volume is related primarily to the transactions needs of firms.[20] The tied accounts are time accounts held by individuals as a repository for their bona fide savings which are entrusted to the banks more or less permanently.[21] Tied accounts are also held by business firms as "the favorite repositories of funds raised through equity accounts and bond issues, pending actual investment expenditure."[22]

The cartel sets the ceiling rates on the various deposit categories,

[20] Cf. "Deposits with Italian Banks," *Review of Economic Conditions in Italy*, March, 1952, pp. 118–119.

[21] *Idem.*

[22] Bank of Italy, *Annual Report for 1961*, p. 51.

but competition determines the actual rates paid for deposits. There is no single deposit market but rather a number of submarkets with varying degrees of insulation from each other. As in the case of loan markets, many influences which determine the size and scope of the deposit markets are associated with size of depositor. In the absence of artificial restraints, large and small depositors would operate in substantially different geographical orbits. The large depositor (e.g., a firm with nationwide business) would operate over a wide area because it would be worthwhile to compare the terms offered by banks in widely separated areas and to shift accounts to the most advantageous locations.[23] By contrast, the mobility of small depositors would be inhibited by lack of information about distant alternatives, the inconvenience of doing business with a distant bank,[24] and the small advantage to be gained from shifting a small account even for a perceptible difference in rate.

The potentially greater mobility of the large depositor is important in analyzing the structure of deposit markets because depositor mobility, unlike borrower mobility, is not restricted by law (or cartel agreement). The territorial competence restriction does apply to depositors but in a much milder form than to borrowers. While it restricts banks from soliciting deposit accounts outside of their zones, it does not prevent them from opening an account for a depositor in a different zone of competence. Thus, the territorial competence restriction does not impede the mobility of an aggressive large depositor.

The major banks have branches in the major cities, but their presence does not have an equal effect on all depositors in those cities. In part, this is because certain banks prefer to concentrate on certain *kinds* of deposits or depositors. The banks of national interest, for example, have no interest in the deposit categories of *piccolo risparmio speciale* or *buoni fruttiferi* (Table 16). Indeed, since those categories are ignored by most banks, they are a virtual monopoly of the savings and first-class pawn banks. On the other hand, the banks of national interest have an exceptionally strong interest in business accounts *(conti correnti di corrispondenza)*, which are far less important (though not negligible) in the liability structure of the savings and first-class pawn banks.

The specialization of different bank categories in particular kinds of deposits appears to be related to their preferences for dealing with depositors of a particular size. Thus, the average-size deposit account

---

[23] For an example of the rate sensitivity of large depositors, cf. Bank of Italy, *Annual Report for 1954*, pp. 58 and 61.

[24] Some small depositors are willing to put up with some inconvenience in dealing with a distant bank to protect the privacy of their affairs.

TABLE 16

Composition of Deposit Structure, by Kind of Bank,
December 31, 1965

| | Deposits held by | | | | | | | | | |
| Deposit category | Public law | | National interest | | Ordinary credit | | People's cooperative | | Savings and first class pawn | |
	Percent	Percent of all banks	Percent	Percent of all banks	Percent	Percent of all banks	Percent	Percent of all banks	Percent	Percent of all banks
Depositi a risparmio										
Liberi										
risparmio ordinario	7.0	15.7	8.9	16.0	13.7	30.1	14.1	15.9	8.8	22.4
piccolo risparmio	7.4	20.6	5.0	11.3	6.0	16.5	7.7	10.8	12.8	40.8
piccolo risparmio speciale	0.2	3.2			0.1	2.8	0.7	7.6	3.7	86.4
Vincolati										
a tempo	26.3	18.5	16.6	9.4	32.4	22.4	41.9	14.9	42.0	34.7
buoni fruttiferi	0.2	3.3			0.2	2.8	0.2	1.2	5.6	92.7
Conti correnti con clienti										
Ordinari	1.9	14.0	3.8	22.7	4.0	29.5	2.5	9.5	2.8	24.3
Di corrispondenza										
liberi	45.7	28.0	49.5	24.5	38.1	23.0	30.4	9.4	21.5	15.1
vincolati	11.3	34.4	16.2	39.9	5.4	16.1	2.5	3.8	1.6	5.7
Totals	100.0		100.0		99.9		100.0		99.8	

SOURCE: Calculated from data in Banca d'Italia, Bollettino.

in the banks of national interest is almost four times larger than in the savings and first-class pawn banks (Table 17). The rank order of the bank categories in terms of mean size of all deposit accounts is banks of national interest, public law banks, ordinary credit banks, people's cooperative banks, and savings and first-class pawn banks. Because of these (and other) differences in the preference patterns of banks, the number of effective alternatives for a particular depositor group in a given major city may not be the same as the nominal alternatives, and these differences will be reflected in different levels of effective concentration for the different depositor groups in that city.

The degree of specialization by size of customer is not necessarily equal between deposit and loan markets. The banks of national interest offer the most striking example. They held 21.8 percent of the total volume of all bank loans with only 3.2 percent of the total number of loan accounts (Table 11), but they held only 18.2 percent of the total volume of all bank deposits with 8.9 percent of the total number of deposit accounts (Table 18). The absolute numbers are also indicative: the three banks of national interest together held less than 150,000 loan accounts but more than 2¾ million deposit accounts.[25]

TABLE 17

Mean Size of Deposit Account, December, 1965
(thousand lire)

Deposit category	Public law	National interest	Ordinary credit	People's cooperative	Savings and first-class pawn
Depositi a risparmio					
Liberi					
risparmio ordinario	457	665	665	578	374
piccolo risparmio	142	177	132	144	97
piccolo risparmio speciale	80		193	87	67
Vincolati					
a tempo	1,200	1,384	1,116	1,111	937
buoni fruttiferi	940		511	568	1,075
Conti correnti con clienti					
Ordinari	595	546	814	656	555
Di corrispondenza					
liberi	3,911	3,656	2,584	2,077	1,944
vincolati	33,199	35,256	10,203	20,061	18,444
Mean size of all accounts	933	1,341	858	704	358

SOURCE: Calculated from data in Banca d'Italia, *Bollettino.*

[25] The Banca d'Italia *Bollettino* provides figures for the number of *deposit accounts* but not for the number of *depositors*. There may be a significant difference between these two figures. Cf. Mario Mazzantini, "Operating Costs of the Italian Banks," Banca Nazionale de Lavoro, *Quarterly Review*, March, 1955, p. 14.

TABLE 18

Amount of Deposits, Number of Accounts, by Kind of Bank,
December, 1965

	Savings accounts		Current accounts		All accounts			
	Number	Amount (million lire)	Number	Amount (million lire)	Number	Percent of all banks	Amount (million lire)	Percent of all banks
Public law	4,246,058	1,898,367	699,573	2,715,551	4,945,631	15.9	4,613,918	22.5
National interest	2,000,157	1,136,461	778,165	2,589,000	2,778,322	8.9	3,725,461	18.2
Ordinary credit	4,370,329	2,382,233	916,680	2,153,901	5,287,009	17.0	4,536,134	22.2
People's cooperative	2,875,603	1,503,742	433,425	824,765	3,309,028	10.6	2,328,507	11.4
Savings and first-class pawn	13,866,835	3,904,000	858,226	1,370,184	14,725,061	47.4	5,271,184	25.8
All banks	27,358,982	10,824,803	3,686,069	9,653,401	31,045,051	99.8	20,478,204	100.1

SOURCE: Banca d'Italia, *Bollettino.*

Small (and medium-size) depositors in different parts of the country, especially outside of major centers, probably do not face a uniform level of market concentration because (as noted earlier) banking facilities are not uniformly distributed throughout the country either by total number or by different bank categories. For example, owing partly to a lower level of economic development, the south and the islands are underrepresented in terms of the total number of facilities. The northern part of the country, with its particularly heavy concentration of savings banks, is an example of uneven geographical distribution by kind of bank.

The nonbank alternatives available to large and small depositors are also different. Small depositors can use cash as a substitute for bank demand deposits, whereas large firms find it clumsy to use cash for some purposes and virtually impossible for others. As might be expected, therefore, "Notes and coins . . . are used predominantly by consumer households, while bank money responds more closely to the needs of enterprises and the movement of production."[26] The Post Office also offers a cash substitute with its giro facilities. Those accounts increased from 33,033 million lire in 1938 to 464,198 million by the end of 1962. In 1963, they increased spectacularly to 962,189 million, and had reached 1,354,000 million by the end of 1965.[27] In spite of this increase, however, Post Office current accounts are not important substitutes for bank accounts.[28]

With respect to tied deposits (broadly speaking, savings accounts and liquidity reserves), the nonbank alternatives available to large and small depositors are also different. Instead of placing their funds in a tied bank deposit, individuals can place their savings with the Post Office, either in a Postal Savings book or in an interest-bearing Post Office bond (buoni postali fruttiferi). The latter, which is by far the more important form of Postal Savings,[29] has no fixed maturity, and the interest is accumulated and paid when the bond is redeemed. Postal Savings are particularly important substitutes for bank savings for small savers. According to one calculation, 40 to 60 percent of total

---

[26] Bank of Italy, Annual Report for 1955, p. 68.

[27] Cf. Banca d'Italia, Bollettino, March–April, 1964, p. 143, and March–April, 1966, p. 119.

[28] Post Office current accounts are "largely influenced by accounts of the Government and public authorities, principally because of the payment of pensions and related movements of funds within the Office of Public Administration. . . ." Cf. Bank of Italy, Annual Report for 1955, p. 55.

[29] At the end of 1965, for example, postal bonds amounted to 2,796,800 million lire, whereas Postal Savings books were only 830,700 million lire. Cf. Bollettino, March–April, 1966, p. 119.

postal deposits are the savings of "subordinate labor" (i.e., low-level wage-earners), and most of the rest consists of savings of "the less important members of the free professions, craftsmen, owner farmers, small traders, and the like."[30] It should be added that, although maximum bank deposit rates are set by the Interbank Agreement, and Post Office deposit rates are set by the appropriate ministry, the extent of competition between banks and Post Office is strictly regulated,[31] since the government uses its authority over rates to influence the flow of savings between banks and Post Office.[32]

Large depositors face a quite different range of alternatives for bank tied deposits. Treasury bills (*buoni del tesoro ordinari*), with maturities ranging from one to twelve months, are high on the list of substitutes. Until May 16, 1962, treasury bills were available on tap at interest rates that remained fixed for long periods. For reasons which will be discussed later (in Chapter VI), the Treasury now regulates the volume of treasury bill issues, but it has ceased to fix the rate (on part of the issue). Although the treasury bill is a real alternative to a bank tied deposit, the extent of possible competition between bank deposits and treasury bills is limited. Indeed, the amount of competition seems to be controlled more carefully under the new system than it ever was under the old system for issuing treasury bills.

Large depositors can also place their funds in securities of business firms and securities issued by public or semipublic bodies.[33] These securities are partial substitutes for bank savings deposits, and the division of funds between bank deposits and the securities market definitely affects the growth of savings deposits, especially in large banks.[34]

---

[30] Cf. Giovanni Scanga, "National Income, Investments, and Savings," *Review of Economic Conditions in Italy*, May, 1959, p. 309. In 1959, the average size of postal deposit was only about 30,000 lire. Cf. *idem.*

[31] Cf. Bank of Italy, *Annual Report for 1955*, p. 53.

[32] It is interesting to note, however, that when the Interbank Agreement raised the maximum bank deposit rate (in 1954), after the government had reduced the interest rate on Post Office bonds (in 1953), the volume of Postal Savings continued to rise, albeit at a somewhat slower rate. Clearly, the Post Office appeals to many savers on grounds other than rate. Cf. Scanga, *op. cit.*, p. 308.

[33] On March 8, 1963, the Italian authorities also extended to all residents the freedom (formerly limited to specified types of institutes, agencies, and finance companies), to invest in foreign securities. Cf. Bank of Italy, *Annual Report for 1962*, p. 39.

[34] For example, cf. Bank of Italy, *Annual Report for 1959*, p. 56; or 1961, p. 52. Ironically, the large banks are partly responsible for this competition because "these banks' own commission business in the placing of security issues diverts some of their clients' money from bank saving into security investment" (Bank of Italy, *Annual Report for 1961*, p. 52).

MODIFICATIONS IN BANK SPECIALIZATION

During the postwar period, the tendency of banks to specialize by size of customer and type of business has somewhat declined. Some large-city unit banks that formerly tended to concentrate on deposit and loan operations with medium-size business firms have begun to diversify the size-distribution of their operations. Prompted in part by the fear of instability from a deposit structure dominated by a few large accounts, some of these banks have opened new branches to attract the deposits of smaller customers.[35] The change in deposit policy has led in turn to a change in loan policy: on the one hand, these banks have been taking on smaller borrowers; as their total size has increased (aided by their branching activities) they have been able to take on larger borrowers as well.[36]

There have also been pressures on the large banks to modify their historic tendency to concentrate their loan business among large firms. At one time, large firms were able to finance their credit needs from internal sources, and this put pressure on the banks to find other loan outlets. When rising costs cut into the self-financing capacity of large firms and made them more dependent on bank financing, the large banks continued to seek for diversification in the size-structure of their loan operations. Some of the pressure on the banks has come from the government in connection with its policy to strengthen medium-size and small firms. While the government has not specifically directed the banks to lend more to such firms, the Bank of Italy has made "suggestions" to this effect. Thus, in 1962, bank loans to business increased by 1,995 billion lire, and 24 percent was credit for large companies. In 1963, the increase was 2,268 billion lire, but only 16 percent was credit for large companies. The Bank of Italy has cited these figures as "eloquent testimony to the fact that a strong flow of new credit in 1963 was directed to the small and medium-sized companies, and not to the big ones—*in line with suggestions the Bank of Italy has more than once addressed to the banks.*"[37]

During the postwar years, some change has also occurred in bank specialization by kind of business. The most striking change was the increase in commercial lending to business firms by the savings banks.

---

[35] Cf. testimony of Stefano Siglienti in "L'intervento dell'Avv. Siglienti ai lavori della Commissione d'inchiesta sui limiti della concorrenza," in Associazione Bancaria Italiana, *Bancaria*, February, 1963, p. 210.

[36] Cf. Luigi Ceriani, *op. cit.*, (see n. 15 above), pp. 126–127.

[37] Bank of Italy, *Annual Report for 1963*, p. 125 (my italics). Cf. also Banca Commerciale Italiana, *Relazione del consiglio di amministrazione, 1963*, pp. 11–12.

Some large savings banks also developed sufficient foreign business operations to be designated agents of the Exchange Office.[38] This greater emphasis on short-term operations in the savings banks has increased the similarities between savings and commercial banks. Partly for this reason, the authorities in August, 1958, added the savings banks to the list of credit institutions required to hold compulsory reserve requirements.[39]

Modifications in the tendency for Italian banks to specialize by size of customer or kind of business could have important effects on medium-size and small customers. First, a change in specialization can substitute for a change in banking structure in terms of market-structure effects. Changes in specialization by large branch banks with extensive regional or nationwide branch systems can be particularly important in increasing the effective alternatives for medium-size and small customers in a large number of local markets. Second, the large branch banks can significantly increase the supply of funds in local markets. They are effective in accomplishing interregional mobility of funds because they collect large interbank accounts from the smaller banks in one province or region and redistribute the funds through their far-flung branches to other provinces or regions. On December 31, 1961, "the total of funds which all categories of banks except the six largest had deposited with other banks amounted to 1,077 billion lire; at the same date, the same banks, again without the six largest, had themselves 530 billion lire in interbank deposits. The rest had gone to the six largest banks."[40] The banking system's efficiency in making interregional transfers, especially to less developed areas,[41] can be particularly important to medium-size and small firms, which are most likely to bear the brunt of a short supply in those areas. On the other hand, although interbranch mobility of funds is an important mechanism for increasing the supply of credit to deficit areas, it is not a substitute for mobility of banks as far as market structure is concerned. Mobility of funds (via branch banking and interbank accounts) can deliver funds to an underdeveloped area, but the terms on which the funds are available depends (within limits prescribed by the cartel) on the extent of market rivalry.[42]

---

[38] Cf. Stefano Siglienti, op. cit., p. 211.

[39] Cf. Bank of Italy, Annual Report for 1960, p. 60.

[40] Cf. Bank of Italy, Annual Report for 1961, p. 95.

[41] The authorities have often expressed their approval of such transfers. For example, cf. ibid., p. 94.

[42] For a further discussion of this point, cf. David Alhadeff, "California Banking and Competition," in California Banking in a Growing Economy, 1946–1975, ed. Hyman Minsky (Berkeley, 1965), p. 179.

V

Competitive Regulations and Market Behavior

THE LEVEL OF CUSTOMER RATES UNDER THE CARTEL

Controls and Bank Efficiency

The restrictions on bank competition affect the level of customer rates by their effect on bank efficiency and costs, and by restricting market rivalry. Controls on competition can affect bank costs and efficiency in at least three ways. First, the system of competitive controls can influence the level of bank costs by moderating the competitive pressures on banks to improve efficiency. In Italy, however, the system of competitive controls (including entry and merger restrictions and territorial competence as well as direct rate controls) is designed to forestall a degree of price competition that might endanger bank solvency, not to relieve the banks from all competitive pressures for efficiency. Moreover, some competitive pressures that are suppressed in the marketplace exert their influence within the cartel because the most efficient banks often try to secure a competitive edge over less efficient rivals by pressing for low minimum loan rates. Second, some competitive controls affect bank costs directly because they add to the total amount of work the bank must do simply to conform to the regulations.[1]

Third, some controls on competition (like the controls on entry and mergers) affect the level of costs through their influence on bank size.

---

[1] Bank costs are also affected by controls that are imposed for reasons other than the control of competition. For example, in the opinion of one informed observer, the increase in bank costs between 1938 and 1949 was due in part to the "lower productivity of the staff due to a number of causes, among which firstly ranks the unproductive work resulting from the numberless controls the banks are compelled to observe in compliance with the laws now in force (extremely intricate foreign exchange operations, for instance). . . ." Cf. C. Bresciani-Turroni, "Interest Rates in Italy," *Review of Economic Conditions in Italy*, January, 1949, p. 14.

As there are no adequate data for relating bank costs and bank size,[2] the government's position on bank size and costs presumably reflects the largely impressionistic views of high officials. It is pertinent, therefore, to record some of those views. As noted earlier, the president of the ABI has expressed doubts about the cost advantages of a merger among big banks; and the governor of the Bank of Italy has stated that free entry for branches would probably raise bank costs. Some officials believe (as they reported to the author in interviews) that the most efficient firms are neither the very small nor the very large but some of the medium-size banks, especially in the Milan area. In their view, small banks generally are not very efficient because of their low turnover, and the smallest banks are not efficient because they fall below the minimum feasible size for a bank. The latter tend to be located in the less developed parts of the country and, at least in the past, could rely on low wages to overcome the worst effects of their inefficiency. As the pressures from a national wage policy become stronger, these officials expect that many of the smallest banks will be eliminated by merger with other (but probably not with the largest) banks.

Some who believe that the largest banks are not the most efficient claim that large banks are vulnerable to cost pressures that seemingly operate in only one direction (especially the wages of bank employees, which are very sensitively adjusted to a cost-of-living index) and more than counter any size economies. While inflationary pressures in the economy are thus promptly translated into higher costs for all banks, the large banks have not generated pressures to cut back other costs. Because the large banks are government-owned, management is exempt from the pressure of private stockholders; and according to these officials, the government has exerted no (or not enough) pressure for cost reduction in the large banks. In part, the government has been reluctant to interfere in the daily operations of the publicly owned banks;[3] and at times, it has been caught in a conflict between efficiency and other goals.[4]

---

[2] For a discussion of data obstacles in analyzing the costs of Italian banks, cf. Mario Mazzantini, "Operating Costs of the Italian Banks," Banca Nazionale del Lavoro, *Quarterly Review*, March, 1955. As noted earlier, the Bank of Italy made a special survey of bank costs and earnings in 1965 but noted that as "the survey was based on official accounts, considerable caution is indicated in the interpretation of the results (Bank of Italy, *Annual Report for 1965*, p. 106).

[3] In the opinion of one highly placed official (as he stated to the author in an interview), the efficiency of the largest banks may suffer from government intervention in the future more than it suffered from nonintervention in the past. This is based on the fear that, with the gradual replacement of the older generation of bank managers who were in office before the banks were nation-

Market Rivalry and Loan Rates

The controls on bank competition also affect the level of customer rates by limiting the amount of market rivalry. On many routine bank services, price rivalry is precluded, because the Interbank Agreement specifies actual, not just minimum, commissions. On bank loans, price rivalry is not proscribed as long as it is contained within the minimum levels set by the cartel. Indeed, the government, which approves of the Interbank Agreement, also approves of loan-rate competition[5] (within the prescribed limits), for its aim in sanctioning restrictive bank agreements is to protect bank depositors, not to expose bank customers to the exploitation of monopoly.

There are no figures available to the public on the actual rates paid by different borrowers. In the opinion of informed observers, large firms with top credit ratings (and even some smaller firms with top-quality ratings) can usually borrow at the cartel's minimum loan rate.[6] Thus, consistent with the earlier findings about the low concentration in the market structures of the large-borrower markets, there appears to be enough competition in those markets to prevent lenders from extracting rates above the cartel's minimum rates. Significantly, the pressure for reduction of loan rates has sometimes come from the medium-sized banks whose "ready reduction of the interest charged on loans proved an incentive for the larger banks to do likewise."[7]

alized, it will be more difficult for the selection of management personnel and the management of bank affairs to be kept free from political considerations which are not related to and may possibly even conflict with considerations of efficiency.

[4] In 1949, for example, one writer reported that "Considerations of a social nature forbid the adoption of strictly economic principles with regard to the staff, such as the dismissal of all surplus clerks. For the same reason, the use of calculating machines, etc. has to be limited. Another drawback, which is characteristic of the present situation, is that a big bank with a number of branch offices spread throughout the country cannot proceed to a rational distribution of its personnel among the various branches owing to the severe housing shortage which makes it difficult to shift clerks from overstaffed branches to understaffed ones." Cf. Bresciani-Turroni, *op. cit.*, p. 14. These particular problems have, of course, long since been overcome.

[5] Official spokesmen in Italy have often noted that the Interbank Agreement is designed not to eliminate competition but to limit it. For example, cf. "L'intervento dell'Avv. Siglienti ai lavori della Commissione d'inchiesta sui limiti della concorrenza," *Bancaria*, February, 1963, p. 213. In keeping with this policy, the Interbank Agreement stipulates limit rates (on loans and deposits) and lets market forces determine the actual rates. Thus, even under the highly regulated circumstances of the banking system in Italy, market forces have a role to play and can influence market behavior.

[6] In mid-1967, some could even borrow at a rate below the official minimum.

[7] Bank of Italy, *Annual Report for 1964*, p. 133.

The ability of large borrowers to secure bank loans at the minimum rate is evidence of some competition in the large-borrower market, but it is not evidence that the cartel's minimum loan rate is a competitive rate (in a pure competition sense). The presumption, indeed, is to the contrary, for it would not be necessary to establish by agreement a minimum rate which is equal to (or less than) the rate which would exist in an unregulated, competitive market. It is important to stress, however, that this general argument can support the presumption of a higher-than-competitive minimum cartel loan rate *only under the given system of deposit controls*. Whether the cartel's minimum loan rate is higher than a competitive loan rate would be if both deposit and loan markets were unregulated and competitive is a different and far more difficult question. As we shall see later, the cartel has probably been subsidizing borrowers at the expense of depositors—that is, as compared with the results that would prevail in unregulated and competitive markets.

The cartel's minimum rate applies only to top-quality borrowers; others must pay higher rates in accordance with their additional risk or cost to the banks. According to the ABI, the effective rates paid by borrowers (i.e., presumably those who do not pay the minimum rates) are much higher than the cartel's minimum rates.[8] In the absence of precise information about the costs, risks, and rates paid by nonprime borrowers (i.e., medium-size and small borrowers), it is not possible to determine whether their higher rates are due entirely to higher costs and risks or to their weaker market position. However, as medium-size and small borrowers face a less favorable market situation than large borrowers located in the same major city, it cannot be taken for granted on grounds of market structure that the loan rates paid by most medium-size and small borrowers exceed the cartel's minimum rates solely by amounts commensurate with the actual differences in costs and risks.

The situation of the small borrowers outside of major cities has been particularly adverse in the less developed southern region of Italy because the low level of regional savings has not been compensated by a sufficient inflow of funds from other areas to eliminate regional differentials in loan rates. In addition, the prewar movement toward concentration eliminated a large number of small banks in southern

---

[8] Associazione Bancaria Italiana, "La Structure du système bancaire italien au point de vue de la liquidité," in *First International Credit Conference, Papers and Proceedings* (Rome, 1953), II, 304. Cf. also European Economic Community, *The Instruments of Monetary Policy in the Countries of the European Economic Community* (1962), p. 166: ". . . banks generally exceed these minimum [loan] rates. . . ."

Italy and left the two major southern banks (the Banco di Napoli and the Banco di Sicilia) in a particularly strong position in their primary areas of operation. Until the Second World War, their market dominance was reinforced by a psychological advantage (the continuing traces of a quasi-feudal mentality) which further weakened the small borrower's bargaining position. In the postwar period, two important developments have been changing the situation in the south. In part as a result of the war, traditional status relationships have been further weakened. In addition, the government has approved the branch applications of the smaller banks, in line with the policy of fostering a reduction of bank concentration in the south.[9]

Market Rivalry and Deposit Rates

In principle, the controls on both the deposit and the loan rates leave room for rate rivalry; in practice, bankers have less flexibility in setting deposit rates than loan rates. In the case of loans, the cartel sets a minimum rate but most borrowers pay more; in the case of deposit accounts, the cartel's ceiling rates are also typically the actual rates. This difference between the two markets may be due in part to the greater ease in standardizing deposit categories than loan categories. In the case of loans, the cartel prescribes only the minimum rate for prime borrowers and leaves it to the banker to determine the appropriate surcharge for costs and risks on nonprime loans. In the case of current-account deposits, the cartel prescribes different ceiling rates according to the maturity and size of the deposit account. The clear inference—sometimes stated explicitly[10]—is that the cartel has already made allowance for maturity differences and for the different handling costs of deposit accounts of different sizes. In the case of savings accounts, the cartel also prescribes different ceiling rates for different maturities, but, in contrast to its practice on current-account deposits, it does not establish different ceiling rates for different sizes of savings accounts, because they are generally small accounts.[11] There are no published figures on deposit rates paid to different depositors (nor even any figures on the total interest paid for broad deposit categories[12])

---

[9] As noted earlier, the large northern banks have not been very active in expanding their activities into the south, but the two major southern banks have shown some interest in expanding into northern cities.

[10] For example, the Bank of Italy explained that the Interbank Agreement of 1954 had allowed higher rates on large deposits because of "the lower cost of handling larger deposits . . ." (Bank of Italy, *Annual Report for 1953*, p. 61).

[11] This explanation was made in a letter to the author by an official of the ABI.

[12] The following excerpt suggests the kind of difficulties that are encountered in trying to use published bank statements to compile information about

but, in the opinion of a knowledgeable informant, no depositor receives less than the cartel ceiling rates.[13] This does not mean, however,
that small and large depositors are treated alike. As shown later, large
depositors sometimes receive rates in excess of the cartel's maximum;
small depositors do not.

The ceiling rates on current-account deposits appear to be determined in the belief that the basic level of current-account deposits is
not significantly elastic with respect to interest rates. For individuals,
it depends on the amount of liquid funds they require to cover un-
foreseeable contingencies; for firms, it is determined by their conception
of a "normal degree of liquidity."[14] Therefore, except for funds in
excess of this basic level, deposit rates do not have to be competitive
with rates on alternative outlets. In keeping with this view, the Interbank Agreement of 1954 reduced the ceiling rate on some current
accounts while at the same time raising the ceiling rates on time-deposit
accounts.[15]

There are a number of reasons for supposing that the cartel sets the
general level of all deposit ceiling rates below an unregulated market
level. First, it would not be necessary to set a ceiling rate if the unregulated market rate was expected to be less than or equal to it. Second,
the extent of the violations of the cartel ceilings makes it clear that
the ceiling rates have sometimes been far below the rates that would
have prevailed in an unregulated market. Third, an important purpose
of the regulatory authorities in supporting a ceiling rate has been to
strengthen the banks by holding their costs below the level of an unregulated market. Thus, the Bank of Italy has stated that "the objective
of safeguarding our credit system . . . requires that interest on deposits
be not excessive, in accordance with a principle which is carefully
observed abroad even in countries favouring the utmost freedom of

---

interest paid for broad deposit categories: "Of the banks whose statements we
examined only 10 indicated both the interest paid on saving deposits and also,
as a separate item, that paid on current accounts. 12 banks make it impossible
to see the amount of interest paid even on saving deposits, indicating this in
items obscurely described, or even lumped together with discount paid, interest
paid on advances and loans received, or brokerage and commission paid, as
well as in some cases with interest paid on current accounts. A further 28 banks
regularly show the interest paid on current accounts, but add such subsidiary
items as depreciation, so that there is ground for supposing that they may have
offset the interest paid on current accounts against the interest received on
lending to customers." Mazzantini, *op. cit.* (see n. 2. above), pp. 4–5, n. 5.

[13] This statement was made in a letter to the author by an official of the ABI.
[14] Cf. Bank of Italy, *Annual Report for 1954*, p. 93.
[15] Cf. *ibid.*, pp. 57 and 93.

competition. . . ."[16] Fourth, the government has encouraged the cartel to establish low deposit-rate ceilings so that the banks could offer low loan rates.[17] Indeed, in pressing for low deposit rates, the government appears to have been motivated as much by a desire to stimulate business investment as to safeguard the banks against excessive competition.[18]

The Spread Between Loan and Deposit Rates

The bank cartel's maximum loan and minimum deposit rates determine the *minimum* "spread" for the banking system as a whole. It is convenient to think of the spread as a conduit charge which borrowers pay the banks for the intermediary service of channeling funds from ultimate suppliers to ultimate demanders of funds. This conduit charge is made up of the banks' fixed and operating costs and their profits. In Italy, where the minimum conduit charge is set by a cartel instead of by competitive market forces, the size of the cartel's minimum spread has been the object of considerable criticism. Critics have charged that the cartel set an "excessive spread" during most of the postwar period. The criticisms, which began right after the war, have not been limited to the banks' customers. In 1945, Governor Luigi Einaudi publicly expressed his concern (to the general shareholders meeting of the Bank of Italy) that, in setting low deposit rates and high loan rates, the bank cartel was behaving like a monopoly, and he warned the bankers that the cartel had to operate in the public interest if it was to justify its existence.[19] In January, 1949, a prominent banker acknowledged that "the so-called 'cartel' among banks is the object of constant criticism, as it is considered to create a bank monopoly."[20]

The criticisms were especially strong in 1948 because the spread between the minimum overdraft rate and the maximum rate on *conti*

---

[16] *Ibid.*, p. 93. The Bank of Italy has also expressed the view that "The growth of deposits . . . should not be entrusted to an increase in the interest paid on them, but rather to an improvement in the standard of living of those who are still far removed from the credit institutions, and who have come to them in recent times only with minimal amounts" (*idem*).

[17] This information is based on the author's interviews. Cf. also the Bank of Italy's observation that "The new Interbank Agreement [of 1954] fits into the trend of the last few years towards a reduction in interest costs to production enterprises" (Bank of Italy, *Annual Report for 1953*, p. 61).

[18] It should also be mentioned that the level of deposit rates at banks also affects the rates the government must offer on treasury bills and Postal Savings.

[19] Cf. Banca d'Italia, *Adunanza generale ordinaria dei partecipanti*, 1945, pp. 35–37. Cf. also Giuseppe Lanzarone, *Il sistema bancario italiano*, ed. Giulio Einaudi (Torino, 1948), p. 516.

[20] C. Bresciani-Turroni, *op. cit.* (see n. 1 above), p. 15.

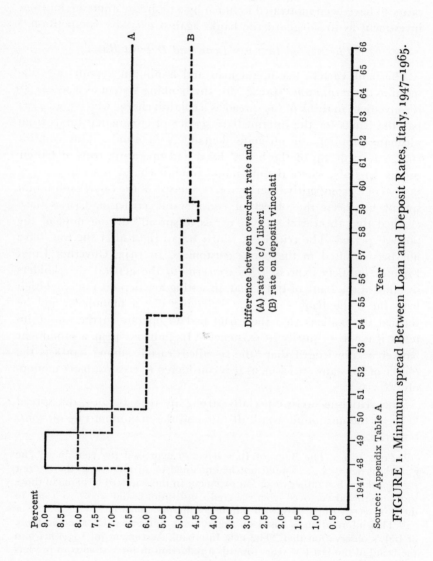

Source: Appendix Table A

FIGURE 1. Minimum spread Between Loan and Deposit Rates, Italy, 1947–1965.

correnti liberi had reached 9 percent (Fig. 1), or even more if the commission on overdrafts is included. This unusually wide spread was defended on three main grounds.[21] First, only the spread between the rates on overdrafts and free current accounts exceeded 9 percent; the spread between the cartel minimum rate on discounts and (say) the maximum rate on deposits tied for three months was much smaller (5.50 percent). Second, the high loan rates were fundamentally due to a low level of savings (relative to the demand for funds), and the low level of savings was due to a combination of a low level of national income and the postwar redistribution of income in favor of high-consumption elements of the population. Finally, the large spread was due to high operating costs which the banks could not reduce: higher wage costs, costs incurred to comply with government regulations on banks (red-tape costs), costs due to obstacles of a social nature which impeded the rationalization of the organization of bank services, and costs due to the "exaggerated number of banks existing in Italy. . . ."

The cartel's minimum spread was larger between September, 1947 (when the overdraft rate was raised to 9.50 percent), and April, 1949, than at any other time during the postwar period. Subsequently, the spread was reduced to 6.50 percent (between the overdraft rate and deposit rate on c/c liberi) and 4.75 percent (between the overdraft rate and the rate on three-month "tied" deposits), and this smaller spread has been in effect since mid-1958 (Fig. 1). This reduced spread has not stilled all criticisms, however. Indeed, some businessmen object to the present spread on the grounds not only that loan rates and commissions are too high but also that deposit rates are too low. In their view, the cartel's policy of holding deposit rates below competitive levels has not (as bankers claim) benefited business borrowers; it has forced the saver to subsidize the banks.

The regulatory authorities strongly reject the view that the present spread is excessive. On the contrary, they insist that the narrower margin now in effect is "the most eloquent possible demonstration of the existing keen competition in the banking world."[22] In fact, however, it is doubtful whether the present size of the minimum spread is a reliable gauge of the underlying market forces. First, since the minimum official margin is established by the cartel and not by the market, the only certain conclusion from a lower margin is that the cartel decided to change it. This does not deny that the cartel may take the underlying market conditions into account in setting the minimum spread, but

[21] Based on *ibid.*, pp. 5–16.
[22] Governor Carli, Bank of Italy, *Annual Report for 1961*, p. 97.

competition is not the only consideration in that decision. Second, a narrower official margin is not equivalent to a narrower actual margin, because the cartel does not compel the banks to implement the official margin but only to treat the prescribed rates as limit rates. Third, as the loan and deposit rates which determine the official minimum margin tend to be effective only for the strongest bank customers, a strengthening of competitive forces in the strongest customer markets which could force the cartel to reduce the official margin, might have little or no effect on the other customer markets. Fourth, a narrowing of the official margin between borrowing and lending rates is a fallible clue to the state of actual competition because of widespread *scartellamento* (violation of cartel rate agreements) during part of the period shown in Figure 1, especially before the Interbank Agreement of 1954.

It should be noted that not even a decline in the overall effective margin[23] would be conclusive evidence per se that competitive forces had become stronger. For example, with no change in the underlying structure of competitive forces, the effective margin could become narrower with a shift in the size-composition of customers. Or a reduction could be due to changes (in demand or supply conditions or both) that altered the optimal spread for the banks while leaving competitive forces unchanged. On the other hand, a reduction due to scartellamento would be evidence of "keen competition"; but since scartellamento violates the control structure, it could only persist until the cartel and regulatory authorities had reasserted their authority over the banks. In 1961, as will be noted later, the monetary authorities joined the officials of the ABI in a strenuous campaign to force the banks back within the framework of the Interbank Agreement.

RATE FLEXIBILITY UNDER THE CARTEL

Flexibility in interest rates in response to changing conditions of demand and supply is achieved automatically in a competitive market. Because full flexibility is precluded in a regulated market by the existence of arbitrary limits on the range of rate variation, changes in the schedules of demand and supply develop strains in the market. In Italy, the cartel provides a certain degree of rate flexibility on an official basis, and the banks have sometimes provided an additional amount unofficially.

---

[23] The effective margin is the difference between the effective rates on deposits (amount of interest paid on deposits divided by the average volume of deposits) and the effective rate on loans (amount of interest paid by borrowers divided by the average volume of loans). As already noted, there is no information available to the public about the effective rates.

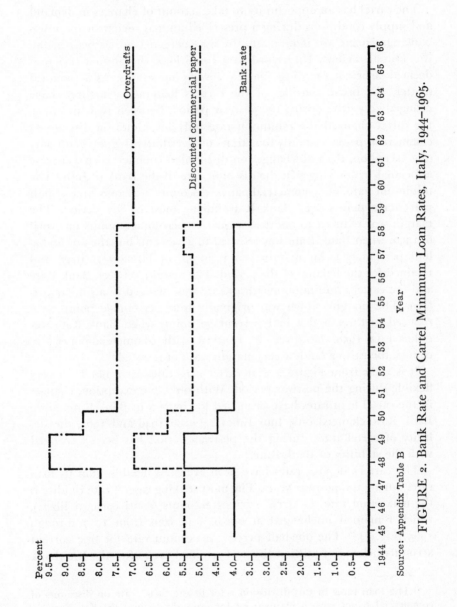

Percent

Overdrafts

Discounted commercial paper

Bank rate

9.5
9.0
8.5
8.0
7.5
7.0
6.5
6.0
5.5
5.0
4.5
4.0
3.5
3.0
2.5
2.0
1.5
1.0
0.5
0

1944 45 46 47 48 49 50 51 52 53 54 55 56 57 58 59 60 61 62 63 64 65 66

Year

Source: Appendix Table B

FIGURE 2. Bank Rate and Cartel Minimum Loan Rates, Italy, 1944–1965.

Official Rate Flexibility

The cartel has an opportunity to take account of changes in demand and supply conditions during a prescribed annual review of the inter-bank agreement (or, if necessary, by an emergency adjustment before the annual review). Under ordinary conditions, the annual review is deemed sufficient to adjust for any developing strains. As a practical matter, the broad outlines of the cartel's loan-rate structure[24] have changed very little during the postwar period. Between 1946 and 1965, the cartel changed the minimum rate only five times on discounted commercial paper and only four times on overdrafts (Fig. 2). With only one exception, the rate changes on discounted commercial paper were associated with changes in the discount rate of the Bank of Italy. The minimum rate on commercial-paper discounts was one and a half percentage points over Bank Rate during most of the period. The margin was reduced to one and a quarter percentage points on April 6, 1950, when Bank Rate was reduced to 4 percent, but the one-and-a-half percentage-point margin was restored on January 1, 1957, and retained for the balance of the period. The margin between Bank Rate and the cartel's minimum overdraft rate was changed in a similar pattern. The margin which was originally four percentage points, was reduced to three and a half percentage points when Bank Rate was reduced in 1950. However, by contrast with commercial-paper discounts, the earlier (and larger) margin was not restored.

It is clear from Figure 2 that cartel loan rates have not been very flexible during the postwar period. With only one exception, changes in the cartel loan rates have been tied to changes in Bank Rate. Since Bank Rate changed only four times between 1946 and 1965, the stability of cartel rates during the postwar period has been associated with the stability of Bank Rate.

The cartel's deposit rates have been even less flexible than its loan rates during the postwar years. The most striking case of rate rigidity is the maximum rate on "free" current accounts (conti correnti liberi), which remained unchanged at one-half percent from 1947 through 1965 (Fig. 3).[25] The one-half percent maximum rate for free current accounts below five million lire was retained even after the Interbank

---

[24] The loan rates in this discussion refer to the cartel rate on discounts of commercial paper with a maturity of four months (sconto di effeti fino a 4 mesi) and the rate on current account overdrafts (crediti in conto corrente). These are the only cartel loan rates which the Banca d'Italia Bollettino reports back for several years.

[25] The Bollettino shows that this rate was the same at least back to September 11, 1944. Cf. Appendix Table C (for Fig. 3).

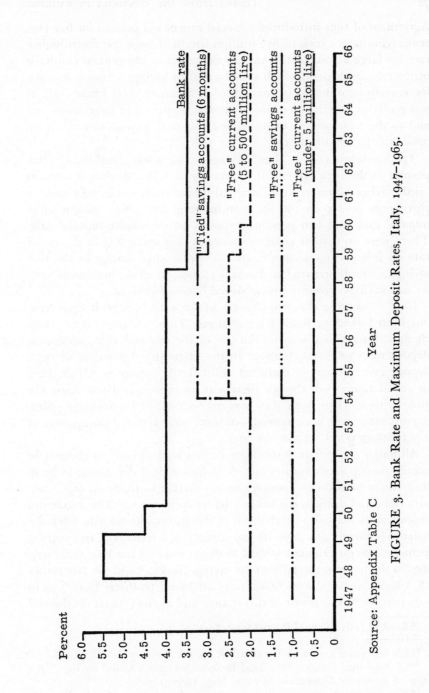

Source: Appendix Table C

FIGURE 3. Bank Rate and Maximum Deposit Rates, Italy, 1947–1965.

Agreement of 1954 introduced a special rate of 2½ percent for free current accounts in excess of five million lire. Although the much higher rate for large accounts—this was an exception to the general emphasis of the new agreement, which raised rates for savings accounts but not for current accounts[26]—was explained in terms of their lower costs, it was probably also due to the high interest sensitivity of large accounts[27] and to the widespread violations of the cartel's deposit-rate structure under the former low rates.

The maximum rate on "free" savings accounts was raised one-quarter percent in the 1954 agreement. By comparison, the maximum rates on "tied" savings accounts were increased substantially— one and a quarter percentage points on the six months' rate, one point on the three months' rate, and two percentage points on the twelve months' rate. There were no further changes (between 1954 and 1965) in the cartel rate on free savings accounts; and the only other change in the tied savings accounts occurred on January 1, 1959, when the maximum rates on tied savings accounts were reduced one-half percent.

Unlike loan-rate changes, changes in the cartel's deposit rates have not been linked to Bank Rate changes. Thus, although Bank Rate changed three times between the end of the war and 1950, maximum deposit rates were not changed. In the Interbank Agreement of 1954, deposit rate ceilings were altered dramatically (partly to adjust them to actual rates) even though there was no change in Bank Rate. On June 7, 1958, when Bank Rate was cut one-half of a percentage point, deposit rates were not changed, but some were reduced one-quarter of a percentage point six months later.

Although changes in Bank Rate do not lead directly to changes in maximum deposit rates, they may do so indirectly if the change in Bank Rate alters rates on competitive money-market instruments (e.g., treasury bills) and disturbs the balance with deposit rates.[28] The maximum deposit rates may also be changed if the authorities wish to alter the balance between bank deposits and competing alternatives. In 1953, for example, the government wished to divert some of the Post Office savings to the banks (especially to the savings banks),[29] and (on November 18, 1953) it reduced Post Office rates on *buoni fruttiferi* from 4.50 to 3.75 percent.[30] As a result of this change and of the rate set (at the end

---

[26] Bank of Italy, *Annual Report for 1954*, p. 57.

[27] Cf. *ibid.*, p. 58.

[28] Cf. European Economic Community, *op. cit.* (see n. 7 above), p. 166.

[29] Cf. Giovanni Scanga, "National Income, Investments, and Savings," *Review of Economic Conditions in Italy*, May, 1959, p. 306.

[30] The reduction was actually a minimum of .75 percent for bonds withdrawn within the first five years to a minimum of .25 percent for bonds left on deposit for 16 to 20 years. Cf. Bank of Italy, *Annual Report for 1953*, p. 54.

of 1953) for the new Interbank Agreement, Postal Savings (bonds) rates were below the cartel's maximum rate on comparable savings (viz., 3.75 percent for the Post Office bonds and 4 percent for bank savings accounts).[31]

The rigidity of the cartel's rates has been noted by the authorities who (in 1965) expressed concern that the Interbank Agreement "prevents the rates from adapting themselves flexibly to the conditions of supply and demand with respect to money resources." On that occasion, the governor of the Bank of Italy put the banks on notice that "This artificiality will have to be removed sooner or later."[32]

Unofficial Rate Flexibility

Because the cartel has provided little flexibility for loan rates and even less for deposit rates, the control system has come under pressure from time to time as demand and supply conditions have changed. In a highly concentrated or highly disciplined banking system, it might have been possible to contain the market strains without impairing the integrity of the controls. Under the less highly concentrated and at times less disciplined situation in Italy, the underlying competitive forces have sometimes disrupted the control apparatus and provided unofficial (and illegal) flexibility in the form of violations of the cartel agreement.

Prior to the Interbank Agreement of 1954, the cartel agreement was being widely violated, and this provided an important form of de facto rate flexibility. Although the violations were supposedly made in secret, their existence was common knowledge. In its Annual Report for 1953, the Bank of Italy reported that, in spite of no change in the official (cartel) rates on loans and deposits during the year, "The Banks however continued to pay to their more important customers, and for the larger deposits, rates of interest higher than those fixed by the agreement; and they applied to their lending operations rates even nearer to the minima."[33] In 1953, when the cartel maximum was one-half percent, the (unofficial) rate paid to large depositors exceeded 4 percent.[34] As pressure of violations was threatening to collapse the entire system of cartel controls, the banks finally got together and renewed their pledge to adhere to a new Interbank Agreement. Significantly, the new agreement gave official recognition to the unofficial flexibility that had

---

[31] Cf. *idem.*

[32] Bank of Italy, *Annual Report for 1964*, pp. 133–134. (The governor makes his report for each year during May of the following year.)

[33] Bank of Italy, *Annual Report for 1952*, p. 63.

[34] Cf. Mazzantini, *op. cit.* (see n. 2 above), p. 11, n.13.

been secured by violations and provided higher maximum rates on large deposit accounts.

In recent years, the inflexibility of the official rate schedules in the face of changing credit conditions led to a renewed outbreak of cartel violations.[35] Since scartellamento is secret and illegal, there is no fully reliable information on it. In 1963, the president of the Italian Bankers Association stated that it was then a marginal element whose importance had been exaggerated by borrowers who used it to get more favorable rates by reporting falsely that other bankers had offered them rates that violated the cartel.[36] It should be noted, however, that even if scartellamento were marginal in terms of the *number* of bank customers, it might not have been marginal in terms of amounts, for it primarily benefits large customers.

The monetary authorities have taken official notice of scartellamento. During 1963, they repeatedly warned the bankers in unmistakable language to adhere to the cartel rate schedule. In this connection, the governor of the Bank of Italy reminded the bankers:

Our policy with respect to interest rates, both for borrowing and for lending, has always been to prefer those types of restraint which work through agreements among the banks themselves. We have no intention of suddenly adopting the kind of intransigent attitudes for which we sometimes chide our colleagues in the banks, and we shall resist the proposals, which are often made to us, to adopt coercive controls which, in our view, are humiliating both for those who impose and for those who are subject to them. On the other hand, we shall not shrink from using the instruments which modern monetary policy puts into our hand, because we believe them to be more effective than admonishments and threats.[37]

In 1967, the Governor suggested that a tax reform might be more effective than coercion as a means of influencing the banks' behavior

---

[35] It is interesting to note that, as far as *scartellamento* is concerned, the behavior of the public banks cannot be distinguished from that of the private banks; publicly owned banks seem to be just as prone as private banks to violate the cartel. One observer cited this (to the author in an interview) as evidence that the publicly owned banks in Italy are "private-minded." Another remarked that rivalry is a "point of prestige" among Italian banks, without distinction between private and public banks. It will be recalled that, at least in the past, there has been general agreement in Italy that the banks should not be subjected to political control and, in keeping with this principle, the publicly owned banks have been directed by the government to behave as if they were private banks.

[36] Cf. "L'intervento dell'Avv. Siglienti ai lavori della Commissione d'inchiesta sui limiti alla concorrenza," *Bancaria*, February, 1963, p. 213.

[37] Bank of Italy, *Annual Report for 1961*, p. 96. The ABI, which is responsible for enforcing the cartel, also condemned the violations. More recently, however, the authorities have relaxed their opposition to the violations of the deposit cartel. See Bank of Italy, *Annual Report for 1966*, p. 137.

on deposit rates. Accordingly he proposed that the tax rate (on the proportional tax which is deducted at source from interest on bank deposits) should be lower when banks paid deposit rates that did not exceed the ceiling rate fixed by the monetary authorities, and higher for any interest paid in excess of the official ceiling.[38]

While scartellamento has introduced de facto flexibility into a rate structure that is outwardly quite rigid, it is discriminatory and benefits the large customers far more than the small. When the pressures of tight money start to crack the deposit cartel, business firms with large deposit accounts are the first to benefit. If the tight-money pressures are not severe, the violations may not extend significantly beyond the large depositors. In very tight conditions, the violations may reach down to medium-size depositors, but not to small depositors, especially in small towns.[39] Similarly, it is the larger borrowers who benefit most when the pressures of excessive liquidity begin to crack the loan cartel. Scartellamento on the loan rate probably does not affect more than 1,000 firms, perhaps from 20 to 30 percent of the credit granted by banks.[40]

---

[38] Cf. Bank of Italy, *Annual Report for 1966*, pp. 137–138.
[39] Cf. *ibid.*, p. 137.
[40] Based on an interview by the author.

VI

Competitive Regulations and Monetary Controls

Competition among Italian banks has been regulated in one way or another for more than four decades. At the outset, the purpose was to increase bank safety by holding down bank costs. The early goal has never been dropped. As a result of the events in recent years, however, the role of competitive restraints was significantly expanded, and they became an integral part of the regulatory mechanism by which the authorities sought to carry out the monetary and economic policies of the government. This chapter examines the nature and causes of the transformation in the historic role of competitive curbs. To put this development in perspective, a preliminary section examines the traditional instruments of monetary control.[1]

CONTROLS OVER THE VOLUME OF BANK CREDIT

The Bank of Italy, like all central banks, is a lender of last resort. It makes its resources available to the banks[2] either through the discount window or by advances against the collateral of government (or government-guaranteed) securities. Since the discounts involve a more cumbersome procedure than advances, most banks are reluctant to rediscount, and the volume of central-bank discounts is accordingly much smaller than its advances. The only exception, an important one, concerns the rediscounts of storage-agency bills in connection with the

---

[1] The central bank can also influence credit conditions by its dealings with the Treasury, but that relationship receives only passing mention in this study, which deals primarily with the control of bank competition. For a good and concise discussion of the Treasury relationship, cf. European Economic Community, *The Instruments of Monetary Policy in the Countries of the European Economic Community* (1962), pp. 175–179.

[2] Under a provision of the Banking Act of 1936, reaffirmed in 1947, the Bank of Italy does not discount for private customers. Moreover, its advances to enterprises and individuals are quite small.

financing of compulsory stockpiles of various agricultural crops (*risconto ammassi*), but variations in the amount of this credit do not necessarily reflect the central bank's credit policy.

The authorities have characterized the rediscount and advances mechanism as "a very powerful means of exerting pressure on commercial banks. . . ."[3] The mechanism does not, however, rely much on Bank Rate changes. In line with a policy which "tends to disassociate measures aiming at domestic monetary equilibrium from those which, with sometimes contrary effects, influence international capital movements,"[4] the Bank of Italy has used Bank Rate very sparingly to influence credit conditions—only four changes (1947, 1949, 1950, and 1958) during the postwar years. Although variations in Bank Rate (which is not a penalty rate)[5] may not deter banks from borrowing at the central bank, they do affect credit conditions because the cartel's loan rate minima are tied to Bank Rate.[6] In addition, a Bank Rate change signals a change in central-bank credit policy and causes banks to adjust their loans accordingly.

Since the authorities cannot rely upon Bank Rate variations to limit bank borrowing-for-profit during boom periods, they also resort to administrative rationing. In Italy, the banks do not have a right to central-bank credit (except for the discount of storage-agency bills); it is a privilege granted by the authorities, who consider the overall credit conditions as well as the particular circumstances of the individual bank.[7] For the most part, the banks can secure central-bank funds only for seasonal or emergency reasons. Until recent years, the amount of discounts and advances usually has not varied greatly.

---

[3] Guido Carli, "Relations Between The Central Banks Of Italy, Switzerland And Austria And The Commercial Banks In Those Countries," in *Relations Between The Central Banks And Commercial Banks,* lectures delivered at the Tenth International Banking Summer School, Garmisch-Partenkirchen, September, 1957, p. 52.

[4] This was the reason for not raising Bank Rate in 1959. Cf. Bank of Italy, *Annual Report for 1959,* p. 95.

[5] The minimum cartel rate has been one and a half percentage points above Bank Rate since 1957; most bank borrowers must pay even higher rates.

[6] Cf. Bank of Italy, *Annual Report for 1964,* p. 134.

[7] In this connection, the governor of the Bank of Italy has stated that "recourse to the Bank of Italy is administered by the latter mainly with reference to the liquidity situation of each separate bank. . . ." (Bank of Italy, *Annual Report for 1963,* p. 124). In part, this emphasis on the circumstances of the individual bank is due to the fact that large banks carry (in the form of interbank balances) much of the liquidity reserves of the smaller banks. When the smaller banks draw on these interbank balances, they put the larger banks under pressure, and the central bank has had to bail them out. The Bank of

A second instrument of control is the compulsory reserve requirement for banks. The present system evolved from an earlier requirement prescribed by the Banking Act of 1926 to protect bank solvency
by preventing banks from extending too much credit in relation to their
capital. The earlier legislation provided that any deposits in excess of
twenty times a bank's capital and reserves had to be either invested in
government securities to be held by the Bank of Italy or deposited in
an interest-bearing account at the central bank. The provision was
largely inoperative during the prewar period because deposits rarely
exceeded twenty times the capital and reserves of banks. It became oper-
ative after the war when the postwar inflation expanded deposits far
more rapidly than capital. The inflation was particularly strong in the
spring of 1947, and the Interministerial Committee for Credit and
Savings introduced a new system of compulsory bank reserves.[8]

Under the new system, 20 percent of a bank's deposits on September
30, 1947 (but not more than 15 percent of total deposits) in excess of
ten times its capital and reserves had to be invested in government
securities to be held at the Bank of Italy, placed in a special interest-
bearing time deposit account (*conti correnti vincolati speciali*) at the
central bank (or, until 1953, at the Treasury), or any combination of
these alternatives. In addition, after October 1, 1947, 40 percent of any
additional amount of deposits had to be set aside in the manner prescribed above as long the the bank's total percentage of reserves did
not exceed 25 percent of its deposits.[9] This high reserve ratio was required for sight, time, and savings deposits, but not for interbank
deposits.

Except for a slight change in 1953 (when the banks were required to
restrict their holdings of government securities as compulsory reserves
to ordinary treasury bills),[10] the system remained unchanged until
January, 1962, when the upper limit of compulsory reserves was reduced from 25 to 22.5 percent "to give the banking system more elbow
room in the fulfillment of its functions."[11] Clearly the overall level of

---

Italy has gone out of its way to explain that, in aiding the large banks, "It
was by no means a case of trying to bolster the big banks' competitive position
vis-à-vis the small and medium ones, but of enabling the former to administer
efficiently the cash pool entrusted to them by the latter" (Bank of Italy, *Annual
Report for 1961*, p. 96).

[8] Cf. Bank of Italy, *Annual Report for 1957*, p. 72.

[9] Cf. Carli, *Relations Between Central and Commercial Banks, op. cit.*, p. 50.

[10] Bank of Italy, *Annual Report for 1953*, p. 64.

[11] Bank of Italy, *Annual Report for 1961*, p. 58. This reduction of reserve
requirements was made possible by the improved cash position of the Treasury
and by the buildup of foreign exchange reserves to a satisfactory level. Cf. *idem*.

the compulsory reserve requirements has not been actively manipulated in the interests of cyclical credit control. On the contrary, as one authority has remarked, ". . . the use made so far in Italy of obligatory reserves has been rather to channel to the public sector a considerable proportion of the expansion of bank credit" instead of to regulate liquidity for business-cycle needs.[12]

As part of the 1962 reforms, the authorities curtailed the banks' freedom to allocate required reserves between treasury securities and central-bank deposits. As of December, 1962, the cash component of the required reserves may not fall below 10 percent of the excess of deposits over capital.[13] The Bank of Italy can, of course, compensate for changes in the composition of bank reserves by altering the proportion of the banks' cash reserves which it would otherwise have invested in treasury securities. Some writers have stressed, however, that the change in the composition of reserves, although it leaves the total unchanged, is a qualitative change "which is anything but insignificant as regards economic effects."[14]

Open-market operations, a third traditional instrument of central-bank control, have not been employed systematically as an important instrument of monetary policy in Italy.[15] Until October, 1962, short-term treasury securities were available on tap and mostly purchased by banks (as part of their compulsory reserve requirements) at rates which moved only with the infrequent changes in Bank Rate.[16] Until the 1962 reform of the Treasury issue, the short-term money market in Italy was almost entirely the market for interbank deposits; and inter-

[12] Paolo Baffi, "Monetary Stability and Economic Development in Italy, 1946–1960," Banca Nazionale del Lavoro, *Quarterly Review*, March, 1961, p. 8.

[13] Cf. Bank of Italy, *Annual Report for 1962*, p. 68. In the late part of 1966, the banks were authorized to include mortgage bonds in their compulsory reserves up to the amount that would be required by any increase in time deposits. On March 31, 1966, this authority amounted to 275 billion lire, but only 135 billion lire had been allocated in this way. Cf. Bank of Italy, *Annual Report for 1965*, pp. 85 and 137.

[14] Cf. Amedeo Gambino, "The Control of Liquidity in Italy," Banca Nazionale del Lavoro, *Quarterly Review*, March, 1960, pp. 17–18.

[15] Some writers have pointed out, however, that the Treasury has been engaged in a kind of open-market operation since 1950, for (with exceptions noted later) it has issued a nine-year security during the first few months of each year to absorb the excess liquidity which appears regularly at year-end and to neutralize the inflationary effects of budget deficits. Cf. Carli, *Relations Between Central and Commercial Banks, op. cit.* (see n. 3 above), p. 53, and Bank of Italy, *Annual Report for 1959*, p. 95.

[16] The only exception since 1944 (the first year reported in the Banca d'Italia *Bollettino series*) was April 6, 1950, when the Bank Rate was reduced but the Treasury security rate was not reduced until two years later on May 10, 1952. Cf. *Bollettino*, March–April, 1964, p. 137.

bank deposit rates also did not change often. The reforms of 1962 laid the groundwork for an organized money market, and it may some day become feasible for the Bank of Italy to add open-market operations to its list of important monetary controls.

The Bank of Italy can also influence the amount of bank resources by its control over foreign exchange operations.[17] Specifically, the central bank can regulate the amount of short-term foreign borrowing by banks and the use of their foreign exchange holdings. The authorities can also regulate the banks' swap transactions (in which lire are exchanged for foreign currencies). Because foreign exchange is important to the Italian banks, central-bank control over foreign exchange operations is a major means of influencing the banks' credit operations. During 1960, for example, as part of a policy "to facilitate internal liquidity control by protecting the domestic market from the potentially disturbing effects of certain short-term capital movements"[18] the authorities encouraged the banks to reduce their foreign indebtedness (incurred when they borrowed at the low foreign rates to relend at the higher domestic rates). The central bank provided the dollars that the banks needed to repay their foreign indebtedness by permitting them to buy spot dollars from the Italian Exchange Office against lire, subject to a repurchase agreement which shifted the dollar exchange risk from the banks to the Exchange Office.

As the usual instruments (rediscount rate, reserve requirements, open-market operations) are inadequate to regulate credit in the Italian banking system, the Bank of Italy relies heavily on requests, backed not only by its prestige but also by the sanctions it can impose on uncooperative banks: withholding rediscount and advance facilities, and (a particularly effective form) refusing permits for new branches. The system of appeals, threats, and sanctions, is not, however, fully effective in controlling bank behavior. It is most successful with large banks and least with some small banks outside of major cities. Moreover, the slow response of small banks to official requests often undermines the cooperation of the large banks as well. Thus, the manager of a local branch office of a large bank will sometimes violate a policy instruction from his own head office if a local bank rival is gaining a competitive advantage by ignoring the government's new policy. Interestingly, public or private ownership of banks seems to have no effect on a bank's propensity to comply with official requests. The public banks do cooperate more fully and more readily than the private banks, but this

---

[17] In this discussion, it is not necessary to distinguish between the power exercised over foreign exchange dealings by the Bank of Italy or the Italian Exchange Office, because their policies are closely coordinated.

[18] Bank of Italy, *Annual Report for 1960*, p. 96.

is due to their size, not their ownership: the public banks are large banks; the private banks are smaller.

CONTROLS OVER THE ALLOCATION OF BANK CREDIT

To influence the allocation of bank credit, the monetary authorities have from time to time proposed broad policy guides to the banks in the form of "suggestions." For example, the Bank of Italy has urged the banks to give preference to customers with "sound development programs" and to refuse accommodation to borrowers for speculative purposes which would provoke inflationary pressures.[19] As noted earlier, the government has also made "suggestions" to the banks in line with its policy to encourage the growth and development of small- and medium-size enterprises. Although they have broad powers (under Article 32 of the Banking Law of 1936 and under more recent confirmation), the authorities have chosen not to dictate directly to the banks about specific allocations of credit. The official reluctance to become more directly involved in allocating short-term bank credit is due in part to the fear that it would be difficult to avoid arbitrariness, given the heterogeneity of medium-size and small business borrowers.[20] As the governor of the Bank of Italy has emphasized, "Regardless of the orientation of the government's economic policy, I believe that the task of the banking sector is to behave impartially."[21] The forbearance has also been due to a desire not to burden the large number of medium-size and small banks that operate in geographically restricted areas, because "If these latter were asked to implement directives implying choices of high-priority sectors, they would be all but paralyzed in practice, or else they would be forced into a concentration of risks incompatible with efficient safeguards for the class of depositors to whom they cater."[22]

The government's "hands off" policy applies to the government-owned as well as private banks and enterprises. In practice, however, the government-owned banks of national interest supply most of the bank-financing for the government-owned enterprises, and some have concluded that this is due to government policy. As one writer put it, "The State-owned corporations which are a legacy of fascism get first

[19] Bank of Italy, *Annual Report for 1958*, p. 116.

[20] Bank of Italy, *Annual Report for 1963*, p. 134.

[21] Cf. Interrogatorio del Dottor Guido Carli, in Camera dei deputati, *Commissione d'inchiesta sui limiti posti alla concorrenza nel campo economico*, seduta del 22 novembre, 1962, p. 4. Governor Carli emphasized that, to achieve this goal, bankers must have independence as well as technical competence and moral integrity (*ibid.*, p. 10). For a similar view about the importance of bankers exercising impartial or independent judgment, cf. Bank of Italy, *Annual Report for 1962*, p. 124.

[22] Bank of Italy, *Annual Report for 1963*, p. 134.

call on capital and on bank credit; the largest banks are State-owned to make sure they get it."[23] There are a number of reasons for doubting that this particular allocation of credit has been due to government policy. First, in testimony before the Parliamentary Commission on Limits to Competition[24] the president of the ABI specifically rejected the notion that the large banks, because of their public ownership, would be less interested in private business customers and more concerned to favor state-owned enterprises in order to safeguard the state's interest in those enterprises. This has not happened, he said, because "the administration of the banks has been left free and there has been no interference."[25] Second, the state-owned banks (like the banks of national interest or the Banca Nazionale del Lavoro) are large banks, and many of the enterprises wholly or largely owned by the government are among the largest in the country. It is possible, therefore, that the state-owned banks lend to state-owned enterprises because they prefer to deal with large customers and not because of any government pressure. Third, the large state-owned banks may lend to the state-owned enterprises because they consider lending to government enterprises as safe as lending directly to the government. Indeed, although all banks make the "mistake" (in the opinion of the governor of the Bank of Italy) of equating credits to government-controlled firms with credits to government itself, "banking firms with a private-enterprise structure seem to be more prone than others to this belief."[26] Finally, the regulatory authorities have made it clear that they are unhappy that government-controlled enterprises can secure bank credit with great ease, because it induces some of them "to rely on bank credit more than is right from the point of view of proper balance among various sources of finance. . . ."[27] In sum, if government companies do have preferred access to bank credit, it does not appear to be due to government intervention or policy and, in some cases, it may occur in spite of the government's wishes.

Although the government has not directly dictated the allocation

---

[23] Neil McInnes, "No Soft Life," *Barron's*, July 27, 1964, p. 14.

[24] This part of the inquiry dealt with the allocation of bank credit and sought to determine whether a concentrated banking system would use its market power to discriminate against medium-size and small business firms in allocating credit and thereby increase industrial concentration. (Cf. statement of Ricardo Lombardi in "L'intervento dell' Avv. Siglienti ai lavori della Commissione d'inchiesta sui limiti alla concorrenza," *Bancaria*, February, 1963, p. 212). Lombardi was not much interested in the implications of banking concentration for the operations of the banking sector.

[25] Testimony of Stefano Siglienti, *ibid.*, pp. 210 and 212.

[26] Cf. Bank of Italy, *Annual Report for 1962*, p. 106.

[27] *Idem.* This problem was serious enough to engage the attention of the Joint Ministerial Committee for Credit.

of bank credit, it has attempted to influence this allocation in other ways. First, as noted above, it has made "suggestions" to the banks with respect to the government's views about priority sectors. Second, it has influenced the allocation of bank credit by its authority to discount for banks and, in particular, by its greater willingness to discount for banks which lend to medium-size and small firms than to banks which specialize in large borrowers.[28] Third, the Bank of Italy has been able to influence the allocation of bank credit under the provision of the Banking Act of 1936 which empowered the Bank of Italy to limit the amount of bank loans to a single borrower.[29] Under this authority, the Bank of Italy has ruled that, unless an exception has been granted by the Bank of Italy, no bank may lend more than 20 percent of its capital and reserves to any single borrower. The original purpose of the regulation (which resembles the corresponding 10 percent rule in American banking) was to protect bank solvency by enforcing a certain minimum amount of diversification in the banks' loan portfolios. This regulation was not unduly restrictive during the prewar period when most banks had large capital positions relative to the size of loan demands made upon them. However, inflation during and after the war severely undermined bank capital positions. As a result, banks were forced to apply more often for central-bank permission to exceed the legal loan limit. In considering applications for exemptions, the central bank takes account of the general credit situation and the purpose of the proposed loan.[30] As the Bank of Italy is normally very strict about granting exemptions,[31] it can influence the use of a bank's credit simply by varying its liberality in granting exemptions. During the Korean crisis of 1950–1951, for example, the central bank used this instrument to encourage the banks to grant credits to finance imports of raw material and finished products.[32] Occasionally, too, it has used this instrument to restrict the use of bank credit for financing fixed plant (other than temporary financing pending recourse to the capital market) or for speculative stockpiling.[33]

---

[28] Cf. Testimony of Stefano Siglienti, op. cit., p. 217.

[29] Cf. Associazione Bancaria Italiana, Raccolta di testi legislativi e normativi in materia creditizia, La legge bancaria, V edizione (Rome, 1962), Article 35, paragraph 2b, p. 42.

[30] Cf. Baffi, op. cit. (see n. 12 above), p. 9.

[31] Cf. Siglienti testimony, op. cit., p. 215. However, it is possible that a loan above the legal limit could be split between two affiliated companies and might not be caught by the supervisory procedures of the Bank of Italy. Cf. idem.

[32] Cf. Donato Menichella, "The Contribution of the Banking System to Monetary Equilibrium and Economic Stability: Italian Experience," Banca Nazionale del Lavoro, Quarterly Review, January–June, 1956, p. 17.

[33] Cf. Baffi, op. cit. (see n. 12 above), pp. 9–10. He stressed that this was done occasionally rather than systematically.

Finally, it has not been necessary for the authorities to intervene directly in order to influence the allocation of credit, especially by size of borrower, owing to the way the banking system has been structured. For example, the prohibition (in the Banking Act of 1936) against mixed banking also influenced the allocation of credit. Indeed, it will be recalled that the fear of an unsound allocation of bank credit was a primary consideration of the opponents of mixed banking. However, the most important structural feature which favors medium-size and small firms is the size-structure of the Italian banking system. As shown earlier, the present size-structure is the product of a conscious government policy in which the authorities, acknowledging the banks' tendency to specialize by size of customer, aimed for a size-structure that would be conducive to a desired distribution of credit. As a result, the Italian banking system now consists of a few large banks to handle the needs of large business firms, and many smaller banks to serve the banking requirements of smaller business firms.

As noted earlier, the government has been particularly anxious to ensure an adequate supply of bank credit for medium-size and small business firms in order to discourage the growth of industrial concentration.[34] Although it is difficult to test the matter statistically (in the absence of the necessary data and information about demand functions of different classes of borrowers and amounts of bank credit they have received), there is prima facie evidence that the banks have not ignored the small and medium-size borrowers. On the basis of information about the allocation of bank credit by kind of borrower (Table 19), it is possible to make reasonable inferences about the size-distribution of bank loans. Thus, a substantial part of the loans to public agencies are presumably loans to large entities. In addition, the firms in the next two categories (government-controlled companies and agencies, and major private companies) are unambiguously large firms, because they have presumed annual sales in excess of 1.5 billion lire. The three large-borrower categories together received (as of the end of 1964) 30.4 percent of the credit granted by banks. The balance was probably allocated mostly to medium-size and small firms and to individuals. There is some uncertainty on this point because the size-composition of the fourth category (other companies, private firms, and individuals) is not known. That category does not include the very largest firms, but it is not clear whether it contains any moderately large firms, and if so, how much of the category's total credit they received. It is also pertinent to record

---

[34] The monetary authorities are satisfied that the allocation of credit under the present banking system has not stimulated industrial concentration. Cf. testimony of Governor Carli, *op. cit.* (see n. 20 above), p. 10.

here the official view that "the great bulk of bank credits goes to sectors comprising innumerable small and very small firms."[35]

COMPETITIVE CONTROLS AS MONETARY CONTROLS

For many years, the monetary authorities tacitly accepted the Interbank Agreement as part of their own bank-control apparatus. In testimony to the Parliamentary Inquiry on Competition, the governor of the Bank of Italy stated that the Credit Committee has not exercised its power (under Article 32 of the Banking Law) to regulate active and passive rates, the conditions of bank operations, and other conditions, because it has been satisfied that the banks' handling of these matters has been consistent with the general interest.[36] In 1963, for reasons explained below, the authorities moved from tacit to overt support of the Interbank Agreement.

Changing Situation in the Capital Market

The Italian gross national product rose at an average annual rate of 6.0 percent in *real terms* (1954 prices) between 1950 and 1961. During

TABLE 19

Allocation of Bank Credit, by Kind of Borrower,
1963 and 1964

Category of borrower	December 1963		December 1964	
	Amount (billion lire)	Percent	Amount (billion lire)	Percent
Public agencies	1,358.5	10.4	1,589.9	11.9
Government-controlled companies and agencies[a,b]	978.9	7.5	1,235.4	9.2
Major private companies[a]	1,122.1	8.6	1,249.6	9.3
Other companies, private firms and individuals	9,545.1	73.4	9,323.9	69.6
Totals	13,004.6	99.9	13,398.8	100.0

a Included in the list of 500 companies and agencies with presumed annual sales exceeding 1.5 billion lire.

b Including ENEL, the nationalized electricity board.

SOURCE: Based on figures in Bank of Italy, *Annual Report for 1963*, p. 86, and *Annual Report for 1964*, p. 104.

---

[35] Cf. Bank of Italy, *Annual Report for 1962*, p. 107. Similarly, the *Annual Report for 1952* (p. 102) observed that "a great or even the greatest part of the large amount of credit distributed in 1952 went to medium-size and small borrowers."

[36] Cf. testimony of Governor Carli, *op. cit.* (see n. 20 above), p. 11.

the last few years of the period (1958–1961), real gross national product rose even more rapidly—at an average annual rate of 7.8 percent.[37] This impressive increase in real output depended on a growing capital market to finance high levels of investment. New security issues of stocks and bonds (both private and government) rose from 336 billion lire in 1950 to the substantial level of 1,301 billion by the end of 1961. The expansion was particularly rapid in the last few years—the volume of new securities roughly doubled between 1950 and 1958 and then doubled again between 1958 and 1961.[38] In spite of this heavy demand for funds, interest rates in the capital markets generally declined. Bond yields fell from 7 percent in 1953 to a low of 5 percent in the early part of 1961, and were about 5½ percent at the end of the year.[39]

The favorable situation in the capital market that was achieved by the early part of 1961 began to change toward the end of 1961 as the market began to lose its capacity to finance investment demand at the same low rates. In part, this was due to the rising demand for investment funds as rising wage and other costs whittled profit margins and reduced the volume of funds available to business firms from internal sources. This increased demand coincided with a reduced flow of savings and a partial redirection of the flow away from the capital market. From 1950 to 1961, investment and exports had gained steadily at the expense of consumption. This pattern was reversed during the next two years when large wage increases[40] caused a redistribution of income. The average annual increase in consumption, which had been 7.6 percent (at current prices) from 1950 to 1961, jumped to 13.4 percent (at current prices) in 1962 and to 17.6 percent in 1963.[41] The reduced flow of savings to the capital market was also due to a shift of investors' preferences away from securities. Favorable expectations for business profits had attracted a large volume of funds to the securities market during the period 1950–1961. As company profits began to dwindle, the attraction of security market investment drastically declined.[42] The attractiveness of the security market was also affected by Law No. 1745 (passed on December 29, 1962) which inaugurated a tax-withholding of dividends by the paying company. The market was further unsettled by the prospects of nationalization of the electricity industry and of the strain on the market to supply the funds to com-

---

[37] Cf. Bank of Italy, *Annual Report for 1962*, p. 16, Table 3.

[38] Bank of Italy, *Annual Report for 1961*, p. 44.

[39] Cf. *ibid.*, p. 41 (Chart 8).

[40] Wage incomes in the public and private sector increased by almost 4,000 billion lire in 1962 and 1963. Cf. Bank of Italy, *Annual Report for 1963*, p. 112.

[41] *Ibid.*, p. 42, Table 13.

[42] Bank of Italy, *Annual Report for 1963*, p. 98.

pensate the owners.[43] The attempt to attract investors' funds into the bond (as distinct from the stock) market was also made more difficult by the rise in the general price level and by the uncertainty about the government's capacity or will to restrain the inflation. Finally, but not least important, the reduced flow of savings to the capital market was due to a narrowing spread between long- and short-term yields. Part of the rise in short-term yields, especially on bank deposits, occurred because a shortage of funds in the capital market obliged business firms to turn to the banks, and this additional pressure on bank funds raised deposit as well as loan rates. It should be stressed that, in many cases, the higher deposit rates violated the Interbank Agreement.

Short-term Response to the Capital Market Problem

In 1958, bond and stock yields on the capital market began a steady decline. In 1956–1957, bonds yielded 7 percent and stocks 5 percent. During 1960, bond yields declined to about $5\frac{1}{4}$ percent and stock yields to an average of about $2\frac{1}{2}$ percent.[44] Indeed, by 1960 and 1961, rates on the Italian capital market were comparable to those in other European capital markets, and the capital market's role in financing investment was compared favorably to the most advanced countries.[45] As difficulties developed in the capital market toward the end of 1961 and in early 1962, the authorities became increasingly concerned that the Italian "economic miracle"[46] would be jeopardized by insufficient funds to finance the investment that was essential for the miracle to continue.[47] In this situation, the authorities looked to the banks to finance the investment demand that the capital market could not supply.[48] The

---

[43] To minimize the shock to the stock market, the authorities and the companies that owned the electricity firms agreed on a gradual approach to pay the owners in ten annual installments instead of a once-for-all compensation. This plan eased but did not completely eliminate the impact on the market. Cf. Bank of Italy, *Annual Report for 1962*, p. 116.

[44] Bank of Italy, *Annual Report for 1961*, p. 44.

[45] *Ibid.*, p. 91; also cf. pp. 89–91.

[46] The "economic miracle" refers to the period of rapid expansion accompanied by price stability which began in mid-1959. Cf. Paolo Baffi, "Monetary Developments in Italy from 1961 to 1965," Banca Nazionale del Lavoro, *Quarterly Review*, March, 1966, p. 19.

[47] The growth of the economy was also threatened by other important developments—rising prices, reduced competitiveness of Italian industry in the world market, growing pressures in the balance of payments, etc.—which are not of primary interest in this study.

[48] Other official measures that eased the pressure on the capital market but did not directly affect the banks are ignored in this context. For example, in order to encourage a larger flow of funds to investment, the Minister of the Treasury decided not to issue nine-year treasury bonds to replace those ma-

banks were expected to meet this challenge in two ways: by increasing their supply of short-term credit to meet the demand that was temporarily diverted from the long-term market, and by increasing their bond purchases to compensate for the reduced demand for securities by other investors.

The Bank of Italy took a number of steps during 1962 and early 1963 to increase the lending and investing capacity of the banks. First, effective January 13, 1962, the Bank of Italy reduced reserve requirements by 10 percent (from 25 to 22.5 percent) "to contain the rise of interest rates in the bond market"[49] and to make it possible "to complete investment programs already begun in the public and private sector alike."[50] This reduction in required reserves was designed to allow the banks to expand bank credit by almost 500 billion lire.[51] Second, the authorities helped the banks to serve their customers by selling the banks substantial amounts of foreign exchange.[52] This helped the banks to balance their foreign commitments but it also reduced their lire liquidity, and toward the latter part of the year, the banks began to feel this liquidity pinch. To relieve the pressure, the Bank of Italy (acting through the Italian Exchange Office) repurchased some foreign exchange which it had earlier sold to the commercial banks and then redeposited it with the banks. In this way, the monetary authorities not only relieved the year-end seasonal pressure on bank liquidity but also developed a new instrument for influencing bank liquidity.[53] Third, to strengthen the lending and investing capacity of the banks, the authorities (in October, 1962) lifted the prohibition against banks' incurring debts abroad. The banks promptly began to borrow abroad on a large scale. During November and December alone, their borrowings were equivalent to 320 billion lire.[54] The accumulation of foreign debts by Italian banks was not stopped until the summer of 1963.

Finally, the banks were able to expand bank credit because the Bank of Italy significantly increased the volume of its rediscounts and advances for the banks (Table 20). The volume of rediscounts and ad-

---

turing on January 1, 1963. Cf. minutes of the meeting of the Interministerial Committee on Credit and Savings, held in Rome on November 16, 1962. The plan succeeded, owing in part to the action of the special credit institutes which issued their own bonds to the holders of the redeemed government securities and channeled the funds into investment. Cf. Bank of Italy, *Annual Report for 1963*, p. 118.

[49] Bank of Italy, *Annual Report for 1961*, p. 92.
[50] Bank of Italy, *Annual Report for 1963*, p. 118.
[51] *Idem.*
[52] Italy had a balance-of-payments surplus in 1961.
[53] Cf. Bank of Italy, *Annual Report for 1961*, pp. 76–77.
[54] Bank of Italy, *Annual Report for 1962*, p. 102.

vances began to rise appreciably in 1961 (24.4 percent) and continued to increase sharply in the following two years (58.6 percent in 1962, and 72.2 percent in 1963). By the end of 1963, rediscounts and advances were at an all-time high level of 1,002 billion lire. The growth of deposits associated with the expansion of bank loans and investments raised required reserves by about 397 billion lire in 1962; the reduction in reserve requirements supplied 226 billion lire; and the balance was borrowed from the Bank of Italy.[55]

The increased bank liquidity from these different sources made it possible for the banks to acquire some of the bonds which other investors were no longer willing to buy.[56] In 1961, the banks purchased 227.9 billion of the 1,301.4 billion lire of new securities, or 17.5 percent

TABLE 20

Bank of Italy's Rediscounts and Advances
to aziende di credito, 1947–1965
(billion lire)

End of year	Rediscounts			Advances[a]	Total
	Ordinary trade bills	Storage-agency bills	Treasury bills		
1947	20.3	43.9	0.03	20.6	84.83
1948	9.3	40.3	3.62	34.7	87.92
1949	11.2	60.2	1.11	46.4	118.91
1950	27.2	69.1	1.56	71.8	169.66
1951	16.6	75.2	0.09	73.2	165.09
1952	12.5	90.5	2.48	104.9	210.38
1953	12.2	116.1	0.08	95.3	223.68
1954	24.0	149.9	0.09	77.1	251.09
1955	7.2	160.5	0.09	70.9	238.69
1956	25.4	206.1	0.07	97.9	329.47
1957	20.5	200.3	0.04	73.9	294.74
1958	3.5	217.6	0.08	28.7	249.88
1959	2.9	224.4	0.07	42.8	270.17
1960	4.9	229.8	0.19	61.1	295.99
1961	14.9	246.3	3.15	103.6	367.95
1962	27.6	298.2	0.01	256.3	582.11
1963	317.8	342.5	8.00	333.9	1,002.20
1964	121.0	363.4	—	281.9	766.30
1965	40.4	386.6	—	307.8	734.80

a Includes advances to Central Institutes of the categories.
SOURCE: Banca d'Italia, *Bollettino*.

---

[55] *Ibid.*, p. 99.
[56] Private investors and companies reduced their new security purchases from 945.1 billion lire in 1961 to 857.5 billion in 1962, and they reduced their bond holdings from 496.2 billion lire to 282.5 billion. Cf. *ibid.*, p. 82, Table 27.

of the new security issues for the year. In 1962, they increased their
security purchases to 506 billion out of 1,642.1 billion lire of new security issues, or almost 31 percent of the new issues in that year.[57] Thus,
in spite of the funds supplied to the banking system, the overall liquidity position of banks was strained. The loan-to-deposit ratio, which had
ranged between 71.3 and 71.7 percent during 1960 and 1961, rose to
74.4 percent in 1962 and to 79.8 percent in 1963; the liquidity-to-deposit
ratio [58] fell steadily: 8.1 percent in 1960, 6.3 percent in 1961, 5.5 percent
in 1962, and 4.8 percent in 1963 (Fig. 4).

Longer-run Structural Reforms

During 1962, the authorities sought to provide the economy with
enough liquidity to finance the investment demand and avoid a slowdown in production but not enough to provoke a rise in prices which
would lead to a balance-of-payments crisis and unemployment. During
1962, the production goal was achieved and a near equilibrium was
maintained in the balance of payments even though prices had started
to rise. In order to forestall a further price rise, the authorities switched
in the summer of 1963 to a more cautious policy in creating additional
liquidity.[59] In spite of this change, prices continued to rise, and by
the end of 1963, after several years of balance-of-payments surpluses, a
deficit was incurred of 1,252 million dollars.

As early as 1962, the authorities had concluded that certain longer-
run reforms were necessary and the events of 1963 confirmed them in
their views.[60] In the view of the authorities, a solution of the capital
market problem required "the creation of a structure of interest rates
susceptible of generating a distribution of the public's liquid assets
more in line with the use to which the investable funds are put."[61] As
the governor of the Bank of Italy explained to a parliamentary commission, it was necessary "to structure the system in such a way as to
eliminate a propensity to liquidity on the part of the public in order
to create an incentive to channel funds towards productive uses."[62]

---

[57] Cf. *idem*. The figures for the total volume of new security issues include
416.8 billion lire of new equity securities in 1961 and 608.2 billion lire in 1962.

[58] The official definition of "liquidity" includes the credit margin with the
Bank of Italy, free treasury-bill holdings, and "other" (cash, deposits with
Bank of Italy, deposits with Treasury, etc., stockpiling bills, and convertible
foreign currencies). Cf. Bank of Italy, *Annual Report for 1961*, p. 57.

[59] For a discussion of these events by the president of the ABI, cf. Stefano
Siglienti, "The Italian Credit System under Present Economic Conditions,"
Review of Economic Conditions in Italy, May, 1964, pp. 159–166.

[60] The reforms discussed below are those which affected the operations of
the capital market by means of control of the banks.

[61] Bank of Italy, *Annual Report for 1962*, p. 112.

[62] Testimony of Governor Carli, *op. cit.* (see n. 20 above), p. 18.

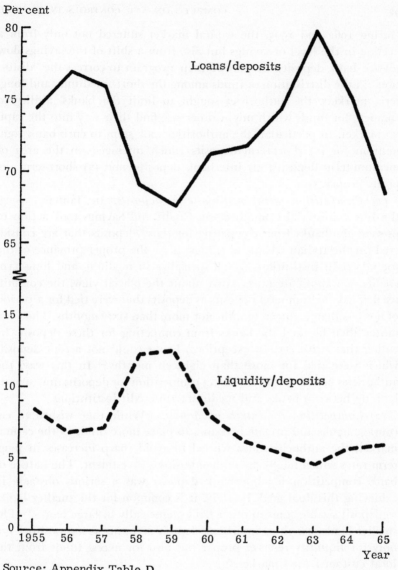

Source: Appendix Table D
FIGURE 4. Measures of Bank Liquidity, Italy, 1955–1965.

During 1962 and 1963, the capital market suffered not only from a decline in the level of savings but also from a shift of the savings flow toward bank deposits. As part of their program to correct the "distortion" in the distribution of funds among the short-, medium-, and long-term markets, the authorities sought to limit the banks' ability to compete for funds which might otherwise find their way into the capital market. In particular, the authorities took steps to curb bank competition for (1) short-term deposits which infringed on the area of medium-term deposits, (2) interbank deposits, and (3) short-term deposits proper.

(1) Competition with medium-term deposits. In January, 1963, the Interministerial Committee on Credit and Savings took action to prevent the banks from competing for those deposits that are considered (in the Italian scheme of things) to be the proper province of the special credit institutions which specialize in medium- and long-term credits. To eliminate uncertainty about the official view, the committee defined medium-term deposits as deposits that were tied for a period of not less than eighteen months nor more than sixty months. The committee then blocked the banks from competing for these deposits by ruling that (with certain exceptions) banks could not accept deposits which were tied for more than eighteen months.[63] In this way, the authorities hoped to prevent direct competition for deposits due to overlapping between banks and medium-term credit institutions.

(2) Competition for interbank deposits. While they wished to encourage banks and private investors to place more funds in the capital market, the authorities also wished to avoid sharp increases in long-term rates which might discourage business investment. The nature of bank competition for interbank deposits was a serious obstacle in achieving this dual goal. In Italy, it is common for the smaller banks to deposit sizable sums in other banks, especially in large banks.[64] The smaller banks use these interbank deposit accounts as a repository not only for liquidity reserves proper but also for excess funds from the local customer loan market.[65]

The large banks' competition for these interbank accounts disturbed

---

[63] At the same time, it was decreed that the special credit institutions could not accept deposits tied for less than eighteen months. Cf. minutes of the meeting of the Interministerial Committee on January 28, 1963; Bank of Italy, *Annual Report for 1962*, pp. 69–70.

[64] At the end of 1961, the amount deposited in interbank accounts by all but the top six banks was 1,077 billion lire. Cf. Bank of Italy, *Annual Report for 1961*, p. 95.

[65] Cf. press release by the Minister of the Treasury after the November 16, 1962, meeting of the Interministerial Committee on Credit and Savings.

the authorities for a number of reasons, but especially because it raised
the general level of short-term rates. As the large banks raised their deposit rates to the smaller banks, the latter were induced to compete
more vigorously by offering higher deposit rates for the deposits of
their own customers, and this further stimulated the large banks to
raise deposit rates for their nonbank customers.

The authorities did not welcome a general rise of deposit rates at a
time when they were trying to protect business investment against
higher costs of borrowing. In addition, the higher interbank deposit
rates encouraged the smaller banks to place their excess funds (available for long-term placement) into interbank accounts instead of into
medium- and long-term securities. Thus, the competition for interbank
accounts aggravated the shortage of funds in the capital market with
resulting pressures for higher long-term rates. Another reason for official concern about the heightened bank competition for interbank
accounts was that the gravitation of interbank accounts to the large
banks increased deposit concentration. It is not clear how the authorities viewed this development in terms of banking or market-structure
effects, but it is clear that they were not pleased by the potential instability of a system under highly pyramided bank reserves nor by the
possible pressure on the Bank of Italy to rescue the system from an
unstable situation.

To curb the banks' power to influence short-term rates and to increase the monetary authorities' ability to do so, the Credit Committee
ruled (on November 16, 1962) that the rate on interbank deposits could
not be higher than the free treasury-bill rate established at the monthly
tender. The new regulation has sharp teeth. The Bank of Italy can
order a bank which violates the regulation to place any part or all of
its interbank accounts in a special time-deposit account at the central
bank. This is an effective penalty because the interest rate on this special account is below the permissible rate on interbank accounts. Moreover, *without any prior determination (or even suspicion) of a violation,*
the Bank of Italy also can require any individual bank or all banks
to place part or all of their interbank accounts into these special accounts.[66] Thus, the new regulation has provided the authorities with
a very effective instrument for regulating the degree of bank competition on interbank deposits.

The Bank of Italy's ability to moderate bank competition for interbank deposits and to encourage a greater flow of funds to the capital
market was further increased by a simultaneous reform of the system

---

[66] *Idem.*

of issuing treasury bills. Under the previous system, treasury bills were available on tap at a fixed rate of interest, and the volume of treasury bills was adjusted neither to the financing needs of the Treasury nor to the views of the monetary authorities about an appropriate level of short-term rates. Since the banks had the option of investing any amount they wished in treasury bills at a fixed rate of return, the central bank could not control the level of short-term rates by increasing bank liquidity. Similarly, the central bank was unable to control long-term rates by increasing the liquidity of the system,[67] because the funds could be siphoned off into treasury bills and thus fail to reach the capital market. In addition to reducing the central bank's ability to influence rates on the capital market, the old system also reduced the banks' incentive to go to the capital market with their excess liquidity.

On October 12, 1962, the old system was changed by a decree of the Minister of the Treasury. Under the new system, treasury bills are no longer available on tap at a fixed rate. They are issued only once a month, and the volume is based on the cash needs of the Treasury and on the amount of treasury bills that the banks require as compulsory reserves. The banks have first call on treasury bills needed for compulsory reserves. These are bought at a fixed rate which is related to Bank Rate, and the balance of the monthly issue is sold on a tender basis to the highest bidders.

(3) *Competition for short-term deposits.* In recent years, deposit competition has led to *scartellamento* (violation of cartel rate agreements). This, too, disturbed the authorities because scartellamento led to higher levels of short- and long-term rates throughout the economy and diverted the flow of funds away from the capital market. In addition, scartellamento could force the central bank to create more liquidity than was desirable. If higher deposit rates offered by banks reduced the public's propensity to hold bonds, bond yields would rise. Higher rates were opposed because of the Treasury's financing problems as well as on grounds of general policy.[68] To counter the higher rates (whether by direct or indirect support of bond prices), the monetary authorities could be led to expand liquidity beyond the level which they deemed to be appropriate.

The governor of the Bank of Italy has stated that "effective liquidity control cannot do without interventions designed to maintain a bal-

[67] However, in each case, the Bank of Italy must pass on the rate of interest and all other conditions which determine effective bond yield for a particular issue. Cf. Bank of Italy, *Annual Report for 1962*, p. 114.
[68] Cf. *ibid.*, pp. 114–115.

anced structure of interest rates."[69] In this view, a balanced structure of rates is one in which short-term rates do not rise enough
to cause a rise in long rates nor fall so much that resources are drained
away from the banking system to other forms of investment which the
authorities are less able to control.[70] The "interventions" mentioned
by the governor included (along with others) the rate limits set forth
in the Interbank Agreement. Although the authorities reserved the
right to determine whether the rates agreed upon by bankers were consistent with the official monetary policy, they did not try to substitute
their own for the bankers' judgments about appropriate short-term
rates.[71] Instead they took steps to reinforce banker compliance with
the Interbank Agreement. At its meeting of January 28, 1963, the
Interministerial Credit Committee officially and formally declared
the agreement to be in the public interest. In addition to this formal
declaration, the authorities (in official speeches) explained their reasons
for emphasizing adherence to the Interbank Agreement and exhorted
the banks to abide by it.[72]

In sum, the importance of the controls on bank competition in recent
years has been due not only to their impact on the safety of bank deposits but also to their part in the larger framework of controls by which the
Italian authorities implement monetary and economic policy. During
a period (like the past few years) when the demand for investment
funds exceeded the amounts which the public was willing to supply at
current rates,[73] the authorities have had to face the choice of let-
ting rates rise to encourage larger bond purchases by the public or
holding rates down by providing the banks with enough liquidity to
buy the bonds. By choosing the latter course, the authorities succeeded
in bringing down market rates[74] but lost their freedom to control the
total volume of credit.[75] Under the circumstances, they deemed it es-

---

[69] *Ibid.*, p. 115.

[70] *Idem.*

[71] They have stated that they prefer to rely on the judgment of bankers who
are in close contact with the market because they "do not consider themselves,
at present, to be possessed of sufficient knowledge to replace the market by
their own rules." Cf. *ibid.*, p. 113 (my italics).

[72] For example, cf. Stefano Siglienti, "Il contributo del sistema creditizio
alla soluzione del problema degli investimenti," *Bancaria,* November, 1962,
pp. 1263–1272; and Guido Carli, "Verso un assetto piu efficiente del mercato
monetario e finanziario," *ibid.*, pp. 1273–1279.

[73] In 1965, there was a revival of fixed-interest investment by individuals
and companies, yet bank purchases of bonds remained very large. Cf. Bank
of Italy, *Annual Report for 1965,* pp. 76 and 77.

[74] Bond yields reached their peak in mid-1964 and were lower throughout
1965. Cf. *ibid.*, p. 78.

[75] *Ibid.*, pp. 116 and 123.

sential to restrain the competitive pressures for higher deposit rates,[76] and in doing so, they accorded the Interbank Agreement a key position in the arsenal of instruments for monetary control.[77]

---

[76] On May 31, 1966 (during the annual stockholders meeting of the Bank of Italy), Governor Carli again condemned the "excesses of competition" and implied that the banks were trying to enlarge their share of the market for reasons of prestige instead of profit. Cf. *ibid.*, pp. 126 and 127.

[77] The controls to restrict competition have received primary emphasis in this discussion of recent monetary policy because the regulation of bank competition is the central focus of this entire study. It is important to stress, however, that the authorities have by no means relied solely on competitive controls to strengthen the capital market and to direct a larger flow of funds into long-term investment. Competitive controls were supplemented by a variety of other controls. Some, like the incomes policy urged by the monetary authorities, were aimed primarily at containing inflation. Others, like the authority of the Credit Committee to pass on both the amount and terms of new security issues of stocks and bonds, were designed to ensure that the demands made on the capital market did not exceed the available supply of savings. In addition, the monetary authorities emphasized the necessity for the government to establish a schedule of priorities for its planned investments and to schedule investments so that they could be financed without resort to inflationary means. At the same time, they explored new ways of stimulating a larger supply of funds to the long-term market, e.g., by encouraging the development of investment trusts, or by authorizing insurance companies and social insurance funds to invest in equities. Cf. Bank of Italy, *Annual Report for 1963*, p. 129.

Part Two
France

VII

Banking Structure in France

THE BANKS INCLUDED IN THIS STUDY

The basic banking law of December 2, 1945, divided French banks into three broad categories: *deposit banks, investment banks,* and *banks of medium- and long-term credit.*[1] This study of French banking is concerned primarily with the commercial banks (i.e., the deposit banks) and secondarily with other banks or financial institutions whose activities significantly overlap the activities of commercial banks. Under the 1945 legislation, deposit banks were not restricted on their loan maturities—most of their lending has nevertheless been short-term—but they were restricted to a maximum of two years on their deposit maturities. This restriction was removed in 1966 in a major reform of the banking structure and system of banking controls. The nature and probable significance of those and other reforms will be discussed at a number of points in this study, but in a study of alternative combinations of regulations of the banking structure and the conditions of competition, it is even more instructive to examine the situation that existed immediately prior to the reforms. An analysis of the situation before 1965 can also provide an excellent framework for appraising the market significance of the later reforms. In order to facilitate the later comparisons, the deposit markets included in this study of French banking are those that commercial banks could enter even under the maturity restrictions (i.e., two years or less) of the 1945 law. Similarly, the French banking structure described in this chapter is based on the banking system that existed before the latest reforms.[2] The modifica-

---

[1] In addition, there are a number of other banks of a public or semipublic nature (Crédit Agricole Mutuel, Crédit Populaire, Crédit Foncier, Caisse Nationale des Marchés de l'Etat, Crédit National, Banque Française du Commerce Extérieur, and others). As indicated below, some of these banks are eligible to be included in this study.

[2] Unless otherwise noted, the banking figures in this chapter refer to the year 1964 (selected as a typical year in terms of the preform banking structure) and are based on Commission de Contrôle des Banques, *Bilans des banques,* 1964.

tions made necessary on these and other points by the reform measures of 1965–1967 have been incorporated at later points in the analysis.

The deposit banks are the preeminent commercial banks in the French banking system, but even under the 1945 legislation they were not the only suppliers of short-term deposits (i.e., those with a maturity of two years or less) or short-term business loans. The most important alternative institutional suppliers (Table 21) of both short-term loans and deposits include the *banques d'affaires* (investment banks), *banques populaires* (popular banks), and the *Crédit Agricole* (agricultural banks). In addition, transactions deposits are provided by the *comptes courants postaux* (Post Office checkery), and short-term time deposits are provided by the *Caisse Nationale d'Epargne Postale* (Postal Savings Bank) and the *caisse d'épargne ordinaire* (ordinary savings bank). Some banks (or institutions that perform bank types of functions) have been omitted from the list of alternative institutional suppliers (Table 21) because of their minor importance as alternative suppliers—for example, the Bank of France (as a minor supplier of short-term loans) or the Treasury (as a minor supplier of short-term deposits, *fonds particuliers au trésor*). Others were omitted because their only overlap with com-

TABLE 21

Number of Banks and Total Resources,
Selected Bank Groups, End of 1964

Bank group	Number		Total resources	
	Banks	Offices	Amount (000, 000 F)	Percent of total
Deposit banks[a]	233	4,098	102,434	43.6
Banques d'affaires	46	101	16,072	6.8
Popular banks	46	1,000[b]	6,104	2.6
Agricultural banks	94	3,200 (approx.)	40,271	17.1
Comptes courantes postaux	—	13,586[c]	18,770[d]	8.0
Caisse Nationale d'Épargne Postale	—	13,586[c]	19,680[d]	8.4
Caisse d'Épargne Ordinaire	570	4,031	31,840[d]	13.5
Totals			235,171	100.0

[a] For composition of deposit banks, cf. Table 22.

[b] Number of branches of popular banks is approximate and includes *guichets permanents and periodiques.*

[c] With the addition of postal agencies, correspondents, and auxiliary offices, the number is increased to 19,860.

[d] Deposits only.

SOURCES: Commission de Contrôle des Banques, *Bilans des banques,* 1964; CNC, *Annexes au rapport annuel,* 1962 and 1964; Caisse Nationale de Crédit Agricole, *Rapport annuel,* 1964, *Annuaire statistique de France,* 1965 and 1966.

mercial bank activities is in areas which are of minor interest in this study.[3] Finally, treasury securities were not included in Table 21, though they have been included later in the discussion of deposit substitutes.

In spite of their common elements, the institutions listed in Table 21 are a heterogeneous group. Since these differences condition the character of the market interaction among them and in some cases the kind and extent of government regulation, it is necessary to identify the important characteristics of each bank category before examining the market and regulatory aspects.

Deposit Banks

The deposit bank group, with total resources of 102 billion francs, is significantly larger than any other group in Table 21. However, these 233 banks are also a heterogeneous assortment, consisting of nationalized credit establishments, nonnationalized credit establishments, Paris deposit banks, foreign banks (including French branches of foreign banks), regional banks, and local banks (Table 22).

TABLE 22

*Number and Total Resources of Deposit Banks,
End of 1964*

Type of bank	Number of banks	Number of Branches	Total resources (000,000 F)
Établissements de crédit (nationalized)	4	2,335	64,424
Établissements de crédit (non-nationalized)	3	168	6.654
Paris deposit banks (other than above)	71	144	5,270
Foreign banks	33	81	8,614
Regional banks	24	1,143	15,260
Local banks	98	227	2,212
Totals	233	4,098	102,434

SOURCE: *Bilans des banques,* 1964.

---

[3] The best example is the group of *établissements financiers.* This heterogenous group of 454 companies, registered with the Conseil National du Crédit (CNC), included 60 *sociétés financiers* (holding companies which own shares in industrial or realty firms), 137 *maisons de titres* (securities firms which act as stockbrokers for clients), 138 *maisons de financement de ventes à crédit* (installment credit companies), 33 *unions meunières* (firms which acted mostly as collection agencies for the milling industry), and 86 *divers* (miscellaneous firms including specialists in financing certain kinds of business). Cf. CNC, *Rapport annuel,* 1964, p. 123. Although they are not banks in the ordinary sense, the établissements financiers are under the same control authority as the banks (viz., Conseil National du Crédit) because they perform some bank types of functions.

(1) Établissements de crédit. The most important deposit banks are the *établissements de crédit.* Before 1966, there were four nationalized credit institutions (Crédit Lyonnais, Société Générale, Banque Nationale pour le Commerce et l'Industrie, and Comptoir National d'Escompte de Paris) and three nonnationalized banks (Crédit Industriel et Commercial, and Crédit Commercial de France, and Société Centrale de Banque). At the end of 1964, the four giant nationalized banks, with total resources of more than 64 billion francs, held approximately 63 percent of the resources of all deposit banks. Because of their size, these four banks were prime candidates for nationalization in the immediate postwar period.[4] In addition, they were the only banks with nationwide branch networks.[5] On December 31, 1946, their combined network consisted of 1,875 branches, and 1,597 were outside of Paris. By comparison, the two large nonnationalized banks (the Crédit Industriel et Commercial and the Crédit Commercial de France) had only 119 branches, and more than half were in the Paris region.[6] It should be added, however, that the Crédit Industriel et Commercial has extensive group-banking connections with eleven regional and numerous other banks. It is the only établissement de crédit with group-bank affiliations.

From the point of view of a market study, it is important to stress that nationalization has not affected business policy or management discretion in the nationalized banks. From a legal point of view, the nationalized banks are commercial enterprises and are subject to the legislation on *sociétés anonymes.*[7] It has been suggested that it was concern about the reaction of bank customers and about foreign reaction to the nationalization which motivated Parliament to preserve the autonomy of the nationalized banks.[8] Whatever the reason, the nationalized banks are expected to behave like private banks, and they do.[9] Since nationalization has not changed either the nature of the banks'

---

[4] According to Dupont, nationalization was motivated primarily by political rather than economic considerations. Cf. P. C. Dupont, *Le Contrôle des banques et la direction du crédit en France* (Paris, 1952), pp. 43–46.

[5] Under the 1945 Banking Law (Art. 13), the Conseil National du Crédit can propose the nationalization of any banks which come to resemble the nationalized banks in terms of size or a nationwide branch network.

[6] Cf. Conseil National du Crédit, *Annexes au rapport annuel*, 1946, p. 95.

[7] This was explicitly affirmed by the law of December 2, 1945 (Art. 10) and again by the decree of May 23, 1946 (Art. 2). (A société anonyme, like a corporation, has limited liability of shareholders.)

[8] Cf. Georges Petit-Dutaillis, *Le Crédit et les banques* (Paris, 1964), p. 453.

[9] As shown later, however, all deposit banks, nationalized or not, have operated under considerable government regulation.

operations or the bankers' concern with liquidity or earnings,[10] the nationalized banks have been included with the private banks as independent sources of supply for short-term deposits and short-term (commercial) credit.

(2) *Paris deposit banks.* The 1946 census of French banks listed 89 Parisian deposit banks (in addition to the établissements de crédit); by 1964, there were only 71 banks in this category. All of the Paris deposit banks—their total resources are more than 5 billion francs—are significantly smaller than any of the établissements de crédit. The largest Paris deposit bank (De Neuflize & Schlumberger) had total resources of 436 million francs whereas the Société Centrale de Banque, the smallest of the nonnationalized établissements de crédit, had 1,296 million francs. At the opposite end of the size scale, the smallest Paris deposit bank (Banque Franco-Serbe) had total resources of only 1½ million francs. The mean size (resources) of the Paris deposit banks was 74.2 million francs as compared with 16.1 billion for the nationalized banks and 10.2 billion for the établissements de crédit.

The Paris deposit banks are a diversified group. Some (like De Neuflize & Schlumberger, Vernes & Cie, Mallet Frères) belong to the group of private bankers known as the *hautes banques.* They deal with wealthy customers (both individuals and business firms) with whom they have had long-standing relationships, and the personal relationship between banker and client is typically very important in the hautes banques. Other Paris deposit banks are specialist institutions, for example, specialists in particular industries (like the Crédit Sucrier et Commercial, or the Banque Cotonnière).

(3) *Foreign banks.* The thirty-three foreign-owned banks or agencies of foreign banks in France had total resources of more than 8 billion francs, but they are less important on the domestic banking scene than the volume of their resources might suggest. Like their counterparts in other countries, these banks do much of their business with their own nationals, especially in financing trade between their own countries and France.

(4) *Regional banks.* There were twenty-four regional banks with total resources of 15 billion francs. These banks, usually well rooted in their particular areas, tend to confine both their branches and their activities to those areas. Except for their size, regional banks generally resemble the large établissements de crédit. Their average size was only 636 million francs, but their size-distribution ranged from the giant Crédit du Nord, with total resources of 3 billion francs, to the tiny

---

[10] For example, cf. Emile James, *Problèmes monétaires d'aujourdhui* (Paris, 1963), p. 216.

Banque Journel, with only 60 million francs (smaller than some of the "local banks" discussed below). The Crédit du Nord is far larger than any other regional bank and somewhat larger than any of the nonnationalized établissements de crédit. Half of the regional banks, holding half of the group's resources, are affiliated with the group-banking complex headed by the Crédit Industriel et Commercial. Indeed, if the resources of its regional affiliates are added to those which it holds directly, the Crédit Industriel et Commercial would have ranked (in 1964) as the fourth largest deposit bank in France.

(5) *Local banks.* There are 98 local banks with total resources of 2.2 billion francs. Almost all are small banks—the smallest had 200,000 francs and the largest had 146 million. Their average size was 22.2 million francs. Sixty-one percent of the local banks are unit banks; the others have an average of between four and five branches each. Because their resources are very limited and their branches few or nonexistent, local banks concentrate on small local customers.

Banques d'Affaires

The 46 banques d'affaires had total resources of 16.1 billion francs (Table 23), about five-eighths in the five largest banks. The resources of the largest (Banque de Paris et des Pays-Bas) were 4.6 billion francs, or more than a quarter of the resources of the entire group. All but six of the investment banks are located in Paris—the others are in Monte Carlo—and typically operate with a single office.

In order to distinguish commercial banks proper from investment banks, the Banking Law of 1945 (and subsequent amendments in 1946) had prohibited the deposit banks but not the banques d'affaires from accepting deposits with more than two years' maturity. Similarly, it had severely limited the participations of the deposit banks, but not of the banques d'affaires. These distinctions between the two bank

TABLE 23
Number, Resources, and Deposits, Banques d'Affaires,
End of 1964

Type of bank	Number		Total resources (000,000 F)	Sight deposits (000,000 F)	Bons et comptes à échéance fixe (000,000 F)
	Banks	Branches			
Sociétés par Actions	40	93	14,155	4,738	1,842
Sociétés de Personnes et Affaires Personnelle	6	8	1,917	931	259
Totals	46	101	16,072	5,669	2,100

SOURCE: *Bilans des banques,* 1964.

categories were dropped in 1966, but even before that date, it would have been necessary to include the banques d'affaires with the alternative suppliers of short-term credit and short-term deposits because of potential overlap with commercial bank activities. Under the law of May 17, 1946 (Article 5 of the amended 1945 law), a banque d'affaire could accept short-term deposits (i.e., demand deposits or deposits fixed for less than two years) from its own personnel, from business firms to which it had granted loans or investment funds, from merchants (whether individuals or firms) acting in their business capacity, and from subscribers of stock (if the bank also handled their security accounts) in firms in which the bank had a participation. Under that law (Article 5), a banque d'affaire could lend at any maturity to firms which might benefit in the past, present, or future from the bank's participations.

The banques d'affaires did not ignore these opportunities to operate in the short-term deposit and credit markets, and often they were virtually as active as the deposit banks. Most of their short-term deposit and loan business was carried on with large firms and wealthy individuals, typically long-time customers. In 1964, the demand accounts of business firms accounted for 30 percent of the total resources of the banques d'affaires—the same percent as in the établissements de crédit. On the credit side, *portefeuille effets* (commercial bills and other short-term papers, including treasury bills) were equal to 47 percent of their resources, as compared with about 66 percent for the établissements de crédit.[11] By contrast, due to legal strictures, their short-term deposits of individuals were far behind those in deposit banks—funds received from individuals (*comptes de chèques* and *comptes spéciaux*) accounted for 5 percent of their total resources as compared with about 35 percent in the établissements de crédit.

Banques Populaires

In 1962, 46 popular (people's) banks had approximately 1,000 *guichets permanents* or *périodiques* operating in all parts of the country.[12] Mutual and cooperative banks in France date from the first half of the nineteenth century, but the basic law under which the popular

---

[11] The growth of the commercial business of the investment banks has been aided by the fact that they acquire the commercial banking business of firms by investing in them but do not lose the commercial accounts of their former subsidiaries when they sell their shareholdings. Cf. Neil McInnes, "Rothschild to Paribas," *Barron's*, October 1, 1962, p. 9.

[12] Cf. CNC, *Annexes au rapport annuel*, 1962, p. 129. In 1946, the number of banks was larger (56) but the number of *guichets* was smaller (698). Cf. "Note sur le crédit populaire," CNC, *Rapport annuel*, 1946, p. 151. For an explanation of the different kinds of guichets, see n. 26 in the next chapter.

banks are now organized was passed in March, 1917. The 1917 legislation (which contained many of the reforms envisaged by the 1912 Pallain Commission)[13] was modified by subsequent legislation, but it continues to be the legal text for the popular banks.

The popular banks are cooperative credit organizations whose capital stock consists of nonnegotiable shares. The maximum interest rate on these shares is limited to 6 percent to ensure that any profit is distributed among the members, in accord with cooperative principles.[14] Deposits, especially demand deposits, are by far the most important source of funds. In 1964, demand and time deposits were 85 percent, and demand deposits alone were 75 percent, of the 6.1 billion francs total resources of the popular banks (including the Caisse Centrale des Banques Populaires).[15]

A major reason for launching the popular banks was the widespread feeling that the large banks were not particularly interested in serving the needs of smaller customers. To counter this neglect, the popular banks engage in educational activities to familiarize potential customers with the mechanics, requirements, and advantages of credit when properly employed.[16] In addition, they concentrate their activity, especially loans, among the smaller business firms: merchants, manufacturers, and artisans.[17] They try to establish permanent relations with their customers, and they work hard to overcome the traditional obstacles to commercial lending to small firms, namely, management problems, and a shortage of capital and of suitable collateral. In 1964, the popular banks devoted 60 percent of their total resources to *autres effets* (commercial bills) and an additional 17 percent to other loans and advances.[18]

Crédit Agricole

The agricultural banks, like the popular banks, are cooperative institutions.[19] They extend medium- and long-term as well as short-term

[13] Cf. Pierre Montfajon, *Le Crédit populaire de France* (Paris, 1957), p. 8.
[14] *Ibid.*, p. 12.
[15] Calculated from Conseil National du Crédit, *Annexes au rapport annuel, 1964*, p. 149.
[16] Montfajon, pp. 26–27.
[17] The popular banks deal almost exclusively with small firms even though it was the intention of their founders that they would serve both medium-size and small firms. Cf. J. S. G. Wilson, *French Banking Structure and Credit Policy* (London, 1957), p. 233, n. 38.
[18] Cf. *Annexes au rapport annuel*, 1964, p. 149.
[19] However, the agricultural banks have greater tax advantages than the popular banks. Cf. Petit-Dutaillis, *Le crédit et les banques*, p. 237.

credit primarily for agricultural purposes. Since agricultural credit is outside the scope of this study, the agricultural banks have been included in Table 21 for their deposit rather than their lending operations. Deposits, however, are not their most important source of funds. Demand and time deposits were only 12.4 billion francs out of total resources of 40.3 billion francs. They secured 12 billion francs from *bons à 3 ans* and *bons à 5 ans* and almost 4 billion in advances from the fonds de Développement Economique et Social.[20] Agricultural bank deposits (which were only about 7 percent of the total resources shown in Table 21), consist almost entirely of the demand accounts of individuals (comptes de chèques)—unlike, say, the popular banks, in which both individual and business deposits are important. In 1960, the regional agricultural banks held 2,077,460 deposit accounts, and more than 2,000,000 were accounts of individuals.[21] In appraising the market significance of the agricultural banks as suppliers of demand deposits for individuals, it is also pertinent to note that they have a large network of about 3,200 offices all over the country.[22]

Service des Chèques Postaux

The Service des Chèques Postaux opened in Paris in July, 1918, as a checkery service for both individuals and business firms. The Post Office checkery is included here because its activities overlap with the deposit operations of the banks. It does not overlap with the banks' loan operations, however, because the Post Office does not lend to customers; the funds it receives are turned over to the government.

The number of Post Office checking accounts increased from 41,803 in 1919 to more than 5,000,000 in 1962. Its deposits were 18.8 billion francs or more than 10 percent of the deposits held by all institutions listed in Table 21. In its early years, the postal checkery probably did not grow at the expense of the commercial banks because it served individuals who probably would have been reluctant to maintain a bank checking account. As the check habit has spread in France, individuals have come to regard the postal checkery as an effective substitute for a bank current account. Although the postal checkery does

---

[20] Cf. *Annexes*, 1964, p. 153. These figures (and the others in this section) about agricultural banks refer to the agricultural banks controlled by the government; less information is available about the other agricultural banks.

[21] Cf. Caisse Nationale de Crédit Agricole, *Rapport sur la situation du Crédit Agricole Mutuel*, December 31, 1960, p. 37.

[22] These are offices of the local agricultural banks which increasingly operate like branches of the 94 regional agricultural banks. (Cf. Petit-Dutaillis, *Le crédit et les banques*, p. 237.)

not pay interest on deposit accounts, it can compete with the banks because it offers other services at a low charge or no charge at all.[23]

Savings Banks

The combined deposits of the two savings bank systems in France were almost 30 percent of total deposits for the institutions in Table 21. The larger system (caisses d'épargne ordinaires), composed of "private" or "autonomous" savings banks and often under municipal sponsorship, held deposits of 31.8 billion francs (Table 21). The smaller system, (Caisse Nationale d'Epargne Postale) with deposits of 19.7 billion francs, comprises the savings facilities at the more than 13,000 post offices. As neither savings bank engages in direct customer lending—both are required by law to turn over their funds to the Caisse des Dépôts et Consignations, a public institution[24]—the savings banks have been included in this study solely for their overlap with the deposit activities of the commercial banks. Since the law limits the maximum size of deposits (15,000 francs after January 1, 1964, and 30,000 francs after December 24, 1965), savings bank accounts are mostly used by small savers. A maximum rate is set for both savings banks, but because they are older, the *caisses ordinaires* were authorized to pay one quarter percent more than the Caisse Postale.[25] Deposit accounts are subject to a fifteen-day notice before withdrawal, but since these can in practice be withdrawn on demand, many depositors use the savings banks as a repository for transactions as well as savings deposits.[26]

---

[23] Cf. J. S. G. Wilson, "France," in *Banking in Western Europe*, ed. R. S. Sayers (Oxford, 1962), p. 13. Others who support the view that the postal checkery competes with the banks are Philippe Aymard, *La Banque et l'état* (Paris, 1960), pp. 284–285, and Pierre Cauboue, "Competition Among Banks in France and the Fixing of their Rates," Banca Nazionale del Lavoro, *Quarterly Review*, June, 1955, p. 89. For a view which holds that the postal checkery is complementary rather than competitive, cf. Henri Germain-Martin, "France," in *Banking Systems*, ed. B. H. Beckhart (New York, 1954), p. 265.

[24] The ordinary and postal savings banks differ in their ability to influence the allocation of their funds by the Caisse des Dépôts et Consignations, but since these differences do not affect commercial lending, they are not germane to this analysis.

[25] Cf. Petit-Dutaillis, *Le crédit et les banques*, p. 415.

[26] *Ibid.*, p. 416.

VIII
Regulation of Bank Concentration

The history of bank concentration[1] in France divides naturally into the periods before and after the Second World War. In the prewar period, banking as such was not specifically regulated by the government, and the size-distribution of banks was not affected by any direct government policy on bank concentration. The postwar size-structure (especially after the Conseil National du Crédit was established in 1946 and given broad powers over the banks, including the authority to regulate entry, mergers, and concentration) definitely does bear the imprint of government policy on bank concentration.

GROWTH OF CONCENTRATION BEFORE 1946

Since the first bank census in France was not taken until 1941— there was not even a legal definition of a bank before 1941—there are no reliable statistics on the course of banking concentration in France before that date.[2] The census revealed that a significant degree of bank concentration had occurred during the period of unregulated banking. At the end of 1942, six large *établissements de crédit* held 55.8 percent of the total resources of all listed banks (*banques inscrites*), and 356 banks held the other 44.2 percent.[3] By the end of 1946, these six large banks had increased their share to 58 percent. Thus, even before the government began to intervene in banking affairs, a few large banks, mostly national in scope, held a substantial percentage of total bank resources;

---

[1] This chapter is concerned solely with changes in banking structure, not changes in the market structure of banking markets. The former includes changes in the distribution of banks by kind or size; the latter refers to changes in market segmentation, market concentration, number of independent alternatives, and so forth. The market-structure effects are discussed in later chapters.

[2] Bank specialists give widely different estimates on the total number of banks and branches in France before 1941. Cf. P. C. Dupont, *Le Contrôle des banques et la direction du crédit en France* (Paris, 1952), p. 284, n. 1.

[3] Cf. *ibid.*, p. 385, Annexe No. 10.

twenty-four banks exercised an important influence in their respective regions; and more than three hundred other banks operated at a local level, in the capital or in provincial cities and towns.

Since bank resources in the period before 1946 were heavily concentrated in a few giant banks, the history of bank concentration can be followed in terms of the growth of each of the Big Four. Three of the Big Four établissements de crédit were organized during the second half of the nineteenth century and had become large banks by the end of the century.[4] In each case, the development of an extensive branch network (overwhelmingly by branches established *de novo*) was an important instrument of growth.

The Comptoir Nationale d'Escompte de Paris, the oldest of the Big Four, was established in 1848 but did not begin its career as a deposit bank proper until 1854. Its growth was slow until 1860, when a government decree opened new growth opportunities by authorizing it to establish agencies in France and abroad. Its deposits grew rapidly thereafter—25 million francs in 1855, 170 million in 1870 (when it was the largest of all the credit establishments), and 235 million francs in 1880 (when it was surpassed by the Crédit Lyonnais with deposits of 385 million francs).

The Crédit Lyonnais was established in Lyons (then the second city of France) in 1863, and under the dynamic leadership of its founder, Henri Germain, soon became one of the country's major banks. Its success was due to its flexibility in attracting depositors by means of different kinds of deposit arrangements and by its rapidly expanding network of branch offices (established almost entirely *de novo*).

The Société Générale was established in 1864, as a combination deposit and investment bank. Its deposits were 118 million francs in 1875 and 240 million francs by 1895. In 1898, its growth was threatened by a technical restriction in its legal structure. This was overcome, however, and after 1900 (when its deposits exceeded 300 million francs), its growth was resumed, primarily as a deposit bank.

A number of influences contributed to the phenomenal growth of these new banks. Good timing was particularly important—these banks were established and grew most rapidly during the last years of the nineteenth and the early years of the twentieth centuries, a period of

---

[4] This description is based on Robert Bigo, *Les Banques françaises au cours de XIXe siècle* (Paris, 1947).

The reader is reminded that a new franc equal to 100 old francs was introduced on November 18, 1959. At a few points in the French study, which can be readily identified in context, I have converted a figure from old francs to new francs to facilitate comparisons.

far-reaching economic change. The banks both assisted and benefited
from these changes. The new banks were also beneficiaries of their
location. Except for the Crédit Lyonnais (which quickly joined the
others), they were all located in Paris. Paris was becoming an important
banking center—its population was growing rapidly, and many large
business firms had headquarters in Paris. In addition, the new banks
took advantage of the emergence of an affluent middle class in the
latter part of the nineteenth century. The old-line bankers largely
ignored this new group and continued to concentrate on their older,
well-established clients, whose fortunes were relatively declining. The
aggressive new banks actively solicited the deposits and other banking
business of the rising middle class, increasing their growth along with
their customers' affluence.

The new banks competed aggressively with the old-line banks on
the basis of both price and product. Thus, they cut discount rates in
areas of high loan demand (with funds secured from areas of excess
supply). Similarly, they took advantage of their strong organization to
cut commissions (by as much as one-half) in order to conclude a deal.
They also engaged in product competition. They maintained large
staffs to provide a wide range of customer services (including the service
of going to a customer's house to make a collection in order to save
the customer the inconvenience of a trip to the bank). They were also
very active in *soliciting* business, especially discountable paper. They
advertised widely and offered many financial services at little or no
cost. Bank advertising was an innovation which the new bankers used
aggressively. In contrast to the old-line bankers, who were discreet and
often mysterious about their affairs, the new breed reveled in publicity.
They published their balance sheets, pointed to their large capital, and
issued press releases on their stockholders' meetings. One writer has
observed that, in their stress on rapid turnover of capital, aggressive
merchandising, and plow-back of earnings, the new bankers shared a
common approach with their contemporaries in the merchandising
field, who were innovating by opening large department stores.[5]

In short, the new bankers were highly aggressive, competitive, and
innovative, and in approximately forty years they had won undisputed
preeminence among French banks. In the process, they replaced many
local and family banks which could not (or would not) employ the
new tactics.[6] As already noted, however, the new banks did not grow
entirely at the expense of local banks, for in many cases, they introduced
branches into formerly bankless areas.

[5] *Ibid.*, p. 182.
[6] Cf. Patrice Grivet, *La Mobilisation des crédits bancaires en France* (Paris,
1962), p. 39.

The two nonnationalized établissements de crédit that were established during the nineteenth century grew less rapidly than the three large banks described above. The Crédit Industriel et Commercial, founded at the end of 1858, moved carefully and slowly. Although it opened five branches in Paris in 1863, its deposits were less than 50 million francs by 1872. In 1887, after it was transformed into a *société anonyme*, it increased its capital and by 1913 had raised its deposits to 234 million francs. The Crédit Industriel et Commercial, unlike the large établissements de crédit, did not develop a nationwide system of branches. Instead it was represented in the provinces by its group-banking relationship with many regional banks.

The other nonnationalized établissement de crédit was the Crédit Commercial de France, founded in 1894. Acquisitions were important in its growth. Its most rapid growth occurred after 1917 when it acquired the Caisse de Crédit de Nice and a bank in Lyons and took its present name. In 1919, it merged with the Banque de Bordeaux, and its resources, which had been 699 millions in 1918, rose to 1,700 millions by the end of 1920. Like the Crédit Industriel et Commercial, the Crédit Commercial did not develop an extensive branch network; but unlike the former, it also did not develop an extensive group-banking system.

Acquisitions have also been important in the growth of the Banque Nationale pour le Commerce et l'Industrie (BNCI). The BNCI (actually its predecessor, the Banque Nationale de Crédit) was established in June, 1913, and promptly started to absorb other banks and to open branches all over France. By the end of 1913, it had 112 branches and 142 million francs in deposits. It continued to absorb small local banks during the First World War, and by the end of that war, the Banque Nationale de Crédit (BNC) had 203 branches and 814 million francs in deposits. The process of expansion by absorption was halted abruptly by a severe internal crisis which forced the bank to suspend payments on September, 1931. To avoid loss to depositors, the government advanced funds to the bank and arranged for it to emerge as a new bank, the Banque Nationale pour le Commerce et l'Industrie, in April, 1932. The BNCI took over the sound assets and branch structure of the BNC. In addition, after 1936, it absorbed many banks which had also been undermined by the crisis of the 1930's.

The process of bank concentration began during the nineteenth century and continued into the twentieth century. In the latter period, the growth in concentration has been aided by advantages which accrue to large banks by virtue of their branch structure. For example, the local branches of a large branch bank have sometimes enjoyed a competitive advantage because they could offer services which local unit bank competitors could not provide. In addition, because of interbranch mobility of funds, local branches of a branch bank have had a competitive edge in areas where the local demand for funds has exceeded the local supply. Similarly, when a branch and a unit bank have been located in an area of declining economic activity, the branch bank could simply close the local office, whereas the unit bank might be forced out of existence. During the depression of the 1930's, many unit banks were absorbed by large branch banks. The large banks have also grown more rapidly because large-scale business firms have continued to grow during the twentieth century, and these firms have concentrated much of their business in the large banks.

CONCENTRATION POLICY AFTER 1946

As noted above, the growth of concentration after 1946 bears the imprint of Conseil National du Crédit (CNC) policy on bank concentration. The Banking Law of 1945 authorized the CNC to regulate the number of banks and branches by deciding which could be opened and which ought to be closed or merged. It is convenient, therefore, to divide this discussion of the CNC's concentration policy into its merger policy and its entry policy.

Merger Policy

The 1945 legislation transferred to the CNC the full power to control bank mergers which the Permanent Committee had exercised under the 1941 legislation. However, the 1945 legislation did not go beyond the earlier legislation in prescribing a guide for the use of this authority —the only guide in the 1941 legislation was contained in Article 34 which defined a *décision de caractère individuel* to include the authority to merge banks when "justified by general or local economic needs." In the absence of any clearly defined legislative guides on bank merger policy, the CNC designed its own policy under the very broad powers contained in the 1945 banking law.

On July 25, 1947, the CNC, following the precedent established by its predecessor organizations (the Comité Provisoire des Banques and the Comité Permanent d'Organisation), issued a *décision de caractère général* to prohibit all bank mergers except by special permission of the CNC.[7] This prohibition did not reflect a general hostility to bank mergers, for the door was left open for the CNC to approve particular mergers by means of décisions de caractère individuel. The purpose of this action was to provide the CNC with an opportunity to supervise

---

[7] Cf. CNC, *Annexes au rapport annuel*, 1947, p. 26. This was repeated in the *décision de caractère général*, December 23, 1954, Art. 9.

the financial and legal details of each merger in order to ensure that the mergers were sound and that they protected the rights of all interested parties. The CNC also wished to prevent the banks from using mergers as a device to form new banks in order to avoid the CNC's authority to regulate entry.[8] At the same time, this decision assured the CNC of an opportunity to evaluate each merger in terms of its effects on the overall banking structure and to block those mergers which might alter the structure in an undesired manner.

Between 1946 and 1964, the CNC struck 154 French banks from the list of banks, and it listed only 52 new banks.[9] Two-thirds of the delisted banks were eliminated by mergers with other banks (mostly large banks absorbing small banks), but the number of formal mergers (101) understates the full extent of de facto mergers. In France, the merger of two banks is often a very gradual process, and the final act in the merger may simply give legal recognition to a de facto situation. In lieu of acquiring a small bank by outright merger, a large bank often prefers to establish close relations with the small bank. Sometimes the two banks become formally affiliated without being formally merged. Chain banking is widespread in France, and the relationship between the large and small bank often begins when the large bank buys shares in the small bank (directly, or perhaps indirectly by holding the shares of another institution which holds the small bank's shares). This permits the large bank to secure effective control over a small bank while retaining the local directors and managers of the small bank. After a period of close relations between the two banks, a formal merger may be carried out, and the small-bank affiliate becomes a branch of the large bank. In other cases, although effective control of the small bank has passed to the large bank, a formal merger is omitted in order to permit the small bank to maintain the image of an independent bank. Between 1945 and 1964, sixty banks were more or less taken over by other banks in this way without the benefit of formal merger.[10]

In its early years, the CNC strongly favored a higher level of bank concentration in France, and it made no secret of its views. In later years (up to the banking reforms of 1965–1966), it made fewer statements about its views of an optimal concentration in the banking structure. As a matter of public record, it followed a policy neither of rejecting merger applications nor (as in the early years) of encouraging them. Moreover, the Annual Reports of the CNC do not reveal any

---

[8] Cf. Dupont, op. cit., p. 203.

[9] Most of the newly-listed banks were in existence and carried on many bank types of activity even before their legal conversion to full bank status.

[10] Cf. CNC, Rapport annuel, 1960, p. 30, and 1964, p. 120.

particular concern about the competitive implications of the drastic reduction in the number of banks. Until the mid-1960's, French banking officials appeared to be generally satisfied with the level of French bank concentration, and the CNC's occasional statements about bank mergers more often referred to the need to rationalize the bank structure and reduce bank costs than to the state of bank competition.

The CNC's seemingly neutral policy toward bank mergers changed in 1966 when the authorities merged two of the country's largest banks, Banque Nationale pour le Commerce et l'Industrie (BNCI) and Comptoir National d'Escompte de Paris (CNEP), to form a new bank, the Banque Nationale de Paris (BNP). It was reported that the government had considered other merger possibilities, including a double merger of the CNEP with Crédit Lyonnais and of BNCI with Société Générale.[11] The final decision to have three rather than two giant banks was due in part to a belief that a merger of CNEP and Crédit Lyonnais would have been too dominating. In addition, the merged banks were somewhat complementary: the BNCI had relatively few Paris branches and more overseas branches than the CNEP; and the BNCI was represented in London while CNEP was represented in New York.[12] Before the merger, BNCI (with total resources of 16,950 million francs and CNEP (10,079 million francs) ranked respectively as the third and fourth largest French banks. After the merger, BNP moved to first place, and the lineup of the Big Three (at end of 1965) was BNP (27,023 million francs), Crédit Lyonnais (25,001 million), and Société Générale (21,047 million).[13]

The two main advantages expected from the merger of the two large banks are greater bank efficiency and greater flexibility in bank credit operations. An improvement in efficiency is expected from the elimination of wasteful duplication in branches and services[14] and from fuller and more effective utilization of electronic bank equipment.[15] The expectation of greater flexibility is related to the bank's larger size. Proponents of the merger point to the trend for larger-sized business firms and to the acceleration in this trend that can be expected as the Common Market makes it possible for more French firms to do business on a European scale. In their view, larger business firms need larger banks

---

[11] Cf. *New York Times*, May 5, 1966.
[12] Cf. *The Banker*, June, 1966, p. 355. (This refers to the English rather than the American journal.)
[13] *Entreprise*, April 14, 1966, p. 35.
[14] Cf. *New York Times*, March 26, 1966, p. 42.
[15] Cf. *Entreprise*, May 12, 1966, p. 17.

to supply their credit needs.[16] As a result of the merger, the BNP became the largest bank in the Common Market (Table 24),[17] and the
eleventh largest bank in the world (Table 25). The BNP's large size
(together with its 38 foreign branches or agencies) will give it greater
"weight" in foreign lending and make it less dependent on foreign
banking consortiums. As a result of its greater flexibility (foreign banking consortiums are limited by the need to reconcile different views of

TABLE 24
Ten Largest Banks in the Common Market, 1965

Bank	Deposits (million $)	Country
Banque Nationale de Paris	5,116	France
Banca Nazionale del Lavoro	5,072	Italy
Crédit Lyonnais	4,640	France
Société Générale	4,044	France
Banca Commerciale Italiana	3,685	Italy
Deutsche Bank	3,464	W. Germany
Credito Italiano	3,248	Italy
Dresdner Bank	2,730	W. Germany
Rheinische Girozentrale	2,728	W. Germany
Banco di Roma	2,685	Italy

SOURCE: *American Banker*, August 1, 1966.

TABLE 25
Twelve Largest Banks in the World, 1965

Bank	Deposits (million $)	Country
Bank of America	14,937	U.S.A.
Chase Manhattan	12,813	U.S.A.
First National City Bank of New York	11,949	U.S.A.
Manufacturers Hanover Trust	6,643	U.S.A.
Barclays	6,460	England
Midland	5,923	England
Chemical Bank New York Trust	5,814	U.S.A.
Morgan Guaranty Trust	5,646	U.S.A.
Royal Bank of Canada	5,408	Canada
Canadian Imperial	5,269	Canada
Banque Nationale de Paris	5,116	France
Banca Nazionale del Lavoro	5,072	Italy

SOURCE: *American Banker*, August 1, 1966.

[16] Before the merger, banking pools consisting of from twelve to twenty
banks and sometimes more have been required to supply the credit needs of
large business firms. Cf. *Entreprise*, April 14, 1966, p. 37.

[17] The BNP would not be the largest if England belonged to the Common
Market. The English Big Five would rank among the eight largest banks in
the Common Market.

the participating banks) the BNP's foreign loan business is expected to increase significantly.[18]

Entry Policy

Under Article 13 of the Banking Law of 1945, the CNC[19] (as inheritor of all powers formerly exercised by the Comité Permanent d'Organisation) has the authority (acting through the intermediary of the Bank of France) to regulate bank entry. The law of June 13, 1941, set forth the criteria for a bank to be "listed" (authorized to operate in France). The criteria prescribe the technical legal form or organization (Art. 6), close the banking business to *faillis non-réhabilités*, that is, persons convicted of certain crimes or bankrupt persons who had not been discharged (Art. 7), and make provision for certain minimum capital requirements depending upon the bank's legal form and whether it has

---

[18] This expectation has led to speculation that French officials may approve further mergers in the future—as one observer has noted, Bank of America is still three times larger than BNP. Cf. *Entreprise*, May 12, 1966, p. 17.

[19] Although the CNC is the locus of real power on entry matters, it has shared a limited amount of its authority over new branches with the APB. Until the reform of 1967, the CNC used to require all new branch applications to be accompanied by an APB recommendation. The APB's recommendations (on new banks and branches) were actually decided by its Governing Council, a group representing the five major bank categories (four representatives for each category) in the APB: the nationalized banks, the other banks headquartered in Paris and organized as *sociétés anonymes*, all other banks located in Paris (private banks, *sociétés en nom collectif*, *sociétés en commandité*), the banks located outside of Paris and organized as sociétés anonymes, and all other banks located outside of Paris. Each member of the council has only one vote, but the council itself is elected by the General Assembly of the APB in which each bank member's vote is weighted according to the amount of the bank's deposits and capital. Thus, while the council is not dominated by direct representatives of the large banks, its members are elected by an assembly in which the large banks have a commanding position. Cf. Association Professionnelle des Banques, *Recueil des textes usuels* (Paris, 1958), Tome 1, pp. 25–31.

In determining its new branch recommendations, the APB tried to resolve conflicting applications before they were formally submitted to the CNC. In preliminary APB negotiations, the banks (especially the large banks) usually arrived at gentlemen's agreements for an amicable division of the prospective market, and thus avoided an official and public conflict if two or more banks wanted to open a branch in an area where only one branch was "needed." The APB also served the CNC by coordinating the banks' applications to keep them in line with CNC instructions or "requests" (e.g., the CNC's wish, expressed at the end of 1960, that the banks reduce their plans for opening new branches in areas already provided with banking facilities). Cf. CNC, *Rapport annuel*, 1961, p. 24. In short, by its intermediary function, the APB sought to ensure that the number of new branch applications accorded with the view of the authorities on the number which could be justified by "economic need."

less or more than two branches (Art. 8). These entry restrictions (which exist in most advanced countries) seek to ensure that banks are soundly financed and under competent and trustworthy management. However, in addition to meeting the preceding requirements, a prospective entry had to be warranted by general or local economic needs (Art. 10).[20] Neither the 1941 nor the 1945 legislation spelled out the criteria of economic need, and the meaning given to this term in practice has changed over the years. It is convenient to divide the discussion of the CNC entry policy into four periods: 1946–1953, 1954–1958, 1959–1966, and after 1967.

1946–1953

When the CNC was first established, it was more interested in closing existing branches than in opening new ones. The Banking Law of 1945 (Art. 13) had instructed the CNC to "participate in the elaboration of all projects having as an object the concentration of banking and the reduction of the general expenses of commerce and banking by improving the organization and methods." As a first step leading to a reduction of branches, the CNC called a halt to the opening of new branches while it made an intensive survey of the number, distribution, and activity of existing branches. When this survey was completed (in February, 1947), the CNC asked all banks with at least twenty branches to submit suggestions with respect to closings and mergers in order to reduce the total number of branches by 10 percent. The CNC announced its intention to evaluate the proposals in terms of the general interest and to avoid eliminating too many branches in one area or leaving too many branches in another and, in any case, to prevent the disappearance of a reasonable amount of competition.[21]

In spite of its declared interest in maintaining a reasonable amount of competition, the CNC in its early years put great emphasis on eliminating "unnecessary" banking facilities—for example, four branch offices of four different banks on the four corners of the *grand'place* of a small city—[22] to reduce bank expenses.[23] In spite of some criticisms,[24]

---

[20] The CNC can also delist a bank for lack of economic need.

[21] Cf. CNC, *Rapport annuel*, 1946, p. 11.

[22] For a critical view of this policy, cf. Georges Petit-Dutaillis, *Le Crédit et les banques* (Paris, 1964), pp. 436–437.

[23] Other cost-reducing activities (not of primary interest in this study) included measures to simplify, mechanize, and modernize bank operations.

[24] Some criticism of the CNC for closing "unnecessary" (in practice, often rural) branches was due to skepticism that the closings would significantly affect general bank expenses or that the giant banks could in practice secure the scale economies which are possible in theory. Cf. Alfred Pose, "Les Banques," *La France économique en 1947, Annuaire de la vie économique française*, pp. 218–219.

the CNC was content with its concentration program and reported that the concentration measures adopted in 1947 had tended essentially to reduce general expenses without causing any significant inconvenience to the banks' customers.[25]

The CNC's survey of existing branches resulted in new rules about entry by *guichets permanents, guichets semi-permanents,* and *guichets périodiques.*[26] Under the new ruling, no guichet permanent or semi-permanent could be opened, closed, reopened, or transferred without CNC permission. Guichets périodiques were exempted from this ruling, but the banks were required to inform the CNC about any changes in that category.[27] From 1946 through 1953, in keeping with the policy on concentration which it had formulated in 1946 and 1947, the CNC followed a basically restrictive policy on entry.

In 1950, the CNC's concentration policy of reducing the number of existing branches and limiting the number of new branches was pursued less vigorously than in earlier years. This change was due to a number of difficulties which had been encountered in the concentration program.[28] First, the concentration policy had altered the branch structure of banks, and although some functions which the older structure had been designed to perform had become less important by 1950, the CNC believed they might become important again. Second, the forced closing of certain old branches created problems for the banks—for example, difficulties in selling a branch (or in reconstituting it if conditions changed), adverse effect on bank personnel, and so forth. Third, it was evident from the growth of postal accounts that the banks needed an extended branch network to collect the public's deposits, but the expanded branch network desired for deposit growth was not compatible with the reduced network desired for economy reasons.

These were not the only problems raised by the concentration program. The CNC also had to face the opposition of bankers who objected to the regulation of their branch activities while other business firms were generally free to do as they wished. The banks regulated by the CNC particularly objected to the fact that the CNC restricted their branch activities but had no authority to regulate the entry of the popular banks and agricultural banks, which operated under a special

---

[25] Cf. CNC, *Rapport annuel,* 1948, p. 15.

[26] *Guichets permanents* are branch offices that are open to the public (however briefly) more than three days per week: *guichets semi-permanents* are open for two or three days per week; *guichets périodiques* are open at least one day per week, and possibly also on fair-days and market-days, but not more than seven days per month; and *bureaux de saison* are open less than four consecutive months during each year.

[27] Cf. CNC, *Annexes au rapport annuel,* 1947, pp. 24–25.

[28] Cf. CNC, *Rapport annuel,* 1950, pp. 8–10.

law. In recognition of this difference, the Minister of Finance (in 1949) urged the CNC to recommend to the government the necessary steps to keep the activities of the popular and agricultural banks in harmony with those of the banks under CNC control.[29] This did not resolve the matter, however, for while the popular banks were generally as restricted as the banks controlled by the CNC, in terms of branch expansion, agricultural banks were not.[30] The result was that, in the interests of equity, the CNC did not press for as much concentration as it wished to have among the banks it did control.

The tax advantages of the popular and agricultural banks aggravated the problem of coordinating the policy on branch expansion between them and the banks that were affiliated with the Association Professionnelle des Banques (APB). An event in 1952 illustrates the kind of complications that arose. Two popular banks had requested permission to establish branches in provincial locations, and the CNC was asked for its recommendations on the proposed branches. The CNC conceded that the existing banks (which were affiliated with the APB) were not fully satisfying the needs of the areas and that the entry of the popular banks could have met at least part of those needs. Moreover, the popular banks presumably thought they could operate profitably in the proposed locations; and the record does not show that the CNC disputed this presumption. In spite of these considerations, the CNC recommended against the proposed entry because the economic activity in the areas was barely adequate to assure the profitability of the branch offices that were already located in the areas.[31] Thus, in trying to meet the criticism of the banks under CNC control, the CNC was open to the charge that it sought to restrain popular-bank entry to protect the interests of the large branch banks that were already established in an area.[32]

1954–1958

At the end of 1954, the CNC revised the entry policy that had been in effect since 1947. Although the CNC believed that its policy had been

---

[29] Cf. letter of December 6, 1949 from the Minister of Finance to the governor of the Bank of France, as vice-president of the CNC (CNC, *Annexes au rapport annuel*, 1949, p. 40).

[30] The CNC does not control the branches of the popular banks, but it may advise the Ministère des Finances. The final decision usually but not always accords with the CNC recommendation. For an occasion when the CNC recommendation was not followed, see n. 31.

[31] Cf. CNC, *Rapport annuel*, 1952, p. 11. In this case, the Minister of Finance ignored the CNC recommendations and authorized the opening of the two new branches. Cf. CNC, *Rapport annuel*, 1953, p. 12.

[32] Cf. Pierre Montfajon, *Le Crédit populaire de France* (Paris, 1957), p. 33.

useful in preventing certain competitive abuses, the policy was complex and sometimes hard to implement.[33] Accordingly, the CNC issued a new regulation.[34] At the same time, it adopted a policy of reviewing entry applications only twice a year. This allowed the CNC more time to consider the nature of the evolving branch network in each region or *place*, and also made it less likely that a new branch would be awarded to a bank simply because it had applied before some other bank. As in the earlier period, the CNC continued to stress economic need in authorizing new branches and to judge economic need in terms of inadequate banking facilities.[35] In practice, this did not prevent authorization of many new branches, especially guichets permanents. Part of the increase was due to the fact that many guichets semi-permanents were converted into guichets permanents after the semi-permanent category was dropped; part was due to the growth of economic activity which increased the need for banking facilities, especially in many rural areas where banking facilities were weak. As a result of these influences, the number of branches increased sharply during 1955.

By the end of 1955, the CNC felt that it had authorized enough new branches to catch up with existing economic needs and declared that it would authorize new branches in the future only "upon the appearance of clearly established new needs."[36] This reversion to a more restrictive entry policy coincided with a new interpretation of economic need. The CNC had been concerned about the high level which interest rates had reached (e.g., the excessive remuneration of certain creditor accounts in some banks and the excessive rates that some financial firms were charging for consumer credit) and this led the CNC to expand the criteria of economic need so that "only those *enterprises which practice moderate rates . . .* can claim to be satisfying an economic need and to obtain as a result their listing."[37] By this announcement, the CNC converted its authority to authorize new branches or to close existing branches into a powerful instrument for promoting the interest-rate levels which it considered appropriate and desirable.[38]

---

[33] Cf. CNC, *Rapport annuel*, 1954, p. 10.

[34] Under the new regulation, the category of guichets semi-permanents was dropped; branches open three or more days per week were classified as guichets permanents; and those open for a maximum of two days per week, regardless of whether one day was a market- or a fair-day, were classified as guichets périodiques (*ibid.*, p. 11).

[35] *Idem.*

[36] Cf. CNC, *Rapport annuel*, 1955, p. 13.

[37] Cf. *ibid.*, p. 42 (my italics). A "moderate rate" was a rate that did not exceed the mean rates in the principal establishments. Cf. *idem.*

[38] According to Dupont, the CNC could stretch its authority to regulate

1959–1966

In the latter part of 1959, the CNC once again modified its entry policy in an attempt to resolve the conflict of goals which made the strict entry policy of the preceding period increasingly unsatisfactory. On the one hand, it wished to encourage the use of checks, and this called for a fairly liberal policy in authorizing new branches, especially in new areas and in expanding suburban areas. On the other hand, it wished to avoid an excessive proliferation of branches in one area in order to prevent too much competition among the banks. In an attempt to resolve this conflict, the CNC set up a special committee to consider the views of those who wanted to preserve a close regulation over entry and those who advocated a return to free entry. On the basis of the committee's report, the CNC decided to experiment with a compromise policy designed to provide the desired increase in new branches without provoking an undue amount of competition.[39]

The new policy retained the existing framework for regulating new entry but significantly simplified the procedure and gave the banks greater freedom of action to complete their branch systems. The banks still had to obtain CNC authorization to open guichets permanents, but approval was quasi-automatic for an important group of applications. While reserving its right to veto any branch application, the CNC provided a simple and rapid procedure whereby a bank which already had a guichet permanent in a particular *place* could obtain approval to open other new guichets permanents in the same *place*.[40] The same simple procedure and quasi-automatic approval was promised for all new branch applications in areas (*places*) where there was no permanent branch of either a bank affiliated with the APB or a popular bank. However, the CNC planned to adhere to its preexisting policy

---

entry for economic need to include the need for the particular kind of banking operation in which a new bank or branch proposed to concentrate. For example, a new bank or branch would not meet an economic need, and its application could be legally denied for that reason, if it planned to emphasize consumer loans at a time when the CNC wanted to restrict those loans. Cf. P. C. Dupont, *Le Contrôle des banques et la direction du crédit en France*, p. 79.

[39] In announcing the new, more liberal entry policy, the CNC also reiterated its firm determination to repress any undue amount of competition. Cf. CNC, *Rapport annuel*, 1959, p. 36.

[40] A *place* referred to every continuous agglomeration (as defined by the *Annuaire statistique de France*). There are 32 such metropolitan areas in France. This more liberal policy did not apply to new branches within the administrative limits of Paris, but the banks located within those limits could generally receive permission to open suburban branches in all other communes of the *agglomération parisienne*. Cf. CNC, *Rapport annuel*, 1959, p. 36.

of carefully scrutinizing all new branch applications for areas where the applying bank did not already have an existing guichet permanent.

Under the new policy the total number of branches had increased to 4,209 by the end of 1964 (Table 26). This greater leniency in authorizing new branches[41] led some observers to claim that the new policy was tantamount to free entry for banks in France ("it is simply a matter of filling out an application"). In fact, however, the more liberal entry policy operated within a basic framework that had been carefully structured to ensure that a more liberal entry policy would *not* result

TABLE 26

Number of Banks and Branches, Banques Inscrites,
1946–1964

End of year	Banks	Branches[a]		Total[b]
		Paris and Seine	Provinces	
1946	444	574	2,975	3,549
1947	430			3,372
1948	418	546	2,780	3,326
1949	415			3,328
1950	412			3,322
1951	410	549	2,789	3,338
1952	401	548	2,788	3,336
1953	387	549	2,792	3,341
1954	376	550	2,809	3,359
1955	372	554	2,912	3,466
1956	366	549	2,902	3,451
1957	357	561	2,913	3,474
1958	350	562	2,937	3,499
1959	338	583	2,997	3,580
1960	338	612	3,073	3,685
1961	338	649	3,166	3,815
1962	339	677	3,258	3,935
1963	341	718	3,365	4,083
1964	338	752	3,457	4,209

a Number of branches *authorized*; actual openings of some branches occurred in later periods. After 1959, the number of branches excludes certain specialized branches which are not authorized to receive deposits from the public. There were two such branches in 1953 and four in 1956.

b Excludes Monaco and overseas branches.

SOURCE: Conseil National du Crédit, *Rapports annuels*, 1946–1964.

<hr>

[41] For several years, entry has meant the opening of a new branch (especially by a large branch bank) but not the opening of a new bank. Most new banks in recent years were *établissements financiers* converted into deposit banks.

in significantly more *effective* entry (i.e., entry which increases the effective number of alternative sources of supply).[42] This was clearly the
intent of the 1959 decision which eased entry restrictions only for
bankless areas or for banks which already had an existing branch in
the area. Indeed, under the new policy, the CNC became even more
restrictive than formerly with respect to new branches for banks which
did not have a branch in an area already provided with banking
facilities.[43]

After 1967

The relaxation of entry conditions that had been put into effect by
the 1959 reform was carried further by a 1967 reform. At its meeting
of January 10, 1967, the CNC announced that the banks inscribed on
the list of banks would no longer have to apply for CNC approval to
open new branches—a simple declaration of intention to open new
offices would suffice. This decision was intended to bring French practice more nearly in line with banking practice in other Common Market countries and also, by facilitating the opening of new banking
offices, to increase the banks' ability to attract more funds into the
banks.[44] It is important to emphasize, however, that this reform did not
introduce free entry into French banking, since the branch entry restrictions were removed solely for existing banks. Presumably, new
banks will continue to have to secure CNC approval for entry, and the
critical (but as yet unanswered) question is whether the CNC's policy
toward new banks will be the same as its new policy toward new
branches by existing banks.

GROWTH OF BANKING CONCENTRATION AFTER 1946

The changes in the banking structure and the growth in bank concentration during the period of CNC control can be measured in a
number of ways: by the changes in the total number of banks and
branches, by the changes in the distribution of banks and branches in
different bank categories, and by the changes in the concentration of
banking resources.

By Number of Banks

Table 26 shows the change in the total number of banks and branches
of the bank population whose operations (including entry, merger, or

---

[42] Cf. D. A. Alhadeff, "California Banking and Competition," in *California
Banking in a Growing Economy, 1946–1975,* ed. H. Minsky (Berkeley, 1965),
p. 186.

[43] The CNC itself called attention to this fact. In 1963, it rejected 16 such
requests for new branches. Cf. CNC, *Rapport annuel,* 1963, p. 34; and 1964,
p 122.

[44] Cf. *Le Monde,* January 5, 1967, p. 16.

closing) are directly controlled by the CNC, namely, the banques inscrites.[45] The CNC's original concentration policy (to reduce the number of branches) is clearly reflected in the change in the number of permanent branches—from 3,549 in 1946 to 3,326 by the end of 1948.[46] After this initial reduction, the number of branches remained approximately stable for a couple of years and then began to drift upward. In spite of a gradual increase, the number of branches in the provinces and in the Paris-Seine region by 1958 was below the 1946 level. In 1959, the CNC changed its policy and eased the entry restrictions. This change had a striking impact on the number of new branches opened in that year. During the preceding decade, the net number (allowing for closings) of branches had increased by more than 25 in only one year; in most years, the increase was much smaller; and it was even negative in some years. Under the new policy, the CNC authorized a *net* increase of 710 branches between 1959 and 1964, or an average of 118 per year.

The CNC's concentration policy affected the number of banks as well as the number of branches. Between 1946 and 1949, more than a hundred banks were struck from the list, and there is no question that the CNC approved of this reduction. By 1956, after a decade of CNC jurisdiction, the number of banks had been reduced by almost 18 percent. The decline in the number of banks was arrested in 1959 and has changed only slightly since that date. Thus, during the period of CNC control, the banking population has been reduced by more than a hundred banks, or about 24 percent of the original number.

---

[45] The *banques inscrites* are the banks which derive their authority to conduct a banking business from the Conseil National du Crédit: the *banques de crédit à long et moyen terme, banques d'affaires (sociétés par actions), banques d'affaires (sociétés de personnes et affaires personnelles), établissements de crédit nationalisés, établissements de crédit non-nationalisés, banques de dépôt parisiennes, maisons de réescompte et divers, banques françaises exerçant leur activité principale dans les pays d'outre-mer ou à l'étranger, agences françaises des banques étrangères ayant leur siège à l'étranger, banques de forme juridique française sous contrôle étranger, banques régionales, banques locales, banques algériennes* (before 1962), and *banques monegasques.* The banks and the bank types of institutions which are *not* on the list of banques inscrites include the Banque Française du Commerce Extérieur; *banques populaires; caisses de crédit agricole; comptes courants postaux; caisses d'épargne nationale* and *caisses privées;* Caisse des Dépôts et Consignations; Crédit National; Crédit Foncier de France; Caisse de Consolidation et de Mobilisation des Crédits à Moyen Terme; Caisse Centrale de Crédit Hotelier, Commercial et Industriel; and others. As already noted, most banks in the second group are not relevant to this study. They are listed here to suggest the range of banks which are and those which are not under direct CNC control.

[46] The percentage reduction was much larger in the provinces than in the Paris-Seine area.

TABLE 27

Distribution of Banques Inscrites, 1946 and 1964

Type of bank	Number of banks 1946	1964	Change
Établissements de crédit (nationalized)	4	4	0
Établissements de crédit (non-nationalized)	2	3	+1
Regional banks	24	24	0
Local banks	214	98	−116
Paris banks	89	71	−18
Banques d'affaires	43	46	+3
Medium- and long-term credit banks	8	24	+16
Foreign banks	28	33	+5
Other banks[a]	34	28	−6
Totals	446[b]	331	−115

a Includes banks which operated outside of metropolitan France and banks of the semipublic sector.

b This figure is sometimes shown as 444. For example, see CNC, *Rapport annuel* 1951, p. 8.

SOURCES: Conseil National du Crédit, *Rapport annuel*, 1946, p. 95; Commission de Contrôle des Banques, *Bilans des banques*, 1964. The *Bilans* reports that there are 338 banques inscrites, but provides information for only 331.

By Kind of Bank

Table 27 shows the change in the composition (by kind of bank) of the same banks shown in Table 26 (banques inscrites). Between 1946 and 1964, the number of banques inscrites fell from 444 to 331. As might have been expected, the banks that were eliminated (by failure or acquisition) were small banks—mostly local banks and Paris deposit banks.

Aymard has identified three main sources of pressure on small banks.[47] First, there have been pressures due to the growing mechanization of banking. The use of checks has grown tremendously since 1940 (partly because of government encouragement), and this has stimulated the trend toward mechanization, including the use of electronic computers. The CNC has followed these developments closely and has encouraged the mechanization of banking. This equipment is economically feasible only for large-scale users, and small banks that have been unable to secure access to this equipment (e.g., by joining together with other banks, or by other means) have been placed at a competitive disadvantage. Second, small banks have also been under pressure because of the growing complexity of conducting the banking business. This

---

[47] Cf. Philippe Aymard, *La Banque et l'état* (Paris, 1960), pp. 278–279. Aymard's arguments are all in general terms; he gives no figures on comparative costs. Cf. *ibid.*, pp. 278–280, 235, and 261–262.

stems in part from the growing complexity and diversity of financial services that banks provide, but it is also due to the large number of (often involved) regulations that have been imposed on banks by a number of agencies which regulate French banks: Bank of France, Treasury, Exchange Office, CNC, Control Commission, Tax Office.[48] Specialization is called for on both counts, but only large banks can afford it. Finally, the growth of concentration was fostered as a by-product of the government's policy in conferring the status of *intermédiaire agréé*. This designation authorizes a bank to conduct foreign exchange operations on behalf of the Exchange Office. In 1960, 190 banks had this authority; 164 registered banks did not. By extending this privilege to other than major banks, the government has created a "class distinction" among banks. In addition to the competitive advantage of a superior image, the favored banks enjoy a competitive advantage because they can provide their customers with foreign exchange services instead of having to work through the intermediary of another bank, a more time-consuming and cumbersome procedure. Moreover, the ability to provide foreign exchange services directly probably attracts other business to the bank as well.

In spite of these pressures—and they have been operating at least since the end of the Second World War—a number of local and regional banks have held their own against the large banks. J. S. G. Wilson has ascribed the durability of the smaller banks to a variety of circumstances.[49] First, there is a demand for the services of the small local banks in France from customers who want individualized attention and believe they are more likely to get it from small private banks than from large branch banks. Second, many customers have secured loans from local or regional banks that they would have been unable to secure from large banks. In some cases, the large Paris banks did not have a local branch in the area, and the local banker, with his special knowledge of the parties involved and of the local economy, was more able and willing than a distant Paris bank to assume the risks. In other cases, especially in earlier years, the large banks were simply not very interested in dealing with smaller customers. Third, some customers support small banks because of a sentiment of particularism which causes them to favor local institutions. The durability of the small banks has also been ascribed to French individualism (which presumably strengthens the small bankers' determination to preserve their

---

[48] To illustrate, the first volume of the *Recueil des textes usuels* (n. 19 above), a codification of banking laws, decrees, and regulations, runs to almost 1,000 closely printed pages; and as Aymard has stated, changes and modifications are issued almost daily.

[49] Cf. J. S. G. Wilson, *French Banking Structure and Credit Policy* (London, 1957), pp. 47–51.

independence). Finally, the larger nonnationalized banks have been reluctant to expand by absorbing local banks for fear of growing too large and becoming candidates for nationalization.

Table 28 shows the changes that occurred among the group of banks and financial institutions that supply short-term business loans or deposits. Although these changes took place during the years when the CNC (assisted by the APB) regulated mergers, entry, and closings, they cannot be ascribed solely to CNC policy. The CNC did not control directly the entry of all banks shown in Table 28, and many influences other than the CNC's concentration policy have affected the growth of each bank category during the CNC's tenure. On the

TABLE 28

Number of Banks and Banking Offices, Selected Bank Categories
1946 and 1964

Type of bank	Number of banks		Number of banking offices		Change in banking offices	
	1946	1964	1946	1964	Number	1964/1946
Établissements de crédit (nationalized)	4	4	1,875	2,335	+460	124.5
Établissements de crédit (non-nationalized)	2	3	119	168	+49	141.2
Paris deposit banks	89	71	119	144	+25	121.0
Foreign banks	28	33	59	81	+22	137.3
Regional banks	24	24	952	1,143	+101	120.1
Local banks	214	98	305	227	−78	74.4
Total, deposit banks	361	233	3,429	4,098	+669	119.5
Banques d'affaires	43	46	50	101	+51	202.0
Popular banks	56	46[b]	303	520[b]	+217	171.6
Agricultural banks[a]	97	94	4,397	3,131[c]	−1,266	71.2
Comptes courants postaux			16,776	19,860	+3,084	118.4
Caisse Nationale d'Épargne Postale			16,776	19,860	+3,084	118.4
Caisse d'Épargne Ordinaire	555	570	2,513[d]	4,031	+1,518	160.4

a Number of banks refers to the regional banks of the Crédit Agricole Mutuel; and number of branches, to the local banks.

b 1962 figure.

c 1963 figure.

d Does not include Alsace and Lorraine.

SOURCES:
1946: CNC, *Rapport annuel*, 1946, p. 95, 151, 148; and 1956, p. 147.
    Annuaire statistique de France, 1951, pp. 272–273.
1964: *Bilans des banques*, 1964.
    Crédit Agricole, Rapport, 1963, and Rapport, 1964.
    CNC, *Annexes au rapport annuel*, 1962, p. 129.
    Annuaire statistique de France, 1965 and 1966.

other hand, given the extremely close official control over bank concentration in France, the CNC's policy must be regarded as a (and perhaps the) dominant influence on the banking structure. Moreover, while it directly controlled entry only by the banques inscrites, the CNC exercised considerable influence over entry in other bank categories—as noted earlier, the CNC was required to submit its recommendations on the entry applications of popular and agricultural banks, and it used this power to coordinate policy between those banks and the banks under direct CNC control.

As noted in connection with Table 27, the greatest decline among the deposit banks occurred among the local banks and to a much lesser extent among the Paris deposit banks. The only other sizable decline (from 56 to 46) occurred among the popular banks. The decline in the number of local and popular banks is particularly relevant to small (and medium-size) customers, overwhelmingly the most important customers in both bank categories.

The distribution of banking offices among the bank categories did not change in the same pattern as the number of banks. All bank categories (except local banks and agricultural banks) held a larger number of branches at the end than at the beginning of the period (Table 28). Overwhelmingly the largest increase (3,084 offices) accrued to the *comptes courants postaux* and the Caisse Nationale d'Epargne Postale, and the second largest (1,518) to the *caisse d'épargne ordinaire*. Sizable increases (but at a much lower level) were also registered by the nationalized établissements de crédit (460) and the popular banks (217). In short, the categories with the largest increases (Post Office and savings

TABLE 29

Distribution of Deposit Bank Resources, by Kind of Bank,
1948 and 1964

Type of bank	Resources			
	Amount (million F)		Percent	
	1948	1964	1948	1964
Établissements de crédit (nationalized)	6,985	64,424	63.7	62.9
Établissements de crédit (non-nationalized)	774	6,654	7.1	6.5
Paris banks	499	5,270	4.6	5.1
Foreign banks	559	8,614	5.1	8.4
Regional banks	1,786	15,260	16.3	14.9
Local banks	355	2,212	3.2	2.2
Totals	10,958	102,434	100.0	100.0

SOURCE: *Bilans des banques*, 1948 and 1964.

banks) are categories that the CNC does not regulate. A comparatively large increase also occurred in the popular banks where the CNC's influence on entry was limited to an advisory opinion. In the categories directly regulated by the CNC, by far the largest number of new branches went to the large banks—giant nationwide branch banks and large regional banks; by contrast, local bank branches fell sharply.

Finally, Table 29 shows the change in the resources of the deposit banks, the most important subset of the banques inscrites. In spite of a considerable change in the total number and distribution of banks in the different deposit bank categories (Table 27), there was comparatively little change in the distribution of resources among them. The large nationalized banks held virtually the same share of total deposit bank resources at the beginning and end of the period; the same was substantially true for the Paris deposit banks and the local banks; and (except for the foreign banks) shares of the remaining categories changed very little.

By Size of Bank

The changes in the banking structure can also be measured by the size-distribution of a given banking population at different moments in time. One important measure of size-distribution is the percentage of total banking resources held by the largest deposit banks. It is easy to identify the largest banks in the country; it is more difficult to select an appropriate banking population as the base for comparisons. Given the framework and purposes of the present study, at least three different bases are eligible for consideration: the banques inscrites (the group of banks directly controlled by the CNC), the suppliers of short-term deposits, and the suppliers of short-term business credit.

Table 30 shows how the concentration of banking resources is affected by the use of the three different bases. At the end of 1964, the four banking giants held more than half of the total resources of the banques inscrites,[50] and the seven largest deposit banks[51] held 59 per-

[50] This figure is based on metropolitan resources of the banques inscrites, because this study does not cover banking markets outside of France in which French banks may operate. The extra-metropolitan resources have been removed from the denominator but not entirely from the numerator because the *Bilans des banques* does not show this breakdown for the individual banks listed in Table 30.

[51] In 1964, one investment bank with total resources of 4,626 million francs (Banque de Paris et des Pays-Bas) would have ranked fifth in the list of banks in Table 30. It was not included in this table because its operations were not fully comparable with those of the other (deposit) banks in the table and, in particular, because a very substantial part of this bank's business is carried on outside of metropolitan France.

TABLE 30

Resources of Largest Deposit Banks as
Percent of Total Banking Resources, 1964

Bank	Total resources (million F)	Percent of		
		Banques inscrites	Suppliers of short-term business credit	Suppliers of short-term deposits
Credit Lyonnais	22,056	17.9	17.7	9.4
Société Générale	18,431	14.9	14.8	7.8
Banque Nationale pour le Commerce et l'Industrie	15,288	12.4	12.3	6.5
Comptoir National d'Escompte de Paris	8,649	7.0	6.9	3.7
Crédit du Nord	3,026	2.4	2.4	1.3
Crédit Commercial de France	2,748	2.2	2.2	1.2
Crédit Industriel et Commercial[a]	2,610	2.1	2.1	1.1
Top four banks	64,424	52.2	51.7	27.4
Top seven banks	72,808	59.0	58.4	31.0
Total, Banques inscrites[b]	123,295	100.0		
Total, suppliers of short-term business credit	124,610		100.0	
Total, suppliers of short-term deposits	235,171			100.0

a Does not include holdings in eleven regional banks with resources of 6,654 million francs.

b Does not include extra-metropolitan resources.

SOURCE: CNC, *Annexes au rapport annuel,* 1964; and *Bilans des banques,* 1964.

cent.[52] The concentration of resources in terms of suppliers of short-term business credit—the most important are the deposit banks, investment banks, and popular banks—is almost identical. However, the concentration of resources in terms of the suppliers of short-term deposits—the most important are the institutions listed in Table 28—is sharply different (27.4 percent for the four banking giants, and 31 percent for the seven largest deposit banks) from the concentration on the other bases. Clearly, no single base is entirely satisfactory, and although (for simplicity) only one base (banks under direct CNC controls, viz., banques inscrites) has been employed for the remaining tables of this chapter, the results must be evaluated in light of the differences shown in Table 30.

As might have been expected (on the basis of the earlier discussion of CNC concentration policy), concentration of banking resources did

---

[52] This figure ignores group-banking relations.

not increase much between 1950 and 1965. The share of the top four banks moved from 51 to 57 percent, and the top seven from 66.5 to almost 70 percent (Table 31). In 1966, however, the authorities arranged the BNP merger, and this single merger raised the concentration of banking resources more than the rise during most of the CNC's entire existence. Thus, whereas the top four banks' share had increased by only six percentage points in the preceding fifteen years, the BNP merger raised it by almost eight percentage points—from 57.1 to 64.9 percent (Table 32). On the other hand, whereas the share of the four top banks (including BNP) rose by almost fourteen percentage points (from 51 to 64.9 percent) in fifteen years, the top seven banks' share rose far less (from 66.5 to 71.0 percent). This different pattern is due to the enormous size of the five largest banks (before the BNP merger) and to the sharp break in the size-distribution of banks between this top group and the next-largest banks. In fact, the resources of the deposit bank that advanced to seventh place after the BNP merger are comparatively so small that the immediate effect of the BNP merger was to raise the share of the seven largest banks by only 1.2 percentage points (from 69.8 to 71.0 percent).

TABLE 31

Concentration of Resources in Large Deposit Banks,
1950 and 1965

Bank	Amount (million F)		Percent of Banques inscrites	
	1950	1965	1950	1965
Crédit Lyonnais	3,204	25,001	16.4	19.3
Société Générale	2,596	21,047	13.3	16.3
Banque Nationale pour le Commerce et l'Industrie	2,280	16,950	11.7	13.1
Comptoir National d'Escompte de Parris	1,870	10,073	9.6	7.8
Crédit Industriel et Commercial[a]	1,814	10,814	9.3	8.4
Crédit du Nord	634	3,086	3.2	2.4
Crédit Commercial de France	578	3,256	3.0	2.5
Total, top four banks	9,950	73,812	51.0	57.0
Total, top seven banks	12,976	90,227	66.5	69.7
Total, Banques inscrites	19,515	129,379	100.0	100.0

[a] Includes regional bank holdings.

SOURCES: For 1950: P. C. Dupont, *Le Contrôle des banques et la direction du crédit en France* (Paris, 1952), p. 389. For 1965: *Entreprise*, April 14, 1966, pp. 35 and 39.

In a second major reform (in 1966) the authorities removed the deposit maturity restrictions on commercial and investment banks. Unlike the BNP merger, the removal of deposit maturity restrictions did not have an immediate impact on the banking structure (number and size of deposit banks and investment banks). However, by blurring the distinction between them, the new regulation could lead to important future changes in the banking structure. First, as deposit and investment banks can now encroach more fully upon each other's traditional markets, the possibility of mergers between them is increased. Second, under the stimulus of an altered liability structure, deposit banks may move more aggressively into medium- and longer-term lending, and as this would threaten the investment banks' position in those areas, it could lead to a regrouping among investment banks.[53] Some possible regroupings could have a considerable impact on the size-distribution of banques inscrites, for some investment banks are quite large.[54] Finally, the size-distribution of banks could be affected if the enlarged opportunities

TABLE 32

Concentration of Resources in Large Deposit Banks,
Before and After Banque Nationale de Paris Merger,
End of 1965

Deposit banks (ranked by resources)	Before merger Amount (million F)	Percent	After merger Amount (million F)	Percent	Cumulative percent Before merger	After merger
Largest	25,001	19.3	27,023	20.9	19.3	20.9
2	21,047	16.3	25,001	19.3	35.6	40.2
3	16,950	13.1	21,047	16.3	48.7	56.5
4	10,814	8.4	10,814	8.4	57.1	64.9
5	10,073	7.8	3,256	2.5	64.9	67.4
6	3,256	2.5	3,086	2.4	67.4	69.8
7	3,086	2.4	1,597	1.2	69.8	71.0
Total Banques inscrites	129,379	100.0	129,379	100.0		

SOURCE: *Entreprise,* April 14, 1966, pp. 35 and 39. Crédit Industriel et Commercial figure includes its regional bank holdings.

[53] This was talked about as early as November, 1965. Cf. *Economist,* November 20, 1965, p. xxxii.

[54] As noted earlier, investment bank resources are highly concentrated. At the end of 1964, the largest (Banque de Paris et des Pays-Bas) had total resources of 4,626 million francs, and the next four largest (Banque de l'Union Parisienne, Union des Mines-La Henin, Union Européenne Ind. et Fin., Banque de l'Indo-chine) together held 5,495 million francs (based on figures in *Bilans des banques,* 1964).

for mutual encroachment should lead to significantly different growth rates (aside from growth due to merger) for different banks than have prevailed in the past.

In a third important reform (in 1967), the CNC removed the restrictions on branch entry by existing banks. While this change did not have an immediate impact on the distribution of bank resources, it could affect the future concentration of bank resources by facilitating different rates of growth for different banks.

IX

Regulation of the Conditions of Bank Competition

PRIVATE AND PUBLIC RESTRAINTS ON BANK COMPETITION

Prewar Regulation by Interbank Agreements

Government regulation of bank competition is of very recent origin in France. Before the Second World War, there were virtually no special regulations for banks as such. With minor exceptions, banks operated under the same commercial legislation as other business enterprises. The question of the advisability of separate regulation for banks was raised from time to time, but no legislation followed. A particularly extensive study was made by a Parliamentary commission (Brunet Commission) shortly before the Second World War, but its recommendations were overshadowed by the outbreak of war.

In the years before the government undertook to regulate bank competition, the field was preempted by various private banking organizations. The most important were L'Union Syndicale des Banquiers de Paris et de la Province; L'Union Syndicale des Banquiers des Départements; La Fédération des Banques Regionales Françaises; Le Groupement Professionnel des Banquiers de France; and Le Syndicat des Maisons de Banque, de Bourse, et de Change.[1] There were also a number of smaller regional banking associations. The Union Syndicale des Banquiers de Paris et de la Province, the most important prewar association, was established in 1871 as the Union des Banquiers en Commerce.[2] This banking association sponsored the first interbank agree-

---

[1] P. C. Dupont, *Le Contrôle des banques et la direction du crédit en France* (Paris, 1952), p. 133, n. 1.

[2] This is Dupont's version of the original name (cf. *ibid.*, p. 133); according to Cauboue, it was the Conference des Banquiers du Commerce de Paris et de la Province. (Cf. Pierre Cauboue, "Competition among Banks in France and the Fixing of their Rates," Banca Nazionale del Lavoro, *Quarterly Review*, June, 1955, p. 86, n. 2.)

ment to restrain bank competition. The agreement, known as the *Entente de Paris et de la banlieue,* became effective in October, 1925.[3] The large banks and chief *banques d'affaires,* which together dominated the Union Syndicale des Banquiers, were the main promoters of the agreement. Their purpose was to restrain the small- and medium-size banks, which had become troublesome competitors to the larger banks under the prevailing tight-money conditions. The agreement stipulated maximum deposit rates for each of three bank categories, established minimum loan rates on overdrafts and advances,[4] and fixed certain commissions. Compliance was secured by moral suasion and by the underlying threat of expulsion from membership. Although membership was "voluntary," the Union made membership attractive (at least more attractive than nonmembership) by requiring nonmember banks to pay the higher customer rates on interbank transactions instead of the lower interbank rates. By December 31, 1939, the Union had 150 members with 95 percent of total bank deposits.[5]

Opinions differ about the effectiveness of the attempts by the Union Syndicale des Banquiers to regulate bank competition. Dupont remarked on the "useful role" of the Union between the First and the Second World War, and cited the 1925 and 1936 interbank agreements sponsored by the association.[6] Cauboue has stated that "the agreement was often ill-observed" but added that "In all these breaches of the agreement, it was not a question of large amounts."[7] On the other hand, Wilson has pointed out that "the banking system was far from homogeneous and control by a central authority was not easy to establish."[8]

Banking Legislation During the Second World War

The Banking Law of June 13 and 14, 1941, significantly increased the bankers' power to organize and regulate their profession. A main objective of the 1941 legislation was to organize the banking system to make it susceptible to *government* control—it was part of the Vichy government's broader policy (set forth in the law of August 16, 1940) to "organize" all sectors of the economy to make them amenable to the government's will. Thus, the major focus of the 1941 legislation was on government control of banks, not on control of credit. However,

---

[3] This description of the agreement is based on Cauboue, *ibid.,* pp. 86–87.

[4] However, the minimum loan rate agreement did not affect competition, for the minimum had been deliberately set at a low level.

[5] Cf. Dupont, p. 133, n. 1.

[6] *Ibid.,* p. 135. The 1936 agreement concerned a collective work agreement—*convention collective du travail.*

[7] Cauboue, p. 87.

[8] J. S. G. Wilson, *French Banking Structure and Credit Policy* (London, 1957), p. 310.

as the 1941 legislation was basically framed by a committee of bankers (the Comité Provisoire d'Organisation des Banques) the legislation, in practice, enlarged the power of the *bankers* to control banking, under the supervision of the state.

The new legislation provided for a new Comité Permanent d'Organisation Professionnelle des Banques, Entreprises et Etablissements Financiers with wide powers over banks and others that performed bank types of activities. Article 33 specifically authorized the Comité to regulate bank ententes, conditions of banks, creation of common services, rules about liquidity, personnel matters, and bank competition. Bankers controlled this committee because the secretary of state for the National Economy and Finances was required (under Article 30) to appoint bankers to all of the six positions on this powerful body. The legislation also created another powerful agency, the Commission de Contrôle des Banques, to supervise the application of the new laws (and any others that might be passed) and to punish violators (by sanctions which included warnings, fines, suspensions, and removal from the list of banks).[9] Bankers exercised important power on this committee, too, because (under Article 49) the commission consisted of the governor of the Bank of France, the president of the Comité d'Organisation, and (the only strictly governmental representative) the director of the treasury of the Department of National Economy and Finances.

Finally, the legislative provisions concerning the professional bankers' associations increased banker control over their own affairs. The law of 1941 (Article 24) abolished all banking organizations, including the Union Syndicale des Banquiers, and replaced them with the Association Professionnelle des Banques (APB). Membership in the APB was compulsory for all listed banks. The APB was assigned the role of carrying out the decisions of the Comité d'Organisation and other banking regulations among its members. It also served as an intermediary between the banks and the Comité d'Organisation, and between the banks and the Control Commission. However, the APB was not solely a passive agent, transmitting rules made by others. On the contrary, the law explicitly required the APB to make recommendations to the Comité d'Organisation about entry of new banks and branches and about the important responsibilities (including the regulation of bank competition) which Article 33 conferred upon the Comité. Thus, the APB shared the authority of the Comité d'Organisation, and in practice this authority was used to prevent the creation of new banks or even of new branches.[10] In addition, on January 19, 1944, the Control Commission

---

[9] Under Article 52, removal from the list was to be accomplished by the Comité d'Organisation.

[10] Cf. Henri Germain-Martin, "France" in *Banking Systems*, ed. B. H. Beckhart (New York, 1954), p. 230.

(acting under Article 26) designated the APB to exercise the disciplinary powers of the Commission (except suspension and removal from the list of banks) with respect to infractions of the *conditions de banque*.[11]

Postwar Control Apparatus

The basic framework of the postwar system of bank controls, including competitive controls, was established by the Banking Act of December 2, 1945 (and the companion legislation of May 17, 1946).[12] Although the war years had been difficult, the French banks were generally sound and intact at the end of the war.[13] In spite of its timing, therefore, the Banking Act of 1945 was not designed to restore a banking system ravaged by war. It was designed to give the government greater influence over the course of postwar economic development by placing the volume and allocation of credit firmly under its control. Although the motivation and character of the governments which sponsored the wartime and postwar banking laws were quite different, the 1945 law generally retained the provisions of the 1941 legislation as long as they did not conflict with the provisions of the 1945 law.

The powers which the Comité Permanent d'Organisation exercised under the 1941 law passed to the newly-created Conseil National du Crédit (CNC) under the 1945 law (Article 13). The CNC, as the main policy-making authority, sets the basic guidelines for the credit policy, which is executed by the Bank of France. The CNC also inherited the power of the old Comité Permanent to regulate competition (by fixing the conditions of banking and by controlling bank concentration), but the composition of the CNC differs strikingly from the Comité Permanent d'Organisation. The latter was a small committee, dominated by bankers; the CNC is a very large committee with representatives from the government and from all sectors of French economic life. The original CNC consisted of a president (the Minister of Finance), a vice-president (the governor of the Bank of France), and thirty-eight additional members. Seven bankers on the CNC represented the deposit banks and an additional seven members represented the public or semipublic financial organizations (Caisse des Dépôts et Consignations, Crédit Foncier de France, Crédit National, Caisse Nationale de Crédit Agricole, Caisse Centrale de la France d'Outre-mer, Chambre Syndicale des Banques Populaires, Chèques Postaux). The CNC's composition was changed in 1957 and again in 1962: there are now eight banker

---

[11] Cf. Dupont, p. 136, n. 1. For a discussion of conditions de banque, see p. 140.

[12] The 1945 act also nationalized the Bank of France and the four giant deposit banks.

[13] Cf. Dupont, p. 27.

representatives and eight representatives from the public and semi-public financial organizations, but the total membership of the CNC has been raised to forty-three, in addition to the president and vice-president of the CNC.[14]

The Banking Law of 1945 also retained the Commission de Contrôle des Banques and expressly endowed it with all the powers of investigation, control, and discipline which it had exercised under the 1941 law. However, the 1945 law sharply altered the composition of the Commission and the extent of banker representation. Under the 1941 law, the president of the Comité d'Organisation was one of the three members of the Control Commission. Under the original 1945 legislation, this banker representative was dropped (and the Comité d'Organisation was eliminated) in favor of the president of the Section des Finances of the Conseil d'Etat. The law of May 27, 1950, restored the seat of the bank representative, but he is only one member on a six-man Commission. The governor of the Bank of France is president of the Commission, three members are government representatives, and one represents bank personnel.

The component parts of the control apparatus established by the Banking Act of 1945 mesh together in operation, as they were intended to do. The law established a triumvirate of control agencies. The CNC exercises both legislative and executive authority. It defines broad lines of credit policy, establishes detailed regulations on bank interest rates and commissions, rules on entry or merger applications, passes on modifications in the financial or legal structure of banks, and imposes sanctions on banks which violate its directives. The Bank of France also has a dual role. It enforces the policy directives of the CNC, but it also shares in policy-making through the governor of the Bank of France, who is ex officio vice-president of the CNC. In addition, the president of the CNC can delegate his powers to the vice-president; in practice, the governor of the Bank of France usually presides over the meetings of that body.[15] The third control agency, the Commission de Contrôle des Banques, exercises technical supervision over the banks' loan and investment operations. It also supervises the banks to ensure compliance with all bank regulations, including regulations issued by the other two agencies. The Bank of France is represented on the Control Commission by the governor of the Bank of France, who is also president of the Control Commission.

The provisions of the 1945 legislation with respect to the bankers association were substantially the same as under the 1941 law. Spe-

---

[14] Cf. CNC, *Rapport annuel*, 1962, p. 15.

[15] One indication of the close relation between the two agencies is that the CNC's offices are located in the Bank of France building.

cifically, the 1945 law retained the Association Professionnelle des Banques together with the compulsory membership requirement for all banks. It also provided that the APB would continue to be an intermediary between the control organizations and the banks, to advise the control agencies, and to mediate among the banks in cases of conflicting interests.

All these things remained unchanged, but the position of the bankers did not. The 1941 law, written and put into operation by bankers, was highly favorable to the banks. The postwar banking law was different not only in authorship but also in spirit, and despite the similarities in the formal control apparatus of the 1941 and 1945 legislation, the bankers' position sharply declined. As already noted, this difference was particularly evident in the sharply reduced banker representation on the control organs, but the more basic changes occurred when the government increasingly took over effective authority from the banks. Under the wartime legislation, the banks had been able to employ the prewar system of self-regulation to moderate interbank competition. Under the postwar legislation, the government continued to sanction the use of competitive restraints in banking, and in the early postwar years, the APB (in cooperation with the CNC) even set the conditions de banque.[16] However, this power steadily waned as the government assumed greater responsibility for controlling the economic life of the country. In the prewar system, the banks determined the competitive restraints, and the government merely reserved a veto power for itself; in the postwar years, the government has by no means been limited to a veto. As we shall observe later, the government on occasion has pressed, against vigorous bank opposition, for changes in the conditions of banking. In short, the government gradually incorporated the system of competitive restraints in banking into a larger framework of general economic controls; although the forms of bank self-regulation were sometimes preserved, the reality of bank self-regulation was substantially undermined.

"CONDITIONS DE BANQUE"

In the prewar years, competition was regulated exclusively by private banking ententes. In the postwar period, the CNC largely took over this role and has controlled bank competition in France in two major ways. First, by its authority to regulate bank mergers and branch openings, closings, or transfers, the CNC influenced bank concentration and thus indirectly influenced the extent of potential bank competition. Second, it has regulated the conditions de banque—that is, the terms and

---

[16] Cf. Philippe Aymard, *La Banque et l'état* (Paris, 1960), p. 105.

conditions under which banks can operate, especially maximum deposit rates and minimum loan rates.

Regulation of Deposit Rates

The CNC prescribes maximum interest rates for each kind of deposit offered by the banks under its control.[17] These include *comptes à vue*,[18] *comptes à terme, bons de caisse,* and *comptes spéciaux* (replaced by *comptes sur livrets* during the banking reforms of 1965–1966). French banks pay interest on comptes à vue (demand accounts), but the service charges often absorb the interest allotted to the accounts.[19] The CNC used to set different maximum demand-deposit rates for different bank categories, depending on bank location and bank size. On June 4, 1964, the rate structure was reformed when the CNC established the following two categories:[20] the first category banks included (in addition to the foreign banks) *sociétés anonymes* with current liabilities (*passif exigible*) at the end of 1963 equal to or greater than 75 million francs, other banks with current liabilities equal to or greater than 150 million francs, and any other bank if more than half of its capital was held directly or indirectly by one or more first-category banks; all other banks were second-category banks.[21] The CNC authorized the small banks to pay a higher ceiling rate on demand deposits than the larger banks (Table 33). This was intended to provide a competitive aid to the smaller banks on the presumption that, without the rate difference, they would be unable (because of their inferior "standing") to compete with the larger banks. It should be noted, however, that a rate category encompassed a considerable range of bank sizes. In Paris, for example, the first-category banks included not only the French giants but also a large number of much smaller deposit banks and banques d'affaires (as

---

[17] There is nothing secret about these rate schedules, which can be obtained from any bank or from the APB. Indeed, in one of his "letters" to the governor of the Bank of France, the Minister of Finance stated that it was "indispensable for the banks to make public the principal elements of their new rates and even to post some of them in their offices." The Minister also urged the banks to simplify their rate schedules because it would be easier to publicize a less complex schedule. Cf. Letter addressed to the Governor of Bank of France by Minister of Finance on December 6, 1949, in CNC, *Annexes au rapport annuel*, 1949, p. 40.

[18] *Comptes à vue* (demand deposits) are divided into *comptes de chèques* (mostly demand accounts of individuals) and *comptes courants* (mostly demand accounts of business firms).

[19] Cf. Pierre Despessailles, *La Banque*, 2d ed. (Paris, 1962), p. P1.

[20] Before this change, there had been three bank categories.

[21] Cf. CNC, *Annexes au rapport annuel*, 1964, pp. 22–23. For this computation, current liabilities include *comptes de chèques, comptes courants, comptes exigibles après encaissement, bons et comptes à échéance fixe*.

TABLE 33

Maximum Rates Payable on Demand Deposits, June 1964
(percent)

Bank category	Paris	Province
First-category banks	½	1
Second-category banks	⅝	1⅛

Source: CNC, *Rapport annuel*, 1964, p. 111.

well as all foreign banks). Under the 1964 regulation, the CNC also set a different ceiling rate on the demand deposits of banks located in Paris and those located in the provinces. The differential was allowed on the grounds that in the provinces it requires a higher rate than in Paris to attract money into the banks. On the other hand, a business or agricultural firm with "real activity" in the provinces could be remunerated at the provincial maximum rates on a Paris demand-deposit account.[22] As of January, 1966, the CNC abolished the two bank categories but retained the differential between the rate in Paris (one-half percent) and in the provinces (one percent).[23]

The conditions de banque also prescribe the maximum interest rates payable on time-deposit accounts (comptes à terme). These accounts are fixed for a predetermined period, and when a depositor opens a time account, he must stipulate in writing (a form letter is prescribed in the conditions de banque) how long he will hold the deposit. A copy of this letter, stating the interest rate to be paid, must be sent to the APB within eight days. Thereafter, the depositor cannot make withdrawals from the account, and the only way he can get his money back before the period agreed upon is to arrange for a loan on his account. The loan cannot be for less than thirty days and the interest rate on the loan cannot be less than the rate payable on his deposit account plus an additional 1 percent, or plus 1½ percent for accounts with a maturity of more than two years.

The maximum rates payable on time deposits (on June, 1964) are shown in Table 34. Deposits fixed for two years or less[24] were divided into four categories: from two months to less than three, from three months to less than six, from six months to less than twelve, and from twelve months to less than twenty-four. The schedule provided higher maximum rates on longer maturities, but no interest could be paid on deposits which were smaller than 100,000 francs and fixed for less than

---

[22] Association Professionnelle des Banques, *Conditions de banque*, April, 1963, p. 5.

[23] Cf. *Annexes au rapport annuel*, 1965, p. 56.

[24] For reasons explained earlier, deposits with a maturity in excess of two years are not included in this study.

TABLE 34

Maximum Rates Payable on Time Deposits, June, 1964

(percent)

Duration of account (months)		Size of account (francs)					
Equal or more than	Less than	Paris 30,000 to 99,999	Provinces 5,000 to 99,999	100,000 to 1,499,999 Paris	100,000 to 1,499,999 Provinces	1,500,000 and over Paris	1,500,000 and over Provinces
For sociétés anonymes							
2	3	0	0	1¾		2	
3	6	1¾	1¾	2		2⅛	
6	12	2	2	2¼		2¼	
12	24	2⅜	2⅜	2½		2½	
24	30	2¾	2¾	3		3	
For other banks							
2	3	0	0	$1\frac{13}{16}$	1⅞	$2\frac{1}{16}$	2⅛
3	6	$1\frac{13}{16}$	1⅞	$2\frac{1}{16}$	2⅛	$2\frac{3}{16}$	2¼
6	12	$2\frac{1}{16}$	2⅛	$2\frac{5}{16}$	2⅜	$2\frac{5}{16}$	2⅜
12	24	$2\frac{7}{16}$	2½	$2\frac{9}{16}$	2⅝	$2\frac{9}{16}$	2⅝
24	30	$2\frac{13}{16}$	2⅞	$3\frac{1}{16}$	3⅛	$3\frac{1}{16}$	3⅛

SOURCE: CNC, *Annexes au rapport annuel*, 1964, p. 24.

three months. Banks which were not organized as sociétés anonymes could pay slightly higher rates than the sociétés anonymes for a comparable account. The banks which are not organized as sociétés anonymes are the smaller banks, and the discriminatory provision was intended to give them an edge in competing with large banks. This differential was a long-established tradition in French banking antedating the CNC and even the APB. It was also traditional for banks other than sociétés anonymes to pay somewhat higher rates in the provinces than in the Paris area. This tradition was preserved (through the 1964 rate schedule) on the grounds that, to attract deposits, banks in the provinces had to offer higher rates than the banks in Paris, but the differential (only one-sixteenth percent) was hardly meaningful for most depositors. Finally, in the 1964 rate schedule, the CNC set different ceiling rates for different-sized accounts. In the sociétés anonymes, the rate differences ranged from 2 percent (between the smallest and largest accounts in the less than three months maturity) to one-eighth percent (in the twelve to twenty-four months category). Significantly, the official schedule did not prescribe a rate differential by size of account until October 25, 1956, when a differential was introduced "to take account of market conditions."[25]

As part of the 1965–1966 reforms, a number of changes were made in the rate schedule shown in Table 34. The purpose of the changes was to raise interest rates on time deposits and to simplify the existing regulations. On time deposits of less than two years' maturity, the maximum rates were raised by an average of about one-third. The 5,000-franc-minimum size of account, which had formerly been in effect only for banks in the provinces, was made uniform for all banks. In addition, only one maximum rate was specified for each maturity, thereby abolishing the differentials that had formerly been allowed for size of account, location of bank, or size of bank.[26]

Like time-deposit accounts, bons de caisse have a fixed maturity, but unlike time deposits, they can be transferred because they can be made out to bearer, to order, or to a specified person. Also like time deposits, bons de caisse cannot be cashed before maturity, but there is a provision (similar to the loan provision for time deposits) whereby a depositor can secure the funds before maturity. Even before the 1965–1966 revision, the CNC did not allow differential rates on the bons de caisse by size of the bons, but it did (and does) specify different ceilings for different maturities; and the ceilings are substantially similar in each maturity range to the ceilings on the corresponding time deposits.

Finally, until the banking reforms of 1965, the CNC used to stipulate a maximum rate for comptes spéciaux. These special accounts, which

25 CNC, *Rapport annuel*, 1956, p. 35.
26 Cf. CNC, *Rapport annuel*, 1965, p. 124.

could be offered only to individuals, could be withdrawn at sight (but only by passbook, not by check). The maximum size of these accounts was restricted to 15,000 francs (after January 1, 1964), and banks could not open more than one account per person. The CNC had authorized this deposit category on March 29, 1957, to bring into the banks some of the funds which individuals had hoarded;[27] and to increase the effectiveness of the new category as a magnet for hoarded funds, the CNC authorized a higher maximum rate on comptes spéciaux than on demand deposits. For example, when the highest maximum demand-deposit rate was 1⅛ percent (on April, 1963) the ceiling rate on comptes spéciaux was 2 percent. To hold down bank costs on these accounts, the CNC set 100 francs as the minimum amount of a withdrawal, deposit, or transfer of funds, and stipulated that larger amounts had to be in multiples of 100 francs.

As already noted, the CNC does not set the ceiling rates for the popular banks, agricultural banks, or savings banks. The Minister of Finance, together with the Minister of Agriculture, sets the limits for agricultural banks; and the Minister of Finance, together with the Minister of Post, Telegraph, and Telephone, sets the limits for the Caisse Nationale d'Epargne Postale. In the interests of equity and balance, the Minister of Finance and the CNC coordinate their actions in changing the rate structures and other deposit terms. On March 4, 1958, for example, the authorities raised the deposit limits at the Caisses d'Épargne from 750,000 to one million francs; and raised the maximum rates from 2¾ to 3 percent at the Caisse Nationale d'Epargne, and from 3 to 3¼ percent at the Caisse d'Epargne Ordinaire; on May 9, 1958, the CNC took similar action—deposit limits of the comptes spéciaux were raised from 700,000 to one million francs and the maximum deposit rate (on deposits which were stable for at least six months) was raised from 2½ to 2¾ percent.[28] Similarly, on May 3, 1962, the CNC reduced the maximum deposit rates which the banques inscrites could pay on bons de caisse, comptes à terme, and comptes spéciaux. On June 7, 1962, the public authorities ordered the new regulations on rates for bons de caisse and comptes à terme to be put into effect at the popular banks, and the Minister of Finance reduced the maximum deposit rates permitted in the agricultural banks. The CNC gave its approval to this action, which prescribed maximum rates very close to the highest maximum rates allowed by the CNC for the various deposit categories in the banques inscrites (Table 35).

---

[27] Cf. CNC, *Rapport annuel*, 1957, pp. 34-35.

[28] Cf. *ibid.*, p. 35, n. 1 It will be observed that rate coordination between savings and commercial banks did not necessarily produce equal rates. Indeed, until the 1965 reforms, the preferential rate treatment of the savings banks was a very sore point with the commercial banks.

TABLE 35

Comparative Deposit Rate Ceilings Set by the Conseil National
du Crédit and the Minister of Finance, June 7, 1962

| Deposit category | Conseil National du Crédit | | Minister of Finance |
	Lowest maximum[a] (percent)	Highest maximum[a] (percent)	Maximum (percent)
Sight	1/2	1 1/8	1 1/4
To six months	2 1/4	2 1/2	2 3/8
To one year	2 5/8	2 3/4	2 3/4
To two years	3	3 1/4	3 1/4

[a] Lowest maximum (sight deposits) refers to the rate at first-category Paris banks, and highest maximum (sight deposits) refers to third-category banks outside of Paris. (Note: After June, 1964, the third category was abolished).

Lowest maximum (time deposits) refers to the rate on the smallest acceptable size of deposit in a bank organized as a *société anonyme*; highest maximum (time deposits) refers to the largest size deposit category in such a bank (viz., 1 1/2 million francs or more).

SOURCE: CNC, *Rapport annuel*, 1962, p. 22.

Regulation of Loan Rates and Commissions

In 1966, the CNC made a major change in the conditions de banque and abolished the minimum loan rate regulation. During the twenty-year period in which it was enforced (1945–1965), the minimum loan rate regulation was a key element in the CNC's control apparatus. Hence, in this study of government regulation of bank competition, it is instructive to examine the nature and operations of that regulation. That examination can also provide a background for the evaluation (in a later chapter) of the probable impact of the reform.

The minimum loan rate regulation specified a set of minimum rates for different forms of bank credit—commercial-paper discounts, overdrafts, and others.[29] The commercial-paper discount, which has a long history in France, is by far the most important form of short-term bank credit. At the end of 1964, the banques inscrites held 62.3 billion francs of *autres effets*[30] (discountable commercial paper), 12.2 billion francs of *comptes courants débiteurs* (overdrawn deposit accounts, or over-

[29] For a discussion of some of the "others," cf. Pierre Cauboue, *Monnaie, crédit, banque* (Paris, 1959), p. 70.

[30] Cf. CNC, *Rapport annuel*, 1964, p. 148. Because commercial paper discounting is slow, cumbersome, and expensive, the Council of Ministers set up a commission (on May 25, 1966) to study alternative ways of financing short-term business loans. Cf. François Sergent, "La Vie financière," *Revue politique et parlementaire*, June, 1966, p. 109. For a discussion of the recommended reforms, cf. "Vers une Réforme du crédit à court terme," *Revue politique et parlementaire*, January, 1967, pp. 70–71.

drafts), 1.4 billion francs of *avances garanties* (another variation on the overdraft), and 3.1 billion francs of *avances et débiteurs divers* (excluding .6 billion francs of long-term loans).[31]

The formulas for computing the minimum loan rates and the commissions for various forms of bank short-term credit are shown in Table 36. A minimum permitted loan rate was composed of a base minimum and a commission. The base minimum was stipulated by reference to the appropriate discount rate of the Bank of France: TB (*Taux Banque* de France) or TAB (for *Taux Avance Banque* de France).[32] On December 17, 1959, T was introduced to denote the discount rate of the Bank of France under certain circumstances. T was defined to be equal to TB when the latter was between $3\frac{1}{2}$ and $4\frac{1}{2}$ percent; when TB was greater than $4\frac{1}{2}$ percent, T was equal to TB plus half of the difference between TB and $4\frac{1}{2}$ percent; and when TB was less than $3\frac{1}{2}$ percent, T was equal to TB minus one-half of the difference between $3\frac{1}{2}$ percent and TB.[33] In 1962 (the date shown in Table 36), the Bank of France discount rate was $3\frac{1}{2}$ percent, and the minimum base rate applicable to the discount of checks was T, or $3\frac{1}{2}$ percent.[34]

The minimum base rate on commercial paper depended on whether the commercial paper was eligible for rediscount at the Bank of France. For example, the Bank of France will not discount *effets prorogés* (bank credits which are renewed upon maturity instead of being paid off)—this paper carried a higher base discount rate on the grounds that a borrower who remains indebted to his bank may be in trouble, and the higher rate was allowed to compensate the banker for the presumed

---

[31] In French banking, the overdraft takes different forms. An *avance* is an overdraft that is granted all at one time and is due on a given maturity date; a *facilité de caisse* is an overdraft that is granted for very short periods, perhaps not more than fifteen days; a *découvert* is an overdraft that is granted for a longer period, perhaps three months to a year, and which is limited in amount. Overdrafts are commonly but not invariably secured. On these and similar technical matters, cf. Cauboue, *Monnaie, crédit, banque*, pp. 101 ff.

[32] TAB is usually higher than TB. In recent years, the difference has ranged from 1 percent (November 14, 1963 to April 7, 1965) to $2\frac{1}{2}$ percent (October 16, 1958 to February 4, 1959). Cf. Banque de France, *Compte rendu des opérations*, 1965, p. 83.

[33] Cf. CNC, *Décision de caractère général*, No. 59–12, December 17, 1959. T was further modified by *décision* No. 63–08, November 21, 1963. Thereafter, T = TB when TB = $3\frac{1}{2}$ percent; when TB $\neq$ $3\frac{1}{2}$ percent, T = arithmetic mean of TB and $3\frac{1}{2}$ percent. (Cf. CNC, *Rapport annuel*, 1963, p. 19. This is discussed further in Chap. XII.)

[34] The CNC regulated not only the minimum discount rate on checks but also the minimum maturity of the discounts. In 1962, the minimum period was three days for checks *sur place* (town checks) and five days for checks *sur une autre place*.

TABLE 36

Selected Minimum Loan Rates Established by CNC, 1962[a]

For checks	
Discount Rate	T
For effets commerciaux	
Réescomptable à la Banque de France	
Bancables	
Base discount rate	T
Commission d'endos	.40% per annum
Déplacés	
Base discount rate	T + .50%
Commission d'endos	.40% per annum
Proroges ou nonréescomptables à la Banque de France en raison de leur durée	
Base discount rate	T + 1.50%
Commission d'endos	.40% per annum
For effets de mobilisation de crédit à court terme	
Crédits réescomptables à la Banque de France	
Base discount rate	T
Commission d'endos	.40% per annum
Commission de signature	.50% per annum
Crédits nonréescomptables à la Banque de France	
Base discount rate	T
Commission d'endos	.40% per annum
Commission de signature	2% per annum
For découverts and avances	
Base rate on découvert	T + 2% (minimum)
Commission de découvert	1/20% per month (minimum)
Commission de confirmation d'ouverture de crédit	1% per annum (minimum)
Avances garanties par des titres[b]	TAB
For engagements par signature	
(avals, ducroires, cautions)	1% per annum (minimum)

[a] The French terms in this table are explained in the text.
[b] Overdrafts secured by stocks.
SOURCES: APB, *Conditions de banque* (re-edition 1959); and Pierre Despessailes, *La Banque*, 2d ed. (Paris, 1962), pp. R4 and R7.

higher risk, and also to induce the borrower to pay off his loan upon maturity.[35] The Bank of France also will not rediscount paper if it has an unacceptable signature, excessive maturity, very short maturity, or

[35] Cf. Cauboue, *Monnaie, crédit, banque*, p. 96.

if it is for very small amounts—this paper also carried higher minimum base rates to allow for the presumed greater risk or for the greater amount of work. The minimum rate on eligible commercial paper depended on whether the paper could be discounted in localities where the Bank of France has a branch or office (*effets bancables*) or in other localities (*effets déplacés*). The minimum base rate for effets bancables was T, but it was T plus .50 percent for effets déplacés. This differential presumably compensated the banks for their higher costs in rediscounting the effets déplacés.[36] The minimum base rate on eligible paper was substantially below (1½ percent less, in 1962) the minimum on ineligible paper.

The CNC also used to set a minimum base rate (equal to T, in 1962) for *effets de mobilisation de crédit à court terme*, the instrument which is used when a bank agrees (in writing) to extend its credit by means of a *découvert*. When this instrument is employed, the borrower signs another document, the *billet à ordre* (promissory note), for the same amount and same maturity as the découvert. This note, in turn, can be rediscounted at the Bank of France. The minimum rate on export credits was also set by the CNC, and it was set at a low level to encourage exports.

The minimum base rate was higher on avances and découverts than on discounts. In part, this reflected the presumed risk difference. Although they are usually secured, avances and découverts are less completely covered than discounts (e.g., the avances and découverts carry only one name, whereas discounts have at least two names). The rate difference probably allowed, too, for different liquidity. The discount is ostensibly self-liquidating; neither the avance nor découvert is automatically self-liquidating, and typically both have longer maturities. The discount is also more liquid because of its eligibility for rediscount at the Bank of France; the avances and découverts can be rediscounted only with central-bank permission.

Before 1957, the minimum base rates for avances and découverts were stated in absolute terms (e.g., it was 6 percent per annum on April 11, 1957, and raised to 8 percent on August 12, 1957). On December 2, 1957, the CNC set the minimum base rate at TB plus 3 percent and provided for automatic changes thereafter with changes in Bank Rate.[37] The minimum base rates on avances were tied to TAB and usually exceeded it by one or two points.[38] In certain cases, like the *avances garanties par des titres*, the minimum base (if the banker ad-

---

36 The Bank of France charges the banks a higher discount rate on *effets déplacés* than on *effets bancables* (cf. *ibid.*, p. 97).

37 Cf. CNC, *Rapport annuel*, 1957, p. 39, and *Annexes*, p. 25.

38 Cf. Cauboue, *Monnaie, crédit, banque*, p. 104.

hered to Bank of France regulations concerning the nature of the securities and the amount of the avances) was TAB (Table 36).

The other component of the minimum loan rate, the commission, was added to the minimum base rate. Commissions are an important and integral part of the French rate structure. Some commissions are service charges imposed for particular services (e.g., the *commission de manipulation*, a handling charge on discounts). The CNC sought to prevent discriminatory pricing among different customers for essentially standardized services by setting the actual commission. Thus, during the years when it was in force, the commission de manipulation was fixed at 10 centimes per discount, regardless of the amount or maturity of the discount.[39]

Other commissions are simply substitutes for an overtly higher base loan rate. The prime example is the so-called "endorsement commission" (*commission d'endos*). The CNC authorized this commission in July, 1947, to help the banks. In 1947, bank deposits were inadequate to supply the demand for loanable funds, and the banks were forced to discount repeatedly at the Bank of France. The Bank of France discount rate was higher than the banks' average deposit rate, and the banks complained that they could not cover their expenses and risks with the prevailing loan rate levels. To relieve the pressure on the banks, the CNC considered raising the minimum base loan rate but decided instead to authorize a special commission to be added to the base rate. This commission was compulsory on all bank discounts (except government securities, since they are riskless).[40] The endorsement commission, originally set at .60 percent per annum, was subsequently reduced to .40 percent.

There are also commissions to compensate a bank for the specific risks of particular loan operations. The *commission de découvert*, for example, is supposed to compensate the bank for the risk of loss when it grants an overdraft credit.[41] This commission was set at a minimum of one-twentieth percent per month (on the largest sum outstanding during the month) and made compulsory for all banks.[42] Other com-

---

[39] The *commission de manipulation* was introduced by a décision de caractère général on July 18, 1946 and implicitly suppressed by another décision de caractère général in December, 1959.

[40] Cf. CNC, *Rapport annuel*, 1947, p. 24.

[41] For a further discussion of this point, cf. Jacques Ferronnière, *Les Opérations de banque* (Paris, 1954), p. 205.

[42] The CNC also set a maximum *amount* on the *commission de découvert*, i.e., one-half of the amount paid in interest per quarter. (Cf. Association Professionnelle des Banques, *Conditions de banque*, 1959, p. 6.) When the interest rate was about 6 percent (and the commission rate was about .0025 per quarter), this ceiling was effective for loans of less than thirty days. It also restricted the *amount* of commission which banks could charge on loans of

missions, like the *commission de confirmation d'ouverture de crédit*, imposed when a bank makes a loan commitment, are supposed to compensate the bank for immobilizing its funds. In 1962, the CNC set the minimum charge for this service at one percent per year. The CNC implicitly acknowledged the relation between this commission and the commission de découvert by providing that the commission de découvert could be reduced to one-eighth percent per quarter for customers who had already paid a loan commitment commission. Finally, some commissions are imposed when a bank extends credit by lending the use of its name to guarantee repayment of funds provided by another bank. This service is offered in a number of different forms—*acceptations, avals, ducroires, cautions*—and the CNC used to set the minimum commission which banks could charge for each form. The minimum limits in each case took account of both the amount and the maturity of the arrangement.

The CNC expected the banks to offer the minimum loan rates (minimum base rates plus minimum commissions) only to borrowers of the highest standing. In fact, discounts to the best borrowers could even be made *franco commission* (except for the commission d'endos).[43] On standardized services (which do not vary with the size or credit standing of the customer), the banks had to offer the CNC's fixed charges to all of its customers.[44] However, if a *commission fixe* was not involved in a customer transaction, the bankers were free to raise the base rates and commissions above the official minimum levels in order to cover the greater risks[45] and expenses of lending to nonprime borrowers. Or, as the CNC once stated, the banks could charge higher rates "to the extent permitted by competition and where required by the borrower's quality . . ."[46]

Under the regime of official minimum loan rates, the authorities used to coordinate the rates prescribed in the different bank groups. Indeed, even before the CNC had been established, loan rates in the commercial and popular banks were coordinated under an instruction of the Minister of Finance which required popular banks to be governed by the minimum loan rates which prevailed in the banques inscrites, unless they could justify a modification in terms of the special law under

---

90–120 (or 180–210, or 270–300) days, but the restriction applied only to the amount of the commission charged for the period in excess of 90 (or 180, or 270) days. Hence, the limit was significant only for very short-term loans. (Cf. Ferronnière, p. 229, and Despessailles, *La Banque*, p. R5.)

43 Cf. Cauboue, *Monnaie, crédit, banque*, p. 99.

44 These rulings were designed to wipe out the former regional differences and to ensure a uniform price for the same service throughout the country.

45 Cf. *Décision de caractère générale*, No. 59–11, December 17, 1959, Art. 4.

46 CNC, *Rapport annuel*, 1959, p. 32.

which they operated. This pattern continued after the CNC came into existence.[47]

Zone of Activity

Under Article 5 of the law of May 17, 1946 (which modified the basic law of December 2, 1945), the CNC can designate the zone of activity within which each bank must operate. If a bank has any offices outside of its zone, the CNC can require it to close those offices. Alternatively, the CNC (working through the Minister of Finance), can arrange for the office to be transferred to a nationalized bank located in the area, and for the transferring bank to receive indemnification.

The objective of this law is not entirely clear. Proponents of the law apparently wished to limit each of the large nationalized banks to a particular geographical area; and there was also a vague notion about protecting the public interest by controlling the expansion of the regional banks.[48] This authority has never been implemented, and French banks have been free to lend all over the country.

Instead of regulating bank competition by restricting zones of activity, the CNC relied on controls on the number and placement of banks and branches, which were regulated in terms of an "economic need" criterion. Since the CNC has very large powers under "economic need" (e.g., it can limit the maximum amount of deposits which a bank can accept, or forbid a bank to do business with certain groups of customers[49]) the CNC did not really need the authority under Article 5 to

---

[47] Cf. CNC, *Rapport annuel*, 1947, p. 27. While the loan activities of the agricultural banks are not directly relevant to this study, it is interesting to note in passing that agricultural bank loan rates were also coordinated with the commercial bank rates. At the beginning of the CNC tenure, the agricultural banks (unlike the popular banks) had operated under favorable rates and conditions. This began to change in 1947 when the agricultural banks decided that they would follow the CNC's minimum rate in their discount operations (cf. *idem*). This coordination was strengthened in the years that followed. For example, when the Bank of France raised its discount rate in 1957, the ministers of Agriculture and Finance (who jointly fix the maximum rate in the agricultural banks) issued a decree on October 15, 1957, to raise the maximum rate on short-term loans at agricultural banks. Cf. CNC, *Rapport annuel*, 1957, p. 41. Similarly, on December 17, 1959, the CNC reduced the minimum loan rate for the banques inscrites by one point, and the Minister of Finance (on March 28, 1960) decreed a one-point reduction (from 6½ to 5½ percent) in the maximum rates for short-term agricultural bank credit. Cf. CNC, *Rapport annuel*, 1959, p. 33, n. 2.

[48] Cf. P. C. Dupont, *Le Contrôle des banques et la direction du crédit en France* (Paris, 1952), pp. 205 and 206, including n. 1, p. 206. Dupont observes that this argument confuses the public interest with the interest of the banks which already had a national branch network.

[49] Cf. *ibid.*, p. 125.

impose geographical restrictions; it could accomplish much the same ends by regulating bank activity in terms of economic need.[50] Nevertheless, Article 5 is potentially an instrument of great power—at least some informed observers believe (as they stated to the author in interviews) that, without being implemented, Article 5 has been a powerful disciplining influence to secure bank compliance with CNC directives.

Enforcement of the Controls on Competition

To implement its decisions about the conditions de banque, the CNC transmits instructions to the APB which in turn passes them on to its member banks. This is a considerable downgrading of the APB's role from its prewar position. Instead of organizing and enforcing banking ententes, the APB is today basically an intermediary between the monetary authorities and the banks. It retains a vestige of its former power in that it receives advance notification of proposed CNC directives and can communicate its reactions to the CNC. When the APB opposes a projected action, it negotiates privately with the CNC to resolve the objections. These negotiations also help the APB preserve the sense that it "collaborates" with the CNC in setting the terms that are imposed on the banks. If the negotiations fail, however, the matter is turned over to the Minister of Finance for a final decision; and, as the Minister of Finance is also the president of the CNC, there is no doubt either in principle or in practice about the real locus of authority to set the conditions de banque.

Any violations of the conditions de banque (or any other CNC instructions to the banks) can result in disciplinary action by the Commission de Contrôle des Banques. Under the law of June 13, 1941 (Article 52), violators are liable to warnings, censures, or fines. The Commission also has authority to prohibit certain operations and impose any other limitations on the banker's exercise of his profession, suspend the responsible management personnel with or without the nomination of a provisional administrator, and delist the bank. In addition, following the 1956 violations of the maximum deposit rates, a new law (Law No. 56–760, August 2, 1956) authorized a fine of not less than 50,000 francs and as much as twenty times the amount of the interest paid.[51]

The APB has a certain moral authority but no legal authority in its own right to discipline members for violations of CNC directives. However, it has exercised the right, delegated to it by the Control Com-

---

[50] However, Dupont has argued that a restriction on a bank's geographical operations for reasons other than "need" would constitute an arbitrary exercise of CNC authority (*ibid.*, p. 206).

[51] Cf. CNC, *Annexes au rapport annuel*, 1956, p. 31.

mission (in January, 1944), to impose sanctions for violations of the conditions de banque.[52] As mentioned earlier, the Commission did not delegate its most powerful sanctions—suspension of responsible officials and delisting. As part of its activity to ensure bank compliance with CNC directives, the APB also supervises the banks. For example, a bank which opens a term deposit account for a customer is required to send a letter to the APB to announce the opening of the account and to state the terms (including rate) on which the account will be operated. Similarly, under the regulatory changes inaugurated during 1956, the banks were required to report the maximum rates they would pay on demand deposits at the end of 1957, and the APB was designated to serve as the intermediary between the banks and the Direction du Service des Banques (of the Bank of France) in connection with the required report.[53]

In spite of this combination of supervisory and disciplinary powers, the authorities have not always been successful in preventing violations of the regulations when the competitive restraints became too unrelated to the underlying market realities. However, this failure cannot have been due to insufficient authority. Given the determination to enforce compliance, the authorities have powers adequate to the task. Moreover, if necessary, they can employ sanctions which were not designed for that purpose. For example, when the CNC (as part of its postwar anti-inflation program) issued instructions to the banks about the granting of credit, the governor of the Bank of France (and vicepresident of the CNC) informed the president of the APB that all banks which did not scrupulously adhere to the CNC's strictures would be exposing themselves to the loss of the usual discounting facilities at the Bank of France.[54]

Bank Controls and Bank Efficiency

In an unregulated *competitive* market, competition spurs each firm to increase its efficiency. As the French authorities undermined this market spur to greater bank efficiency by restraining bank competition, they have employed various administrative measures to compensate at least in part for the weakened market pressures. Thus, from the beginning, the CNC has been interested in improving bank services and

---

[52] One banker expressed the opinion (to the author in an interview) that important violations do not remain secret because of "indiscretions" by disgruntled employees. For a discussion of the procedure to be followed when one bank charges another with violating the conditions de banque, cf. APB, *Conditions de banque de Paris,* Re-edition of April 1, 1957, "Principes Généraux," p. 3.

[53] Cf. CNC, *Annexes au rapport annuel,* 1956, p. 34.

[54] Cf. letter from governor of Bank of France to president of APB in CNC, *Annexes au rapport annuel,* 1947, p. 29.

reducing bank costs; and one of its earliest actions was to set up its own research section (Comité d'Etudes Techniques et de Normalisation Bancaire) to study the rationalization of bank organization (especially by greater bank concentration), techniques for simplifying procedures and handling, possibilities for standardization and greater mechanization of bank operations. The CNC continues to give considerable attention to these matters and especially (in recent years) to the use of electronic computers in banks. Its concern to modernize and simplify bank procedures applies to medium-size and small banks as well as to large banks. In short, instead of relying entirely on market forces to spur efficiency, the CNC has accepted responsibility for seeking out ways to improve bank efficiency and for persuading the banks (by moral suasion and other means) to adopt the improved techniques and procedures.

Second, the CNC generated pressure for greater efficiency as a by-product of its efforts to reduce the general level of bank charges to customers (whenever this could be done without injury to the banks). In 1959, for example, the CNC put tremendous pressure on the APB to reduce a number of bank rates and commissions. Significantly, the CNC pressed for the reductions in spite of bitter opposition by the banks (both private and nationalized) to an action that would reduce gross profits by 20 to 25 percent.[55] At least on that occasion, the CNC pressed the banks with the relentlessness of an impersonal market force; and to this extent, administrative pressure substituted for the pressures of a competitive market.

The CNC's policy on the failure of marginal banks also stimulated greater bank efficiency. When the CNC's policy of protecting bank solvency conflicted with other goals (like the desire to reduce bank charges), the outcome was often a compromise. This did not mean, of course, that the CNC jeopardized the solvency of major banks. Indeed, when the APB could show that a reduction in loan rates or commissions proposed by the CNC would have forced most banks, especially major banks, to operate below cost (as measured by general bank costs of the preceding year), the CNC took such facts into account before issuing its final decision. However, the CNC did not *as a matter of policy* withhold a projected rate-reduction to protect some marginal banks. The CNC seems to have been mostly concerned with the expected effects on the half-dozen major banks; and although it took no action that inflicted serious injury on a very large number of small banks, it did not ordinarily solicit their views, and was not unduly influenced by them. The official attitude seems to have been that smaller banks had to make their way as best they could, and that a merger could be arranged with a larger bank if they got into serious trouble. Since the CNC had no policy bias against bank mergers (especially of a weak bank), it was not

---

[55] Cf. Philippe Aymard, *La Banque et l'état* (Paris, 1960), pp. 107–108.

constrained to set official rate schedules to cover the costs of literally all banks. To this extent, the CNC again behaved like an impersonal market force and was not deterred by the prospect of causing a bankruptcy.

Although bank efficiency was spurred in these ways, the enormous and complex superstructure of regulations to restrain bank competition and to control their activities in other ways had a negative effect on efficiency. First, because of frequent changes in the extensive and detailed set of regulations, the banks required specialized personnel just to keep up with the steady flow of new regulations. Second, the regulations impaired efficiency by hampering bank flexibility. Third, they diverted the bankers' attention from credit risk evaluation to "la risque de pénalisations" in granting a credit which, while sound and desirable from a banking point of view, would be disapproved under existing government regulations.[56] Costs rose, too, when bankers expended excessive effort in tailoring a proposed loan application to fit the regulatory code.[57] The CNC was aware of these negative aspects of its control apparatus and had taken some action (even before the major reforms of 1965–1966) to avoid the sclerosis which some critics felt was threatening the banks.[58]

BANKING REFORMS OF 1965–1966: A MAJOR RETREAT FROM CONTROLS

During the two decades following the Banking Act of 1945, the changes made in the structure and controls of French banking left the basic regulatory structure substantially intact. This pattern was broken in 1965–1966 when the French authorities, in a set of reforms which one authority has termed potentially the most important changes in banking practice in almost a hundred years,[59] made a major retreat from the system of banking controls.[60] The reforms were instituted to improve the banking system and to make it a more effective instrument of government policy in furthering the Fifth Economic Plan, especially raising the level of investment.

---

56 *Idem.*

57 Cf. *ibid.*, p. 282.

58 Cf. *ibid.*, p. 107.

59 Cf. Pierre Besse, *Entreprise*, May 12, 1966, p. 121.

60 An earlier, partial retreat from the limits imposed on bank competition occurred in 1953, when the CNC, in an effort to reduce bank charges to customers, lifted the regulatory controls on certain bank charges. The CNC stated at the time that the most significant part of its action was not the reduction of some charges but the fact that it had made the first retreat from the limits imposed on bank competition since the laws organizing the banking profession had been put into effect. Cf. CNC, *Rapport annuel*, 1953, p. 19.

The framers of the Plan considered it essential for French industry to modernize its plant and equipment in order to compete effectively against producers in other Common Market countries.[61] In addition, they desired a higher level of investment to promote domestic economic expansion. In the latter part of 1963 and during 1964, the goals of the Fourth Economic Plan had been set aside to pursue a policy of economic stabilization. The stabilization policy had succeeded in preventing inflation but at the price of restricting economic expansion, and in the discussions which preceded the Fifth Plan, there was a consensus in favor of resuming the domestic economic expansion.

The commercial banks were assigned a key role in promoting the investment goals of the Fifth Economic Plan. As the country's major financial intermediaries, they were strategically located to carry out the twin roles of collecting the public's savings and supplying business finance; and the banking reforms of 1965–1966 (in this study of banking markets, the changes of particular interest are the merger of two giant banks—discussed in Chapter VIII—the elimination of minimum loan rates, the abolition of deposit maturity restrictions, and the authority for the deposit banks to open passbook accounts on the same terms as the savings banks) were aimed at increasing the effectiveness of the banks in this dual role.

The abolition of the minimum loan rates on discounts and advances on March 18, 1966, restored the banks' freedom to set those rates as well as all commissions that had been regulated.[62] This step was taken to introduce more competition in the loan market, and (on the grounds that more competition cannot help but be favorable to borrowers) presumably to facilitate the goal of raising the level of investment.[63]

To finance a higher level of investment without inflation, it was clear that the level of savings would also have to be increased. Accordingly, the government took a number of steps to increase the public's inducements to save, especially in the form of medium- and long-term savings. Some reforms (e.g., discontinuing the Treasury's progressive interest rate securities[64]) were aimed at making short-term savings less attractive; others (e.g., tax-exemption for the first 500 francs of bond interest, or the ten-year savings plan on which interest would be tax-

---

[61] Cf. Louis Beaupère, "Les Récentes réformes financières," *Revue politique et parlementaire*, February, 1966, p. 62. In recent years, private business investment fell short of the goals set by the Fourth Economic Plan and also failed to keep pace with investment in other Common Market countries. Cf. Vera Lutz, *French Planning* (Washington, 1965), p. 72, and *Entreprise*, April 14, 1966, p. 33.

[62] Cf. Banque de France, *Compte rendu des opérations*, 1965, p. 31.

[63] Cf. *Le Monde*, February 18, 1966, p. 2.

[64] Those securities had tax advantages which tended to deflect savers away from medium- or long-term placements.

free under certain conditions[65]) were aimed at increasing the attractions of longer-term savings.

The measures to reform the banking structure were an integral part of this program to raise the level of savings. Specifically, by giving the banks greater freedom to operate in the savings field, the authorities hoped to make the banks more effective mobilizers of the public's savings. At the same time, they hoped to prepare the banks to play a more important part in financing the higher level of planned investment. The banks were expected to face a larger demand for investment funds not only because higher target levels were set by the Fifth Plan but also because business firms' capacity for self-financing had declined in the postwar years. In the years 1956–1958, self-finance had provided almost 45 percent of gross fixed investment in the economy; in the years 1959–1962, the ratio had declined to 40 percent.[66]

To prepare the banks for a larger role in the financing of business expansion, the authorities took steps to improve their competitive position with respect to savings deposits. One important handicap had been the prohibition (in the Banking Law of 1945) against deposit banks accepting deposits for more than two years. This prohibition was removed (along with restrictions on investment bank operations in demand deposits or deposits fixed for less than two years).[67] Another handicap was the commercial banks' inability to offer rates as favorable as those the savings banks could offer. The government moved to eliminate this competitive disadvantage by authorizing the commercial banks to offer comptes sur livrets (savings book accounts) with identical limits[68] and identical rates as the savings book accounts in the savings banks.[69]

---

[65] Cf. Banque de France, *Compte rendu des opérations*, 1965, p. 36.

[66] Cf. Lutz, p. 46. The declining capacity of business firms to finance expansion from internal funds has been ascribed to the greater competition and progressive disappearance of tariff protection associated with the opening of the frontiers under the Common Market agreement. (Cf. Jacques Riboud, "Réforme bancaire et développement du crédit," *Revue politique et parlementaire*, September, 1965, p. 39.) In this connection, it should be noted that raising the level of business saving is another important goal of the Fifth Plan.

[67] Cf. CNC, *Rapport annuel*, 1965, p. 103; and CNC, *Annexes au rapport annuel*, 1965, p. 14.

[68] The *comptes sur livrets* replaced the *comptes spéciaux*. The decree of December 24, 1965, authorized the savings banks to open accounts for individuals up to a limit of 30,000 francs—15,000 francs in one passbook (livret A) and 15,000 in a second (livret B).

[69] The maximum interest rate on both accounts as well as on the comptes sur livrets was set at 3 percent. Cf. CNC, *Rapport annuel*, 1965, p. 125. On June 29, 1967, the CNC reaffirmed the 3 percent ceiling rate but abolished the restriction on size of account.

The abolition of restrictions on deposit maturities in commercial banks was also intended to increase the effectiveness of the commercial banks in their role as suppliers of funds. There have never been any legal restrictions on commercial bank loan maturities, but because of the limitations on their deposit maturities, the banks have traditionally refrained from placing more than a small part of their funds in longer-term assets. As a result, the commercial banks have not performed as effectively as the authorities would like in financing investment, constructions, or exports. By removing the restrictions on deposit maturities, the authorities hoped to increase the banks' flexibility and to encourage them to extend more medium- and long-term credit. As the banks will have to pay higher interest rates for long-term deposits, they will also be under pressure on this account to lengthen loan portfolios.[70]

OBJECTIVES IN RESTRAINING BANK COMPETITION

The forms of the competitive restraints (such as limits on rate competition, fixing of commissions) remained unchanged for many years, but the objectives of the competitive restraints changed considerably. As already noted, bank competition in France was regulated by private organizations for many years before the govenment decided to enter this field. The earliest and most enduring purpose in restraining bank competition was to protect the safety of deposits. During the prewar period of regulation by the Union Syndicale des Banques, the protection of bank profits was an additional motivation to restrain bank competition. After the First World War, bank competition had become sufficiently vigorous to impair bank profitability, and this impelled banks to form an *entente interbancaire* to limit the "excesses" of competition.[71] The interbank agreements continued to operate during the thirties, but they were not inspired by the economic difficulties of the post-1929 period.[72]

---

[70] To encourage the commercial banks to make longer-term loans, the Bank of France announced that it would be willing (under certain conditions) to rediscount medium-term credits up to a seven-year maturity instead of five years. However, to encourage banks to rely on private rather than on central bank resources, the Bank of France also announced that only two-year paper could be rediscounted at the official discount rate and that a slightly higher rate would be charged for the additional year on three-year paper. Cf. Banque de France, *Compte rendu des opérations*, 1965, p. 37.

[71] Cf. Jacques Ferronnière, *Les Opérations de banque* (Paris, 1954), p. 209.

[72] During the depression years, individual banks encountered difficulties, but there was no general bank crisis in France. Cf. Ferronnière, p. 210, Germain-Martin, "France" (see n. 10 above), pp. 228–229, and Dupont, *Le Contrôle des banques* (see n. 48 above), pp. 23 and 29.

The Banking Law of 1941 conferred official government approval on the system of competitive restraints originated by the bankers. The bankers who wrote that law and its provisions to control competition were presumably motivated by the same kinds of considerations that had led bankers to curb bank competition before the war; but the government, in sanctioning the bank ententes, was mainly concerned with other matters. Under the policy laid down by the law of August 16, 1940, the government wanted to organize all sectors of the economy to make them amenable to government control, and the 1941 legislation was intended to apply this policy to banks.

A new and quite different government passed the Banking Act of 1945, and the CNC, while it took over the system of competitive controls that had been originated by the banks and confirmed by the wartime authorities, had other objectives in mind.[73] In the first year of its operation, the CNC took action on fifty-one matters concerned with fixing and approving the rates which banks could charge their customers. Its dual purpose was to unify rates all over the country (while continuing to respect certain local conditions), and to make the application of those rates uniform for all customers (by suppressing the exceptions which benefited certain firms operating under a special law.)[74]

In its early years, the CNC also regulated bank commissions and deposit and loan rates in the interests of general price stabilization. In discussions with government officials about ways to reduce prices, business representatives frequently claimed that high bank charges impeded their efforts to reduce operating costs. Those discussions convinced the authorities that "an easing of the rates charged by banks on credit operations would permit the reduction to a degree which is not negligible of the operating costs of firms."[75] Accordingly, the Minister of Finance proposed and the CNC put into effect a number of measures to reduce the cost of bank services to business firms. In June, 1950, for example, the CNC sought to reduce business loan rates by lowering the minimum overdraft rate from $5\frac{3}{4}$ percent in Paris and 6 percent in the rest of the country to a uniform level of $5\frac{1}{2}$ percent for the entire country.[76] Thus, at a comparatively early date, the CNC had

---

[73] The protection of deposit safety was not a major consideration in the Parliamentary deliberations which preceded the Banking Act of 1945. Cf. Dupont, p. 43.

[74] Cf. CNC, *Rapport annuel*, 1946, p. 21.

[75] Letter of December 6, 1949, from M. Petsche, Minister of Finance, to governor of the Bank of France in CNC, *Annexes au rapport annuel*, 1949, p. 39.

[76] CNC, *Rapport annuel*, 1951, p. 15. This change served the double purpose of unifying as well as reducing bank rates. For other changes, cf., *ibid.*, p. 16.

made clear that one of its permanent objectives was to reduce (within the limits of bank safety) bank charges to business.[77]

In 1952, the CNC reexamined its earlier position that the cost of bank services affected the general price level by its "not negligible" effect on business operating costs. The CNC particularly wanted to know whether an increase in the cost of short-term credit would raise French prices enough to be a serious obstacle to the expansion of French exports.[78] It concluded that the interest cost generally had a very modest effect on prices and exports. Thus, a one percentage point reduction in interest would represent a one percentage point change in a business firm's sale price only if its bank loan was equal to its annual sales volume. As the bank loan was more likely to be equal to 10, 20, or perhaps 30 percent of annual sales, a one percentage point reduction in loan interest rate would make possible only a .1 percent, .2 percent, or .3 percent reduction in sales price.[79] Although this analysis reassured the CNC that the (1952) increase in loan rates had not aggravated prices or significantly impeded French exports,[80] they reduced the commission d'endos and various other commissions (in 1958), and announced that "this reduction is particularly desirable as the coming into force of the Common Market places French firms in a regime of enlarged competition."[81]

The authorities also utilized the competitive controls (on bank loan rates and other bank charges) to stimulate or retard the level of business spending. In 1959, for example, the CNC took a number of steps to reduce the cost of bank services "in order to encourage the resumption of private investment. . . ."[82] At an earlier date, the CNC had noted that the level of loan rates may have a great impact upon business profits, for while a one percentage point increase in interest rates may have little effect on the net profit of a firm with little debt and a strong profit position, it could convert profit into loss in a firm with a weak profit position and large bank indebtedness. Thus, by their effects on

---

[77] Cf. CNC, *Rapport annuel*, 1953, p. 22; or 1956, p. 33.

[78] Cf. CNC, *Rapport annuel*, 1952, p. 16.

[79] The Service Central des Risques calculated a number of possible relations between loan volume and sales price. This is presented as a table, Annexe No. 17, in CNC, *Annexes au rapport annuel*, 1952, p. 55.

[80] CNC, *Rapport annuel*, 1952, p. 18. Most chambers of commerce (which had studied the problem on the urging of the Conseil Économique) also concluded that variations in the cost of short-term bank credit had only a very small direct effect on the sales, prices, or costs of business firms (cf. *idem*).

[81] *Décision de caractère général*, No. 59–02, February 5, 1959, in CNC, *Annexes au rapport annuel*, 1958, p. 27.

[82] CNC, *Rapport annuel*, 1959, p. 11.

firms' net profits, higher loan rates induce a reduction in bank borrowings or at least retard a further increase.[83]

In addition to supporting the competitive controls for broader economic objectives, the authorities (at least until the reforms of 1965–1966) also favored competitive curbs to avoid "excessive" competition. When bank competition occasionally exceeded the acceptable limits, proponents of controls were quick to point to the results as confirming the need for controls.[84] On the other hand, there has always been an opposition view which favored greater bank competition. This view was significantly advanced as a result of the reforms of 1965–1967 when the authorities, in a major retreat from the philosophy of controls, sought to enlarge the scope for individual bank action. The probable market consequences of those changes will be examined further in later chapters.

---

[83] Cf. CNC, *Rapport annuel*, 1952, pp. 16–17. For another view about the effect of loan rate variations on borrowing, cf. Patrice Grivet, *La Mobilisation des crédits bancaires en France* (Paris, 1962), pp. 200–201.

[84] In a typical expression of this view, one writer summed up his discussion of bank competition in the first half of the 1950's with the observation that "The restoration of freedom in the matter of fixing of banking conditions showed the disadvantages of entirely unrestricted competition in rates. . . . " (Pierre Cauboue, "Competition Among Banks in France and the Fixing of their Rates," Banca Nazionale del Lavoro, *Quarterly Review*, June, 1955, p. 98.)

X

Competitive Regulations and Deposit Markets

STRUCTURE AND OPERATIONS OF DEPOSIT MARKETS

The market structure of deposit markets depends upon the system of financial institutions (banks and nonbanks) that exists in a country and upon the legal, institutional, and other factors that affect the mobility of those financial institutions and of their depositors. Because the banking reforms of 1965–1967 made changes in both the financial structure and the legal framework of banking, this discussion begins with a description of the structure and characteristics of deposit markets immediately prior to the reforms, and then shows how those markets have been, or are likely to be, affected by the reforms.

Transactions-deposit Markets

The Paris transactions-deposit market has a special significance for large depositors. As there are no legal impediments in France to interfere with the expected association between depositor mobility and depositor size, large depositors have access to alternatives all over the country. In practice, however, their alternatives are adequately represented by those in Paris, because all large branch banks as well as numerous other banks have offices in the country's financial center.

The deposit banks with Paris offices are the most important suppliers of transactions deposits in Paris, but all are not equally important alternatives: 33 are foreign banks which tend to deal with their own nationals; 71 (the Paris deposit banks proper) held less resources (in 1964) than the nonnationalized *établissements de crédit*; and 4 giant établissements de crédit held almost ten times more resources than the nonnationalized établissements de crédit (Table 29). In addition to the deposit banks there were 46 banques d'affaires. They increased the number of alternatives (at least for some large depositors), but had a proportionately smaller effect on the reduction of concentration, since the combined resources of all the banques d'affaires were only 25 percent as large as the resources of the Big Four (in 1964). In short, the structure of the large-demand-deposit market in Paris has been oligopolistic with a competitive fringe.

In some ways, the small-transactions-deposit market in Paris is more concentrated than the large-transactions-deposit market. Although not legally prohibited from dealing with small depositors, many of the seventy-one Paris deposit banks have retained the *haute banque* tradition of concentrating on a comparatively small number of wealthy customers. Similarly, the banques d'affaires have not been a significant element in the market for small deposits. Until the reform of 1965, the banques d'affaires were obliged (by the Banking Law of 1945) to restrict their deposit services to a selected group of deposits, which virtually eliminated them as possible suppliers to the typical small depositor (and even to some large depositors). Moreover, many of those banks operated under the same self-imposed restrictions as many of the Paris deposit banks; and this, too, eliminated them as effective alternatives for small depositors. In short, the banks that provided a competitive fringe to dilute the oligopolistic concentration in the large-deposit market have been virtually unavailable to the small-deposit market in Paris.

This is not the full story, however. Whereas large depositors have dealt mostly with deposit banks and banques d'affaires, small depositors have turned to cash (a better substitute for the transactions needs of small than of large depositors), to the popular banks, and especially to the *chèques postaux*. In 1963, for example, the Post Office had more than five million checking accounts in all of France. The Post Office does not pay interest on credit balances in postal checking accounts, but this has not deterred small depositors, because the ceiling rates on commercial bank accounts have been very low (one-half to five-eighths percent in Paris in recent years). The Post Office checking account is an excellent substitute for a bank checking account and superior in some ways—for example, the Post Office can provide a daily balance, whereas banks provide statements to customers only at quarterly intervals; the Post Office also provides other related services at a lower cost than banks, and sometimes at no cost.

In each local area outside of Paris, the number of bank alternatives available to small depositors varies with the size and economic importance of each town or city. Table 37 shows the number of bank alternatives[1] available to small depositors in all French towns and cities (except Paris), on the assumption that the city limit is probably a

---

[1] Multiple offices of the same bank were not counted as independent alternatives if they were in the same town.

reasonably good approximation of the relevant local market for most small depositors. The banks in the table include deposit (other than foreign) banks, popular banks, and agricultural banks. Foreign banks and banques d'affaires were excluded because they have typically not been available to small depositors. Post Offices were also excluded, but only to distinguish bank alternatives from Post Office alternatives. Since every town that has a bank (and many which do not) also has a Post Office, small depositors have one more alternative in each town than the table indicates. Most local areas offer a small number of bank alternatives: 44.3 percent have only one bank; 63 percent have two or fewer banks; 76.2 percent have three or fewer; 83.8 percent have four or fewer; and 88.1 percent have five or fewer banks. Thus, even with the addition of the Post Office facilities, the market structure of most small-depositor markets outside of Paris is at best highly oligopolistic.

The oligopolistic structure of the small-depositor markets is not a good clue to their market behavior. In part, of course, this is because small depositors (to a much greater extent than large depositors) can

TABLE 37

Number of Suppliers of Transaction Deposits for Small Depositors, France, 1961

Number of "banks" in town or city	Number of towns or cities	Percent of all towns or cities with a "bank"
1	820	44.3
2	347	18.7
3	244	13.2
4	141	7.6
5	80	4.3
6	76	4.1
7	51	2.8
8	47	2.5
9	31	1.7
10	7	a
11	1	a
12	1	a
14	1	a
18	1	a
19	1	a
21	1	a
Totals	1850[b]	99.2

a Less than 1 percent.
b Excludes Paris.
SOURCE: Association Professionnelle des Banques, *Répertoire par localités* (des guichets permanents en France metropolitan), 1961. Multiple offices of the same bank were not counted as separate "banks" if they were in the same town or city.

use cash as a substitute for a bank transactions account.[2] In addition, the postal checkery has been a significant element in the transactions-deposit market for small depositors, partly because of its large size[3] but even more because of its policy. The postal checkery has used its powerful market position, not to maximize postal checkery profits, but to serve broader goals of public policy; and the government's terms on postal checking deposits have also determined the level which banks had to match to be competitive in the market for small transactions deposits.

Savings Deposits[4]

Large depositors have the same Paris bank alternatives (and subject to the same reservations) for their savings deposits (with a maturity up to two years)[5] as for their transactions deposits, namely, the établissements de crédit, the 71 Paris deposit banks, and the 46 banques d'affaires. The banks' savings facilities are in the form of *bons et comptes à échéance fixe*.[6] In evaluating these alternatives, it is important to note that the deposit banks (at least in the past) have not deliberately tried to attract savings.[7] As a result, perhaps, their fixed deposits were less than 14 percent of their total deposits (Table 38). This low figure is dominated by the four (before 1966) nationalized banks, which had a 13.4 percent ratio; but the highest ratio for any deposit bank category was only 23.6 percent (foreign banks). The banques d'affaires had a higher ratio (27.0 percent) than any deposit bank category.

Large depositors also have the option of placing their funds in treasury securities with comparable maturities; but there has been a very

---

[2] Traditionally, individuals have held large amounts of cash. At the end of December, 1965, the total amount of currency and coin in circulation was 66.3 billion francs, about 37 percent of the money supply. Cf. CNC, *Annexes au rapport annuel*, 1965, p. 90.

[3] At the end of 1965, bank sight deposits were 87.1 billion francs; *comptes courants postaux* were 20.6 billion francs (cf. *idem*).

[4] These are called "savings deposits" for convenience. Some deposits which are fixed for a relatively short period may actually be quasi-demand deposits rather than true savings deposits. Cf. CNC, *Rapport annuel*, 1955, p. 56, or 1956, p. 51.

[5] As explained earlier, the deposit markets included in this study of French banking are those that commercial banks could enter even under the maturity restrictons of the 1945 banking law (i.e., two years or less).

[6] This balance sheet entry is a composite of *comptes à échéance ou à préavis* (also called *dépôts bancaires à terme*) and *bons de caisse*.

[7] Cf. Henri Fournier, "The Problem of Controlling Liquidity in France," Banca Nazionale del Lavoro, *Quarterly Review*, December, 1960, p. 317. This may change in the future, perhaps as a result of the reforms in the deposit maturity restrictions (discussed later).

close relationship between maximum rates for fixed deposits at banks and the rates on comparable maturities of treasury securities (Table 39). This is not due to chance, for the CNC takes account of the rates on treasury securities in setting the maximum rates on fixed deposits in banks.[8] For the five years shown in Table 39, the rates on treasury securities were identical to the maximum rates permitted on bank de-

TABLE 38

Sight Deposits and Fixed Deposits, December 31, 1964

Bank category	Sight deposits (million F)	Fixed deposits (million F)	Fixed deposits as percent of total deposits in each category (percent)
Deposit banks	61,119	9,383	13.3
Nationalized banks	41,300	5,541	13.4
Nonnationalized banks	3,988	742	15.7
Paris banks	3,005	453	13.1
Foreign banks	1,995	615	23.6
Regional banks	9,395	1,753	15.7
Local banks	1,436	279	16.3
Banques d'affaires	5,669	2,100	27.0

SOURCE: Commission de Contrôle des Banques, *Bilans des banques*, 1964.

TABLE 39

Interest Rates on Bank Deposits and Treasury Securities of Same Maturity, 1961–1965

End-of-year	One-year maturity			Two-year maturity		
		Bank deposits			Bank deposits	
	Treasury securities[a]	comptes à terme	bons de caisse	Treasury securities[a]	comptes à terme	bons de caisse
1961	3	3	3	3½	3½	3½
1962	2¾	2¾	2¾	3¼	3¼	3¼
1963	2½	2½	2½	3	3	3
1964	2½	2½	2½	3	3	3
1965	2½	2½	2½	3	3	3

a *Bons du tresor sur formule.*
SOURCE: CNC, *Rapport annuel*, 1965, p. 76.

---

[8] In 1962, for example, the CNC reduced the maximum rate on certain deposit categories because the rate on treasury securities had been reduced. Cf. CNC, *Rapport annuel*, 1962, p. 18. For another example, cf. *Rapport annuel*, 1963, p. 22.

posits of comparable maturity.[9] Since a large depositor did not have to settle for a bank deposit rate below the CNC ceiling rate, the official view (that the CNC set only the maximum deposit rate but allowed competition to determine the actual rate) is misleading. In practice, the CNC arranged the situation so that the maximum rate for large depositors became their minimum rate as well. In this sense, the CNC set the actual as well as the limit rate for those deposits.

Small savings depositors do not face the same alternatives as large depositors. For the same reasons mentioned in connection with transactions deposits, small savers have not dealt much with the banques d'affaires, most of the Paris deposit banks, or the foreign banks. The large deposit banks also have not been important outlets for their savings, partly because small savers often prefer to deal with smaller banks, and partly because the large deposit banks have not deliberatly tried to attract any savings deposits, and especially not small savings.

On the other hand, small savers have had other alternatives which large savers do not have. Between 1957 and 1965, the banks offered small savers the facilities of the *comptes spéciaux*, on which the CNC allowed a preferential interest rate.[10] Although comptes spéciaux have often appeared in deposit statistics (e.g., *Bilans des banques*) as part of a composite category, "comptes de chèques et comptes spéciaux," they resembled savings more than checking accounts—for example, a *carnet* (passbook) was required with the comptes spéciaux; the use of checks was strictly forbidden; and—the most eloquent evidence of substitutability between comptes spéciaux and other savings accounts—the CNC altered the terms (rate and maximum size of account) for comptes spéciaux whenever the corresponding terms were changed in the savings banks. Small savers clearly liked the comptes spéciaux—in 1963, for example, they increased their deposits in comptes spéciaux from 2.92 billion (in 1962) to 3.94 billion in spite of a reduction in interest rates on those accounts.[11]

Small savers can also use the facilities of the popular banks and the agricultural banks; the law permits anyone to use these banks,[12] but their savings clientele is actually composed of small savers. The Minister of Finance (jointly with the Minister of Agriculture, for the agricultural

---

[9] The rates shown for the fixed deposits in banks is the maximum rate in Paris (i.e., the ceiling rate on the largest-size category).

[10] It has been suggested that *comptes spéciaux* were instituted to meet depositor complaints that banks offered illusory rates on creditor accounts. Cf. Pierre Cauboue, *Le Chef d'entreprise et ses banquiers* (Paris), p. 30. As noted earlier, the comptes spéciaux were replaced in 1966 by *comptes sur livrets*.

[11] Cf. CNC, *Rapport annuel*, 1964, p. 84.

[12] Cf. Association Professionnelle des Banques, *Recueil des textes usuels* (Paris, 1958), pp. 500 and 578.

banks) sets the maximum rates on these savings accounts, and he has cooperated with the CNC to keep them in line with the maximum rates at deposit banks.

It is clear from Table 40 that none of the foregoing (comptes spéciaux, popular banks, or agricultural banks) has been the really important repository for the savings of small depositors—in 1964, the *combined* savings deposits of these institutions were only about 6 billion francs (83 percent in comptes spéciaux). The really important repository for small savings has been the savings banks (the Caisse Nationale d'Epargne Postale and the *caisses d'épargne privées*)[13]—in 1964, almost 52 billion francs, or 89 percent of the total savings accounts shown in Table 38.

Until the reforms of 1965, the savings banks were authorized to pay higher deposit rates than the other banks.[14] For example, at the end of November, 1964, the Paris ceiling rate on small fixed deposits at the commercial banks was 2.375 percent for *comptes à terme* up to one year, and 2¾ percent for accounts up to two years; on the same date, the Caisse Nationale d'Epargne Postale could pay up to 2.80 percent on its deposits, and the *caisses ordinaires* up to 3 percent.[15] The difference in the ceiling rates of the two institutions was greater than appears,

TABLE 40

Savings Deposits in Selected Institutions, 1964
(million F)

Comptes spéciaux	
Popular banks	5,076[a]
Agricultural banks	643
Caisse National d'Epargne Postale	403
Caisse d'Epargne Ordinaire	19,680
	31,840
Total	57,642

[a] The popular banks held 604 million francs and the *banques inscrites* held 4,472 million francs.

SOURCE: CNC, *Annexes au rapport annuel*, 1964.

[13] It has been suggested that the size of savings bank accounts is restricted to preserve the "popular" composition of savings bank clientele. (Cf. Pierre Cauboue, "Competition Among Banks in France and the Fixing of Their Rates," Banca Nazionale del Lavoro, *Quarterly Review*, June, 1955, p. 97, n. 20.)

[14] Their rates were less flexible, however. By law, the Minister of Finance can set the savings bank deposit rate only once a year; but the CNC can change the ceiling rate on bank time deposits at any time.

[15] Cf. CNC, *Rapport annuel*, 1964, p. 86. As of January 1, 1964, the savings banks' deposit rates fell to 2.40 percent after the interest on a savings book account reached 280 francs at the Caisse Nationale, or 300 francs at the Caisse Ordinaire (*idem*).

because savings bank interest is paid on funds that are immediately available to the depositor;[16] hence, the 2.80 ceiling rate at the Caisse Nationale d'Epargne Postale was, in effect, a ceiling rate on a quasi-sight deposit.[17] The commercial bankers used to complain that such rate differences constituted unfair competition by the savings banks; but others have argued that the competition was not serious, because most savings bank accounts are too small to be profitable for a commercial bank.[18] As a result of the 1965 reform, it will be possible to test these opposing views. Whatever the future may hold, there can be no doubt about the past success of the savings banks in attracting the deposits of small savers.[19]

Small savers can also place their savings in treasury securities (*bons sur formules*), with maturities of one or two years (or three to five years).[20] It should be noted, however, that the ceiling rates on savings bank deposits (like the ceiling rates on fixed deposits in deposit banks, agricultural banks, and popular banks) have been kept in line with the rates on the Treasury's bons sur formules.[21]

The overwhelming importance of the savings banks in the small-savings-deposit market has meant that small savers (whether located in Paris or outside of Paris) have been operating in a highly concentrated market. On the other hand, the savings banks that dominate this market are state (or quasi-state) enterprises; and the deposit rates are set as a matter of government policy, not in terms of profit-making considerations. Moreover, as it was government policy (until the 1965 reforms) to allow *higher* ceiling rates on savings bank deposits than on commercial-bank fixed deposits, the commercial banks have been under pressure to offer savers their maximum rates. To this extent, it is

---

16 If necessary, the savings banks can require a 15-day delay. Cf. Association Professionnelle des Banques, *op. cit.*, p. 352.

17 By the law of April 3, 1955 (Art. 6), interest is earned on deposits from the first or the sixteenth day of each month after the day the funds are placed in the bank, and ceases to accrue at the end of fifteen days preceding the day of withdrawal. On December 31 of each year, the interest accrued is added to the principal and also begins to draw interest. Cf. *ibid.*, p. 351.

18 Cf. Cauboue, "Competition Among Banks in France and the Fixing of Their Rates," p. 97.

19 In 1962, the Caisse Nationale d'Epargne Postale had 13 million depositors. Cf. L'Administration des Postes et Télécommunications, *La Caisse Nationale d'Epargne* (Paris), p. 4.

20 Until October 22, 1964, the Treasury also offered securities with progressive interest (*bons à intérêt progressif*), a particularly popular form with small and medium-size savers in the countryside. Cf. Emile James, *Problèmes monetaires d'aujourdhui* (Paris, 1963), pp. 210–211.

21 Cf. Henri Fournier, "The Problem of Controlling Liquidity in France" (n. 7 above), p. 319. Cf. also CNC, *Rapport annuel*, 1964, p. 86.

misleading to say that the authorities merely designated maximum rates (for small savings depositors) and allowed competition to determine the actual rates. In effect, the authorities have used their strong position as suppliers in the small-saver market to set the actual rates in the different institutions, under the guise of setting maximum rates.

Market Effects of the Banking Structure Reforms

In 1966, the CNC abolished deposit maturity restrictions and merged two giant banks. Before those reforms, the market structure of the large-transactions-deposit submarket was oligopolistic with a competitive fringe. The market concentration varied somewhat for different large depositors, depending on whether they had access to the deposit facilities of a banque d'affaire. For those who did not, the new authority for banques d'affaires to deal without restrictions in demand deposits is potentially a liberalizing influence. By contrast, the merger of the two formerly independent banks (BNCI and CNEP) has intensified the oligopolistic concentration in the large-transactions-deposit market. On balance, the market-structure effect of the merger is likely to be more important in the short run than the market-structure effect of removing the deposit restriction.

The longer-run effects could work in either direction. If the banques d'affaires enter the transactions-deposit market aggressively and manage to capture a sizable share of that market, their action will dilute the oligopolistic dominance of the major deposit banks. If they do not try (or do not succeed), the long-run effect will be dominated by the merger effect, and concentration in this market will have been increased. Finally, even if they succeed, concentration may not be significantly reduced (as compared with the prereform period) if the success of the banques d'affaires as a group should be associated with mergers (between banques d'affaires or between banques d'affaires and deposit banks) which counteract the tendency of their relative growth in the large-transactions-deposit market to reduce concentration.

A quite different situation exists in the market for small transactions deposits. Before the reforms, this market was overwhelmingly dominated by the chèques postaux, owing partly to the comparative attractions of the postal checkery and partly to neglect of the demand-deposit business of small depositors by the large deposit banks. Unlike the large deposit banks, the banques d'affaires faced legal barriers to full participation in the small-demand-deposit market. To this extent, the banking reform that opened the demand-deposit market to the banques d'affaires has potentially increased the alternatives available to small transactions depositors. Whether it will lead to a significant change is another matter. As noted earlier, the banques d'affaires have traditionally concentrated on a comparatively small number of large customers. Even if they change their historic preference and try to enter the small-demand-deposit market in an aggressive way, they will face a serious handicap (especially in comparison with the major deposit banks) because of their very limited branch network. Thus, the banking reforms per se will probably have no more than a negligible effect (or none) on the structure of the small-transaction-deposit markets in Paris and in the provincial cities and towns.

In the large-savings-deposit market (for deposits fixed for two years or less), the reform of the restrictions on deposit maturity increased the number of possible suppliers to include the banques d'affaires. This structural change is not likely to alter rate behavior on those deposits, which have never been the exclusive domain of the deposit banks. Some large savers had access to the fixed-deposit facilities of the banques d'affaires even before the latest reforms, and all of them had the option of placing their funds in treasury securities of appropriate maturities. The latter was particularly important because, as shown earlier, the CNC set the maximum bank deposit rates to keep them in line with the rates on treasury securities of comparable maturities, with the result that the CNC's maximum bank deposit rate in practice tended to be the banks' actual rate as well. As long as the public authorities set the actual (under the guise of setting the maximum) fixed-deposit rates, the addition of the banques d'affaires as suppliers in this regulated field could not lead to any change in the market's rate behavior.[22]

The reforms also potentially increased the alternatives of small savers: the banques d'affaires can now offer small savers fixed maturity deposits of less than two years, and deposit banks can now offer *comptes sur livrets* on the same terms as the savings banks on their corresponding accounts. It should be noted, however, that the banques d'affaires have

---

[22] Although fixed deposits with a maturity in excess of two years are beyond the scope of this inquiry, it may be noted in passing that the market behavior effects are similar to those described above for deposits with less than two years' maturity. Under the banking reforms of 1966, the deposit banks can enter this formerly prohibited area. This structural change can have no significant effect on rate behavior, for the rate offered by banks must be competitive with the rate on treasury securities of comparable maturities. As the treasury security rates and the CNC's maximum bank deposit rates are likely to be kept in line with each other, the banks will be under pressure to offer their maximum rates. Thus, in this case, too, the market's rate behavior will normally be determined by the government's action in setting treasury security rates and bank ceiling deposit rates rather than by the market-structure effects of the latest reforms. On the other hand, it is important to note that, even if savers' terms are not affected by the reforms, the deposit banks can be significantly affected, for they now have access to a pool of funds formerly denied to them.

always been able to supply small savers with fixed deposits for more than two years' maturity, but they did not do so. As for the deposit banks, they have always been able to operate in the small-savings markets (less than two years' maturity), but did so only to a very limited extent. If this was due (as bankers have long claimed) to their competitive handicap vis-à-vis the savings banks in the small-savings field, the removal of the rate disadvantage could make a significant impact on the market structure of the small-savings market; but if their failure to enter this field to any great extent has also been due to the possible unprofitability of small savings accounts, or simply (in the case of large deposit banks) to indifference, the reforms may have little or no effect on market structure.

Even if both the banques d'affaires and the deposit banks (which are now more concentrated as a result of the BNP merger) decide to enter aggressively into the small-savings field, there is little (if any) scope for small savers' rates to be affected. As long as government continues to set the actual rates (under the guise of setting maximum rates) in the deposit banks and banques d'affaires, those banks will obviously have to match the terms available at the savings banks, if they are to make any significant headway in the small-savings market. In short, the small saver will benefit (i.e., in terms of savings deposit rates) only to the extent that the government wishes him to benefit. Clearly, whatever benefits might thus accrue could have been put into effect independently of the latest structural reforms in the banking system. On the other hand, the structural reforms could become important in terms of market behavior if the deposit ceiling rate were ever abolished.[23] Finally, as in the case of the large savings deposits, the banking reforms could benefit the banks (even if they do not affect the depositors), because the banks can (if they choose) participate in a broader savings-deposit market.

As noted earlier, the CNC introduced another important reform on January 10, 1967, by removing all restrictions to branch entry by existing banks. In the large-depositor market, this liberalization has no direct effect because large depositors have access to suppliers all over the country—the liberalized entry regulations may lead to a larger number of bank offices, but not to a larger number of independent bank alternatives for large depositors. The large-depositor market could be affected indirectly if the new entry policy led to a redistribution of banking offices and thus to a change in market concentration. In the local market

---

[23] At present, some bankers would not welcome such a move. Cf. Maurice Schlogel, *directeur général adjoint* of the Crédit Lyonnais, in *Entreprise*, June 2, 1966, p. 21.

areas where small depositors operate, market structure might be affected by the entry reform; but market behavior probably would not be affected as long as the authorities retain a strong position in the small-depositor markets and continue to set the terms that banks must meet to be competitive.

DEPOSIT-RATE FLEXIBILITY

Maximum Deposit Rates

It is the purpose of this section to examine how much flexibility the CNC has allowed on deposit rates during the entire period in which it has been responsible for regulating French banking. Since, however, the CNC establishes maximum deposit rates for a large number of deposit categories (by kind, maturity, size of deposit, et cetera), it is cumbersome to trace the changes in all maximum rates for almost two decades. Instead, the CNC's policy on rate flexibility has been examined in terms of three selected deposit-rate series: sight deposits (first-category Paris banks), deposits tied for six months to one year, and deposits fixed for one to two years (Fig. 5). After 1956, the CNC set maximum rates for comptes à terme (fixed deposits) by size of deposit, but only the smallest-deposit-size category (in Paris banks) is shown in the chart —the size of this category (30,000 to less than 100,000 francs) has not changed since it was established in 1956.

It should be stressed that the changes in the maximum deposit rates shown in Figure 5 do not fully reflect all of the flexibility allowed by the CNC. On occasion, flexibility has been achieved without any change in the structure or level of maximum rates. In 1960, for example, the CNC changed the effective maximum rates for some banks by reclassifying those banks with respect to maximum rates on sight deposits while leaving unchanged the structure of permitted maximum rates on sight deposits.[24]

The CNC has followed a low-rate policy on deposits throughout its existence, but especially in the most recent years (until 1966). With minor exceptions (mostly in the early years of CNC operations), the authorized maximum rates on fixed deposits have been below Bank Rate;[25] and the maximum rate on sight deposits has invariably been far below Bank Rate. This reference to Bank Rate is not meant to suggest that the CNC has related maximum deposit rates to changes in

---

24 Cf. CNC, *Rapport annuel*, 1960, p. 21.

25 During 1947 and 1948, the Bank of France had two discount rates. Figure 5 shows the rate on *effets commerciaux*.

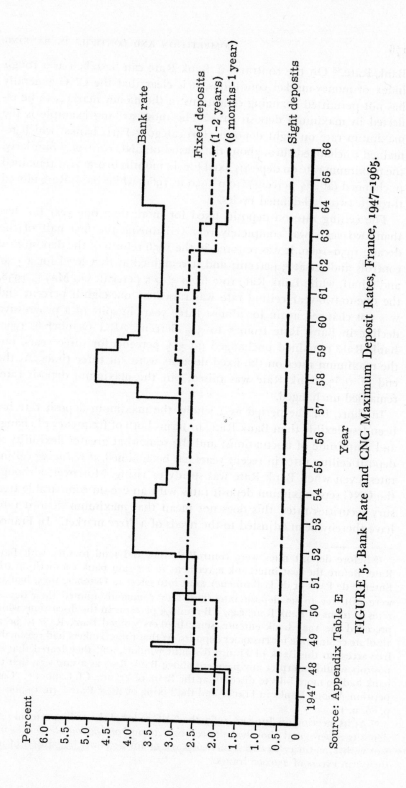

FIGURE 5. Bank Rate and CNC Maximum Deposit Rates, France, 1947–1965.

Source: Appendix Table E

Bank Rate.[26] On the contrary, if Bank Rate can be taken as a rough index of money-market conditions, it is clear that the CNC generally has not permitted changing conditions in the money markets to be reflected in maximum deposit rates. The most striking example is the maximum rate on sight deposits (first-category Paris banks) which remained unchanged throughout the period of CNC control.[27] Similarly, the maximum rate on deposits fixed for six months to one year remained unchanged (at 2¾ percent) from 1950 to 1960, while Bank Rate moved through two well-defined cycles.

The ceiling rate on deposits fixed for more than one year but less than two years was completely removed during the first half of the decade 1950–1960. It was restored in the 1956 reform of the deposit-rate controls and set at 3 percent; and it remained at that level for a year and a half, while Bank Rate rose from 3 to 5 percent. On May 9, 1958, the one-to-two-year ceiling rate was raised by one-eighth percent and was not changed again for almost three years in spite of a progressive decline in Bank Rate from 5 to 3½ percent. After October 6, 1960, Bank Rate remained unchanged (at 3½ percent) for three years, but the maximum rates on the fixed deposits were cut three times. At the end of 1963, Bank Rate was raised, but the maximum deposit rates remained unchanged.

In short, for the period as a whole, the maximum deposit rate has been less flexible than Bank Rate, in terms both of frequency of change and amplitude of fluctuations; and the somewhat greater flexibility of deposit ceiling rates in recent years has been aimed at *reducing* ceiling rates, even when Bank Rate was steady or rising. Moreover, although the CNC sets maximum deposit rates with an eye on comparable treasury securities rates, this does not mean that maximum deposit rates have thereby been adjusted to the needs of a "free market." In France,

---

[26] Before deposit rates were controlled, they did tend to vary with Bank Rate. Before the first interbank agreement to restrain bank competition (the Entente de Paris et de la Banlieue) went into effect in October, 1925, bankers were still free to set deposit rates, and they commonly quoted their deposit rates in terms of Bank Rate, e.g., TB minus 3 percent. In the discussions which preceded the 1925 bank entente, some bankers wanted Bank Rate to be an absolute ceiling rate for customer deposits. At that time, bankers had reasonably free access to the Bank of France discount window, and they feared that depositors would interpret any payment above Bank Rate as a sure sign that the bank had no more bills to discount at the Bank of France. Cf. Cauboue, "Competition Among Banks in France and the Fixing of their Rates" (n. 13 above), p. 86, n. 1.

[27] At its meeting on June 28, 1967, the CNC reduced the ceiling rate on sight deposits to zero, and abolished the ceiling rate on *bons et comptes à échéance fixe* with a maturity in excess of two years, or for accounts (regardless of maturity) in excess of 250,000 francs.

there is no free (nor even a true) money market in which competitive forces determine an equilibrium rate between the demand and supply of short-term capital. The government sets the actual or limit rates on all important outlets available for the public's funds; and the authorities have determined the rate spectrum primarily in terms of the desired flow of funds.

Violations of Deposit-rate Ceilings

A certain amount of deposit-rate flexibility has been achieved by means of violations of the CNC maximum deposit rates. Toward the end of 1951, the monetary authorities intensified their tight-money policy (by closing loopholes which they had formerly tolerated). This put the banks under very great pressure to attract deposits, and for a few years during the decade of the '50's rate competition became very vigorous, and many banks offered deposit rates in excess of the official ceilings. Although it is impossible (in the nature of the case) to document the extent of the violations, there is a consensus among informed observers that the violations were widespread—to the point that a question was raised about banks which did not violate the rate ceilings![28] Significantly, the nationalized banks appear to have been just as guilty as the private banks.

The illegal rates, offered for large deposits which bankers expected to be stable,[29] were quite high.[30] There is uncertainty about the exact amount of the rate concessions, which were made in secret and were often disguised to avoid the appearance of a direct violation. In spite of the uncertainty about the exact levels of the illegal deposit rates, it seems pretty clear that they were even higher than Bank Rate during part of the period. The CNC repeatedly warned about the dangers of such vigorous competition for deposits[31] but did not control it until October 25, 1956 (and in a subsequent *décision de caractère général* on March 29, 1957) when it revised its regulations on maximum depositor rates and other conditions "to adapt them better to actual conditions

---

[28] Apparently it was assumed that nonviolators either were not under (liquidity) pressure, or were not very enterprising. Cf. Cauboue, "Competition Among Banks in France," p. 94.

[29] Cf. CNC, *Rapport annuel*, 1954, pp. 34–35.

[30] Cf. J. S. G. Wilson, *French Banking Structure and Credit Policy* (London, 1957), p. 67. Cf. also Cauboue, "Competition Among Banks in France," p. 93. By a large deposit, Cauboue meant a deposit in the tens of millions (old francs).

[31] For example, cf. CNC, *Rapport annuel*, 1954, pp. 34–35. Again, in its 1955 Report, the CNC noted that deposit competition had remained very lively and onerous during the year. Cf. CNC, *Rapport annuel*, p. 42.

in the market . . ."[32] Although the violations occurred when the APB had responsibility for enforcing the regulations and began to disappear as soon as enforcement was transferred to an inspectorate under the jurisdiction of the monetary authorities, they were not due solely (as some have alleged) to the APB's unwillingness or inability to enforce the regulations. The CNC also knew about the violations, and its failure to act (roughly from 1951 or 1952 to 1957) was tantamount to tacit approval of the violations.

It is interesting to speculate from a market-structure viewpoint on how the violations occurred and why they were limited to large deposits. As already noted, the violations were provoked by the credit-tightening measures taken by the authorities in late 1951; but how did this pressure lead to rate rivalry? In a purely competitive market, deposit-rate competition would have been a natural and expected outcome in a period of tight money. As shown earlier, however, in spite of a large competitive fringe, the large-deposit market is essentially quite concentrated. Under the circumstances, it would be natural for large suppliers to take account of their mutual dependence and (even if there had been no question of a legal violation) to avoid a rate war.

One plausible hypothesis is that the rate war developed as an unintended consequence of secret rate concessions. At the outset, individual bankers may have believed that, due to the confidential nature of the banker–customer relation, they could raise deposit rates selectively to certain large depositors and gain a temporary advantage over other banks without inviting any competitive retaliation. Each may also have believed that the authorities were unwilling to tolerate widespread violations and counted on this to prevent a mass retaliation by other bankers. As it happens, the authorities did tolerate widespread violations, and failed to crack down on the violators for a few years; but this could not have been predicted with confidence at the outset, and by the time the CNC's tacit acquiescence became apparent, the situation had progressed too far to be easily retrieved.

Another plausible hypothesis is that the violations originated as sporadic activity by some banks in the competitive fringe.[33] They may have expected that rate concessions to selected customers would not provoke serious (if any) competitive retaliation, because the concessions were secret, illegal, and confined (for each banker) to an insignificant

---

[32] CNC, *Rapport annuel*, 1956, p. 34. The purpose of the revisions was also "to fill certain lacunae" (*idem*). For details of the new regulation, cf. *ibid.*, pp. 35–38, and CNC, *Rapport annuel*, 1957, pp. 33–42.

[33] The facts on this point are unclear: Some observers think the violations originated in the nationalized banks; others, in the *hautes banques*. (Cf. Cauboue, "Competition Among Banks in France," p. 92.)

fraction of the total large-deposit volume. However, if the pressures of a tight-money policy had already primed the large banks for rate concessions, a spark transmitted from one of the smaller banks could have been sufficient to ignite the chain reaction of rate concessions in the large banks as well.

The rate concessions were accorded overwhelmingly to large but not to small depositors. Such discriminatory treatment is inherent in the illegal nature of the transaction. Although a small depositor's account is inconsequential to any bank, the accounts of small depositors as a group might not be trivial (especially to a smaller bank); but it is difficult for any bank to attract a sizable number of small depositors by offering illegal rates. Clearly, the banks could not openly announce an illegal-rate offer; they also could not depend on word of mouth to spread the news, because such "public secrets" would probably have seemed too brazen to escape official sanction. Moreover, whereas rate concessions for large depositors were often concealed and indirect, this would have been more difficult to do for small depositors because most do not carry on enough other banking business to provide cover for an illegal deposit rate.

XI

Competitive Regulations and Short-Term Business Loan Markets

MARKET STRUCTURE OF LOAN MARKETS

Before the Reforms of the Banking Structure

The market boundaries of the short-term business loan markets are determined by the mobility of bankers and borrowers. A bank's geographical mobility is generally confined to the area in which it is located. The large nationalized banks, with their nationwide branch systems, are located in virtually all parts of the country, whereas the regional banks and local banks are located (as their category names suggest) in particular regional or local areas. Borrower mobility also affects the market boundaries of the short-term business loan markets. Since borrower mobility is strongly associated with borrower size, the markets for large and small borrowers are discussed separately.

(1) Loan market for large borrowers. Because the largest business firms typically have very high credit ratings which are usually widely known, they have access to banks in any part of the country. Since, however, most of the major banks (which are their natural suppliers) are located in Paris or have a Paris office, it is sufficient for large business firms to exercise their mobility primarily among banks with Paris offices.

Large borrowers have the same commercial-bank alternatives as large depositors, namely, the *établissements de crédit,* Paris deposit banks, foreign banks, and regional banks. The nationalized établissements de crédit are the dominant suppliers in this group. In 1964, a typical year in terms of the prereform banking structure, they supplied 51.5 billion francs of short-term credits out of a total of 75.2 billion francs for the entire group.[1] This high level of concentration was modified by the

---

[1] Computed from Commission de Contrôle des Banques, *Bilans des banques,* 1964. These figures (and those cited in Table 41) can only suggest the extent

addition of the short-term credit facilities supplied by the banques d'affaires. The forty-six banques d'affaires significantly increased not only the number of alternative sources in Paris, but also the total supply of short-term credit: in 1964, they supplied 9.3 billion francs, or 18 percent as much as the large nationalized banks.[2] On the other hand, the banques d'affaires did not dilute market concentration for all large borrowers since they were inclined to reserve their short-term credit facilities for customers to whom they also provided long-term investment financing. In fact, a good deal of their short-term lending was extended in connection with longer-term financing. However, even if all large borrowers had access to the resources of the banques d'affaires, market concentration in the large-borrower market would have been high because of the vast differences in size among the bank suppliers. In 1964, about half (53.6 percent) of the major suppliers of short-term business credit to large borrowers held just under 3 percent of the resources of the entire group whereas slightly more than 2 percent of the banks (consisting of four giant banks) held 56 percent of the group's resources (Table 41).

The significance of this comparatively high level of concentration is increased by the fact that self-financing (which was an important source of funds for large firms before the war) has sharply declined. On the other hand, the market concentration in terms of domestic suppliers of short-term business credit is moderated for some large borrowers by their access to sources of loan supply outside of France. This moderating influence, however, is contingent upon the absence of official restrictions on borrowing abroad and upon the borrower's ability to tap foreign suppliers directly instead of through the intermediation of either domestic banks or foreign-owned banks (or branches) that are located in France. In practice, this moderating influence has not been fully effective because French companies could not borrow foreign currencies except by permission of the authorities, and this permission was granted only to a restricted class of companies (e.g., major importing companies, oil companies, and some companies engaged in exporting).[3]

---

of concentration in the large-borrower, short-term loan market. These figures are not limited to business short-term credits but include total short-term credit; and they are not restricted to credits to large business firms.

[2] Cf., *ibid.* For reasons explained in the preceding footnote, these figures, too, are mostly suggestive. They do not refer exclusively to short-term *business* lending, since they are the sum of *portefeuille effets* (which includes short-term lending to the Treasury as well as "autres effets"), *avances, garanties,* and *comptes courants.*

[3] Cf. Oscar L. Altman, "Recent Developments in Foreign Markets for Dollars and Other Currencies," in Joint Economic Committee, *Factors Affecting the United States Balance of Payments* (Washington, 1962), p. 507. The government exercises this control under Decree 47–1337 of July 15, 1947, which pro-

The effective level of market concentration among the domestic suppliers of short-term business credit has been raised by institutional arrangements in connection with syndicated loans (*crédits consortiaux*; also known as *crédits syndicaux* or *crédits collectifs*). Syndicated loans in France seem to have originated during the depression years of the 1930's. The banks were disturbed by the fact that a business firm which needed large amounts of credit could (and commonly did) borrow from several banks, without necessarily notifying each bank lender about its indebtedness to other banks. In many cases, bankers did not find out

TABLE 41

Concentration of Resources among Suppliers
of Short-term Business Credit to Large
Borrowers, End of 1964

Size class (resources) (million F)	Banks		Banking resources	
	Number	Percent	Amount (million F)	Percent
Under 20	34	19.4	340	0.3
20 – 50	34	19.4	1,155	1.0
50 – 100	26	14.8	1,719	1.5
100 – 200	25	14.3	3,740	3.3
200 – 300	17	9.7	4,170	3.6
300 – 500	13	7.4	5,145	4.5
500 – 1,000	8	4.6	5,391	4.7
1,000 – 2,000	9	5.1	12,470	10.9
2,000 – 5,000	5	2.9	15,823	13.8
5,000 – 16,000	2	1.1	23,937	20.9
over 16,000	2	1.1	40,487	35.4
Totals	175	99.8	114,377	99.9

SOURCE: Compiled from data in *Bilans des banques*, 1964. The banks included in this table are the établissements de crédit, Paris deposit banks, regional banks, foreign banks, and banques d'affaires. (The private banques d'affaires were not included because individual bank figures are not available. The combined resources of the entire group, however, were only 1.5 billion francs).

vided that "Any natural person having his usual residence in France, any French juridical person or any foreign juridical person insofar as its agencies in France are concerned, shall be forbidden, except upon authorization of the Minister of Finance, to enter into a contract with a party . . . when the obligations originating from said contract would be stipulated in terms of a currency other than the franc" (Art. 59). Cited in *idem.* Cf. also Organization for Economic Cooperation and Development, *European Monetary Agreement, 1963*, p. 77. This was liberalized somewhat at the end of January, 1967; but to ensure that such borrowings "will not go counter to the general credit policy" of the government, funds borrowed abroad in excess of two million francs must (with certain exceptions) secure the prior approval of the government. See *Le Monde*, January 31, 1967, p. 18.

about these other debts until they were called to a creditors' meeting after a customer had asked for a debt moratorium.[4] To avoid these difficulties, bankers got together on syndicated loans in which the number of participating banks and the amount of each bank's loan were arranged in advance.

In one of its first acts, the CNC established a Service Central des Risques,[5] and required the banks to inform the central risk bureau of the amount of all loans above a certain size together with the borrower's name. With this information, the risk bureau was able to tell prospective bank lenders how much a prospective borrower already owed to other banks. The CNC hoped this would eliminate the difficulties that had arisen in the past from inadequate banker information, and that it would also curb the temptation of borrowers to spread their borrowing among a large number of banks.[6] Although the establishment of the Service Central des Risques removed the original reason which led banks to make syndicated loans, they continued to do so for other reasons. First, syndication provided a banker with risk diversification on large loans. Second, many bankers felt that it would be more efficient to have a single bank (known as the *chef de file*) handle a large loan for an entire group of participating banks.[7] Third, the CNC had ruled that all bank loans above a certain size to a single borrower could be granted only with the prior authorization of the Bank of France.[8] Since the decree specifically stated that it made no difference whether the minimum credit was granted by one or several banks, it behooved the banks to syndicate large loans, not only to facilitate the procedure of securing the "prior authorization," but also to protect themselves against inadvertent violations of the decree.

Loans to the nationalized enterprises, the metallurgical firms, and the large public works firms are almost always syndicated.[9] The nationalized enterprises do not restrict their bank dealings to the nationalized banks, and the principal nonnationalized banks often join the nationalized

---

[4] Cf. Georges Petit-Dutaillis, *Le Crédit et les banques* (Paris, 1964), p. 134.

[5] Cf. CNC, *Rapport annuel*, 1946, p. 167.

[6] This practice disturbed the CNC, which feared that such dispersion could be dangerous in a crisis. Cf. CNC, *Rapport annuel*, 1947, p. 22.

[7] However, the participating bankers must "tell all" to the *chef de file*, and some bankers consider this a severe disadvantage of syndicated lending, especially since the chef de file often does not reciprocate and give full information about the operation of the account to the participating banks. Cf. Jacques Ferronnière, *Les Opérations de banque* (Paris, 1954), p. 227.

[8] Cf. CNC, *Annexes au rapport annuel*, 1947, p. 21. Under this requirement (originally promulgated as a *décision de caractère général*, January 9, 1947), credits of at least 30 million francs to a single borrower, whether made by one or several banks, required the prior approval of the Bank of France (Cf. Art. 4).

[9] Cf. Ferronnière, p. 227.

banks in arranging syndicated loans to the nationalized enterprises.[10]
Since syndicated credits[11] are particularly common for medium-term
credits, commercial banks also join with banques d'affaires to make such
loans.[12] Syndicated credits are also employed for short-term credits[13] but
less than for medium-term credits.

In a market analysis, it is useful to distinguish two variations of the
syndicated loan. In the crédits consortiaux proper, all arrangements
and negotiations with the borrowers are handled by a chef de file on
behalf of the *pool bancaire*. In a *crédit concerté* (also called *crédit
global*), each bank is allotted a participation in the loan, and within
that limit the borrower can negotiate other details with each banker.[14]
In the case of a large firm which is controlled by a bank (usually a
banque d'affaire) which directly or indirectly owns or controls its shares,
the controlling bank is automatically the chef de file and handles all
financial arrangements for the firm. In other cases, bank control is not
involved.

Once a large firm has established a relationship with a particular
bank as its chef de file, the relationship tends to be perpetuated by a
tacit understanding among the other banks in the syndicate. If a large
firm (other than a firm that had been taken over by a bank which
purchased its shares) tried to change its chef de file, it would be difficult
and perhaps impossible to find another bank to assume the role. If by
some chance the firm did find another chef de file, the other banks in
the syndicate would express their solidarity by refusing to remain in
the pool.[15] This extremely powerful banker–customer relationship
operates in both directions, and a bank chef de file is stuck with its
borrowing customer just as much as the reverse. Moreover, the bankers'
sense of obligation to accommodate old customers appears to extend
even to the member banks of a pool, and they will take a share (but
perhaps a reduced share) in the pool even when they prefer to be left
out entirely.[16]

---

[10] Cf. J. S. G. Wilson, *French Banking Structure and Credit Policy* (London,
1957), p. 29, n. 11.

[11] Syndicated credits can be arranged in any of the different technical forms
in which banks grant credit, but the *avance* form is particularly common. (Cf.
Ferronnière, p. 227.)

[12] Cf. Philippe Aymard, *La Banque et l'état* (Paris, 1960), p. 109. They are
also common among *banques d'affaires* for investment financing. Cf. Wilson,
p. 118.

[13] Cf. Petit-Dutaillis, *Le Credit et les banques*, p. 134, and Pierre Cauboue,
Monnaie, crédit, banque (Paris, 1959), p. 104.

[14] Cf. *ibid.*, p. 227, or Petit-Dutaillis, p. 134.

[15] Cf. Pierre Cauboue, *Le Chef d'entreprise et ses banquiers* (Paris), p. 45.

[16] Cf. *idem.*

It follows from what has been said above that the practice of loan syndication can increase effective concentration in the large-borrower loan market. Loan syndication in the form of a crédit consortial drastically impairs, if it does not completely eliminate, large-borrower mobility among the bank suppliers in the large-loan market; loan syndication in the form of a crédit global does not. In short, market concentration was comparatively high in the nonsyndicated sector and even higher in the syndicated sector (especially for crédits consortiaux) of the large-borrower market for short-term business loans.

(2) Loan market for small borrowers. An excellent credit rating can assure wide-ranging mobility for large but not for small borrowers. The typical small borrower, even if he is an excellent credit risk, is not known beyond his local area of operations; and it is difficult for a banker in a distant area, unfamiliar with the relevant local circumstances, to appraise the small borrower's situation. For these and related reasons, a small borrower is typically restricted to alternatives in his local (or nearby) area where he and his operations are known to local lenders.

In each local area, the number of banks which supply short-term business credit is not always equal to the number of effective alternative suppliers for the small-business borrowers in that area. In the Paris small-borrower market, the Paris deposit banks would have to be excluded, for they tended to concentrate their loan operations on large customers with whom they had had long-standing relationships. By and large, the foreign banks would also have to be excluded, for they tended to concentrate on financing the trade relations of their own nationals with their home countries. For the most part, the banques d'affaires also were not important suppliers of short-term credit to small business firms.

It is doubtful whether the établissements de crédit ought to be included among the suppliers of short-term business credit to small business either in Paris or in other towns and cities, because it is doubtful whether the large banks were very interested in serving the credit needs of small business. Before the Second World War, they paid little attention to small customers;[17] in the postwar years, they have exhibited a much greater interest,[18] but there remains a real question about how far the large banks have altered their historic attitudes about lending to small business. Accordingly, the inclusion of the établissements de

---

[17] Cf. Christian Pineau's statement at the October, 1937, VIe Congres International de Science et de Technique Bancaires in Paris. Cf. Cauboue, *Le Chef d'entreprise et ses banquiers*, p. 12.

[18] This change was motivated by a number of considerations. Cf. *ibid.*, pp. 52–53.

crédit among the possible suppliers for the tabulation in Table 42[19]
errs on the side of overstating rather than understating the alternatives
in small-borrower markets.

The regional banks were included as prospective suppliers, and of
course the numerous local banks (with their particular concentration
on the business of small, local customers) were also included. The agricultural banks were excluded because this study is concerned with
short-term business loans, not with agricultural loans. Finally, the popular banks were included in the list of prospective suppliers. The latter
unquestionably belong in this category because, in keeping with the

TABLE 42

*Number of Suppliers of Short-term Business Credit
to Small Borrowers, France, 1961*

Number of "banks" in town or city	Number of towns or cities	Percent of all towns or cities with a "bank"
1	556	41.2
2	308	22.8
3	166	12.3
4	109	8.1
5	69	5.1
6	63	4.7
7	40	3.0
8	20	1.5
9	9	a
10	1	a
11	1	a
13	1	a
16	2	a
19	1	a
Totals	1347[b]	98.7

a Less than 1 percent.
b Excludes Paris.
SOURCE: Association Professionnelle des Banques, *Répertoire par localités* (des
guichets permanents en France metropolitain), 1961. Multiple offices of the same bank
were not counted as separate "banks" if they were in the same town or city. The
banks included in this table are the établissements de crédit, regional banks, local
banks, and popular banks.

---

19 The tabulation in Table 42 contains an overstatement in terms of present
alternatives because the BNP merger was not included in the count (which
was based on 1961 figures).

purpose for which they were originally established, they concentrate on loans to small- and medium-size firms.[20]

It is important to stress that the list of banks included in Table 42 describes the maximum number of bank alternatives available to small borrowers as a group. Because of inherent limitations on small-borrower mobility (sometimes supplemented by self-imposed restrictions on lender mobility), some small borrowers do not have full mobility among all of the suppliers even in this selected list of small-borrower suppliers.

In 1961, 1,348 towns and cities in France had one or more banking offices of the banks included above as suppliers of short-term credit to small business. Table 42 shows how the number of "banks"[21] was distributed in cities and towns other than Paris. About 41 percent of these local areas had only one "bank"; almost 23 percent had only two "banks"; almost 85 percent had four or fewer "banks"; almost 95 percent had six or fewer "banks"; and amost 99 percent of the localities had eight or fewer "banks." Only four cities (excluding Paris) have a somewhat larger number of "banks," and in those cities, the range is only from 13 to 19. Thus, the overwhelming majority of French towns and cities which have banks are at best oligopolistically structured.

The extent of small-borrower market concentration in most of those cities is probably not fully suggested by the limited number of alternatives available, since banking resources (in towns with more than one "bank") are not equally distributed among a bank population that may consist of tiny local banks, small popular banks, and branches of giant national or large regional banks. In addition, as noted above, the large branch banks have not been fully interested in cultivating their small-business loans. In short, in 99 percent of the towns and cities with banks, the market structures of the small-business loan markets have been too concentrated to *ensure* competitive behavior in small-business loan markets, and the market position of most of those banks was not seriously threatened by potential entry. For similar reasons, it is doubtful whether market structures have been sufficiently unconcentrated to ensure competitive behavior even in the large cities where there are a large number of "banks." However, in the absence of figures on loan

---

[20] Since the authorities do not get full information about smaller loans from the Service Central des Risques, they have on occasion regarded the volume of loans granted by the popular banks as an important clue to the total amount of credit granted to small and medium-size business firms. Cf. CNC, *Annexes au rapport annuel*, 1949, p. 108.

[21] The term "bank" as used in connection with Table 42 refers to independent alternatives only. Thus, multiple branches of the same bank in a town or city were counted as one "bank."

volume to small borrowers by different banks in each city, the point is moot.

After the Reforms of the Banking Structure

The two major reforms of the banking structure that could directly affect the market structure of loan markets were the BNP merger (1966) and the liberalization of entry restrictions (1967). The BNP merger unambiguously increased market concentration in the large-borrower market. As shown earlier (Table 41), before the BNP merger about half of the major suppliers of short-term business credit to large borrowers held just under 3 percent of the resources of the entire group, and slightly more than 2 percent of the banks held 56 percent of the group's resources. The BNP merger raised this comparatively high level of bank concentration among the suppliers of short-term business credit to large borrowers because the new Banque Nationale de Paris was formed by a merger of two banks (BNCI and CNEP) that had been in the top group of banks.

By eliminating an independent source of supply, the BNP merger also raised concentration in numerous local (i.e., small-borrower) markets where the BNCI and CNEP both had offices. The full effect of the nominal reductions depends, however, on the extent to which the merged banks had cultivated their small-borrower business and how much interest will be shown in small borrowers by the BNP. At present, there is no information on the former (i.e., no public figures on loan volume to small borrowers by different banks in each city), and it is too soon to have reliable information on the latter.

On January 10, 1967, the CNC removed the restrictions on branch entry by existing banks. This has no direct effect on the market structure of the large-borrower market: it may lead to a larger number of banking offices; but inasmuch as large borrowers have access to suppliers all over the country, it will not increase the number of independent bank alternatives available to large borrowers. The new entry policy could conceivably have an indirect effect on the market structure of the large-borrower loan market if it led to a change in the concentration of banking resources among the major lenders in the short-term business loan market.

In the small-borrower markets, the effect of the more liberal entry provisions will depend upon the resulting amount of actual (or potential) *effective* entry into those markets. It is important to stress that free branching for existing banks is by no means the equivalent of the theoretical concept of free entry. Thus, in any given small-borrower market, additional entry by banks already represented in that market would increase the number of banking offices, but not the number of effective alternatives available to small borrowers in that market. The latter would require entry by banks which are not already represented in that local market.

The possible entrants into small-borrower markets are établissements de crédit, regional banks, small unit banks from nearby localities, popular banks, and banques d'affaires. There is very little scope left for the nationalized établissements de crédit to increase the number of effective alternatives in local markets, because the three banking giants already have nationwide networks of branches. It is also doubtful whether the nonnationalized établissements de crédit—there are only four—will add to the number of effective alternatives in a significant number of local areas, because of their concern about growing too large and becoming candidates for nationalization.

As for the regional banks, they have traditionally maintained a strong identification with their respective regions and have generally confined their operations to nonoverlapping areas. Moreover, there are only twenty-four regional banks in the entire country. Thus, if they are to make a significant impact in local markets in all parts of the country, the majority of those banks would have to abandon their traditional regional character and consciously embark on a policy of nationwide branch banking, with the attendant risk of growing too large and being nationalized.

It is also unlikely that there will be much effective entry by the small unit banks in each locality, because any branch expansion by local banks is likely to be confined to the same (or a nearby) locality. The popular banks, too, are not a likely source of a significant amount of effective entry into local markets, for they are already widely distributed throughout the country.

Finally, while there will doubtless be some branch expansion by the banques d'affaires, there is not likely to be a significant amount of effective entry in a large number of local markets. In part, this is because most investment banks are small and neither able nor interested in undertaking widespread branch expansion. Moreover, they are virtually all located in Paris, and any branch expansion is more likely to mean a duplication of existing facilities within the Paris region than a branching into distant parts of the country. In addition, the principal investment banks (i.e., the most likely prospects for extensive branch expansion into more distant areas) have established closer links with the commercial banks[22] (e.g., loan agreements, reciprocal exchange of

---

[22] For example, the Banque de Paris et des Pays-Bas with the Crédit Industriel et Commercial, and the Banque de l'Union Parisienne with the Compagnie Française. Cf. *Le Monde*, January 5, 1967, p. 16. Cf. also R. J. Truptil and H. Viaux, "Changes in French Banking," *The Banker*, April, 1967, p. 317.

shares and directors, et cetera), and this, together with their fear of nationalization if they become too large,[23] may impair their incentive to seek additional funds by opening new branches.

In sum, it is most likely that an additional entry under the 1967 entry liberalization (i.e., entry in excess of the amount that would have been authorized even before the 1967 reforms) will take place primarily in areas that already have banks (especially Paris)[24] and will be undertaken by banks that are already represented in those local markets. Thus, as far as most small borrowers are concerned, the possible increase in branch entry will not increase effective entry by a corresponding amount.

MARKET BEHAVIOR IN LOAN MARKETS

Market behavior in short-term business loan markets is potentially affected by the abolition of the minimum loan rate (in 1966) as well as by the market-structure changes which resulted from the reforms of the banking structure. In order to assess the probable effects of freeing loan rates, it is necessary to examine market behavior before the change, and especially three aspects of the minimum loan rate: its relation to actual loan rates, to competitive rates, and to the rates that probably would have prevailed if there had been no official loan rate controls.

Minimum Rates and Actual Loan Rates

From the inception of the CNC in 1945 and until the effective date of April 1, 1966, French banks operated subject to a minimum loan rate imposed by the CNC. Although there are no published French banking statistics about the rates paid by borrowers for short-term business credit from banks, informed observers of French banking agree that banks used to charge their large prime borrowers the minimum rate permitted by the CNC[25] on short-term credits.[26] Moreover, this was

---

[23] Cf. "De Gaulle Tackles the Banks," *Economist*, November 26, 1966, p. xix.

[24] Cf. *Le Monde*, January 5, 1967, p. 16.

[25] It is interesting to compare the bankers' behavior in the deposit and loan markets. It will be recalled that tight credit conditions during 1951–1957 led to widespread violations of the deposit ceiling rates. By contrast, under the comparatively easy credit conditions in 1961–1963, the oligopolistic discipline of the bankers appears to have held firm, and violations of the minimum loan rate regulations were neither common nor important. This different bank behavior could have been due to the fact that the tight-money period generated stronger pressures than the easy-money period. However, even if the pressures had been identical, the bankers probably would not have violated the minimum loan rates as they had earlier violated the deposit ceiling rates. In the case of syndicated loans, it is not feasible to keep any rate concessions secret from other members of the syndicate. Moreover, even if it were possible, a secret rate

as true of syndicated as of nonsyndicated loans.[27]

It is implicit in the banking literature (and it was also the view of the French bankers and officials interviewed by the author) that this behavior was due to the "keen competition among the banks." There is an initial plausibility to this view, for it is consistent with the fact that the CNC set minimum loan rates but permitted competition to determine actual loan rates. Since large borrowers typically paid the minimum rate, the action of interbank competition would appear to be confirmed.

In spite of its widespread acceptance, the "keen competition" hypothesis is very doubtful, for it rests on the twin assumptions that the "keen competition" was due to the large number of banks (almost 350 banques inscrites) and to their strong competitive spirit. Neither assumption is convincing. First, the large number of banks in France does not mean that the large-borrower, short-term loan market is atomistic. As shown earlier, the nonsyndicated sector of this market is concentrated in a few very large banks, and the syndicated sector (especially for crédits consortiaux) is even more highly concentrated. Indeed, the syndicated sector borders upon the monopolistic for some borrowers because bank understandings seriously impair their mobility in seeking alternative syndicate suppliers or even a different chef de file. Second, in spite of the alleged strength of their competitive spirit, the bankers have often restrained their competitive inclinations. Thus, even before the CNC existed, the large banks had organized the Union Syndicale des Banques to restrain bank competition. Similarly, the banks' competitive spirit did not deter them from coming to understandings and gentlemen's agreements about matters such as dividing areas for new branches or refusing to deal with a borrower who wanted

---

concession by one banker would not secure a larger share of the syndicated credit for the rate-cutter. In the case of a nonsyndicated loan, a banker might secure a temporary advantage from a secret rate concession for as long as it remained secret. However, the authorities would ultimately learn about any important violation either through their normal inspection activities or perhaps through the "indiscretion" of a disgruntled bank employee. Moreover, whereas the original violators of the deposit rate ceilings may have believed (as was suggested in the earlier hypothesis about deposit rate violations) that the CNC would not tolerate mass violations of the deposit regulations, the bankers in the '60's had reason to believe that the CNC would not have tolerated even isolated violations of the loan regulations.

[26] For a typical expression of this view, cf. Pierre Cauboue, "Competition among Banks in France and the Fixing of their Rates," Banca Nazionale del Lavoro, *Quarterly Review*, June, 1955, p. 95; or Cauboue, *Le Chef d'entreprise et ses banquiers*, p. 54.

[27] Cauboue, *Le Chef d'entreprise*, p. 47.

to change his chef de file. Moreover, in spite of their opposition to some of the CNC's actions on rates, the banks generally accepted and supported the CNC regulations aimed at curbing bank competition.

The history of competitive curbs in French banking suggests that rate rivalry in the large-borrower market, sufficient to bring rates down to their legal minimum levels, was not due to the fact that large banks were unaware of, or indifferent to, their oligopolistic interdependence. On the contrary, it is clear that the oligopolists behaved in a "competitive" manner (in the prime loan market) in spite of their recognized mutual dependence. Indeed, they offered the minimum rates to their best borrowers even when they believed that the CNC minimum rates were too low to meet the banks' legitimate earning needs. An hypothesis which fits these facts is not that the banks were blinded by their competitive spirit from recognizing their mutual dependence, but that they were motivated by the psychological prod of the overhanging authority of the government. The weight of this authority is very great in a country where the largest banks have been nationalized, where the CNC has been authorized to recommend further nationalization if desirable, and where the government has left no doubt about its determination to harness the credit mechanism to accomplish its economic goals.[28] Under these circumstances, a reduction in the official minimum loan rate would be interpreted not simply as permission for lower rates, but as an indication of the rate levels desired by an organ of great actual (and even greater potential) authority to enforce its views. As a result, even when they bitterly opposed the necessity to do so, the oligopolists granted the official minimum rate to the largest borrowers of highest credit standing.

A number of considerations reinforce the credibility of the preceding hypothesis. First, the banks' bitter opposition to certain reductions in the official minimum rates is better understood, given the oligopolistic structure of the large-borrower market, if the minimum is interpreted as tantamount to a mandatory rather than a limit rate. Second, until the CNC reversed its policy in 1966, its actions were consistent with the interpretation that it would have been willing, insofar as it was feasible, to fix loan rates much as it fixed certain commissions. Its efforts to set the minimum loan rates at certain levels in spite of vigor-

---

[28] The weight of government controls led Aymard to question whether French banking would "remain a commercial profession operating within a capitalist structure and governed by the law of profit? Or is it gradually being transformed into a *banking function*, exercised in the superior interest of the collectivity, subordinated to the demands ever more precise of economic policy and in which the spirit of public service prevails over the driving power of individual profit?" Cf. Philippe Aymard, *La Banque et l'état*, p. 282.

ous bank opposition appear to have been aimed at this goal, at least as far as prime borrowers are concerned. The matter is more complicated for the other borrowers because loan risk must be evaluated on a case-by-case basis. Presumably that is why the CNC in effect stipulated only a prime rate and then added that "the rates and conditions applicable to credit operations . . . can be increased by the banks *as a function of risks incurred.*"[29] Third, it would not have been possible for the banks to ignore the minimum rate for large prime borrowers and hope to escape CNC notice. Although loan terms are negotiated privately between banker and borrower, they could not be kept secret from the CNC, which keeps under surveillance the effective minimum rates applied to bank customers. Fourth, the banks could not have taken refuge in the risk estimate to deny the minimum rate to a large prime customer. Reasonable men may differ about how much risk is involved in a nonprime loan, but there is far less scope for disagreement about the credit risk (or the identification) of a prime loan to a large firm. Finally, the banks were aware that the authorities had great power to enforce their views about interest rates without having to ask Parliament for additional support. If necessary, the Bank of France could have enforced the CNC's offiical minimum rates by using its authority to discount directly for private customers. This has declined to very small amounts, but there is nothing to prevent the central bank from reactivating this enforcement device.[30]

It is more difficult to analyze the rate behavior in the small-borrower markets than in the large-borrower market. In the small- as in the large-borrower market, there are no official statistics published about rates paid by borrowers. In the small- as in the large-borrower markets, the rate behavior cannot be deduced from a knowledge of the market structure, because the market structures are not sufficiently unconcentrated to ensure competitive behavior (within the limits set by the CNC's minimum loan rate). On the other hand, competitive behavior cannot be ruled out on grounds of market structure in either case; although competitive behavior in a concentrated market is less likely than non-competitive behavior, it is not impossible.

It was possible to get around these difficulties in the case of the large-borrower market because it is common knowledge (among informed observers) that the typical large borrower paid the minimum rate permitted by the CNC—and that fact is presumptive evidence that the large-borrower market behaved as competitively as CNC rules then

---

[29] *Décision de caractère général*, No. 59–11, December 17, 1959, Art. 4.

[30] Simon states that business firms would turn to the Bank of France for direct loans if the banks became too exacting in their rates. Cf. Philippe Simon, *Le Financement des entreprises* (Paris, 1961), p. 134.

permitted. Among informed observers, there is also a consensus that the typical small borrower did *not* borrow at the minimum rate permitted by the CNC, but paid something more to cover (alleged) higher risks (and costs). The critical question, of course, is *how much* more. The prevalence of a rate above the CNC minimum is not presumptive evidence of noncompetitive behavior in the small-borrower market. Most small borrowers do not have credit ratings of the highest order. To cover their higher risks and costs, they might have to pay more than the prime borrowers (i.e., more than the CNC minimum) even in a competitive market.[31]

The question that needs to be answered is whether the excess (over the official minimum rate) paid by small borrowers was just sufficient or more than sufficient to cover their (alleged) higher risks and costs— that is, whether the excess was due solely to bona fide risk and cost differences or also to the effects of a noncompetitive market structure. In the absence of the necessary statistics, it is not possible to answer the question directly, but it may be possible to do so indirectly. Whatever the level of the small-borrower rate, if the excess above the CNC minimum had been due solely to a risk (and cost) difference, a reduction in the official minimum rate, *ceteris paribus*, would have been associated with a comparable reduction in the new rate paid by small borrowers.

This last point is not clearly dealt with in the banking literature, but bankers and banking officials have stated (to the author in interviews) that there was a tendency for the small-borrower rate to fall by the same absolute amount as the change in the official minimum rate but that this was by no means invariably true. The issue seemed to hinge on the credit standing of the borrower. According to one loan officer, "A full reduction was automatic in the case of short-term credits for the high-grade borrowers, but it was neither automatic nor obligatory for borrowers of lesser standing." In other words, high-grade small borrowers tended to this extent to be treated like large borrowers;[32] others were not. However, according to another informant, even a very highly rated small borrower did not always get a rate reduction equal to the full reduction in the official minimum rate unless he protested to his banker. Indeed, even with a protest, he could not be sure that he

---

[31] The base rate for small borrowers is typically increased by various additional charges which are not asked from or are much less important in the full rate of the large customer. Cf. Laufenburger, cited in Patrice Grivet, *La Mobilisation des crédits bancaires en France* (Paris, 1962), p. 200, n. 9.

[32] Even with identical credit ratings, small borrowers might have had to pay higher rates to cover the banks' higher costs (per dollar of loan) of negotiating small loans.

would get the full reduction unless his case was very strong (i.e., he was an excellent credit risk) and unless he pressed the point with sufficient vigor and determination.

An hypothesis similar to that advanced for the large-borrower market can also account for the behavior in the small-borrower markets. According to the earlier hypothesis, any tendency toward competitive behavior (within limits authorized by the CNC) in the large-borrower market was not due to a competitive market structure but to the psychological prod of the overhanging authority of the government. It seems likely that this prod also operated in the small-borrower market but with much less force than in the large-borrower market. It was probably most effective for small borrowers of excellent credit standing (especially if they were sufficiently aggressive) and least effective for small borrowers of lesser credit standing. As the prime rate was normally equal to the CNC minimum rate, a change in the latter was a clear signal for a corresponding change in the prime rate. However, the loan rate for small borrowers (especially those of lesser credit standing) did not bear a precise relationship to the CNC minimum rate because it contains a risk premium which (however legitimate in principle) is in practice amorphous, ill-defined, and hard to measure. As a result, a change in the CNC minimum rate did not signal the need for a corresponding change in the small-borrower rate as clearly as it did for the large-borrower rate, and a banker who failed to cut the small-borrower rate by the full amount of a reduction in the CNC minimum rate would not have been as clearly vulnerable to the charge of opposing the CNC's wishes for lower loan rates as if he had failed to reduce the rates to borrowers of higher credit standing (for whom the risk premium was a less important part of the total loan rate).[33] It seems probable, too, that bankers were under less (and perhaps no) pressure from their small borrowers (especially those of lesser credit standing). Those borrowers do not consider themselves to be in the same orbit of comparison as the prime borrowers and probably would not have expected their loan rates to be cut by the same amount as the official minimum rate, which (as the CNC often stated) was intended to apply only to

---

[33] It is interesting in this connection to note the following observation, made in 1950 by the CNC, after it had taken a number of steps designed to reduce the level of bank charges to customers: "It is difficult to evaluate the exact measure in which the decisions taken in 1950 in the matter of bank rates have lightened the charges of firms having recourse to credit. One remembers, in effect, that the conditions decided by the CNC are minimum conditions below which the banks are forbidden to descend. The banking charges vary as a function of particular situations, and notably according to the value of the signature and of the risks run by the bank with respect to the operations they finance" (CNC, *Rapport annuel*, 1950, p. 17).

the best (riskless) borrowers. Moreover, they certainly do not have the same market mobility as the customers of higher credit standing, and this, too, probably held down protests from small borrowers (or made them less successful).

Minimum Rates and Competitive Loan Rate Levels

Since the CNC minimum loan rate was also the actual loan rate for prime borrowers, the next question to consider is whether the minimum loan rate (before it was abolished) was set at the level that would have prevailed in a purely competitive market. Clearly, if the minimum loan rate was already at a competitive level, prime loan rates (and, *a fortiori*, nonprime loan rates) could not be expected to fall below that level solely as a result of abolishing the minimum loan rate.

It is not possible to match the CNC minimum rate directly against a competitive rate because there has been no fully competitive loan market in France to serve as a standard of comparison. However, for the reasons set forth below, it is doubtful that the prime rate in France was always (if ever) equal to a purely competitive loan rate (taking as given all the other operating conditions of French banks and especially of the deposit rate controls) during the years of the CNC minimum loan rate. In other words, it is doubtful that the minimum loan rate at all times (if ever) covered nothing more than the actual costs and actual risks of prime borrower loans[34] plus a markup for "normal" (competitive) profits.

First, there is evidence that, at least at the outset, the CNC did not establish floor rates geared to prime-borrower risks. In one of its earliest actions, the CNC homologated the existing interbank agreements that had been formulated under the aegis of the Association Professionnelle des Banques. However, the base level of the *conditions de banque* in those agreements was set to cover (at least) the normal (i.e., average) risk which banks assumed. Thus, the conditions de banque which the CNC took over and homologated subjected borrowers with very little risk to a base rate that was geared to the banks' average risk.[35] In later years, the banks sometimes violated the official minimum loan rate for their prime borrowers,[36] and this, too, casts doubt on the probability of a purely competitive relation between the banks' risks (and costs) on prime loans and the CNC's minimum loan rate.

Second, there is not enough information available about bank costs—

---

[34] This analysis is expressed in terms of the prime loan rate because the prime rate was in fact equal to the CNC minimum rate and because the CNC intended the minimum rate to apply only to the best (least risk) customers and expected others to pay higher rates commensurate with their higher risks and higher costs.

[35] Cf. Aymard, *La Banque et l'état*, p. 105.

[36] Cf. Cauboue, *Le Chef d'entreprise et ses banquiers*, p. 54.

either variable costs or the allocation of fixed costs—to permit bank charges to be related to bank costs with precision.[37] Moreover, it appears that at least one important bank cost, the money cost, has been over-stated. This is implicit in the widely held view that, as the banks no longer have access to the *marché hors Banque*, they can no longer lend to their best customers at Bank Rate, much less below Bank Rate (as they sometimes used to do). Specifically it has been argued that a prime rate equal to Bank Rate would leave *nothing* over to compensate the bank for its operating costs and risks.[38] The pertinent question in the present context is not whether a prime rate equal to Bank Rate would cover *all* of a bank's costs, but whether it could cover *any* of the bank's operating costs and risks. In other words, is Bank Rate an appropriate measure of a bank's money costs for its total loan portfolio, as is implied in the preceding view? The answer depends on the amount and cost of bank borrowing at the Bank of France as compared with other sources of funds. While central-bank discounts are unquestionably important as a source of funds for French banks (especially in tight-money periods), they are far less important than customer deposits.[39] Under the circum-stances, it is particularly pertinent to note that the CNC's official ceil-ing rates on deposits have normally been below Bank Rate. Indeed, on sight deposits, the most important deposit category, the one-half per-cent ceiling rate (in first-category Paris banks) was far below Bank Rate (Fig. 5).[40] As the average money costs of banks (especially the large banks that are the natural suppliers of prime borrowers) have been below Bank Rate, a prime loan rate equal to Bank Rate could normally cover the banks' money costs and make some contribution toward cov-ering other bank costs as well. In this connection, it is pertinent to note that in January, 1965, the base rate used to determine the minimum loan rate was cut from 3.75 to 3.60 percent (as a result of a modifica-tion in the manner of figuring the rate rather than as a result of a change in Bank Rate) with the result that the minimum loan rate (including the .40 percent *commission d'endos*) on a commercial-paper discount fell to 4 percent, exactly equal to Bank Rate on that date.[41]

Third, the CNC sometimes miscalculated the minimum loan rates

---

[37] Cf. Ferronnière, *Les Opérations de banque*, p. 204.

[38] For a typical statement of this position, cf. *ibid.*, p. 248.

[39] For example, at the end of 1964, the volume of Bank of France rediscounts for the banks was approximately 12 billion francs, but the total deposits of the banks were more than 76 billion francs. Cf. Banque de France, *Compte rendu des opérations*, 1965, p. 42, and CNC, *Annexes au rapport annuel*, 1964, p. 148.

[40] At its meeting of June 28, 1967, the CNC reduced the ceiling rate on sight deposits to zero.

[41] Cf. Banque de France, *Compte rendu des opérations*, 1964, p. 30; and CNC, *Rapport annuel*, 1965, p. 120.

which were necessary to cover the costs and risks of prime borrowers. For example, in January, 1948, the CNC authorized the banks to raise their tariffs to cover their costs (including risks). Two years later, however, the Minister of Finance acknowledged that the increases had been predicated on expectations that were too pessimistic. In particular, he recommended a reduction in the rates on *engagements par signature* because they were "often too high in view of the risks run by the banks."[42] He also recommended a revision of the increase that had been granted on the commission d'endos, and following upon his letter, the commission d'endos was reduced from one-quarter percent per quarter (one percent per annum) to one-twentieth percent per month (0.60 percent per annum). However, since the commission d'endos had been compulsory even for prime borrowers, it is apparent that, before the reduction, the official minimum loan rate (including the compulsory commission) must have been more than adequate to cover the minimum risk of prime borrowers.

Finally, it is doubtful whether the CNC would have wanted to push the minimum loan rate to a purely competitive level for fear of jeopardizing bank solvency. It is true that the CNC generally exerted pressure on the banks (sometimes in the face of stiff banker resistance) to reduce their charges to customers, but that program was presumably carried out in conformity with the view that "If it is undeniable that they [French banks] ought to grant business reasonable terms, it is also clear that the economy of our country would have nothing to gain from a deficit administration of the banking apparatus."[43]

Minimum Rates and Unregulated Loan Rate Levels

For the abolition of the minimum loan rate per se to have the desired effect of leading to lower rates, it is necessary but not sufficient for the minimum loan rate to have been above competitive levels. In addition, the minimum loan rates had to be above the rates that would have prevailed in an unregulated loan market. Since the original purpose of rate regulation was to protect bank solvency by placing a floor under loan rates, it might appear that the regulated (minimum) loan rate was invariably above the level that would have prevailed in an unregulated market. However, there are a number of reasons for believing that, in the absence of an official minimum loan rate, the unregulated market rate would not have fallen below and might even have been above the CNC's minimum loan rate.

First, in order to protect depositors and bank solvency, the minimum

---

[42] Cf. letter of December 6, 1949, from Minister of Finance to governor of Bank of France and vice-president of CNC, in CNC, *Annexes au rapport annuel*, 1949, p. 39.

[43] Cf. CNC, *Rapport annuel*, 1950, p. 18.

rate had to be above a purely competitive level, but there is no necessary implication that it also had to be above the level of an unregulated
market rate. Moreover, while minimum loan rates may have originated
in a desire to protect depositors, they were subsequently employed by
the authorities as an instrument of monetary and economic policy, and
during most of the postwar period, the CNC sought to reduce loan rates
when possible.

Second, in pursuing its general policy of cutting the cost of bank
services to business firms, the CNC was not always constrained by the
banks' views about the appropriateness of proposed reductions; on
various occasions, the authorities pressed for rate reductions against
vigorous bank opposition. The last occasion was in 1965 (the last full
year of the minimum loan rate) when the banks strongly objected to
the action of the Bank of France in reducing T because of the adverse
effect on bank earnings and profits.[44] These experiences undoubtedly
contributed to the growing sentiment among realistic bankers that
they might be better off under a regime of unregulated loan rates than
under the "false protection" of the CNC's minimum loan rates.[45]

Third, the existence of an officially sanctioned minimum loan rate
provided bank borrowers with a psychological weapon of considerable
persuasive power in their dealings with bankers. As a result, many
borrowers, both large and small, were almost certainly enabled to negotiate lower loan rates with the banks than would otherwise have
been possible.[46]

Fourth, it is unlikely that an unregulated market rate would have
been a competitive rate, for as noted above, the market structure in the
large- as well as in the small-borrower markets is too concentrated to
ensure competitive behavior. Indeed, the CNC appears to have been
concerned that, in the absence of regulation, the loan rate levels would
have been higher than the authorities desired in terms of economic
policy. According to Berger, one of the dual objectives in regulating the
banking profession was "to prevent the banks from coming to understandings which would completely nullify any attempt by the Government to control the formation of the rates of interest on the short-term
money market."[47] In Berger's opinion, ". . . it may be asserted that such

---

[44] Cf. *Le Monde*, February 18, 1966, p. 2.

[45] Cf. *Economist*, November 20, 1965, pp. xxxii and xxxv.

[46] Cf. Pierre Berger, "Interest Rates in France," Banca Nazionale del
Lavoro, *Quarterly Review*, September, 1964, p. 278.

[47] *Ibid.*, p. 277. In this connection, cf. the CNC's 1952 statement that the
official measures (which the CNC had taken to reduce bank charges) "would
have no real effect except in the measure where the banks assure their loyal
application without looking for ways to paralyze their effect or to reduce
their impact by the play of private ententes" (CNC, *Rapport annuel*, 1952,
p. 13).

understandings, if not controlled, would undoubtedly have led to higher terms being charged."[48]

If, as seems likely, the minimum loan rate regulation held loan rates below the levels they might otherwise have reached, its abolition per se would not be cause for expecting lower loan rates.[49] In the official view, the abolition of the minimum loan rate is supposed to remove an obstacle to greater competition among banks, but this ignores the oligopolistic concentration in the short-term business loan markets in France. As a result of this concentration, the major banks are keenly aware of their interdependence. Before the CNC existed, the large banks had formed interbank ententes to prevent destructive competition. They cannot restore those prewar arrangements,[50] but they could approximate the effects of overt collusion by tacit collusion based on an oligopolistic rationale.[51] While this kind of tacit collusion is a possible, not a necessary, result in an oligopoly market, the authorities have made it more likely by authorizing the BNP merger and thereby raising the concentration in business loan markets. In short, the release of artificial restraints on bank rivalry cannot assure competitive behavior in such concentrated markets.

---

[48] Berger, p. 278. Berger concluded that "It seems certain, therefore, that, all things considered, the effect of regulation by the National Credit Council has been to lower the cost of credit." His view is based in part on the fact that deposit rates have been limited.

[49] In this connection, it is pertinent to note that some French experts do not expect more than a symbolic reduction of loan rates as a result of the "return to competition." Cf. *Le Monde*, February 18, 1966, p. 2. The CNC has also stated that it does not expect this reform to lead "automatically and in all cases" to lower loan rates. Cf. CNC, *Rapport annuel*, 1965, p. 21.

[50] There now exists a legal ban on consultation between bankers. Cf. *Economist*, November 20, 1965, p. xxxii.

[51] For an example of bank action taken after the abolition of the minimum loan rate but "which looks uncommonly like a cartel arrangement," cf. *Economist*, December 3, 1966, p. 1063.

XII

Competitive Regulations and Monetary Controls

The government implements its credit policy by regulating the volume, allocation, and terms of bank credit. It is the purpose of this chapter to discuss the major instruments of credit policy[1] and to show how the competitive controls functioned as an important and integral part of the set of monetary controls.

CONTROLS ON THE VOLUME OF BANK CREDIT

Rediscount Mechanism

The rediscount mechanism has been by far the most important of the traditional instruments (rediscounting, reserve requirements, open-market operations) by which the Bank of France has controlled the volume of bank credit. This is partly related to the importance of commercial-bill discounting in French banking practice; but it has also reflected the French banks' dependence on the discount window of the Bank of France—at the end of 1965, the volume of bank rediscounts at the Bank of France was almost 13 billion francs.[2]

The Bank of France has made extensive use of discount rate changes to influence the volume of rediscounts. Between 1946 and 1965, Bank Rate was changed eighteen times, and ranged from a low of 1.625 percent (at the beginning of the period) to a high of 5 percent (during a fourteen-month period between August, 1957, and October, 1958). However, in part because of conflicting policy objectives, the Bank of France has not relied exclusively on rate changes to regulate rediscounts.

At the end of the Second World War, when the government was pre-

---

[1] Each monetary control has been listed according to its primary effect on bank credit—volume, allocation, or terms; in a discussion of the use of competitive controls as monetary controls, the possible multiple effects of monetary controls have not been stressed.

[2] Banque de France, *Compte rendu des opérations*, 1965, p. 42.

occupied with the numerous problems of restoring a peacetime economy, two major objectives were to restore production and to avoid inflation. The former called for monetary ease; the latter, for monetary restriction. During 1947, Bank Rate (on commercial paper) was raised from 1.625 percent to 3 percent. The authorities became convinced, however, that manipulation of Bank Rate, within the range deemed acceptable, would not be sufficient to combat the inflation. Accordingly, on September 30, 1948, they began to regulate rediscounts by means of rediscount ceilings.[3] Under the new system, each bank was assigned a ceiling (*plafond*) on the volume of commercial paper that it could rediscount at the central bank.

The use of ceilings to regulate the volume of bank discounts was not new—some individual banks had been subjected to discount ceilings before 1948—but the postwar system had some novel features. The earlier ceilings had been imposed on medium-size and small banks but not on large banks (because they had no liquidity problems and did not rely much on the central bank). The purpose of the ceilings was also different: the earlier ceilings were imposed to limit the risks of banks;[4] the 1948 ceilings were explicitly intended as a monetary control.

The Bank of France soon encountered difficulties with the ceilings imposed at the end of September, 1948. The first difficulty was that the ceilings did not remain firm for very long: the Bank of France began to revise them as early as the second quarter of 1949; in the following year, it raised the ceilings again—by 25 percent between January and September, 1950.[5] The pressure for higher ceilings was two-fold. Because of their particular ceilings, some banks were placed at a competitive disadvantage vis-à-vis other banks, and the Bank of France tried to adjust the situation by raising the ceilings of individual banks. In addition, the Bank of France raised ceilings generally for all banks in an attempt to combat a slowdown in economic activity.

A second difficulty arose because the original directive had left some gaping loopholes. Perhaps the most serious was that the banks could ignore the ceilings completely in the case of medium-term credits which had been approved in advance by the Bank of France (and by certain specialized institutions). A third difficulty was purely technical. As a convenience, the original ceilings had applied to the volume of discounts that were outstanding at the end of the month, which permitted the banks to go above their ceilings between the end-of-month dates. In the beginning, the banks had no trouble in bringing their discounts

---

[3] Cf. "Communiqué du Ministère des Finances," CNC, *Annexes au rapport annuel*, 1948, p. 54.

[4] Cf. Philippe Aymard, *La Banque et l'état* (Paris, 1960), p. 41.

[5] CNC, *Rapport annuel*, 1950, p. 31.

down to the ceiling level by the end-of-month settlement date; as the practice grew, they could not have continued to do so without placing undue pressure on the short-term credit markets. To protect the latter, the Bank of France was obliged to bail out the banks, which it did by supplying through open-market operations the resources that had been denied at the discount window—by October, 1951, more than 150 billion francs in excess of official ceilings.[6]

In October, 1951, the authorities tried to improve the effectiveness of the ceilings by establishing new ceilings and enforcing them strictly. In an effort to set realistic ceiling levels, the authorities took account of the amounts which the central bank had in fact supplied to the banks in the preceding period, and also made provision for the larger amounts of credit which a growing economy required. As a result, the new ceilings for all banks together were increased by 500 billion francs.[7]

At the same time that the authorities were planning stricter enforcement, they were also making provision for the banks to borrow above their ceilings in the event of exceptional and temporary needs. This additional recourse, which was provided "en pension temporaire" at the Bank of France, was not strictly a discount operation.[8] The purpose, of course, was to introduce flexibility in the system; but to prevent abuses, the authorities prescribed penalty rates for the "en pension" arrangements: 2 percent above Bank Rate on amounts that exceeded the ceiling by less than 10 percent, and 5 percent above Bank Rate on amounts that were more than 10 percent above the ceiling.[9] The authorities hoped that the penalty rates would effectively limit bank borrowing, since the banks would be unable "in principle" to pass their higher money costs on to their customers[10] (presumably because customer loan rates were related to Bank Rate but not to the penalty rates).

Finally, to increase the effectiveness of the discount mechanism in regulating the volume of bank credit, the authorities introduced a new Bank Rate, T, in lieu of TB.[11] Since this change loosened the link between Bank Rate and the customer loan rate, it was expected that a change in Bank Rate would have a stronger effect on bank borrowing at the central bank. The rationale for this policy was similar to the rationale for the penalty rate; that is, it was presumed that a higher borrowing cost at the central bank (whether from a penalty rate or a

---

[6] CNC, *Rapport annuel*, 1951, p. 40.

[7] Cf. *ibid.*, p. 51.

[8] "En pension" (in pawn) arrangements are essentially repurchase agreements.

[9] In banking circles, the penalty rates were promptly dubbed "taux d'enfer" and "taux de super-enfer."

[10] Cf. CNC, *Rapport annuel*, 1951, p. 41.

[11] This change is discussed later in this chapter.

higher Bank Rate) would act as a deterrent to bank borrowing at the central bank, because the higher costs could not "in principle" be fully passed on to the customer.

Reserve Requirements

The French authorities have employed three major kinds of reserve requirements to influence the total volume of bank lending.[12] The first, which was instituted in September, 1948, required a minimum holding of treasury bills (called a *plancher*, or floor). This requirement, a companion measure to the rediscount ceilings, was expected to reinforce the ceilings by restricting the banks from liquidating short-term government securities (as they had already begun to do) to increase their supply of loan funds. The plancher was originally set at 95 percent of each bank's treasury bills on September, 1948; in addition, each bank was required to hold additional treasury bills equal to 20 percent of any increase in its deposits after that date.[13]

The plancher requirement was not entirely satisfactory. In the second half of 1951, for example, the Bank of France (with the Treasury's approval) had to allow certain derogations of the plancher requirement to help the banks meet their end-of-month ceiling requirements. This unsatisfactory state of affairs led to various reforms (e.g., the plancher had to be maintained on a daily rather than a monthly basis) which were taken in conjunction with the early attempts to enforce the ceilings on rediscounts.[14] In 1956, the plancher requirement was modified. When the requirement was introduced in 1948, the required treasury securities averaged 26 percent of the banks' liabilities; by mid-1956, the proportion had declined to 21 percent. To increase the effectiveness of the plancher, the authorities dropped the base date of September 30, 1948; after July 19, 1956, each bank had to maintain a minimum portfolio of treasury securities equal to 25 percent of its liabilities. This had the advantage of eliminating the interbank differences which existed under the original requirement, inducing the

---

[12] Another reserve requirement, the *coefficient de liquidité*, is not imposed for monetary control purposes, but it has a small monetary control effect. Under this control, the Banking Control Commission requires French banks to maintain in the form of cash or highly liquid assets (treasury bills, rediscountable commercial paper, etc.) at least 60 percent of their sight and short-term liabilities. Although this control is aimed at bank liquidity, its incidental monetary control effect is due to the fact that finance bills can be included only if they are rediscountable at the Bank of France. Cf. Bank for International Settlements, *Eight European Central Banks* (London, 1963), p. 163, n. 1.

[13] Cf. CNC, *Rapport annuel*, 1956, p. 42.

[14] Cf. CNC, *Rapport annuel*, 1951, pp. 40–42.

banks to reduce their lending to the economy—and easing (by 800 million francs) the Treasury's financing problems.[15]

A second reserve requirement, the *coefficient de trésorerie*, was introduced in 1960 in response to the new liquidity pressures generated by an improvement in the external balance. Together with other measures, the devaluation of the franc (at the end of 1958) had led to a rapid improvement in the balance of payments in 1959 and (at a reduced rate) in 1960. The result was a substantial increase in the economy's liquidity. In addition, the banks had significantly increased the total volume of their credits—the relative increase for the banks and the Bank of France was the largest since 1956.[16] In this context, the authorities were particularly concerned about the large volume of medium-term paper held by the banks, because that paper could be rediscounted at the Bank of France without the restrictions of the rediscount ceilings.

In October, 1960, the CNC decided to plug this loophole in the ceiling system by instituting a coefficient de trésorerie. Under this new control, each bank was required to maintain the volume of a specified list of assets—cash, deposits at the *chèques postaux* or at the Bank of France, treasury securities, and the portfolio of paper (principally medium-term paper) which could be rediscounted at the Bank of France without reference to the ceilings—equal to at least 30 percent of its deposits.[17] Although the purpose of the control was to restrain bank lending, the CNC did not anticipate that a 30 percent requirement would have an immediately restrictive effect. On the other hand, the imposition of the new reserve requirement made it possible, without risking a new expansion of bank credit, to reduce the plancher of required treasury securities. In view of the change in the Treasury's position, this was considered desirable. To give the banks time to adjust to the new requirement, the new control did not become effective until January 31, 1961.

The original 30 percent minimum level of the coefficient de trésorerie remained in force throughout 1961; at the beginning of 1962, the Bank of France raised it to 32 percent. The plancher of treasury securities, which had been reduced from 25 to 20 percent when the new coefficient de trésorerie went into effect, was further reduced in 1961 and 1962.[18] In 1963, the coefficient de trésorerie was raised from 32 to 36 percent, and the banks were instructed not to increase their total credits by

---

[15] Cf. CNC, *Rapport annuel*, 1956, p. 43.

[16] Cf. CNC, *Rapport annuel*, 1960, p. 10.

[17] Cf. *ibid.*, p. 11. For a more detailed description of the regulation, cf. *Annexes au rapport annuel*, 1960, pp. 12–14.

[18] Cf. CNC, *Rapport annuel*, 1961, p. 14; and *Annexes*, pp. 11–12.

more than 12 percent during the following twelve months.[19] The basic level of the coefficient de trésorerie was 36 percent in 1964 and 1965, and 35 percent in 1966.[20]

In an attempt to secure more direct and flexible control over bank lending, the CNC announced a major overhaul of the system of reserve requirements at its meeting of January 10, 1967: it eliminated the coefficient de trésorerie and the system of planchers and introduced a system of compulsory reserve requirements. Under the terms set by the CNC, the Bank of France can set the required reserves at a maximum level of 10 percent without having to refer back to the CNC. These reserves, which must be deposited at the Bank of France and will not earn interest, have been made compulsory for the popular banks and agricultural banks as well as for the banks under direct CNC control.

General Ceiling on Bank Lending

The system of rediscount "ceilings" and "floors" of treasury securities did not give the authorities as much control over inflation as they wanted. Accordingly, on February 7, 1958, they imposed an additional control in the form of a general ceiling on bank credits.[21] Under the new regulation, no bank was allowed to expand its total credits (both short-term and medium-term) beyond the arithmetic mean of its outstanding credits on September 30 and December 31, 1957.[22] An exception was allowed for new export credits: to stimulate exports, the banks could exceed the ceiling in the case of new export credits by an amount equal to 3 percent of the total credits on December 31, 1957.[23] To ensure compliance with the new regulation, the authorities decreed that any bank which exceeded its maximum credit volume would be penalized by a reduction in its rediscount ceiling.

Because of the effectiveness of this and other measures taken in 1958 (including a devaluation of the franc), the CNC was able to rescind

---

[19] CNC, *Rapport annuel*, 1963, p. 12. This was reduced to 10 percent in September, 1963.

[20] Because of seasonal variations in bank liquidity, it was two or three points lower in some months.

[21] Aymard has stated that this measure was taken under the pressure of external as well as internal developments—M. Monnet was in Washington to negotiate a loan, and the French authorities hoped that this measure of internal credit restraint would be accepted as evidence of their determination to attack their problems along orthodox lines. (Cf. Aymard, *La Banque et l'état*, p. 55, n. 17.)

[22] CNC, *Rapport annuel*, 1958, pp. 11, 29–30. The reason for using two dates was to reduce the chance of inequity to individual banks from the selection of any single date.

[23] *Idem.*

the general ceiling on bank credits as of February, 1959. On February 28, 1963, however, the banks were instructed not to let their total credits (in metropolitan France) increase by more than 12 percent between February 28, 1963, and February 29, 1964; at the same time, they were urged to give priority to credits for financing exports and productive investment. The 12 percent figure was reduced to 10 percent, as of September, 1963, and remained at that level until it was suspended at the end of June, 1965. Even after the control was removed, however, the banks were required to provide proof that they were being moderate in extending credit, and to continue to provide the central bank with monthly reports (for large banks) or quarterly reports (for others) on their loan activities.[24]

Open-market Operations

Although the Bank of France has been empowered to conduct open-market operations since June 17, 1938,[25] it has not employed that tool very much for purposes of credit control, but has used it to expand the credit-granting capacity of the banks and to supply them with the funds required for day-to-day balancing of their cash accounts.[26] The central bank makes its open-market purchases, which are confined by law to short-term securities, either outright or "en pension." At the end of 1965, the Bank of France held only 6.2 billion francs in securities as a result of open-market operations (including "pension" operations).[27] The comparatively unimportant role for open-market op-

---

[24] Cf. Banque de France, *Compte rendu des opérations*, 1959, p. 33; 1962, p. 27; 1963, p. 29; and 1965, p. 30. Although formally suspended, the regulation continued to be enforced at the request of the Minister of Finance. Cf. *Le Monde*, February 18, 1966, p. 2.

[25] The first open-market operations were undertaken in 1928 after the devaluation of the franc, but they were on behalf of other central banks. Cf. Michel Mitzakis, "Relations Between the Central Banks of France and the Benelux Countries and Their Respective Commercial Banks," in *Relations Between the Central Banks and Commercial Banks*. Lectures delivered at Tenth International Banking Summer School, Garmisch-Partenkirchen, September, 1957, p. 102.

[26] Cf. P. C. Dupont, *Le Contrôle des banques et la direction du crédit en France* (Paris, 1952), p. 320; and Henri Fournier, "The Problem of Controlling Liquidity in France," Banca Nazionale del Lavoro, *Quarterly Review*, December, 1960, p. 327. More recently, the role of open-market operations has begun to change. Cf. R. J. Truptil and H. Viaux, "Changes in French Banking," *Banker*, April, 1967, p. 320.

[27] Banque de France, *Compte rendu des opérations*, 1965, p. 42. Money-market transactions are shown on the Bank of France balance sheet as *"Effets négociables achetés en France."*

erations in France was, of course, one reason why the authorities sought other means to control bank credit.

CONTROLS ON THE ALLOCATION OF BANK CREDIT

In France, the allocation of bank credit is determined partly by the market and partly by government intervention.[28] The government intervenes both indirectly and directly. Indirect intervention, in a variety of forms, has been aimed at making it more attractive for banks to lend in the officially approved directions. In a system where many bank activities are regulated, one form of indirect inducement is to exempt a particular activity from regulation or to give it a preferred position in the control structure (e.g., granting new export credits a limited exemption from the general ceiling on bank credits imposed in 1958). Another form of indirect intervention also in favor of exports was the preferential discount rate, which has remained steady at 3 percent in spite of considerable fluctuations in the Bank Rate applicable to ordinary discounts, including the period (from mid-1957 to late 1958) when Bank Rate was 5 percent.

Throughout the postwar years, the government has also intervened directly, with measures which ranged from recommendations to strict supervision of bank loans, to influence the allocation of bank credit. In 1946, the governor of the Bank of France (and vice-president of the CNC) made a number of "recommendations" to the banks, including a recommendation that banks refuse credit to borrowers for a speculative build-up of inventories.[29] Subsequently, a *décision de caractère général* (January 9,1947) formalized the recommendations and brought bank loans under strict supervision, by requiring the banks to supply the Service Central des Risques with full details (including a justification) on all credit requests,[30] and to secure the Bank of France's prior approval (*accord préalable*) for all credits to borrowers whose total credits, whether from one or many banks, exceed a certain minimum amount.[31] Although the Bank of France was not required to explain its

---

[28] For a discussion of government intervention in other than the credit-granting process, cf. Jean-Paul Delcourt, "Means by which the State can Influence Economic Development under the Plan," in European Committee for Economic and Social Progress (CEPES), *French and Other National Economic Plans for Growth*, pp. 23–27.

[29] Cf. letters of February 7, 1946, and July 19, 1946, from governor of Bank of France to president of APB. CNC, *Rapport annuel*, 1946, pp. 178 and 179.

[30] There were certain exceptions. Cf. CNC, *Annexes au rapport annuel*, 1951, p. 35.

[31] The original minimum was 30 million francs. Cf. *Annexes au rapport annuel*, 1947, pp. 20–22.

decisions on requests for prior approval, its criteria were presumably the same as those contained in the CNC instructions to the banks. The banks were told to examine all credit requests from three points of view.[32] First, they were to evaluate the loan in terms of the traditional banking criteria of safety and profitability, and they were free to reject any borrowers who were unworthy by this test. Second, they were to judge the economic utility of the loan in terms of the CNC's social priorities—no credit for nonessential purposes (e.g., purchase of real estate or shares), and very high priority for loans for food production or for key industries. Third, they were to consider the borrower's need for funds—even firms in high-priority sectors had to justify their need for bank funds with convincing evidence that they could not raise the necessary funds outside of the banks; and all loans were to be for the minimum time possible.

The operations of the Service Central des Risques made it possible for the authorities to be informed about the amount of credit that was going to the different sectors; and the prior-approval requirement made it possible for them to allocate funds in accord with government policy. They were able to ensure the banks' cooperation with the government's credit allocation program by threatening to withhold the very valuable rediscounting privileges at the Bank of France.[33]

In their direct intervention to influence the allocation of credits, the authorities did not try to secure bank loans for particular firms—only for particular sectors. Although the banks were free to judge each applicant from a strictly banking point of view, the authorities urged the banks, in choosing between applicants who were otherwise equally acceptable by traditional banking criteria, not to prefer a well-known over a lesser-known applicant. The choice, the authorities stressed, was to be made on the basis of the applicants' economic utility, not their size.[34]

The precedent inaugurated in the CNC's early years for direct government action to influence the allocation of credit has been continued

---

[32] Cf. CNC, *Rapport annuel*, 1947, pp. 56–60.

[33] Cf. *ibid.*, p. 62.

[34] Cf. letter by governor of Bank of France, *Annexes au rapport annuel*, 1951, p. 40. The CNC subsequently made an investigation to find out whether the banks, under the pressure of limited resources and of the official steps taken in October, 1951, had neglected small and medium-size borrowers in favor of the most important borrowers. They concluded that this had not happened because the records of the Service Central des Risques showed a steady increase in the number of firms that received credit. They also inferred (from the increase in commercial-paper discounts) that large business firms were extending credit to small and medium-size business firms. Cf. CNC, *Rapport annuel*, 1951, pp. 43–44.

in later years as well—with instructions, requests, or recommendations to favor certain industries, to reduce credit to others, and so forth. Although some of the forms of intervention have not changed, the goals of intervention have been different at different times. In the early years, the government sought to guide the distribution of bank credit to counteract inflationary pressures (e.g., by preventing credit from going into speculative increases in inventories); in more recent years, the government has also used its influence on the allocation of credit to foster its program of economic development (e.g., by urging banks to grant loans for industrial decentralization, or to open new business firms in the less developed areas of the country).[35]

RATE CONTROLS AS MONETARY CONTROLS

The general monetary controls (described above) have all played a part in making it possible for the CNC to influence the terms on bank credit, but none of the monetary controls provided as direct and precise control of bank credit terms as the minimum loan rate regulation, which was originally designed as a competitive control.[36] As noted earlier, the minimum loan rate set by the CNC (between 1945 and March, 1966) became the actual rate for prime borrowers and even some nonprime borrowers.

Before the CNC existed, customer loan rates used to be set with reference to the Bank of France discount rate. In easy-money periods, private banks sometimes quoted their best customers a rate below Bank Rate—for example, TB minus one-half percent;[37] and the banks, in turn, negotiated that paper at still more favorable terms on the *marché hors Banque*.[38] During the CNC period, the practice of lending below Bank Rate was discontinued—minimum rates (including the compulsory *commission d'endos*) on *effets commerciaux* were above Bank Rate (except for a few months in 1965), and minimum rate on *découverts*

---

[35] Cf. *Annexes au rapport annuel*, 1962, p. 29.

[36] As noted earlier, the maximum deposit rate (another competitive curb) also influenced the terms on bank credit because low deposit rates supported low loan rates.

[37] Cf. Philippe Simon, *Le Financement des entreprises* (Paris, 1961), p. 134.

[38] That is no longer possible, and banks must now have recourse to the Bank of France. In the "marché hors Banque," established before the First World War as an interbank market outside the Bank of France, rates were below the discount rate of the Bank of France. For a discussion of the "marché hors Banque," cf. Pierre Cauboue, "The French 'Money Market,'" Banca Nazionale del Lavoro, *Quarterly Review*, December, 1955, pp. 189–199; cf. also Jacques Ferronnière, *Les Opérations des banques* (Paris, 1954), p. 248.

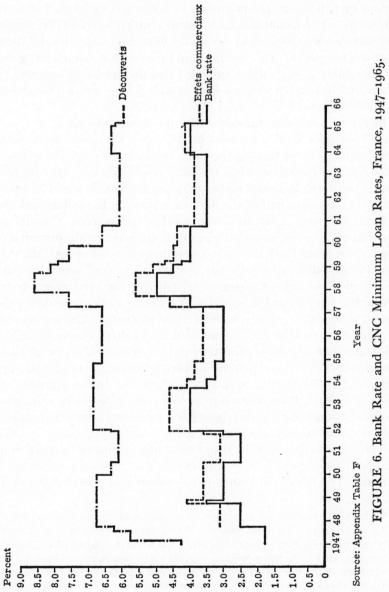

Percent

Découverts

Effets commerciaux
Bank rate

9.0
8.5
8.0
7.5
7.0
6.5
6.0
5.5
5.0
4.5
4.0
3.5
3.0
2.5
2.0
1.5
1.0
0.5
0

1947 48 49 50 51 52 53 54 55 56 57 58 59 60 61 62 63 64 65 66

Year

Source: Appendix Table F

FIGURE 6. Bank Rate and CNC Minimum Loan Rates, France, 1947–1965.

were well above Bank Rate (Fig. 6)[39]—but the CNC continued the earlier practice of adjusting minimum loan rates to changes in Bank Rate. Before 1957, however, the minimum loan rate was designated in absolute terms, which meant that each change required special CNC action, and that the correspondence between the minimum loan rates and Bank Rate was not perfect. This was changed by a décision de caractère général (December 2, 1957) which provided that the minimum loan rate be designated in relation to Bank Rate (e.g., TB + 3 percent) instead of in absolute terms.[40]

In the 1957 decision, the spread (for the découvert) was set at 3 percent. Two years later, a decision of December 17, 1959, introduced a new formula (T) for figuring the base. As noted earlier, the base T was to be equal to Bank Rate when the latter was between 3½ and 4½ percent; when Bank Rate was higher than 4½ percent, T would be equal to 4½ percent plus half of the difference between Bank Rate and 4½ percent; and when Bank Rate was less than 3½ percent, T would be equal to 3½ percent minus half the difference between 3½ percent and Bank Rate. Since Bank Rate was 4 percent at the end of 1959, the new base formula did not require any change in the minimum loan rate; also Bank Rate did not change. Nevertheless, the minimum rate on découverts was changed to accord with a change in the formula for the spread (from T + 3 percent to T + 2 percent).[41] The spread also changed whenever the fixed commission was changed—for example, the minimum rate plus minimum required commission d'endos on effets commerciaux was 5.10 percent before February 5, 1959, and 4.75 percent after February 5, 1959, as a result of a one-quarter percent reduction in Bank Rate and a 0.10 percent reduction in the minimum required commission d'endos (from 0.60 percent per annum to 0.50 percent per annum on February 5, 1959).[42]

The introduction of T in 1959 represented a further integration of the competitive control on loan rates into the framework of monetary controls. The minimum loan rate regulation had provided the CNC

---

[39] The CNC used to set minimum loan rates and commissions for many different kinds of short-term business loans; for convenience, Fig. 6 shows only the minimum loan rates on effets commerciaux ("bancables") and on découverts. In Fig. 6, the minimum rate on effets commerciaux includes the compulsory minimum commission d'endos; and the découvert rate includes the compulsory commission de découvert (one percent per annum till the end of 1949, and one-twentieth percent per month thereafter).

[40] Cf. CNC, Rapport annuel, 1957, p. 39, and Annexes, p. 24–25.

[41] Cf. Association Professionnelle des Banques, "Conditions de banque" (re-edition of December 17, 1959), p. 6.

[42] Cf. Décision de caractère général No. 59–02, February 5, 1959, in CNC, Annexes au rapport annuel, 1958, pp. 27–28.

with a considerable degree of control over the terms of bank credit both before and after the 1959 reform. In addition, however, the CNC sought, after the 1959 reform, to utilize the minimum loan rate mechanism to increase the effectiveness of Bank Rate as a device for influencing the volume of bank credit. Specifically, the authorities had hoped that, when Bank Rate rose above 4½ percent, the banks would be less willing to borrow from the central bank, not only because it was more costly but also because they would be unable (under the new system) to pass on to their customers the full amount of the increase in their cost of borrowing. Conversely, when Bank Rate fell below 3½ percent, it would behoove the banks to increase their customer loans, not only because it was cheaper for the banks to borrow at the central bank but also because they would not have to pass on to their customers the full reduction in bank costs.[43]

In 1963, the CNC once again changed the method of calculating the base to be used for determining the minimum loan rates. The CNC was motivated by the fact that the benefits expected from the 1959 reform had not been realized, and the CNC was looking for another way to increase the effectiveness of Bank Rate to influence bank borrowing from the central bank. The problem with the 1959 reforms was that, by 1963, Bank Rate had not moved out of the 3½ to 4½ percent range where the new rate T would become effective. As a result, the spread between minimum loan rates and Bank Rate had remained constant from 1959 to 1963. Moreover, the one-half percent increase in Bank Rate, which had been announced for November 14, 1963, would have brought Bank Rate only to 4 percent, and thus still within the insensitive inner bounds of the 1959 decision. To break the impasse and to secure the benefits which had been anticipated from a looser tie between Bank Rate and minimum loan rates, the CNC decided, only one week after Bank Rate was raised in November, 1963, to change the base on which minimum loan rates were determined. T would be equal to Bank Rate whenever Bank Rate was equal to 3½ percent; when Bank Rate was above or below the 3½ percent level, T would be equal to the arithmetic mean of Bank Rate and 3½ percent.[44] Under the new ruling, the Bank Rate increase from 3½ to 4 percent raised minimum loan rates one-quarter percent, and not one-half percent (as under the 1959 regulation).

The CNC's attempt to employ the minimum loan rate to influence the volume of bank borrowing at the central bank did not mean that

---

[43] In the CNC's view, this was equivalent to an increase of the commission d'endos. Cf. CNC, *Rapport annuel*, 1959, p. 32.

[44] Cf. CNC, *Rapport annuel*, 1963, p. 19.

it abandoned its long-standing interest in that device as a means of influencing the terms of bank credit. During the last year of its existence, the minimum loan rate was twice reduced—on January 28, 1965 (by a redefinition of T), and in April, 1965 (by a reduction in Bank Rate).[45] Finally, to remove a presumed obstacle to competition, the CNC abolished the minimum loan rate in March, 1966. It is not necessary to repeat here the earlier evaluation of the probable impact of this reform, but it is pertinent to recall that the implicit administrative pressure of the authorities appears to have been a critical factor in converting the minimum loan rate from a limit rate to an actual rate (at least for prime borrowers). The abolition of the minimum loan rate removed an important formal constraint on the freedom of bank action, but it did not alter the realities of the basic relationship between government and banks any more than it altered the market structure of short-term business loan markets. Under the circumstances, it remains to be seen whether the elimination of this formal control marks the end of the government's efforts to control the terms of bank credit, or whether it marks a transition from a more formal to a more informal method of control.

The competitive controls on deposit rates, like those on loan rates, have also been adapted to the needs of monetary and economic policy, especially to influence the flow of funds among financial institutions. During the banking reforms of 1965–1966, for example, the authorities deliberately manipulated the deposit-rate controls in this manner. As shown earlier, their goal was to improve the position of the commercial banks in mobilizing the public's savings in order to strengthen the banks' ability to finance more business expansion, as called for by the Fifth Economic Plan.

---

[45] Cf. Banque de France, *Compte rendu des opérations*, 1965, pp. 30–31; and CNC, *Rapport annuel*, 1965, p. 119.

Part Three
England

Part Three
England

XIII

Banking Structure in England

The English financial system, with its large and complex network of bank and nonbank financial institutions, is one of the most highly developed in the world. As a result, although this study is primarily concerned with the English commercial banks, it must take account of other financial institutions whose activities impinge on the primary activities (deposit and loan business) of the commercial banks. The most important are the *merchant banks, savings banks, building societies, hire-purchase companies,* and *discount houses.*

COMMERCIAL BANKS

Deposits and advances (especially for short-term business credit) are the two primary activities of the English commercial banks. Their deposit business is divided into current accounts (demand deposits) and deposit accounts (time and savings deposits). Deposit accounts are repayable on seven days' notice and generally there is no provision for other fixed maturities. At the end of 1965, gross deposits of the commercial banks were £10,622 million—52.1 percent in current accounts and 37.1 percent in deposit accounts.[1] In their loan operations, the English commercial banks (as a matter of policy, not because of any legal restraints) do not invest in industrial securities nor engage in long-term lending. This policy has been due to a persisting belief that it would be unsound banking and also to the fact that various specialized institutions have traditionally handled medium- and long-term credits for individuals and business firms.[2] In recent years, banker attitudes on this

---

[1] Bank of England, *Quarterly Bulletin.* The balance (£1,138 million) was in "other accounts" (credits in course of transmission, suspense accounts, and internal funds of the banks).

[2] Cf. Economic Intelligence Department, Westminster Bank, "Bank Liquidity—Control of Inflation," in Associazione Bancaria Italiana, *Papers and Proceedings of the First International Credit Conference* (Rome, 1953), II, 252–253; and John E. Wadsworth, "Banking Funds and Government Policy in Britain," *ibid.,* p. 210.

matter have somewhat relaxed[3]—the traditional preference of commercial bankers for short-term business lending of the "self-liquidating" variety[4] has been modified to include temporary finance, and under the pressure of declining demand for loans, "temporary" has been given an elastic interpretation.[5] In spite of these modifications, the main emphasis remains on short-term financing.[6]

Domestic Banks

At the end of 1965, there were 127 commercial banks with offices in England and Wales[7]—23 *domestic banks* and 104 *foreign and overseas banks* (Table 43).[8] The domestic banks (so classified because they mostly do a domestic banking business) are the *London clearing banks*,[9] the *Scottish banks, North Ireland banks*, and certain other banks (see note 8

---

[3] Cf. Sir Oliver Franks, "The United Kingdom Deposit or Clearing Banks," in Institute of Bankers, *The City of London as a Centre of International Trade and Finance* (London, 1961), pp. 76–77.

[4] As Sayers has noted, although the naïve theory of self-liquidating loans has been discredited, it remains true that the average banker is better qualified to appraise a short-term credit (which emphasizes the borrower's balance-sheet) than a long-term credit (which requires a forecast of the borrower's long-run earning power). Cf. R. S. Sayers, *Modern Banking*, 6th ed. (Oxford, 1964), pp. 185–186.

[5] Cf. R. S. Sayers, "The Concept of Liquidity in English Banking," in Associazione Bancaria Italiana, *op. cit.*, pp. 229–230.

[6] The Committee of London Clearing Bankers described this aspect of their business as follows: "The banks provide the credit which is needed to finance the short-term requirements of industry, trade and commerce and of private customers . . . only in exceptional circumstances do banks lend for other than short periods and then only to the extent of a limited proportion of their deposits. This is because current account bank balances are repayable by the banks on demand and bank deposit accounts at short notice and it is therefore necessary to maintain the utmost flexibility" (Great Britain, Committee on the Working of the Monetary System, *Principal Memoranda of Evidence* (London, 1960), II, 54 [cited as Radcliffe Memoranda]).

[7] Hereafter, references to England will (in the language of the Act of 1746–1747) be "deemed and taken to comprehend and include the Dominion of Wales."

[8] Table 43 excludes a few small banks which are not shown separately in official statistical sources. The excluded banks are C. Hoare and Company, Isle of Man Bank Limited, Lewis's Bank Limited, the English offices of the Royal Bank of Ireland Limited, Yorkshire Bank Limited, and the Banking Departments of the Co-operative Wholesale Society Limited and the Scottish Co-operative Wholesale Society Limited. Cf. Bank of England, *Quarterly Bulletin*, December, 1963, p. 288. Table 43 also excludes the Banking Department of the Bank of England—the official classification places it with the domestic banks (cf. *idem*)—because its deposit and loan business with private customers is a small and vestigial activity.

[9] In English banking literature, there is no uniform terminology to describe

above) whose United Kingdom business is concerned mainly with domestic banking.

The London clearing banks are the eleven banks which belong to the London Clearing House: Midland, Barclays, Lloyds, Westminster, National Provincial, Martins, District, Williams Deacon's, National Bank, Glyn Mills, and Coutts. These banks, with 89 percent of do-

TABLE 43

Distribution of Deposits Among Commercial Banks,
End of Year, 1965

Bank group	Number of banks	Deposits (million £)
Domestic banks		
London clearing banks	11	9,454
Scottish banks	5	962
Northern Irisha	7	206
Total domestic	23	10,622
Overseas banks		
British overseas and Commonwealthb	35	1,676
Americanc	9	1,432
Foreign banks and affiliatesd	20	523
Other overseas banks in United Kingdome	40	922
Total foreign and overseas	104	4,553
Total all commercial banks	127	15,175

a Includes all commercial banks operating in Northern Ireland except the National Bank (which is included with London clearing banks).

b Members of the British Overseas and Commonwealth Banks Association, except for British and French Bank Limited, which is included with foreign banks and affiliates. Cf. *Quarterly Bulletin*, September, 1961, p. 23, and March, 1966, p. 96.

c Members of the American Banks in London. Cf. *ibid.*, p. 96.

d Members of the Foreign Banks and Affiliates Association. Cf. *idem.*

e For names of banks included in this group, cf. *Quarterly Bulletin*, December, 1962, p. 268; December, 1964, p. 340; December, 1965, p. 397; March, 1966, p. 96.

SOURCE: Bank of England, *Quarterly Bulletin*.

the different bank groupings. "Joint-stock bank" in *Bar* used interchangeably with "commercial bank" (e.g., cf. Sayers, *Mod* ," *efe* *ng*, p. 18). In some cases, "joint-stock banks" or "commercial ba*kg* specifically to the London clearing banks (e.g., cf. Economic In*f ce* Department, Westminster Bank, "Bank Liquidity—Control of Inflat*n*," *op. cit.*, p. 233). In the Radcliffe Report, "joint stock banks" referred to the London clearing banks, Scottish banks, and Northern Irish banks; "commercial banks" referred to the preceding three groups, the foreign and overseas banks, and the merchant banks (including the accepting houses). Cf. Great Britain, Committee on the Working of the Monetary System, *Report* (London, 1959), p. 5 (cited as Radcliffe Report). Unless specifically noted otherwise, the present study uses the terminology shown in Tables 43 and 44.

mestic bank deposits (in 1965), are by far the dominant commercial banks in the country. Six clearing banks (Barclays, Lloyds, Midland, National Provincial, District, and Martins) have a national network of branches; two (Coutts and Glyn Mills) are London banks; one (Williams Deacon's) is largely a regional bank in Lancashire; and the remaining bank (National Bank Limited), which had many offices in Ireland until 1966, is included among the London clearing banks because of its offices in London and other important cities in England.

The five Scottish banks are the Bank of Scotland, Royal Bank of Scotland, British Linen Bank, National Commercial Bank of Scotland Limited, and Clydesdale and North of Scotland Bank Limited. All but one are under common ownership with London clearing banks. The Royal Bank of Scotland owns Williams Deacon's Bank and Glyn Mills and Co., Barclays owns the British Linen Bank, Lloyds Bank owns a substantial share in the National Commercial Bank (which has owned the National Bank Limited since 1966), and Midland Bank owns Clydesdale and North of Scotland Bank. In spite of this common ownership, the affiliated banks appear to operate independently. In particular, the Scottish banks that are owned by the London clearing banks are controlled entirely by Scottish boards—as one Scottish banker explained, "anything else would have inflamed Scottish opinion."[10] In their London offices, the Scottish banks observe the arrangements of the London clearing banks, but they follow a different cartel in their Scottish offices.

In Bank of England statistics, the Scottish banks are included among the "domestic banks," and with nine percent of domestic bank deposits (end of 1965), they are by no means a negligible part of the domestic banking system. They do not have much direct impact, however, on the deposit and loan markets in England. For historical reasons, Scotland has a separate banking system, and the English clearing banks do not operate in Scotland under their own names. Although the Scottish banks do maintain London offices and even have a few branches in the northern counties of England, the overwhelming majority of their 1,700 branches are in Scotland, and the Scottish banks consider that their primary business is t.. .rily r. banking services in Scotland. They maintain London offices pri City the convenience of their Scottish customers, and they maintain ces to facilitate access to the money market and the Bank of Eng [11] Accordingly, the Scottish banks have not been included among the domestic banks for the purposes of this study.

---

[10] Testimony of A. P. Anderson, general manager, British Linen Bank, representing the Committee of Scottish Bank General Managers, in Great Britain, Committee on the Working of the Monetary System, *Minutes of Evidence* (London, 1960), p. 339 (cited as Radcliffe Hearings).

[11] Cf. Radcliffe Memoranda, II, 69.

Although this study ignores their direct impact on the deposit and loan business in England, their indirect influence on English loan markets will be considered later in connection with the discussion of the impact of the London discount market on domestic loan markets.

The Northern Ireland banks (Table 43) are the members (other than the National Bank Limited) of the Northern Ireland Bankers' Association. The National Bank Limited is also a London bank, and its deposits (except the deposits of its banking offices situated in Northern Ireland) are included with the London clearing banks. Although the Northern Ireland banks are officially classified as "domestic banks," they have not been included among the domestic banks for the purposes of this study. They devote most of their resources to the service of customers in their own area, and they are a negligible part of the domestic banking system—less than two percent of the total deposits of domestic banks (end of 1965).

Foreign and Overseas Banks

The foreign and overseas banks are a heterogeneous grouping consisting of at least four subgroups (Table 43). The most important, the *British overseas and commonwealth banks*, comprises thirty-two African, Australasian, Canadian, and Eastern (Asian) banks. At the end of 1965, they held almost 37 percent of the London deposits held by the entire foreign and overseas bank category. The second most important subgroup, the *American banks* in London, held 31.4 percent of the deposits of the foreign and overseas banks.

For the most part, the foreign and overseas banks establish London offices to finance and service the trade between their own countries and the United Kingdom. Since London is a market and distributing center for raw materials and other commodities from all parts of the world, some of these banks use their London offices to service trade between their own countries and countries other than the United Kingdom. These banks generally do not poach on the domestic deposit business of the domestic banks,[12] and their London deposits are overwhelmingly

---

[12] Cf. memorandum from Canadian and Australasian members, Radcliffe Memoranda, II, 66–67. Cf. also the testimony of S. W. P. Perry-Aldworth, chairman, British Overseas Banks Association, London manager, Hongkong and Shanghai Banking Corporation: "We are really trying here to stress that we do not go out and try to compete with the clearing banks to get extra money" (Radcliffe Hearings, p. 327). The American banks in London have a gentlemen's agreement with the British banks not to scramble—they do not refuse local business, but they may not solicit it. Cf. Neil McInnes, "The Continental Touch," *Barron's*, November 28, 1966, p. 3.

of foreign origin.[13] The foreign and overseas banks also do not carry on much direct lending to borrowers for domestic purposes.[14] They do, however, lend through the back door by means of the funds they place with the discount houses. In addition, the American banks in London have not felt as constrained as other foreign banks to confine their business to overseas transactions. In their domestic business, however (whether in the deposit or short-term business loan markets), the foreign and overseas banks generally adhere to the agreements and understandings among the London clearing banks. Typical is this statement by the Canadian members of the British Overseas Banks Association: ". . . the London offices of the Canadian banks . . . consider themselves bound to conform with any agreements or conventions generally accepted by the domestic banks. . . ."[15]

MERCHANT BANKS (ACCEPTING HOUSES)

The merchant bankers originally were merchants who expanded beyond their regular commercial activities and provided a variety of financial services for their customers. As might be expected, the emphasis on the purely financial activities varies widely among the group of merchant bankers (most broadly defined). For the purposes of this study, the subset of particular interest is the group known as the *accepting houses*. This group places a strong emphasis on financial activities and especially, as their name suggests, on acceptance business.[16] The accepting houses provide short-term credit by "accepting" their customers' bills of exchange.[17] The "acceptance" of a well-known house enhances the negotiability of a bill of exchange and permits the customer to con-

---

[13] According to one banker, "At least 90 per cent of the London resources, i.e., deposits and branch funds, of a typical eastern bank are of overseas origin or association" (S. W. P. Perry-Aldworth, in Radcliffe Hearings, p. 326).

[14] On the other hand, one Canadian banker explained that "While the total of deposits and advances of U.K. residents may not be very large in relation to the resources of the London branches, U.K. residents are important to us as depositors and borrowers and do deal with us in a substantial way in respect of their overseas operations" (J. S. Rodgerson, London Manager, Canadian Bank of Commerce, *ibid.*, p. 318).

[15] Radcliffe Memoranda, II, 66.

[16] Several accepting houses also perform a number of financial services which are not covered in this study—issue business, trustee business, registrar and disbursing agent for companies, activities in the bullion market, investment counseling, etc.

[17] The Bills of Exchange Act of 1882 defined the bill of exchange as "an unconditional order in writing, addressed by one person to another, signed by the person giving it, requiring the person to whom it is addressed to pay on demand or at a fixed or determinable future time a sum certain in money to or to the order of a specified person or to bearer." Cited in "Commercial Bills," Bank of England, *Quarterly Bulletin*, December, 1961, p. 26.

43

vert it readily into cash through the mechanism of the discount market.[18] Although some acceptance credits are employed in internal trade, most acceptance business has traditionally been associated with the financing of overseas transactions. The accepting houses also grant some cash overdrafts in connection with commercial credit business.

In their deposit business, the accepting houses accept both demand and time deposits. Although accepting-house deposits tend to be held in a few large accounts,[19] the Accepting Houses Committee has stated that "the keeping of current accounts on which their customers draw by cheque is a substantial business for many of them."[20] Some deposit business is from ordinary users but most is an adjunct of the other financial services which they provide for customers. A substantial part of their deposits is owned by banks or other companies abroad.[21] In the past, the accepting houses did not try to attract a large number of current accounts from the general public;[22] more recently, they have made some efforts to broaden their clientele.[23]

The accepting houses included in this study are the members of the Accepting Houses Committee.[24] The committee came into being on August 5, 1914, when twenty accepting houses met in a hurriedly called meeting to decide on common policy in handling the problems of the moratorium which had been declared. For many years, the committee was housed in the offices of one of the accepting houses, which also provided its secretarial needs. In 1936, the committee took on a more formal existence and acquired its own office space and staff. At that point, the members considered whether they ought to have some rules or a constitution, but after discussion, they decided that "we could get on very well without any, and so have no written rules at all."[25] Although there are no written rules on the point, there appear to be at least two

---

[18] The overseas banks and (to a limited extent) the domestic banks also do an accepting business.

[19] Cf. J. Macartney-Filgate, "Merchant and Other Banking Houses," in Institute of Bankers, *The City of London as a Centre of International Trade and Finance,* pp. 89–90.

[20] Radcliffe Memoranda, II, 3.

[21] Sir Edward Reid, chairman, Accepting Houses Committee, and a managing director, Baring Bros. & Co., Radcliffe Hearings, p. 390.

[22] Cf. J. Macartney-Filgate, pp. 89–90.

[23] Cf. "Merchant Bankers on the Road," *Economist,* June 6, 1964, p. 1133.

[24] In 1964, the members of the Accepting Houses Committee were Baring Bros.; M. Samuel; Samuel Montagu; Hambros Bank; N. M. Rothschild and Sons; S. G. Warburg; J. Henry Schroder Wagg; Guinness, Mahon; Lazard Brothers; Morgan-Grenfell; Arbuthnot Latham; Wm. Brandt's; Brown, Shipley; Antony Gibbs; Philip Hill, Higginson, Erlangers; S. Japhet; Kleinwort, Benson. M. Samuel and Philip Hill announced their merger in January, 1965. Cf. *Economist,* January 16, 1965, p. 250.

[25] Sir Edward Reid, Radcliffe Hearings, p. 389.

minimum criteria for membership: (1) a substantial part of the house's business must consist of accepting bills to finance the trade of others, and (2) its acceptances must command the best rates in the discount market and be taken (i.e., be eligible for rediscount) by the Bank of England.[26] Although membership of the accepting houses Committee is not fixed, only four firms were elected to membership between 1940 and 1966. In 1965, there were sixteen members with total deposits of £1,030 million (Table 44).

SAVINGS BANKS

Post Office Savings Banks

The Post Office has offered savings facilities to small savers for more than one hundred years. Under the Act of 1861, which authorized the Post Office Savings Bank, the government provides deposit facilities for

TABLE 44

Distribution of Deposits Among Selected Financial Institutions, End of Year, 1965

Financial institution	Number	Deposits (million £)
Commercial bank		
Domestic	23	10,622
Foreign and Overseas	104	4,553
Accepting houses[a]	16	1,030
Savings banks		
Post Office savings banks	21,000 (offices)	1,822
Trustee savings banks	79[b]	2,030[c]
Other financial institutions		
Building societies	650 (approx.)	5,159[d]
Hire-purchase companies	16[e]	654
Discount houses[f]	12	111
Total		25,981

[a] Members of the Accepting Houses Association.

[b] With 1,374 branches at end of 1965.

[c] Includes both ordinary and special investments deposits.

[d] Includes both shares and deposits.

[e] Members of Finance Houses Association. They held about 90 percent of total hire-purchase company deposits.

[f] Members of the London Discount Market Association.

SOURCES: Bank of England, *Quarterly Bulletins*; Central Statistical Office, *Financial Statistics*; Central Office of Information, *The British Banking System* (London, 1964); *The Banker*, April, 1966; Whitaker (almanac), 1966.

[26] Radcliffe Memoranda, II, 3.

small savings and guarantees the deposits and any accrued interest. In keeping with its social purpose of encouraging thrift among small savers, the Post Office Savings Bank sets a ceiling on the amount it will accept from any depositor. The limit originally was an annual maximum of £30 and an overall maximum of £150. The overall maximum was subsequently raised to £5,000, but most accounts are far below this ceiling. In 1964, the Post Office Savings Bank had 21.7 million active accounts.[27]

The Post Office has paid an interest rate of 2½ percent per annum for a hundred years.[28] The first £15 of interest is exempt from income tax. The law requires the Post Office to repay a depositor within ten days' application; in practice, however, a depositor can get his money with not more than four days' notice, and £10 per day can be withdrawn on demand. This last provision has fostered a tendency (which the Post Office Savings Bank does not encourage and does not want)[29] for some depositors to treat their accounts like current accounts in paying household bills. During the Second World War, the volume of Post Office deposits rose rapidly—from one-half million pounds to almost two billion by the end of the war. This peak level was not maintained during the postwar years. Although the level has started to rise again, it had only reached £1.8 billion by the end of 1965 (Table 44). By law, these deposits must be invested in gilt-edged securities.

In mid-1966, the Post Office introduced investment accounts on which depositors with a minimum balance of £50 could earn higher interest rates than in their ordinary accounts. The investment accounts are held to a maximum of £5,000; they are subject to one month's notice of withdrawal; and interest is liable to income tax. The rate paid depends on the earnings of the deposits when invested by the Post Office; in mid-1966, the rate was 5½ percent.

Trustee Savings Banks

The *trustee savings banks* are even older than the Post Office savings banks. The trustee savings banks, which resemble the Post Office savings banks in many ways, were established in the early years of the nineteenth century by public-spirited men who "recognized the importance of individual thrift to the well-being of the community" and who

---

[27] In 1956, when the number of active accounts was similar to 1964, only 8.4 percent of the depositors had more than £300, and only 0.8 percent had more than £1,000. The former owned 59 percent of total Post Office deposits, and the latter owned 17 percent. Cf. Radcliffe Memoranda, I, 211–212.

[28] Cf. Radcliffe Hearings, p. 452.

[29] Cf. G. D. Frazer, Director of Savings, Post Office Savings Department, *ibid.*, p. 453.

wished to reduce the dependence of the poorer classes on the Poor Law.[30] The banks are quasi-governmental institutions, managed by local trustees and managers under the supervision of the government, which guarantees the security of the deposits and accrued interest. The Ordinary Department of the trustee savings banks operates much like the Post Office savings banks. In particular, individual depositors face a £5,000 ceiling; they earn interest at the rate of 2½ percent per annum— with no income tax on the first £15; and they can withdraw on demand all but large sums (for which a short notice is required). Business firms, even though small, may not hold these accounts. The funds collected by the Ordinary Department are invested by the National Debt Office in various government securities.

The Special Investment Department is available to any depositor who holds at least £50 in the Ordinary Department. The trustees of each bank determine investment policy, but within the constraints set by law—namely, government stocks; municipal stocks; various local authority mortgage loans; Commonwealth and Colonial stocks; stocks of certain water boards, of the Agricultural Mortgage Corporation, and of the Scottish Agricultural Securities Corporation. In the Special Investment Department the deposit ceiling is £5,000; the required withdrawal notice is at least one month, and as much as three or six months in some cases. The interest rate, which depends on the earnings of the Special Investment Department, has generally been much higher than the interest paid by the Ordinary Department. The rate varies from bank to bank; in mid-1966 the mean nominal deposit rate was 5¼ percent.[31]

The trustee savings banks have grown far more rapidly than the Post Office savings banks during the postwar period. By the end of 1965, the Post Office savings banks had not fully regained their peak levels of 1946, whereas the trustee savings banks grew from £670 million in 1946 to £2.0 billion by the end of 1965. The Ordinary Department of the trustee savings banks (which strongly resembles the Post Office savings banks) grew from £557.7 million to more than £1 billion[32] and the Special Investment Department grew from £112.6 million to the im-

---

[30] Radcliffe Memoranda, II, 77 and 80.

[31] Central Statistical Office, *Financial Statistics*.

[32] The number of active accounts in the Ordinary Departments more than doubled between the end of the Second World War and November, 1962, when they had reached 8,635,000. Cf. "The Other Branch Banks," *Economist*, June 29, 1963, p. 1368. At the end of 1963, there were more than one million accounts in the Special Investment Departments. Cf. Bank of England, *Quarterly Bulletin*, June, 1965, p. 141.

pressive sum of £996 million by the end of 1965. In 1965 (as noted later), the trustee savings banks were authorized to operate checking accounts for their customers.

OTHER FINANCIAL INSTITUTIONS

Building Societies

The first building society in England was established in Birmingham in 1775. The original building societies were cooperative, self-help organizations. Since they were intended to enable individuals to acquire homes by pooling their savings, they accepted funds only from prospective borrowers. During the middle years of the nineteenth century, the societies gradually changed in two ways which made possible their subsequent emergence as a major agency for mobilizing the public's savings and providing home mortgages: (1) they became established as permanent societies, and (2) they severed the link between savers and borrowers.[33] In spite of these changes, they did not grow much for many years. At the end of the First World War, there were 1,311 building societies with total assets of only £77 million. During the interwar years, their assets grew tenfold, even though the number of societies had been reduced by 27 percent. Growth slowed again during the war years, when their assets increased by £100 million. Substantial growth resumed after the Second World War, and total assets rose from £877 million in 1946 to £5.6 billion in 1965. This growth was also accompanied by a decline in the number of societies—from 874 in 1946 to 650 in 1965.[34]

Building-society deposits are far less important than their share accounts—in 1963, shares accounted for 93 percent of the combined total of shares and deposits in the building societies.[35] The law provides for a notice on small-deposit withdrawals and for a longer notice for large sums; there are similar provisions for share withdrawals, but notification is usually waived for small sums. In law, a depositor is a creditor, and a shareholder is an "owner" of a building society; but in practice the position of the two is very similar. However, since creditors can claim a legal precedence over owners, the deposit interest rate is usually one-half and occasionally one-quarter percent below the rate

---

[33] The Building Societies Act of 1874 conferred corporate status upon the societies.

[34] "The Financial Institutions," Bank of England, *Quarterly Bulletin*, June, 1965, p. 137.

[35] Computed from Central Statistical Office, *Annual Abstract of Statistics*, 1964, p. 316.

paid to shareholders. The rate of interest offered by the building societies is tax-free, because the societies pay the tax on behalf of their
depositors and shareholders.[36] Thus, the effective rate on building-
society funds is substantially higher than the nominal rate.

Each society is free to determine its own interest rate policy on shares
and deposits; in practice, they follow the rate structure recommended
by the Council of the Building Societies Association.[37] It is pertinent
to observe in this connection that, although there are several hundred
building societies, their resources are rather highly concentrated. In
1965, the largest (the Halifax Building Society)[38] held more than 16
percent of the total resources of all building societies,[39] the five largest
held almost 47 percent, and the eleven largest (each with assets in
excess of £100 million) held more than 62 percent of total building-
society assets. At the other extreme, 373 societies, each with less than £.5
million assets, had combined assets of only £52.5 million, or slightly
less than one percent of total building-society assets.[40]

The building societies are included in this study because of their
deposit and share business, not their mortgage lending activities. The
building societies very much prefer to attract the funds of small rather
than large savers. In part, this is because funds placed by large savers

---

[36] The income tax paid by a society is calculated as a "composite rate" representing an average of the income tax rate payable by all investors in all
building societies, and this rate is settled annually in discussion between the
Building Societies Association and the Inland Revenue. Cf. Radcliffe Memoranda, II, 18.

[37] This important fact was explicitly affirmed in testimony to the Radcliffe
Committee by the Building Societies Association: "The Council of the Association makes recommendations to members from time to time on the rates
which it considers should be paid to investors and charged to borrowers. These
recommendations are in no way binding upon members but they are, in
practice, generally followed" (Memorandum of Evidence Submitted by the
Building Societies Association, Radcliffe Memoranda, II, 20).

[38] For many years, the Halifax Society was not a member of the Building
Societies Association, but this appears to have been "for reasons of personal
incompatibility rather than anything more fundamental." Cf. Paul Bareau,
"The Financial Institutions of the City of London," *Journal of Institute of
Bankers,* October, 1961, p. 357. Thus, the rate policy of the Halifax Society
also tended to conform with the Association's recommendations. For an
example, cf. *Journal of Institute of Bankers,* August, 1960, p. 224. In 1964,
the Halifax Society joined the Association. *Economist,* December 26, 1964,
p. 1447. This left only 4 percent of building society assets outside of the
Association.

[39] Cf. Seymour J. Price, *Building Societies: Their Origin and History* (London, 1958), p. 562.

[40] *Stock Exchange Gazette,* May 13, 1966.

are more volatile in periods of credit restriction.[41] In addition, the special tax rate paid by the societies on behalf of their investors applies only to the interest on accounts of £5,000 or less; interest on larger accounts is taxed at standard rates. As a result, almost all societies limit the combined holdings of a husband and wife to £5,000. In competing for the savings of the public, the building societies regard the Post Office savings banks, various government securities, insurance companies, local authorities, trustee savings banks, and hire-purchase companies as their chief competitors.[42]

Hire-purchase Companies

The *finance houses* and the *industrial banks* which provide medium-term credit to consumers (for the purchase of consumer durables) and to business firms (for the purchase of various kinds of capital equipment) are known collectively as the hire-purchase companies. Although they are very active lenders in these areas, the hire-purchase companies are included in this study because of their deposit activities.[43] By far the most important hire-purchase companies are the finance houses.[44] Only the largest of the about 1,200 finance houses are members of the Finance Houses Association. At the end of 1962, the latter held more than 90 percent of all finance houses' deposits.[45] The smaller finance companies have a large number of small deposit accounts, whereas the deposit facilities of the large finance companies are aimed primarily at medium-size and large savers.[46] In the small companies, minimum acceptable deposits range from £5 to £100; in the large companies, the minimum might be £5,000 or more.[47]

Unlike the clearing banks, the finance houses accept deposits for varying terms (generally three or six months' notice),[48] and vary the

---

[41] Cf. testimony of Fred Bentley, a director of Halifax Building Society, in Radcliffe Hearings, p. 480. It has been reported that substantial sums from corporations account for no more than 2 percent of building society assets. Cf. *Economist*, December 26, 1964, p. 1447.

[42] Cf. Radcliffe Memoranda, II, 19.

[43] As noted elsewhere, consumer lending is not included in this study, and medium-term business lending is included only incidentally.

[44] The industrial banks have only a minor amount of deposits, and for convenience, their activities are not further considered in this study.

[45] Cf. "Sources of Funds of Hire Purchase Finance Companies, 1958–1962," in Bank of England, *Quarterly Bulletin*, December, 1962, p. 259.

[46] Cf. Percy Livsey, Radcliffe Hearings, p. 356.

[47] Cf. "Sources of Funds of Hire Purchase Finance Companies," p. 257.

[48] Most finance houses prefer deposits at six months' notice. Cf. P. J. Greaves, a director of North Central Wagon and Finance Co., Ltd., in Radcliffe Hearings, p. 356. However, the most popular term of such borrowing is probably three months, although a considerable amount is for terms up to twelve months. Cf. "The Financial Institutions," (n. 34 above), p. 141.

interest rate accordingly. All of the large finance houses offer about the same rates to depositors. Deposits are a major source of funds for finance houses—in a survey of 440 finance companies (including thirteen large companies with assets of £10 million or more), deposits accounted for more than half of their total funds (including capital and reserves).[49] This dependence on deposits is interesting because the hire-purchase companies originally went into the deposit business with great reluctance. Before 1947, they secured their borrowed funds primarily from the banks (in the form of overdrafts and acceptance credits), and they regarded their bank credits as "the most desirable form of borrowing in that they were flexible for coping with fluctuations in the flow of business and reasonably cheap."[50] They turned to direct solicitation of deposits from the public only when subsequent credit restrictions curtailed the flow from their customary sources.

Discount Houses

The discount houses occupy a special place in the English financial system. The famous London discount market consists of the twelve major discount houses—the members of the London Discount Market Association—and perhaps an additional twelve, consisting of minor discount houses, running bill brokers, exchange brokers, bullion brokers, and some stockbrokers who deal in money.[51] Historically, the discount market became prominent because of its commercial-bill business; at present, the discount houses are primarily underwriters and dealers in government securities. However, their commercial-bill business has not disappeared—at the end of 1965, they had £333 million of discounted United Kingdom bills[52]—and one minor reason for including the discount houses in this study is that they supply short-term business credit.

The discount houses are also involved in the deposit market. They accept deposits on a day-to-day basis and at seven days' notice, and they pay interest on the former as well as the latter. However, deposits are a

---

[49] Cf. "Assets and Liabilities of Hire Purchase Finance Companies," *Board of Trade Journal*, October 19, 1962, p. 787.

[50] Radcliffe Memoranda, II, 27. In this connection, Percy Livsey, managing director, Mutual Finance Ltd., testified that "For many years we borrowed from the joint stock banks, and it was a very happy relationship; we were only paying for money as we used it, and we had a feeling of security, and the banks knew just to what extent one was credit-worthy, and how far one should go. I am quite sure that it is the most satisfactory form of borrowing for our business" (Radcliffe Hearings, p. 355).

[51] Radcliffe Memoranda, II, 23.

[52] United Kingdom bills refers to bills drawn on United Kingdom residents but also includes treasury bills of the Northern Ireland government and refinanceable export credits. Cf. Bank of England, *Quarterly Bulletin*.

minor source of borrowed funds; almost all of their borrowed funds is call money from domestic and overseas banks. At the end of 1965, the member houses of the London Discount Market Association had total borrowed funds of £1,381 million; deposits were only £111 million. The deposit business of the discount houses is small not only in comparison to their own total funds but also (and this is more important) in comparison to total bank deposits.

Clearly it would not have been necessary to include the discount houses in this study solely for their business loan or deposit activities. However, they also perform certain other roles in the English financial system. In particular, they make an important contribution to liquidity management in the commercial banks because they stand ready to absorb any surplus funds from the commercial banks or to supply them with needed liquidity. Their role as suppliers of liquidity is made possible by their special relation with the Bank of England which permits them (but generally not the banks) to borrow at the Bank of England. Another important role is their special relation to the Treasury. Under this arrangement, the discount houses undertake to tender for the full amount of each week's issue of treasury bills. As will be shown later, the arrangements in connection with these activities of the discount houses have important implications for competition in banking markets.

XIV
Regulation of Bank Concentration

English governments did not undertake to regulate bank concentration until 1918. Even before that date, however, they had influenced the growth of bank concentration indirectly as a by-product of certain key pieces of banking legislation, especially the laws which regulated the legal form in which banks could be organized. Accordingly, it is convenient to divide this examination of the government's role in the growth of bank concentration into the periods before and after limited-liability banking was authorized in 1858.

BANK CONCENTRATION BEFORE LIMITED-LIABILITY BANKING

Private Banking Before 1825

The period before 1825 cannot, strictly speaking, be called the pre-joint-stock banking period because William and Mary had chartered the Bank of England as a joint-stock bank in 1694. That was, however, the only exception. Although some other banks were well-established institutions (some were more than a hundred years older than the Bank of England), the Act of 1708 made it necessary for them to remain private banks with no more than six partners. In this early period, the English banking system consisted overwhelmingly of small unit banks. During the eighteenth century, branch banking was extremely limited, not because of any legal prohibition of branch banking, but because the prohibition against joint-stock banking held down bank size. In addition, the development of branch banking was restricted by poor transportation facilities and the concentration of wealth.[1]

During the latter part of the eighteenth century, the number of banks began to multiply rapidly under the stimulus of rapid industrial and commercial expansion. It has been estimated that there were

---

[1] Cf. Joseph Sykes, *The Amalgamation Movement in English Banking, 1825–1924* (London, 1926), p. ix.

probably no more than a dozen country bankers in England (and Wales) in 1750. The number had risen to 230 by 1797, and to 721 by 1810.[2] However, in the ten years after the end of the Napoleonic War, the total number of banks declined, mostly through failures, from 940 to 542.[3]

The large number of bank failures was due to many serious weaknesses both in individual banks and in the banking structure:[4] (1) Many banks were run by nonspecialists as an adjunct of an ordinary commercial business. (2) Bankers were not regulated with respect to the quality and quantity of their assets, and many bankers were unable to achieve sufficient diversification. (3) The limitations on the number of partners made it difficult for many banks to secure adequate capitalization. (4) The public lacked reliable information on the condition of banks—the banks were not required to and did not publish their statements—and this often proved to be a fertile ground for rumor and speculation. (5) The banks had no system for mutual support in the event that one or more faced a run. Thus, even before the rise of joint-stock banking, weaknesses in the early banking system caused many bank failures and left many survivors vulnerable to the competition of the new banks.

Joint-stock Banking with Unlimited Liability

After the Banking Act of 1826 was passed, English banks entered a transition period which lasted for three decades. The new banking legislation terminated the Bank of England's exclusive privilege to engage in joint-stock banking and authorized the establishment of joint-stock banking without limit on the number of shareholders and with right of note issue. This liberalization was subject to two important restrictions: (1) the shareholders retained unlimited liability for the bank's debts, and (2) no joint-stock bank could be organized in London or within a sixty-five-mile radius of the metropolis. The new legislation favored the Bank of England not only by protecting its preeminent London position against encroachment by provincial banks but also by giving it the exclusive privilege of opening branches anywhere in the country. As a result of the new legislation, the Bank of England did open branches outside of London. In addition, joint-stock banks were organized in the provinces, and they, too, established branches in the major provincial cities. The momentum established by the 1826 act was signicantly accelerated by the Banking Act of 1833 which broke the

---

[2] Cf. W. F. Crick and J. E. Wadsworth, *A Hundred Years of Joint Stock Banking* (London, 1936), p. 13.

[3] Cf. Sykes, p. 123.

[4] Cf. Crick and Wadsworth, pp. 13–14.

Bank of England's London monopoly on joint-stock banking and authorized joint-stock banks to be established in London as long as they did not issue notes—and, by 1833, note-issue had ceased to be a serious consideration for the private banks in London.

As a group, the joint-stock banks were highly successful. In 1825 (just before joint-stock banking was authorized), there were 542 private banks and one joint-stock bank, the Bank of England. By 1841, the number of joint-stock banks had increased by 117, whereas the number of private banks had declined (through failure or merger with joint-stock banks) by 231.[5] In part, the private banks succumbed to weaknesses which had plagued them even before joint-stock banking was authorized. In addition, many private banks were overwhelmed by the joint-stock banks with their greater financial resources, their often superior management, and their aggressive competition (especially for business which the private banks had largely neglected: small traders, merchants, and manufacturers).

The reform legislation of 1844 abruptly interrupted the rapid expansion of joint-stock banking which the acts of 1826 and 1833 had set in motion. The problem of note issue was a primary concern of the Bank Charter Act of 1844 and many restrictive provisions against joint-stock banks were incidental to that primary concern. Thus, at least some of the restrictive provisions applied to the private as well as to the joint-stock banks. For example, the act forbade any bank to issue notes unless it had been authorized to do so as of May 6, 1844 (Article X);[6] it forbade even the latter to increase the volume of their notes in the future (Article XI); and it provided that any bank which was authorized to issue notes would permanently forfeit its right to do so if it became bankrupt or discontinued business (Article XII). Some restrictive provisions were applicable only to joint-stock banks. Specifically, a bank which was authorized to issue notes did not lose that right after a merger as long as the number of partners after the merger did not exceed six (Article XI). Similarly, if two private banks merged, the right of issue for the merged institution would be the sum of the issue rights for each separately as long as the total number of partners in the merged bank did not exceed six (Article XVI). On the other hand, in a merger between an issuing private bank and an issuing joint-stock bank, or between two issuing joint-stock banks, the right of issue for the merged institution would not be the sum of the issue rights of each

---

[5] Cf. Sykes, p. 1.

[6] For the original and current texts of the Bank Charter Act, 1844, cf. Hans Aufricht, *Central Banking Legislation* (Washington, 1961), pp. 230–250.

separately but only the issue rights of the absorbing bank.[7] Similarly, if a joint-stock bank with issue rights merged with either a private or another joint-stock bank which was located in London or in a sixty-five-mile radius, the merged bank lost the right to issue. Finally, if a provincial joint-stock bank opened a London office or within sixty-five miles, it lost its issue rights.

The sharp blow dealt to joint-stock banking by the Bank Charter Act of 1844 was reinforced by the restrictive provisions of the Joint Stock Bank Act of the same year. Whereas the former imposed restrictions on their expansion by merger, the latter imposed restrictions on their expansion by entry. In part because of these severe restrictions, and in part because of adverse economic developments which reinforced the legislative restrictions, the formation of new joint-stock banks virtually ceased for more than a decade.[8] The virtual cessation of new entry was a golden opportunity for the existing banks to extend their positions without having to face any additional competition. In the artificial shelter thus provided, the existing joint-stock banks made substantial progress both in the provinces and in London. By 1854, their progress in the capital was so impressive that the joint-stock banks were admitted to membership in the London Clearing House. This action, taken in recognition of an achieved position, also aided their further growth by facilitating the expansion of their increasingly important check business.

The years of sanctuary provided by the 1844 legislation came to a close when the Banking Act of 1857 repealed all provisions of the Joint Stock Bank Act of 1844; during the intervening years, however, the joint-stock banks had significantly improved their position vis-à-vis the private banks. In 1844, there were 208 private issuing banks and 72 joint-stock issuing banks; by 1857, failures and amalgamations had reduced the number of private issuing banks to 157, while 63 of the joint-stock issuing banks remained in existence. In short, although the

---

[7] This and the next two points mentioned in the text do not appear explicitly in the Bank Charter Act of 1844. They have been included here on the basis of Crick and Wadsworth, pp. 24–25.

[8] Although there is little doubt that joint-stock bank entry was drastically curtailed, there is some uncertainty about *exactly* what happened. According to the *Economist*, February 13, 1858 (cited in Sykes, p. 21, n. 1), "no new banks have been established since 1844. . . ." Sykes (p. 21) states that "only one new joint-stock bank was set up between 1846 and 1860." Crick and Wadsworth (p. 27) state that only three joint-stock banks were established during the decade following 1844 and that not more than ten attempted to establish themselves between 1844 and 1857. However, they also cite the Select Committee on Bank Act, 1857, Appendix 21, which suggests that the number was not ten but eight.

1844 legislation hindered the growth of concentration by placing some obstacles in the way of the joint-stock banks, it inadvertently fostered greater concentration by protecting the existing joint-stock banks against competition from new joint-stock banks.

BANK CONCENTRATION AFTER LIMITED-LIABILITY BANKING

Although the 1857 law removed the restrictive provisions against joint-stock banking, the feature of unlimited liability was retained. This remaining obstacle to large-scale banking was removed by three major pieces of banking legislation. The first, the Banking Act of 1858, authorized limited liability for banks, but did not extend limited liability to note issues, and retained the provision (originally enacted by the Joint Stock Bank Act of 1844) for a minimum bank share of £100. The Companies Act of 1862 removed these obstacles, and a period of bank mergers and promotion of new banks ensued, under limited-liability provisions. The Companies Act of 1879 gave another important boost to limited-liability banking. This legislation appears to have been inspired in part by a prominent bank failure (City of Glasgow Bank) in 1878. Before that failure, limited-liability banking had spread to many banks, but it was far from being universal. In 1874, for example, only 49 banks in England and Wales had limited liability, whereas 69 banks continued to operate with unlimited liability.[9] Before the City of Glasgow Bank failed, many bankers believed that unlimited liability was essential to retain public confidence; after the failure, they revised their thinking because the shareholders of the failed bank were called upon to pay as much as twenty-seven times more than their nominal shareholdings.[10] The legislation of 1879 sought to combine the protection which limited liability conferred on shareholders with the protection which unlimited liability was supposed to confer on depositors. The resulting law was a compromise which preserved the principle of limited liability but allowed for additional shareholder liability in the event of liquidation. Significantly, however, the law put definite limits on this additional liability.

1858–1918

The authorization of limited-liability banking made possible a significant increase in bank concentration. From the point of view of bank concentration, the period of limited-liability banking which began in

---

[9] Cf. A. M. Allen, *et al., Commercial Banking Legislation and Control* (London, 1938), p. 232, n. 1.

[10] Cf. Sykes, p. 38.

1858 can be divided into two parts. During the first period, 1858 to 1918, there were neither legal nor political barriers to impede the growth of concentration. The second period began with the Colwyn Committee Report of 1918 and extends to the present. The increase in concentration during the first period was impressive. In 1857, there were an estimated 400 banks in England.[11] By 1918, after sixty years of unrestrained merger activity, the number of banks had been reduced to 40.[12] There is a striking contrast in the rate of merger activity (relative to the banking population) before and after limited-liability banking was authorized. During the transition years 1826–1857, there were 153 mergers (Table 45), or an average rate of 5 mergers per annum; between 1858 and 1918, there were 373 mergers, or an average rate of 6 mergers per annum. However, since the total bank population fell sharply during the second period, the average annual number of mergers in each period as a percentage of the average banking population of that period was much higher in 1858–1918 than in 1826–1857.

After 1858, the nature of bank mergers also changed dramatically. In the period 1826–1857, joint-stock banks were the acquiring banks in 80.4 percent of all mergers, but a joint-stock bank was the acquired bank in only 11 percent of the mergers. Between 1858 and 1918, joint-stock banks were again responsible for almost 80 percent of the mergers, but a joint-stock bank was the acquired bank in 37 percent of the mergers during the period. This change in the composition of the merging banks reflected a change in the character and scope of the mergers. During the period from 1858 to 1918, there were many mergers of the mopping-up variety, but there were others in which large banks were merged to form even larger banks.

The permissive legal environment (limited-liability banking and no

TABLE 45

Merger Activity in English Banking, 1826–1918

| Period | Acquiring bank/Acquired bank | | | | |
| | Private | Private | Joint Stock | Joint Stock | |
	Private	Joint Stock	Joint Stock	Private	Total
1826–1857	30	0	14	109[a]	153
1858–1918	73	2	137	161	373

[a] Includes 17 bank mergers of unknown dates.

SOURCE: Joseph Sykes, *The Amalgamation Movement in English Banking, 1825–1924* (London, 1926), Appendix I, pp. 193–195.

[11] This rough estimate is an interpolation based on Sykes' statement that there were 429 banks in 1842 and 368 in 1870. Cf. Sykes, pp. 1 and 36.

[12] Cf. Report of the Treasury Committee on Bank Amalgamations (Colwyn Committee), reproduced in Sykes, Appendix III, p. 220.

barriers to merger) was a necessary but not a sufficient condition for the growth of concentration from 1858 to 1918. The driving force for the growth in concentration came from a number of other sources. The desire to achieve large size (partly for prestige) was one of the earliest motivations for bank mergers[13] and one of the most durable.[14] A large size was desired for reason of prestige, but especially for the economies which many believed to be associated with large size. Furthermore, especially during the later years of the period, many bankers thought that the concentration movement in industry necessitated an increase in banking concentration to serve large business firms. Some mergers of London banks and provincial banks were due to the provincial bank's desire for the prestige and convenience of a London office;[15] this was matched by the London banker's desire for provincial representation as an outlet for unused lending capacity in the London banks.[16] In addition, of course, many large banks wanted to establish a nationwide system of branches. This desire was often facilitated by the fact that some of the acquired banks were clear candidates for absorption—they were weak, mismanaged, or victims of fraud. The Baring crisis of 1890 and the events which followed also undermined many private banks. Some acquired banks were private banks which were vulnerable in a crisis because they lacked adequate reserves; others were simply unable to resist the attractive offers made by the large joint-stock banks. In part, the merger movement generated its own momentum—that is, the merger activities of the most active banks put pressure on others to undertake defensive mergers to maintain their relative positions. During the latter years of the First World War, some important mergers were spurred by the bank mergers that were taking place in other countries (especially Germany), and were part of the preparation for the banking opportunities that were anticipated for the postwar reconstruction period.[17]

By the end of the First World War, the merger activity had produced five branch banks of particularly impressive size: Midland, Barclays,

---

[13] This reason was mentioned in an 1869 merger. Cf. Sykes, p. 41.

[14] For example, cf. Sykes, p. 49.

[15] Owing to the growing importance of checks, those mergers were not seriously impeded by the restrictive provisions about note issue in the Bank Charter Act of 1844. It is interesting to note in passing that the Bank of England did not achieve a complete monopoly on note-issue until 1921, when the last private issuing bank lost its issue rights after it was acquired by a clearing bank. Cf. "The Note Circulation," Bank of England, *Quarterly Bulletin*, March, 1965, p. 39.

[16] Cf. Sykes, p. 48.

[17] Cf. Sykes, p. 74.

Lloyds, Westminster, and National Provincial. Westminster Bank was the only one of the Big Five which did not originate in the provinces. The National Provincial established itself in London by opening a branch; the other banks secured London offices as a result of mergers with banks already in the capital. Mergers played a critical role in the dominant size attained by each of these banks by 1918. One measure of this role is the large number of mergers involving the Big Five. In his 1926 study of bank mergers in England, Sykes attempted to trace the individual mergers which had led to the Big Five.[18] His investigation, compiled from all available sources, revealed 102 mergers for Barclays Bank between 1832 and 1918, 73 for National Provincial Bank between 1826 and 1918, 91 for Midland Bank from 1829 to 1918, 66 for Westminster Bank between 1826 and 1918, and 133 for Lloyds Bank between 1826 and 1918. These figures can only suggest the role of mergers in the growth of the Big Five by 1918. Information about some of the earlier mergers is not available, and there are difficult problems in trying to trace straight lines of development for banks which have been involved in many mergers and name changes over a long period. In addition, of course, the number of mergers is not a substitute for more detailed information about the size of the merging banks in each merger. The ratio of acquired branches to branches established *de novo* is one alternative way to measure the role of mergers in the growth of the Big Five. Table 46 shows this information for the Midland Bank between 1836 and 1919. Over the entire period, Midland Bank opened 537

TABLE 46

Midland Bank

Origin of Branches, 1836–1919

Date	De novo	Acquired	Closed
1836–1879	1	2	—
1880–1889	16	8	—
1890–1899	111	149	8
1900–1909	135	247	3
1910–1919	274	517	5
Totals	537	923	16

SOURCE: W. F. Crick and J. E. Wadsworth, *A Hundred Years of Joint Stock Banking* (London, 1936), p. 333.

[18] Cf. Sykes, Appendix II, pp. 196–214. Under the term "amalgamation," Sykes included "all agreements for fusion, irrespective of the individual circumstances governing each agreement: e.g., banks which were in difficulties or had actually failed are included" (p. 196).

branches *de novo,* but it acquired 923 branches by merger—a ratio of
about one-third offices established *de novo* and two-thirds acquired by
merger.[19]

1918—the Colwyn Committee and Restraints on Bank Mergers

By the end of the First World War, the enormous amount of merger
activity among English banks had resulted in considerable concentration among the remaining banks. The elimination of unit banks had
proceeded without opposition; but the growing concentration among
the remaining banks aroused a good deal of uneasiness, partly because
of the high levels of the concentration but also because of the changing
nature of the mergers at the end of this period. In many earlier mergers,
concentration had increased because unit and small branch branks were
incorporated into the branch network of large branch banks. There was
generally no serious public opposition to those mergers, because the
increase in bank concentration was gradual, and because attention was
usually focused on the advantages which were supposed to be associated
with large branch systems. During the closing years of the war, however,
several mergers took place between large banks which already possessed
sizable branch networks covering wide areas. Those mergers aroused
widespread fears that a money trust was in the making, and on March
11, 1918, the Chancellor of the Exchequer appointed a committee
(called the Colwyn Committee) "to consider and report to what extent,
if at all, amalgamations between banks may affect prejudicially the
interests of the industrial and mercantile community, and whether it
is desirable that legislation should be introduced to prohibit such amalgamations or to provide safeguards under which they might continue
to be permitted."[20]

The Colwyn Committee deliberations were a momentous event in the
history of the growth of banking concentration in England. For the
first time, an English government seriously considered whether to call
a halt to bank mergers. The committee considered the two main arguments in support of mergers by large banks. According to the first,
mergers served the convenience and needs of business by extending the
area of operation for branch banks; but the committee noted that this
argument could not justify mergers within London, and that the argument did not cover all mergers of large banks nor in the same degree.
According to the second argument, large banks could better accommodate the needs of large business borrowers; but the committee found
that the existing large banks were large enough to satisfy the needs of

---

[19] This ignores the sixteen closed offices.

[20] Treasury Minute dated 11 March, 1918, announcing the composition and
purpose of the committee. Reprinted in Sykes, p. 218.

REGULATION OF BANK CONCENTRATION   241

many large borrowers from existing resources. For the rest, they questioned whether large firms could not meet their needs by using two banks instead of one, or by having the banks form themselves into consortiums when necessary.

The Colwyn Committee very reluctantly[21] concluded that "some measure of Government control is essential." Although the committee believed that "the absolute *necessity* (sic) of large new amalgamations is not clearly proved," this was not the basis for their recommendation that the government ought to control future mergers.[22] Their recommendations were based on the conviction that "the possible dangers resulting from further large amalgamations are material enough to outweigh the arguments against government interference . . ."[23] The committee was particularly concerned about the danger that additional amalgamations might soon produce a money trust powerful enough to dominate in its transactions with private individuals and perhaps to impede the monetary policy of the Bank of England or the economic policy of the government itself.

To preclude this development (and the resulting demands for the nationalization of banking), the committee proposed legislation to require prior government approval for all future bank mergers. The committee did not propose that all mergers be prohibited—it did not object to mergers which absorbed small local banks, or which served the public interest by securing important new facilities for the public, or which significantly extended the geographical branch network of the acquiring bank. It did object to mergers of banks with branch networks in much the same areas, or to mergers which conferred "undue prominence" on the larger bank.

Although the recommendations of the Colwyn Committee did not lead to legislation, they led to an understanding between the commercial banks and the authorities that all future mergers would be submitted for the prior approval of the Treasury and the Board of Trade. During the 1920's, the view that "further amalgamation of banks would not be viewed with favor" was reiterated as government policy on various occasions.[24] Although this position had never been publicly repudiated by the government or monetary authorities of a later period, the National Board for Prices and Incomes reported to Parliament (in

---

21 "We should very much have preferred to avoid the necessity for any interference by Government with the administration of banking" (Sykes, p. 226).

22 In the committee's view "the absence of proof of the public necessity for business re-organisations is not, in itself, any reason for objecting to them, and it is a serious step at any time to interfere with the natural developments of trade" (Sykes, p. 223).

23 Sykes, p. 226.

24 "Big Seven into Big Five?" *Banker*, September, 1962, p. 581.

May, 1967) that "The Bank of England and the Treasury have made it
plain to us that they would not obstruct some further amalgamations if
the banks were willing to contemplate such a development. . . ."[25]

After 1918

The Colwyn Committee Report and the subsequent informal understandings between the banks and the Treasury about further mergers
did not mark an end to bank mergers. Between 1919 and 1924, there were
26 more mergers (16 between joint-stock banks and the balance between
joint-stock and private banks).[26] The 1918 agreements also did not
arrest the trend for a decline in the total number of banks.[27] As noted
above, there were 40 banks in 1918—34 joint-stock banks and 6 private
banks; by 1939, there were only 14 banks—12 joint-stock banks and two
private banks;[28] and by 1948, the number of joint-stock banks had
fallen to eleven (i.e., the clearing banks), and the other banks occupied
a negligible position alongside the clearing banks.

Although the number of banks continued to decline after 1918, a
few large banks had already achieved an overwhelming dominance in
English banking by the time the government decided to intervene in
the growth of bank concentration. Between 1884 and 1918,[29] the largest
bank's deposits[30] rose impressively from 7.5 to 20.5 percent of total deposits (Table 47). The largest bank's share continued to climb (more
slowly) to a level of 23.5 percent by the end of 1965. Similarly, concentration of deposits in the five largest banks had already reached 79.8
percent by 1918, and rose thereafter to 86.9 percent by the end of 1965.

---

[25] Cf. National Board for Prices and Incomes, *Bank Charges* (London, May,
1967), p. 53.

[26] Cf. Sykes, Appendix I, p. 195.

[27] It is difficult to be precise on this point because of the ambiguity in the
definition of a bank. Some enterprises were unambiguously banks but others
(especially some merchant banks) conducted a substantial commercial banking
business along with other activities.

[28] Cf. *Economist*, Banking Supplement, May 20, 1939; and criticism by
Thomas Balogh, *Studies in Financial Organization* (Cambridge, 1947), pp. 14–
16.

[29] The figures (in Tables 47 and 48) on the early (nineteenth century and
before) banking system are only suggestive because some of the earlier banks
did not issue statements and because of the ambiguity about the definition of
a "bank." Significantly, as late as the Radcliffe Committee Hearings, there was
no single published figure for the deposit liabilities of the British banks as a
group! Cf. Great Britain, Committee on the Working of the Monetary System,
Minutes of Evidence (London, 1960), pp. 293–294.

[30] Bank concentration was measured in terms of deposits rather than resources because figures for total resources of banks are not available.

The deposit share of the eleven largest banks increased from 36.7 percent in 1885 to 91.5 percent in 1918, and for all practical purposes, had reached 100 percent by 1938.

By 1918, a few large banks had also achieved a dominant position in terms of branches. Unlike the monetary authorities in many other countries, the Bank of England has never regulated entry, officially or unofficially. The clearing banks do not even have to notify the Bank of England about planned branch openings. Between 1884 and 1918, the total number of branches more than tripled. During the same period, the branches of the eleven largest banks (in terms of deposits) increased by more than ten times, and the branches of the five largest increased almost sixteen times (Table 48). To put it another way, the five largest banks held 16 percent of the total number of branches in 1884 and almost 83 percent by 1918; the eleven largest held 26.3 percent in 1884 and 94.2 percent in 1918. In short, the largest banks had achieved such an overwhelming dominance in the distribution of total branches by 1918 that, barring a merger among the clearing banks, there was little scope left for the largest banks as a group to increase their share of total banking offices. By the end of 1962, the largest bank held 21.8 percent of all branches; the five largest held 85.7 percent; and the eleven largest held (for all practical purposes) 100 percent.

For roughly three decades, the Big Five have held a combined share of approximately 85 to 87 percent of total bank deposits. This remarkable stability is due in part to the high level of the top group's share, but it is also due to the stability of the shares held by the individual banks. For this period of almost thirty years, eight of the eleven clearing banks each experienced a change of less than one percentage point in its share of total bank deposits, and two of the eight experienced no change whatever (Table 49). Among the three banks whose shares each changed by more than one percentage point (Barclays, Westminster, and National Provincial), Barclays gained almost five percentage points, largely at the expense of the other two.

By the conventional measures of bank concentration used above (i.e., percentage of London clearing bank resources held by the largest banks), there is a massive concentration[31] of banking resources in the Big

---

[31] For reasons explained earlier, the Scottish and Northern Ireland banks were excluded from the relevant banking group in all of these calculations. If they had been included in the domestic bank category, the Big Five's deposit share (1965) would have been 77.4 percent of total domestic bank deposits. (The figure for total clearing bank deposits includes the deposits in the Irish offices of the National Bank because there are no separate figures for the latter.)

TABLE 47

Commercial Bank Deposits, England and Wales, for Selected Dates, 1884–1965

A. Amount (in £000)

Bank (deposit size)	1884	1895	1904	1913	1918	1928	1938	1951	1965
Largest	32,231	44,124	56,164	93,834	334,898	394,591	457,000	1,321,000	2,224,700
2	27,007	37,628	50,693	91,512	266,808	352,157	419,000	1,270,000	2,010,400
3	24,335	28,638	47,673	85,395	262,858	335,081	397,000	1,170,000	1,666,700
4	16,364	25,514	44,394	67,882	239,382	294,087	343,000	865,000	1,252,000
5	13,564	16,051	36,392	60,806	200,865	290,310	310,000	806,000	1,064,900
6	11,432	15,505	34,237	43,199	47,867	82,933	100,000	314,000	465,500
7	9,823	14,808	29,049	41,260	44,530	52,255	83,000	239,000	328,300
8	5,989	13,959	28,492	39,224	31,779	32,221	38,000	139,000	162,600
9	5,586	13,453	27,155	37,583	26,347	22,097	36,000	77,000	147,300
10	5,474	13,446	16,351	25,917	21,650	19,578	36,000	76,000	68,000
11	5,417	12,808	15,438	21,063	19,245	18,069	21,000	48,000	63,300
Top eleven	157,222	235,934	386,038	607,605	1,496,229	1,893,379	2,240,000	6,325,000	9,453,700
All banks	428,296[a]	525,623	629,654	836,441	1,634,683	1,982,482	2,262,000[b]	6,325,000[c]	9,453,700[c]

B. Percent

Largest	7.5	8.4	8.9	11.2	20.5	19.9	20.2	20.9	23.5
Top five	26.5	28.9	37.4	47.8	79.8	84.0	85.1	85.9	86.9
Top eleven	36.7	44.9	61.3	72.6	91.5	95.5	99.0	100.0	100.0

a From W. F. Crick and J. E. Wadsworth, *A Hundred Years of Joint Stock Banking*, p. 34.

b Deposits of the eleven largest banks plus deposits of Union Bank of Manchester and Hoare. A few private or very small banks are not included. Cf. Thomas Balogh, *Studies in Financial Organization* (Cambridge, 1947), pp. 14–16.

c A few very small, specialized banks are not included in this total. Cf. Bank of England, *Quarterly Bulletin*, December, 1963, p. 288.

SOURCES: The *Economist*, Banking Supplement, October 18, 1884; October 19, 1895; May 20, 1905; May 23, 1914; May 17, 1919; May 11, 1929; May 20, 1939; June 7, 1952; and *London Times*, December 30, 1965.

Total deposit figures are estimated for the earlier dates. The basic data for those years have gaps and ambiguities because the line between commercial banking and merchant banking or other financial activities was not clearly defined, and because some banks (usually small private banks) did not publish any information.

In this table, Bank of England deposits (which the *Economist* included in Total Deposits for some years) were omitted from the figure for total deposits.

The National Bank is included in the table even though a great part of its business is in Ireland.

TABLE 48

Distribution of Branches, by Deposit-Size Ranking of Banks,
Selected Years, 1884–1962

A. Number of branches

Bank (deposit size)	1884	1895	1904	1913	1918	1928	1938	1951	1962
Largest	151	171	413	867	1,301	2,013	2,138	2,213	2,402
2	160	175	231	679	1,389	1,813	2,131	2,063	2,332
3	9	198	446	342	698	1,979	1,912	1,729	1,900
4	6	17	242	324	1,332	1,009	1,098	1,278	1,611
5	5	24	348	570	492	1,277	1,324	1,067	1,283
6	56	10	150	275	240	560	584	584	600
7	50	65	233	113	221	387	569	539	576
8	17	75	163	280	120	197	209	209	248
9	3	116	35	304	0	1	274	2	250
10	51	0	39	208	124	182	2	254	6
11	35	14	101	196	1	165	6	6	4
Top eleven	543	865	2,401	4,155	5,918	9,583	10,247	9,944	11,006
All banks	2,064[a]	2,677	4,426	5,792	6,285	9,595	10,247[b]	9,944[b]	11,006[b]

B. Percent of branches

Bank (deposit size)	1884	1895	1904	1913	1918	1928	1938	1951	1962
Largest	7.3	6.4	9.3	15.0	20.7	21.0	20.9	22.2	21.8
Top five	16.0	21.8	38.0	48.0	82.9	84.3	84.0	84.0	85.7
Top eleven	26.3	32.3	54.2	71.8	94.2	99.9	100.0	100.0	100.0

[a] Crick and Wadsworth, p. 34.
[b] A few small, specialized banks are excluded from the data.
SOURCES: See sources (and notes) for Table 47. For 1962, see *Economist*, June 29, 1963, p. 1379. The total number of branches is estimated for the earlier dates, and the data limitations mentioned in the notes to Table 47 also apply here.

Five,[32] and an even greater concentration when common-ownership links are taken into account.[33] The concentration of resources in the Big Five looks rather different when viewed against the total resources of all financial institutions that engage in either of the two principal activities (deposits or short-term business loans) of the commercial banks. The principal suppliers of short-term business credit are the London clearing banks, foreign and overseas banks, accepting houses, and discount houses. The combined deposits of the eleven clearing banks were 62.4 percent of this base (Table 50). The Big Five's deposit share was 54.2 percent of the total group (as compared with 86.9 percent of clearing bank deposits).

The principal suppliers of deposits are the London clearing banks,

TABLE 49

Concentration of Deposits Among London Clearing Banks,
1938, 1951, and 1965
(percent)

Bank	1938	1951	1965	Net change 1938 to 1965
1. Midland	20.4	20.9	21.3	+0.9
2. Barclays	18.7	20.1	23.5	+4.8
3. Lloyds	17.7	18.5	17.6	−0.1
4. Westminster	15.3	12.7	13.2	−2.1
5. National Provincial	13.8	13.7	11.3	−2.5
6. Martins	4.5	5.0	4.9	+0.4
7. District	3.7	3.8	3.5	−0.2
8. Williams Deacon's	1.7	2.2	1.7	0
9. National	1.6	1.2	1.6	0
10. Glyn Mills	1.6	1.2	0.7	−0.9
11. Coutts	0.9	0.8	0.7	−0.2
Totals	99.9	100.1	100.0	

SOURCE: *Economist*, Records and Statistics, June 7, 1952, pp. 425, 426; and *London Times*, December 30, 1965. Totals do not add to 100 percent because of rounding.

[32] There is also a high degree of concentration within the Big Five. The largest (in terms of deposits) is more than twice as large as the fifth, and almost as large as the fourth and fifth banks combined. Indeed, the Big Five are giant banks not only by English standards—the largest is almost 35 times larger than the smallest clearing bank—but also by world standards. In a 1963 list of the world's largest banks (based on total resources), the top three clearing banks ranked fourth, six, and tenth; and the two other clearing banks were twenty-second and twenty-seventh. Cf. *Stock Exchange Gazette*, June 14, 1963. p. 47. In 1965, however, their relative positions declined to sixth, tenth, seventeenth, thirty-first, and thirty-eighth respectively. Cf. *Stock Exchange Gazette*, June 17, 1966, p. 65.

[33] Common-ownership links raise the deposit share of the Big Five from 86.9 to 91.0 percent of total clearing bank deposits (1965).

foreign and overseas banks, merchant banks (Accepting Houses Committee), Post Office Savings Bank, trustee savings banks, building societies, hire-purchase companies, and discount houses. At the end of 1965, the deposit suppliers listed in Table 51 had total deposits of almost £25 billion. The Big Five held 33.1 percent of this total. Thus, on this base, the apparent concentration of resources in the Big Five is only 38 percent as large as it is when measured on the usual base of total clearing bank deposits.

Finally, it should be stressed that all of the concentration figures presented in this chapter refer entirely to the extent of concentration in the English banking structure (including alternative bank groupings). The discussion of market concentration in different banking markets is reserved for later chapters.

TABLE 50
Distribution of Deposits,
Principal Suppliers of Short-term Business Credit,
End of Year, 1965

Bank category	£ (millions)	Percent of total
London clearing banks	9,454	62.4
Big Five	8,219	54.2
Others	1,235	8.2
Foreign and overseas banks	4,553	30.0
Accepting houses	1,030	6.8
Discount houses	111	.7
Totals	15,148	99.9

SOURCE: Bank of England, *Quarterly Bulletin*; and *London Times*, December 30, 1965.

TABLE 51
Distribution of Deposits, Principal Deposit Institutions,
End of Year, 1965

Bank category	Percent of total deposits
London clearing banks	38.1
Big Five	33.1
Others	5.0
Foreign and overseas banks	18.3
Accepting houses	4.2
Post Office savings banks	7.3
Trustee savings banks	8.2
Building societies	20.8
Hire-purchase companies	2.6
Discount houses	0.4
Total	99.9

SOURCE: See Table 44; and *London Times*, December 30, 1965.

XV

Regulation of the Conditions of Bank Competition

THE BANK CARTEL

There are laws in England to regulate monopolies and restrictive practices in commerce and industry,[1] but none to prohibit restrictive practices or other anticompetitive agreements among banks. In the absence of legal barriers to collusion, the banks have openly formed a powerful cartel which regulates the conditions of bank competition. Although the government does not regulate the conditions of bank competition directly, it does so indirectly by giving tacit approval to the bank cartel and to the actions of the cartel.

At present, the main organ of the English bank cartel is the Committee of London Clearing Bankers,[2] an association of the eleven large banks described in the preceding chapters. The London Clearing Bankers Committee is a constituent part of the British Bankers Association, an organization which also includes the Scottish and Northern Ireland banks, Commonwealth banks with branches in the United Kingdom, Eastern Exchange banks, other British banks operating overseas, and a

---

[1] Two major pieces of postwar legislation are the Monopolies and Restrictive Practices Act of 1948, and the Restrictive Trade Practices Act of 1956. For a discussion of this legislation, cf. Michael Albery and C. F. Fletcher-Cooke, *Monopolies and Restrictive Trade Practices* (London, 1956).

[2] The first enduringly successful efforts to organize British banks were made in the final quarter of the nineteenth century. The Association of English Country Bankers was formed (as a result of the efforts of George Rae) in 1874 and remained in existence until the country banks which it was formed to represent had virtually disappeared from the English banking scene; the Institute of Bankers was founded in 1879; and the Central Association of Bankers came into existence in 1895. Cf. W. F. Crick and J. E. Wadsworth, *A Hundred Years of Joint Stock Banking* (London, 1936), pp. 427–428; and Joseph Sykes, *The Amalgamation Movement in English Banking, 1825–1924* (London, 1926), p. 149, n. 2.

few smaller British banks which do not belong to the London Clearing Bankers Committee. Although there are fifty-six banks in the British Bankers Association,[3] the Committee of London Clearing Bankers is easily the dominant member of the British Bankers Association, and normally the British Bankers Association has the same president and secretarial staff as the Committee of London Clearing Bankers.[4] In spite of the fact that the committee has no legal basis or executive power, it is the locus of whatever authority exists in British banking.[5] At its monthly meetings, which are informal and intimate, the members of the committee discuss matters of mutual interest to the banking fraternity, including issues of broad banking policy in which the monetary authorities have a direct interest. The authorities do not explicitly approve the committee's actions, but they are fully informed about its deliberations and decisions. Indeed, at least four times a year, the committee holds its meetings at the Bank of England, and the governor of the Bank of England is normally present at those meetings.

A key committee of the bank cartel is the Chief Executive Officers Committee of the London Clearing Bankers, consisting of certain senior general managers from each of the clearing banks. This committee, which also meets on a monthly basis, considers the entire range of practical banking problems which the clearing banks encounter in their regular operations. The recommendations of the Chief Executive Officers Committee are relayed for action to the Chairman's Committee. The decisions of these banker committees carry the greatest weight in British banking circles, which invariably follow a lead given by the Committee of London Clearing Bankers.[6] It should be stressed, however, that the effectiveness of the system relies entirely on the moral

---

[3] This is based on the 1961 figure. Cf. J. Macartney-Filgate, "Merchant and Other Banking Houses," in Institute of Bankers, *The City of London as a Centre of International Trade and Finance* (London, 1961), p. 86.

[4] Cf. Great Britain, Committee on the Working of the Monetary System, *Principal Memoranda of Evidence* (London, 1960), I, 5 (cited as Radcliffe Memoranda).

[5] This description is based on Sir Cecil Ellerton, then deputy chairman, Barclays Bank, "Relations Between the Bank of England and the Commercial Banks of the United Kingdom," in *Relations Between the Central Banks and Commercial Banks*, lectures delivered at the Tenth International Banking Summer School, Garmisch-Partenkirchen, September, 1957, p. 117.

[6] The cartel operates with a small central staff; yet, as the chairman of Barclays Bank (and chairman of the Clearing Bankers' Committee) once remarked, "I can't think of anything that we bankers would like to have got done that we haven't got done because of the present system." Cf. *Economist*, September 4, 1965, p. 900.

authority of the committees,[7] not on formal sanctions in the event of a violation of a cartel agreement.[8]

In sum, the bankers of the cartel have ample opportunities for mutual discussion, there are no legal obstacles to inhibit them from making agreements, and the cartel's deliberations and agreements receive the tacit approval of the authorities. In spite of its quasi-official position, the interbank cartel has chosen not to publicize many of its arrangements. In general, there is somewhat more public information on matters that are handled by formal bank agreements and much less information on matters that are arranged informally.

RATE AGREEMENTS ON BANK DEPOSITS

Current Accounts

At present, the clearing banks have an agreement not to pay interest on current accounts. This agreement was formally announced by the Committee of London Clearing Bankers on October 19, 1945, to be effective from November 30, 1945,[9] but the practice of not paying interest on current accounts began much earlier. According to King, "Efforts to solve the problem of deposit allowances were at first equally unsuccessful." However, ". . . by 1877 all the London banks had abolished all current account allowances."[10] Similarly, in his 1928 volume on the English joint-stock banks, Sykes noted that "Current accounts do not obtain interest in London and certain of the provincial districts."[11] The practice of paying interest on provincial current accounts had begun to decline even before the Second World War, but apparently this was not due to a formal agreement among the banks. During the Second World War, the banks agreed not to compete for deposits by means of interest allowances, and this agreement was continued after the war.

The formal agreement not to pay explicit interest on current accounts has been supplemented by additional agreements with respect

---

[7] This traditional system has been bolstered by many personal, social, and economic ties among prominent bankers—the so-called "old boy network."

[8] There is a similar situation in the London Discount Market Association. Cf. testimony of London Discount Market Association representatives in Great Britain, Committee on the Working of the Monetary System, *Minutes of Evidence*, (London, 1960), pp. 257–258 (cited as Radcliffe Hearings).

[9] Cf. "Notes on Recent Events," *Journal of Institute of Bankers*, January, 1946, p. 5.

[10] W. T. C. King, *History of the London Discount Market* (London, 1936), p. 290.

[11] Joseph Sykes, *Present Position of English Joint Stock Banking* (London, 1928), p. 48.

to service charges on current accounts[12]—for example, charges for some specified types of customers, for particular types of transactions, for the current-account transactions of the Post Office, government departments, and the nationalized industries, for the handling of trustee savings bank checks and credit transfers, and for the terms (known as "ICI" terms) extended to certain wage and salary earners (e.g., employees of public-sector bodies or of major firms in the private sector).[13] On the other hand, the clearing banks do not have a formal agreement on current-account service charges for the general run of depositors. Neither individually nor collectively do the clearing banks publish their scale of charges, and they do not even inform all of their customers about the basis for their charges. Each bank adopts its own guidelines for its branch managers. In general, the charge is set with reference to a stated proportion of the account's turnover or to some target cost per entry, and a rebate is imputed in line with the average size of the balance maintained;[14] the branch manager, however, generally has authority to adjust the charge to take account of a number of other features of the account which influence its present cost or prospective benefits to the bank.[15]

One result of the secrecy which surrounds the banks' service charges is that the banks are able to discriminate among their depositors; and in the opinion of the Jones Committee, "the net result may well be to favour the more powerful customer, who is disposed to bargain, as against the less powerful, who is not."[16] Another result is that, with respect to the general level of bank service charges, it is not possible to test whether (or to what extent) the absence of formal agreements may have been compensated by informal agreements or tacit understandings among the banks to limit interbank rivalry in this area.

Deposit Accounts

The cartel has formally set the rate of interest on deposit accounts since October 19, 1945, but English bankers had cooperated in deter-

---

[12] The clearing banks also have agreements on charges for services other than interest rates and commission on current accounts. Cf. National Board for Prices and Incomes, *Bank Charges* (London, May, 1967), Appendix IX (cited as Jones Report).

[13] Jones Report, p. 40

[14] The implicit rate on the rebate is normally slightly below the long-term average of deposit rates; but, as noted earlier, there is a collective agreement against paying interest on current accounts, and that agreement precludes any positive payments in connection with balances maintained. Cf. *ibid.*, pp. 72 and 40.

[15] Cf. *ibid.*, pp. 40–41, and Appendixes VI and VII.

[16] *Ibid.*, pp. 45–46.

mining deposit account rates long before that date. Some of the earliest efforts at cooperation were inspired by the aggressive competitive behavior (including deposit-rate competition) which gave the joint-stock banks their early success. The early arrangements to bring this competitive activity under interbank control broke down. On May 6, 1866, however, Bank Rate was raised from 2 to 3 percent, and the banks reacted by widening the margin on their London deposit allowances to 1½ percent under Bank Rate. This pattern then became the general rule, unless Bank Rate fell to 2 percent or rose above 5 percent, in which case the margin became 1 and 2 percent respectively.[17] The level of deposit rate was held at Bank Rate minus 1½ percent until 1920.[18] In 1921, the London clearing banks adopted the figure of 2 percent under Bank Rate.[19] At that time, the agreement among the banks applied only to London deposits at seven days' notice, but the agreement did not preclude higher rates when a longer withdrawal notice was required.[20]

The cartel agreement among the banks was strengthened during the Second World War. While the prewar cartel agreement took care of the rates on deposit accounts in the Greater London area, there was no agreement to cover deposits (including current accounts) in the provinces, and rates were not uniform throughout the country. During the 1930's, for example, the London time-deposit rate was set at one-half percent but one percent was probably usual on country deposits.[21] During the war, the banks agreed not to attract deposits from each other by means of higher rates, and this agreement was carried over into the postwar period. In October, 1945, the banks agreed to fix the rate on deposit accounts at one-half percent, subject to fourteen days' notice of withdrawal.[22] These terms were to apply to the operations of all branches (with minor exceptions in certain parts of the provinces) in all parts of the country. Under the 1945 agreement, the clearing banks also agreed not to offer special rates for varying terms of deposit. This action was taken because the banks were underloaned (compared with

---

[17] Cf. King, *History of the London Discount Market*, p. 299.

[18] Thomas Balogh, *Studies in Financial Organization* (Cambridge, 1947), p. 90.

[19] Sykes, *Present Position of English Joint Stock Banking*, p. 37.

[20] Seven days was the usual period for bill-broker loans, and the banks wanted their deposits to be fixed for the same period as their large loans. Cf. Luther A. Harr, *Branch Banking in England* (Philadelphia, 1929), pp. 217–218. Sykes (*Present Position of English Joint Stock Banking*, p. 115) suggests that the longer period referred to more than a fortnight.

[21] A. C. L. Day, *Outline of Monetary Economics* (Oxford, 1960), p. 185, n. 2.

[22] "Notes on Recent Events," *Journal of Institute of Bankers*, January, 1946, p. 5.

the prewar period), and feared that higher deposit rates would lead to higher loan rates in the banks.[23]

At present, the cartel establishes a rate for deposit accounts for seven days' notice and (with minor exceptions) does not permit higher rates to be paid for deposits fixed for longer periods. The cartel reviews the deposit-rate agreement whenever Bank Rate changes, and a change in Bank Rate is a signal for the Committee of London Clearing Bankers to convene promptly to decide what change if any to make in the deposit rate.[24] Since 1955, the deposit rate has been two points below Bank Rate.

In his testimony to the Radcliffe Committee, a banker who represented the Committee of London Clearing Bankers explained why the deposit rate was linked to Bank Rate: "It has not always been tied exactly to two percent under the Bank Rate; there have been occasions when it has differed. But tying it to Bank Rate seems to work well. We must have some rate which we will pay on deposit, and that rate must control our lending rate, because, with overheads as they are, we have to have a given margin. It is related to the Bank Rate because, I suppose, the Bank Rate is the fundamental rate of the country."[25]

INTEREST RATES ON BANK ADVANCES

English banks extend credit in the form of loans or overdrafts.[26] The overdraft arrangement became more prominent after joint-stock banking was introduced into England, but the bill of exchange was still the most important instrument in domestic trade in the last quarter of the nineteenth century. The overdraft however, had some important advantages which encouraged its wider use—for example, the overdraft rules about repayment were more flexible than those applied to the bill system; also, many traders did not like to have their names appear as borrowers on bills which were circulating in the market. The decline of the bill system was also due to industrial mergers, which reduced the occasions for bill financing, and to the development of the check mechanism, which was far superior to the bill of exchange as a means of transmitting funds (one of the uses of bills of exchange). By the early part of the twentieth century, the bill of exchange was no longer much used in domestic trade;[27] by the '20's, the overdraft system had become quite

---

[23] Radcliffe Memoranda, II, 54.

[24] *Ibid.*, p. 50.

[25] Testimony of D. J. Robarts, Radcliffe Hearings, p. 289.

[26] In recent years, the banks have begun to charge a commitment fee when granting an overdraft. Cf. "Levering up Bank Lending Charges," *Banker*, September, 1964, pp. 552–553.

[27] Cf. W. F. Crick and J. E. Wadsworth, *A Hundred Years of Joint Stock Banking*, p. 337.

general in the provinces; and it was becoming more popular in London, too; at present, the overdraft is by far the most common form of bank advance in English banking practice.[28]

Rate Structure on Advances

There is a lot of *unofficial* information about rates on advances, but as Day has remarked, "No *firm* information was (or is) published about the interest rates charged on advances. . . ."[29] Although several years have passed since the Radcliffe Committee made its plea for more published statistics on bank operations, there is still no official series on loan rates. The Bank of England's *Quarterly Bulletin* reports current information about short-term money rates, including the London clearing banks' call-money rate and deposit account rate, but nothing whatever about the clearing banks' rates on advances.

Much of the unofficial information about the banks' rate policy on advances is based on the published statements of informed observers. According to one such observer, "The cartel agreements on this side are mostly comparatively recent, and are much less comprehensive and clearcut than they are over deposit accounts."[30] According to another, "Overdraft rates are a matter for individual banks themselves to arrange with their customers."[31] The Committee of London Clearing Bankers did not even mention the cartel in describing (to the Radcliffe Committee) the mechanism for determining advances rates: "Rates charged on loans and overdrafts are arranged on a formula agreed with customers establishing generally a stated margin above Bank Rate subject to a minimum. Neither the margin nor the minimum is uniform; they vary with the type of borrower and the lending risk. The rate automatically changes with the change in Bank Rate unless the minimum rate is applicable. On occasion borrowing rates may be changed by mutual agreement between bank and customer in appropriate circumstances."[32] In spite of such authoritative statements that make no reference to the cartel's role in the determination of advances rates, it is generally accepted that "The market for commercial bank credit in Britain has long been an artificial one, with rigid *lending rates fixed by agreement* . . ."[33]

In November, 1951, when the authorities decided to restore the use

---

[28] This is common knowledge, but it is not possible to demonstrate the point statistically, because loans and overdrafts are not shown separately in the regular advances series of the Bank of England, *Quarterly Bulletin*.

[29] *Outline of Monetary Economics*, p. 178 (my italics).

[30] "More Competition in Banking," *Banker*, February, 1964, p. 81.

[31] Sir Cecil Ellerton, *op. cit.* (n. 5 above), p. 113.

[32] Radcliffe Memoranda, II, 50.

[33] Cf. *Economist*, June 30, 1962, p. 1328 (my italics).

of a flexible Bank Rate as an instrument of monetary policy, the members of the bank cartel met to decide upon a common policy on advances. According to press reports,[34] the arrangement which the clearing banks devised at that time distinguished four main classes of borrowers: nationalized industries and similar institutions, top-grade industrial and commercial companies, smaller companies and business concerns, and personal borrowers.

The nationalized industries and others whose debts are guaranteed by the government have paid the most favorable rates. In the immediate postwar years,[35] when Bank Rate was 2 percent, the nationalized industries usually paid from 3 to 3½ percent. When Bank Rate was raised from 2½ to 4 percent on March 11, 1952, the new cartel agreements (which had been arranged after the change of November, 1951) came into effect. They provided that loan charges to this group should in general be a matter of negotiation between banker and borrower, but in some instances, existing arrangements provided for an automatic link with Bank Rate. In January, 1958, a representative of the clearing banks told the Radcliffe Committee that the rate to the nationalized industries was Bank Rate (7 percent) with a minimum of 3 percent.[36] In April, 1959, when Bank Rate was 4 percent, a Treasury official stated that "The rate charged [on advances to nationalized industries] is Bank Rate or 4 percent, whichever is higher . . . but if Bank Rate fell to a very low level the formula would probably be renegotiated with the banks."[37] Since Bank Rate has not fallen below 4 percent since that time, there has been no opportunity to discover how low the minimum advances rate might go under easier credit conditions.

The minimum rate for the second category of borrower—a group the Radcliffe Committee characterized as "exceptionally credit-worthy private borrowers"—was probably 4½ percent during the '20's, and it may have been 4 percent during the '30's. After the March, 1952 increase in Bank Rate (and pursuant to the November, 1951 cartel agreement), these borrowers were charged one-half or one percent above Bank Rate, without any minimum. In the banker testimony (cited above) to the Radcliffe Committee (in 1958), it was reported that these borrowers paid one-half percent above Bank Rate, but there was still no mention of a minimum for this group. Toward the end of 1964, however, it was re-

---

[34] This and the other references in this section to the November, 1951, cartel agreement are based on the report in *Financial Times*, March 14, 1952.

[35] This and other information in this section on lending rates during the 1920's, '30's, and '40's is based on Day, *Outline of Monetary Economics*, pp. 178, 185–186, and 192.

[36] Testimony (January 24, 1958) of D. J. Robarts, Radcliffe Hearings, p. 277.

[37] Testimony of W. Armstrong, a Third Secretary of H. M. Treasury, in Radcliffe Hearings p. 931.

ported that the banks had taken action to protect themselves against future reductions in Bank Rate by increasing the agreed minimum rates, and that the new minimum for large blue-chip companies was to be $4\frac{1}{2}$ percent "rather than $3\frac{1}{2}$ percent or 4 percent as hitherto."[38]

The third category of borrower, with by far the largest number of borrowers, consisted of ordinary commercial borrowers with a very good but not exceptional credit rating. Five percent was their absolute minimum throughout the boom period of the '20's, the depressed years of the '30's, and during the war years as well. When Bank Rate was raised in March, 1952, this group usually paid (in keeping with the November, 1951 cartel agreement) 1 percent above Bank Rate with a minimum of $4\frac{1}{2}$ percent. In 1958, this group paid Bank Rate plus 1 percent with a minimum of 5 percent.[39] Toward the end of 1964, the minimum rate for this category was raised to $5\frac{1}{2}$ percent.[40]

The fourth category of borrower encompassed most personal borrowers and probably marginal business borrowers as well.[41] In March, 1952, this group was charged 1 percent above Bank Rate with a minimum of 5 percent, but it was generally recognized that this relatively favorable treatment was likely to be temporary. Even at the time, it was widely anticipated that those rates would soon be raised to $1\frac{1}{2}$ percent or some wider margin over Bank Rate, with a minimum of $5\frac{1}{2}$ or even 6 percent.[42] In March, 1958, when the ordinary commercial borrower was paying one percent over Bank Rate, marginal borrowers were paying between one and a half and two percentage points above Bank Rate.[43] In the 1964 rate revisions, the minimum for this group was raised to 6 percent or more.[44]

In 1964, the cartel began a complete overhaul of the rates charged on advances; and the changes were largely completed by 1965. The

---

[38] Cf. *Economist*, August 22, 1964, p. 743; and "Levering up Bank Lending Charges," *Banker*, September, 1964, p. 553.

[39] Robarts, in Radcliffe Hearings, p. 277.

[40] Cf. *Banker*, September, 1964, p. 553.

[41] In the 1951 rate agreements, smaller companies were placed in the third category of borrowers, and personal borrowers in the fourth category. (Cf. *Financial Times*, March 14, 1952.) In a 1958 report, the *Economist* referred to the state boards, blue-chip companies, good "average" borrowers (including some personal borrowers), and marginal borrowers. Cf. *Economist*, March 22, 1958, p. 1060. In its report for the 1964 rate agreements, the *Economist* placed personal borrowers with "other good business customers" and reported that marginal borrowers consist mostly of small business, rather than personal, customers. Cf. *Economist*, August 22, 1964, p. 743.

[42] *Financial Times*, March 14, 1952.

[43] *Economist*, March 22, 1958, p. 1060.

[44] Cf. *Economist*, August 22, 1964, p. 753; and *Banker*, September, 1964, p. 554.

TABLE 52

Cartel Loan-Rate Agreements, Mid–1967

Type of customer	Rate charged	Details
Nationalized industries (with Treasury guarantee)	Bank Rate with minimum 4 percent	Some lending is at Bank Rate plus ½ percent, reflecting the use of funds advanced in hire-purchase business
Local authorities Building societies Insurance companies Other first-class industrial and commercial borrowers	Bank Rate plus ½ percent with minimum 4½ percent	The "blue-chip" rate
Hire-purchase companies	Bank Rate plus 1 percent with minimum 6 percent	Minimum rate
Export loans (guaranteed by E.C.G.D.)[a]	(i) Bank Rate, minimum 4½ percent (ii) Fixed rate of 5½ percent	For loans up to 2 years For loans for 2–15 years (subject to 1 percent commitment fee to cover whole term)
Other industrial and commercial borrowers and all private customers	At discretion, but above the "blue-chip" rate	

[a] Export Credit Guarantee Department.
SOURCE: National Board for Prices and Incomes, *Bank Charges* (London, May, 1967), p. 36.

cartel's principal loan-rate agreements (mid-1967) are shown in Table 52, on the basis of information provided in the Jones Committee Report.[45] The table contains five groupings of borrowers, but one stipulates a rate for a particular industry (hire-purchase companies), and another sets a special rate for a special kind of loan (export loans with Export Credit Guarantee Department guarantee).[46] Thus, the present agreement is based on three main classifications of borrower: nationalized industries, prime ("blue-chip") borrowers, and other industrial and commercial borrowers and all private customers (a composite of the former third and fourth categories of borrower). As a result of the changes begun in 1964, the spread in rates between the borrower categories has been widened. The "blue-chip" rate remained at one-half percent over Bank Rate; but many customers who were previously charged 1 percent over Bank Rate were increased to 1½ percent over, and many others to 2 percent over. In addition, the new agreement raised minimum rates and extended the practice of levying commitment fees.[47]

Loan Rates to the Discount Market

The cartel formally sets the minimum rate on call loans to the discount market, and it has been doing so for decades. In order to conduct their business in commercial and treasury bills, the discount houses secure funds (in the form of call loans) from the clearing banks and others. The clearing banks are by far their most important suppliers— for example, at the end of 1965, they supplied £849 million out of total borrowed funds of £1,381 million. The clearing banks make different kinds of loans to the discount houses. The "regular" money (also known as "basic" or "good" money) is nominally on a call basis, but "this balance is rarely disturbed except in time of dire need."[48] The money which is truly on a call basis is the "day-to-day" money. The banks also lend on an overnight basis, but "overnight" money must be repaid in the morning, and it is not renewed.[49] Unlike the volume of regular money, which tends to be rather stable, the volume of overnight money fluctuates from day to day. Another kind of loan is "privilege" money, which originated as an accommodation to the discount houses to enable them to meet calls from American sources after the hour at which they could have recourse to the Bank of England. At present, the discount

---

[45] Jones Report, p. 36.

[46] This special rate was due to the special mediation of the Bank of England. Cf. *ibid.*, p. 37.

[47] Cf. "How the Banks Compete for Deposits," *Banker*, July, 1967, p. 583.

[48] Radcliffe Memoranda, II, 24.

[49] Cf. Balogh, *Studies in Financial Organization*, p. 127.

houses use privilege money solely to balance their books. By agreement with the various clearing banks, they can borrow a small additional amount for this purpose at the end of the day, but it must be repaid on the next business day. The volume of privilege money is small—not more than £5 million for the entire discount market.[50]

The "basic rate" (i.e., the minimum rate of regular money) is set by the cartel, not by the market. By long-standing tradition, the cartel changes the basic rate whenever Bank Rate is changed. The traditional hour for announcing a change in Bank Rate is at 11:45 on a Thursday morning—occasionally, the Chancellor of the Exchequer has made the announcement in the House of Commons after banking hours—and before the end of the day, the chief executive officers of the Committee of London Clearing Bankers will have met to settle the range of rates to be applied to loans to the discount market.[51] The cartel sets the basic rate with reference to Bank Rate—since November 20, 1958, at Bank Rate minus $1\frac{5}{8}$ percent—and necessarily also with reference to the deposit rate. Since 1958, basic rate has been three-eighths percent higher than the deposit rate (and privilege money has been one-half percent over basic rate).

In the banking literature, the cartel rate on call loans to the discount market is usually described as a minimum rate; at least for part of the regular money, it is also the actual rate.[52] The balance of regular money is loaned at a somewhat higher rate.[53] Except in times of very easy money, the "basic rate" is usually below the rate on day-to-day money (which varies with monetary conditions).[54] The reason the cartel sets a loan rate that is generally below the market rate is imbedded in the origins and historical development of cartel activity in this market. The cartel agreement to set a minimum rate on call loans to the discount market originated (apparently with official encouragement) after the First World War. According to one view, the agreement was part of a

---

[50] Cf. C. W. Linton, "Commercial Banks and the London Discount Market," in Institute of Bankers, *The London Discount Market Today* (London, 1962), p. 43.

[51] Radcliffe Memoranda, II, 50.

[52] Cf. *Economist*, Banking Supplement, June 25, 1955, p. 2.

[53] Cf. H. F. Goodson, "The Functioning of the London Discount Houses," in *London Discount Market Today*, p. 23. There are no figures published on the division between the amount of regular money that is loaned at the basic rate and the amount that is not; but it has been suggested that the amount loaned at the basic rate is related to the average weekly bill requirement of the banks concerned. Cf. Linton, p. 43.

[54] In very easy money periods, the average rate on funds that the discount houses borrow from overseas, foreign, and merchant banks may fall below the clearing banks' basic rate, but none of the clearing bank money is ever loaned below basic rate. Cf. Radcliffe Memoranda, II, 24.

program to develop a market for treasury bills. Although treasury bills were introduced in 1877, they were not used much until the First World War. Between 1914 and 1925, the authorities encouraged the agreements because they wanted "to develop the market's appetite for short-term debt and believed that extremely orderly (if not dragooned) short-term markets alone could assure the necessary flow of funds into the Treasury."[55] According to another view, the agreement originated after 1925, in order "to underpin sterling when [England] went back to the gold standard."[56] The return to gold at the unrealistic prewar parity aggravated the unemployment and balance-of-payments problems which had existed since the end of the war. This presented the authorities with a conflict of goals: they wanted to avoid a high level of interest rates in order to combat the unemployment, but they needed a high level of rates to protect sterling. The Bank of England tried to resolve the conflict by forcing open-market rates closer to Bank Rate without provoking an undue increase in Bank Rate. The cartel agreement was an integral part of this plan. By agreeing to hold the basic rate close to Bank Rate, the cartel could also set a floor to the treasury bill rate, since the discount houses would not buy treasury bills at rates below their borrowing cost at the clearing banks. In short, whether the authorities encouraged the cartel agreement on call rates to sell treasury bills or to underpin sterling after the return to gold, it gave them greater control over the level of market rates, which they hoped to stabilize between an upper limit of Bank Rate and a lower limit of the cartel rate on call money.

The cartel's minimum rate on call loans was probably Bank Rate minus 1 percent during much of the '20's.[57] The cartel held to this formula even after Bank Rate fell to 2 percent in 1932, but open-market rates did not remain at 1 percent. Under the pressure of excessive liquidity, the banks began to invest directly in open-market paper at rates far below the cartel rate on indirect lending (i.e., via the discount houses) to the market. In the process, the open-market rate fell to one-quarter percent on commercial paper and to one-eighth percent on three months' bills. This put the discount houses in an intolerable squeeze and would have forced them out of business, but neither the Bank of England nor the banks wanted the discount houses to be eliminated. The Bank of England wanted to preserve the discount houses

---

[55] Radcliffe Report, p. 218.

[56] Wilfred King, "The Market's Changing Role," in *London Discount Market Today*, p. 6.

[57] There is some uncertainty about this point. Cf. King, *ibid.*, p. 6; Day, *Outline of Monetary Economics*, p. 179; and Balogh, *Studies in Financial Organization*, p. 179.

because they made a market for short-term bills, a market that could be manipulated in the interests of central-bank policy; the banks wanted to preserve the discount houses because they provided an outlet for the banks' temporarily surplus funds; and to maintain London's position as an important international money center, which they both wanted, the bill business (which was expected to revive with a return to more normal business conditions) had to be preserved.

The measures taken to save the discount houses continue to affect the operation of the market to the present day. The first and most urgent step was for the cartel to cut the rate on basic money. In November, 1934, the cartel cut that rate to one-half percent, thereby immediately increasing the spread for the discount houses' operations. In a second step, the banks agreed not to buy commercial bills from the market below the rates at which they were willing to lend to the discount houses. Finally, and more important, they agreed not to compete with the discount houses in the direct tender for treasury bills but instead to buy treasury bills (for their own account) only from the discount houses.

The cartel's agreement not to compete with the discount houses in the open market raised open-market rates slightly above the cartel's basic rate. However, the cartel's anticompetitive agreements did not cover competition among the discount houses. As a result, when the self-restraining agreements of the banks improved profit opportunities in the market, the discount houses began to tender vigorously for treasury bills. To prevent the discount houses from jeopardizing the cartel arrangements, it was agreed (May, 1935) that the discount houses would not submit competing bids at the Treasury tender but would settle in advance on a common bid and allocate their collective share among the different houses.[58]

The arrangements that were worked out in 1934 and 1935 have been modified in subsequent years, especially after November, 1951, when Bank Rate was raised for the first time (with a brief and negligible exception after the outbreak of war) since 1932. In September, 1953, the clearing banks introduced three separate rates for loans to the discount houses. Loans against treasury bills carried the lowest rate, $1\frac{3}{4}$ percent —the same as the banks' deposit rate; loans secured by commercial bills were 2 percent; and by bonds, $2\frac{1}{8}$ percent.[59] On January 27, 1955, the banks abandoned the three-rate system in favor of a uniform margin

---

[58] According to King, the system of syndicated tenders began not in 1938 (as stated by the Radcliffe Report) but in May, 1935. Cf. King, in *London Discount Market Today*, p. 8. Dacey listed the syndicated tender among the measures taken in 1934 and 1935. Cf. W. Manning Dacey, *The British Banking Mechanism*, 4th rev. ed. (London, 1962), p. 63.

[59] H. F. Goodson, in *London Discount Market Today*, p. 25.

of one-quarter percent between their deposit rate and their call rate to the discount houses. However, by creating a spread between their deposit and call rates, the banks increased the risk that some depositors would shift their funds from deposit accounts to the money market. To reduce this risk, the banks further agreed to cut the notice period from twenty-one to seven days on deposit-account withdrawals. Seven days is considered to be the minimum period for distinguishing between deposit accounts and current accounts—and "the banks are very fearful of pressure for a revival of interest allowances on the latter."[60] As noted earlier, on November 20, 1958, the cartel increased to three-eighths percent the margin between deposit rate and (minimum) call rate to the discount houses, and that spread has been maintained to the present.

The cartel at present has at least four strong reasons to support the discount houses by offering them a basic rate that is generally below the market rate on call money, and by agreeing not to compete with the discount houses at the weekly tender for treasury bills. First, the clearing banks are not anxious to participate in the direct tender for treasury bills, because they generally prefer to hold treasury bills which have only a few weeks to run instead of their whole life of ninety-one days.[61] This preference is related to the difficulties of forecasting their future cash needs. Since the banks (unlike the discount houses) generally cannot go to the Bank of England when they are short, they find it more convenient to let the discount houses conduct the direct dealings with the Treasury.[62]

Second, the discount houses provide an extremely important service for the banks: they stand ready to absorb (at a rate not less than the current minimum rate) any surplus funds the banks may have, and because of their direct access to the Bank of England, they can guarantee to repay any part or all of those funds upon demand. This service contributes to the management of the liquidity component of banks' portfolios by making call money "fully as effective a second-line reserve as rediscountable bills."[63]

Third, the present cartel arrangement with the discount houses is advantageous to the Treasury. It has enabled the discount houses to take responsibility (since 1940) for covering the entire tender,[64] and has

---

[60] *Economist*, Banking Supplement, June 25, 1955, p. 2.

[61] Cf. Bank of England memorandum on London discount market in Radcliffe Memoranda, I, 11.

[62] However, the banks do participate in the tender on behalf of their customers.

[63] Dacey, *British Banking Mechanism*, p. 57.

[64] This is an informal understanding which the discount houses have accepted even though there are normally many tenders besides the discount houses' syndicated tender. Cf. "The Management of Money Day by Day," Bank of England, *Quarterly Bulletin*, March, 1963, p. 16.

provided assurance to the Treasury that it can market its securities at comparatively low, stable rates. It is also part of a broader arrangement which increases the Bank of England's ability to control market rates. The fact that the authorities favor the present discount-market arrangements is thus another element to be considered by the cartel.

Finally, the bank cartel is in a powerful position to protect its own interests in dealing with the discount houses. As the Radcliffe Committee remarked: "The clearing banks keep a lively eye on the market's profit margins on bills, and are quick to squeeze the discount market by altering the terms on which they lend money to the market." In this way, "Any monopoly profit [of the discount houses] is thus merged in the total profit position of the clearing banks . . ."[65] It has been suggested, doubtless correctly, that the relations between the clearing banks and discount houses are "not dictated primarily by considerations of immediate or short-run profit."[66] On the other hand, it also seems to be true that the cartel does not leave the discount houses with excessive earnings.[67]

---

[65] Radcliffe Report, p. 60.

[66] Balogh, p. 126.

[67] Cf. Jones Report, p. 39. In this connection, cf. the statement of A. W. Trinder (a representative of the London Discount Market Association) that the clearing banks had not made an effort to buy their way into the discount business because "it is not a good enough business." Cf. Radcliffe Hearings, p. 263.

XVI

Competitive Regulations and Deposit Markets

It is the purpose of this chapter and the following one to examine how the market structures of deposit and loan markets have been affected in a country whose banking system is dominated by five giant banks. Since banking markets are segmented and some substitutes for bank services are not included in a calculation of banking concentration, the extent of banking concentration, however measured, does not translate directly into market concentration. Hence, the market structure of each banking market must be examined separately.

CURRENT–ACCOUNT MARKETS

Market Structure

In characterizing the activities of the clearing banks, the Bank of England has stated that "Their main function is that of the deposit banker, namely the acceptance of money on deposit and the payment of cheques drawn thereon."[1] The clearing banks supply transactions deposits in the form of current accounts,[2] and they are overwhelmingly

---

[1] Bank of England memorandum, in Great Britain, Committee on the Working of the Monetary System, *Principal Memoranda of Evidence* (London, 1960), I, 5 (cited as Radcliffe Memoranda). In a similar statement, Sir Oliver Franks has written that "Apart from lending, their most important function is the provision of a safe and inexpensive system for the transfer of funds throughout the country . . ." ("The United Kingdom Deposit or Clearing Banks," in Institute of Bankers, *The City of London as a Centre of International Trade and Finance* [London, 1961], p. 73).

[2] The part of current accounts that is held as a liquid reserve rather than for transactions purposes is included later in the discussion of time and savings deposits.

In this discussion of the market structures of transactions-deposit markets, allowance must be made for the existence of cash as a substitute for a bank current account—a possibility that is clearly more important for small than for large depositors.

the most important suppliers of transactions deposits in England. The transactions-deposit market is segmented, however, especially by size of depositor, and the clearing banks hold somewhat different positions in the different submarkets.

The main suppliers of transactions deposits to large depositors (especially large business depositors) are the London clearing banks, foreign and overseas banks, and accepting houses—a total of about 130 institutions. Although London clearing banks are decidedly the dominant component of this set of suppliers, it is not possible to calculate the exact extent of their dominance in this submarket because the official statistics are not broken down (except for the London clearing banks) between current accounts and deposit accounts. Under the circumstances, the concentration figures (based on total deposits in lieu of the unavailable current-account figures) are only suggestive.[3] At the end of 1965, the London clearing banks held 89.3 percent of the nonbank United Kingdom residents' total deposits in the approximately 130 banks; the foreign and overseas banks held 6.6 percent; and the accepting houses held 4.2 percent.[4]

Although these figures suggest a very high level of concentration in the submarket for large transactions deposits, the actual concentration is even greater. First, the clearing bank figures are strongly dominated by the deposit figures of the Big Five. Second, with a limited qualification for the American banks, the foreign and overseas banks tend to specialize in foreign finance. Hence, their depositors (other than overseas residents) are normally recruited from the subset of United Kingdom residents who have business dealings with the particular bank's home country. Third, the accepting houses tend to draw their depositors (other than overseas residents) from the subset of United Kingdom residents consisting of certain large corporations which borrow from the accepting houses or have various connections with them, and of

---

[3] These concentration figures, which are based on deposits of United Kingdom residents only, have a certain amount of error. In the official statistics, the deposits of United Kingdom and overseas residents are shown separately for the foreign and overseas banks and the accepting houses but not for the clearing banks. Although the clearing bank deposit figure contains some deposits of overseas residents, the effect on the concentration ratios is probably not significant, because clearing bank deposits are overwhelmingly the deposits of United Kingdom residents.

These concentration figures are also restricted to the deposits of United Kingdom residents other than United Kingdom banks.

[4] The deposit figures used in this computation were as follows: clearing banks, £9,454 million; foreign and overseas banks, £694 million; and accepting houses, £442 million. Cf. Bank of England, *Quarterly Bulletin*.

certain large individual depositors with either business or family connections.[5] As a representative of the Accepting Houses Committee told
the Radcliffe Committee: "An industrial company in this country
would not keep an account for drawing its wage cheques and so on
with us. It would keep it with the clearing banks."[6] Finally, the effective level of concentration is heightened by interbank agreements and
understandings. As shown earlier, the clearing banks have agreed not to
pay interest on current accounts. Typically, the foreign and overseas
banks also adhere to the deposit agreements of the cartel, at least with
respect to United Kingdom residents; and the accepting houses, too,
have agreed with the clearing banks to maintain the principle of no interest on current accounts.[7]

Until the recent entry of the trustee savings banks into the checking
field, the submarket for small transactions deposits was virtually a private preserve of the clearing banks. The small depositor normally does
not have access to the transactions-deposit facilities of the foreign and
overseas banks or of the accepting houses. To a certain extent, small
depositors have used their Post Office Savings Bank accounts (Ordinary
Department) like current accounts—the full notice period is normally
not enforced and withdrawal can be made on demand for small sums;
the management of the Post Office Savings Bank neither encourages nor
approves of this behavior. Deposits in the trustee savings banks (Ordinary Department) have also sometimes been used like current accounts,
because small amounts can be withdrawn on demand; and much the
same has been true in the building societies. Although small depositors
have to this extent had alternatives for current accounts at the clearing
banks, these alternatives have not been perfect substitutes for a bank
current account, because (until recently) only a bank current account
could be transferred by check; this limitation was partly overcome in
1964 when the trustee savings banks were authorized to operate check-

---

[5] Cf. J. Macartney-Filgate, "Merchant and Other Banking Houses," in Institute of Bankers, op. cit., p. 89.

[6] Sir Edward Reid, Great Britain, Committee on the Working of the
Monetary System, Minutes of Evidence (London, 1960), p. 390 (cited as Radcliffe Hearings).

[7] Ibid., p. 391. This may be modified in practice because the accepting
houses can set deposit accounts for any period, including on call. Although
they have reserved the right to pay interest on call deposits, the accepting
houses do not engage in unrestricted rivalry with the clearing banks. As Sir
Edward Reid told the Radcliffe Committee: "We work with them, and keep
in line with them when we can, but as our business is not stereotyped we always
reserve to ourselves the liberty to treat exceptional cases in exceptional ways;
at the same time *they have our assurance that that liberty will not be abused*"
(*idem*, my italics).

ing accounts for their customers.[8] Finally, the Post Office facilities for transferring funds by registered letter, postal order, and money order also are not perfect substitutes for a bank checking account.

Although the clearing banks have had an opportunity for many years to develop the small-transactions-deposit market, they failed to do so. According to one estimate (in 1958), "Most 'upper middle class people' have banking accounts. Comparatively few 'lower middle class' people have and very few working class people."[9] Until recent years, the banks have not been much interested in catering to the small depositor on current account, and they have manifested their lack of interest in a number of ways. As one critic remarked: ". . . There are few banks willing to open a new account without either a thumping first deposit or a reference for the would-be depositor's probity and regularity of employment. Quite rightly, small depositors anxious about their money think it is the bank, rather than they, that should provide a reference: They are doing it a favour."[10] The banks' lack of interest in small depositors has also been reflected in their banking hours, which are inconvenient for most wage-earners, and in their service charges, which are considered high for small depositors.[11]

While the banks have not done much to attract current accounts of small depositors, it is also true that wage-earners have not exhibited much interest in this service. This was evident, for example, in their reaction to the Payment of Wages Act of June, 1960,[12] which made it legally permissible to pay wages by check. Some expected this act "to bring to the bank more new customers than any other single event in the history of banking. . . ."[13] It may do so in time, but it certainly did not launch any quick expansion of the banks' current-account customers. Both bankers and their would-be customers have lacked enthusiasm. The bankers are reported to be ". . . strongly disinclined to be

---

[8] Cf. J. S. Campkin, review of C. L. Lawton's *Banking Law for Trustee Savings Banks*, in *Journal of Institute of Bankers*, December, 1964, p. 491. The effective date was in 1965. No interest is paid on the part of the deposit which is subject to check withdrawal.

[9] Sir Oscar Hobson, "Towards a Banking Democracy," *Banker*, November, 1958, pp. 710–711.

[10] *Economist*, June 6, 1964, p. 1138. The same writer went on to observe that " . . . even supposing the wage-earner . . . is tenacious enough in his desire to have at least his money among the nobility and gentry, 'WELCOME' is not a word he will find on the bank's mat, nor an attitude he will find persisting in the almost inevitable minor adversity" (*ibid.*, p. 1139).

[11] *Idem.*

[12] For the main provisions of the act, Cf. J. Milnes Holden, "Legal Notes for Bankers," *Journal of Institute of Bankers*, August, 1960, p. 248.

[13] *Idem.*

turned into proxy wage clerks and merely shift the risk of cash and loss from X's payroll office to their own branch."[14] The lack of enthusiasm among their prospective customers has been ascribed to the "impenetrable conservatism" of weekly-paid Britons.[15]

In recent years, the clearing banks have begun to modify their traditional position with respect to small-deposit customers. In September, 1958, for example, Midland Bank introduced a "personal cheque" account (sometimes called a "cloth cap checking account") with a fixed charge of fourpence a check, plus stamp duty. Midland Bank has not claimed great success for its plan nor have the other banks followed Midland's example.[16]

The banks made a more general attack on the problem by means of the credit-transfer system—"probably the most important single development in banking as it affects most of the people in this country, that has been undertaken for a great many years."[17] This made it possible for anyone, without having a checking or other bank account, to pay a bill or to have cash credited to a bank account anywhere in Britain, by using the facilities of any of the thousands of branch offices of the clearing banks.

The original charge of sixpence an item for the credit-transfer facilities was substantially less than the ninepence per item that some banks wanted to charge for each transfer.[18] This sudden interest in the small depositor occurred at a time when the clearing banks still held a largely unchallenged position in the field of current accounts for small depositors;[19] but it was apparently a response to the threat of an official giro—"the alternative that is most dreaded in all banking circles."[20] The Radcliffe Committee wanted a simple transfer service for small customers who did not have bank checking accounts, and it recom-

[14] *Economist*, June 29, 1963, p. 1384.
[15] This "conservatism" has been ascribed to "suspicion of falling into the hands of capitalist institutions . . . ; reluctance to disclose to their wives how much their earnings really are (presumably in fear of being found out in previous undisclosed deductions); and a conviction that their money will not be available when they need it" (*idem*).
[16] Cf. "How Much do the Banks Want the 'Little Man'?" *Banker*, June, 1963, p. 407. Cf. also *Economist*, September 4, 1965, p. 898.
[17] Sir Oliver Franks, *op. cit.* (n. 1 above), p. 75.
[18] Cf. *Economist*, Banking Supplement, June 30, 1962, p. 1343. The 6d charge per item was the same as the charge that (it was believed) the Post Office had contemplated for a giro.
[19] The clearing banks introduced the new plan (which had been available for more limited purposes since 1930) in July, 1959, five years before the trustee savings banks acquired the right to offer checking services.
[20] *Economist*, June 29, 1962, p. 1371.

mended that a giro system (like the Continental and Japanese systems which provide for transfer of payments through the Post Office) be investigated.[21] This provided the irresistible pressure to introduce the new credit-transfer system.[22] On March 4, 1963, the Assistant Postmaster-General told Parliament that a postal giro might easily be a losing venture, and he recommended that the government defer a decision until it became clear that the clearing banks were unable to provide a satisfactory alternative;[23] two years later, a different government announced that a postal giro would be introduced in 1968 or 1969.[24]

Current Accounts and Service Competition

The unyielding opposition of the cartel to any rate competition for current accounts has been based on a conviction that "Competitive interest rates on the broad mass of these accounts would be prohibitive to the banks, and unnecessary too, for the great bulk of them are kept by the customer for his own convenience and not for what he might make out of them—otherwise they would not have remained with the banks."[25] In lieu of rate competition, the competition for current-account deposits takes the form (as bankers and others repeatedly assert) of "extremely keen" service competition. In this connection, one bank spokesman told the Radcliffe Committee about a bank that, over a period of years, had received more than 20,000 current accounts transferred from other banks, and he explained that "The reasons for the change are known in the main to be the result of the extremely keen competition to provide a slightly better service."[26]

---

[21] Cf. Great Britain, Committee on the Working of the Monetary System, *Report* (London, 1959), pp. 331–332 (cited as Radcliffe Report). The main difference between the credit transfer and the giro system is that the latter centralizes all accounts under one roof. Cf. Sir Oliver Franks, *op. cit.*, p. 75.

[22] In blunt language, the *Banker* stated that " . . . whatever doubts some bankers may still feel about the drive for new business are best expressed privately. It is obviously a good thing, from every social point of view, to substitute wherever possible the transfer of credit for the transfer of notes and coin. . . . The pressure is on, and not merely from the press: it does not become the banks to appear to drag their feet on a matter on which so many people have made up their minds" (*Banker*, June, 1963, p. 405).

[23] *Idem.*

[24] Cf. Anthony Bambridge, "Living with the Giro," *Banker*, September, 1965, pp. 579–584. For a discussion of the probable size of the giro deposits, cf. "Who's Afraid of the Giro?" *Economist*, Banking Supplement, June 18, 1966, pp. xxv ff.

[25] "Has Banking a Future?" *Economist*, January 26, 1963, p. 331.

[26] A. D. Chesterfield, Radcliffe Hearings, p. 268. Whether this is a large number for the period involved must be judged in terms of the total number of such accounts, but the latter information is not provided in the regularly published official sources.

Notwithstanding such statements, it is necessary to be cautious in drawing inferences about the nature and extent of service competition for demand deposits. First, a certain amount of service competition is really disguised price competition (i.e., in connection with services provided without explicit charge in exchange for customer balances maintained at the bank); but despite the references to "keen competition," this implicit price competition is probably sharply restricted. Although it is not possible (because of the banks' secrecy on these matters) to make a direct evaluation of the intensity of this form of service competition, it is probable, given the keen awareness of their mutual dependence, that the banking oligopolists in England do not permit the profits from the prohibition of explicit rate competition for demand deposits to be wiped out (or significantly reduced) by unrestrained implicit price competition. Second, some of the most important forms of service competition—two major examples are improved methods of accounting and better and more widespread branches[27]—probably would have existed even if the cartel had not prohibited rate competition for demand deposits.[28] Third, in lieu of formal agreements, the banks appear to have evolved informal (and perhaps tacit) standards of "ethical competition" to limit the intensity of service rivalry in the deposit market. One example is the bankers' attitude toward "touting": although banks try to attract depositors by offering improved services, they would generally be horrified by outright soliciting for business.[29] Fourth, the fact that banker-depositor relations are on the whole quite stable is consistent with the hypothesis that bankers put limits on their service competition and resist depositors who try to improve their current-account terms by playing off one banker against another.

---

[27] Cf. Duncan Stirling, chairman of Westminster Bank Limited. Cf. *Economist*, January 26, 1963, p. 355. However, some depositors do not like the "improved" accounting methods—under the new system, it will not be possible "to enter any words on customers' statements. . . . This was a convenience to those who used their statement as a Cash Book and we regret the need to discontinue it . . ." (from Westminster Bank Annual meeting, reported in *idem*).

[28] The extent of branch openings has aroused some concern about over-banking in England. Between 1958 and 1962, the clearing banks averaged 162 net branch openings per year. Cf. "Is *England* (sic) Over-Banked?" *Economist*, June 29, 1963, p. 1379. Cf. also National Board for Prices and Incomes, *Bank Charges* (London, May, 1967) pp. 51–53 (Jones Report).

[29] As the *Economist* has noted, "Outright soliciting for business is generally viewed with horror except, significantly, by an occasional young assistant manager confiding (when his superiors are safely out of earshot) that he personally can see nothing frightful in it" (*Economist*, June 6, 1964, p. 1121).

THE MARKET STRUCTURE OF
DEPOSIT-ACCOUNT MARKETS

Time Deposits for Large Depositors[30]

Commercial banks offer time-deposit facilities to the public in the form of deposit accounts. Large savers have a number of possible substitutes for commercial-bank deposit accounts (or current accounts held as liquid reserves), such as similar facilities at noncommercial banks and at various nonbank financial institutions, and certain short-term government securities.[31] The market-structure significance of each alternative is considered below.

Although there are more than a hundred commercial banks in England, the market-structure significance of this large number of possible suppliers must be evaluated in terms of the high level of banking concentration and the market agreements and conventions among the banks. The clearing bank cartel presents large depositors with a united front—namely, Bank Rate minus 2 percent for deposits at seven days' notice. Moreover, because of the enormous resources represented by the cartel, its influence extends beyond its own member banks—for example, foreign and overseas banks, which do not belong to the clearing bank cartel, normally offer the same rate as the cartel on *resident* sterling deposits.[32] At the end of 1965, the total[33] deposits (of United Kingdom residents other than United Kingdom banks) in the foreign and overseas banks were £694 million; clearing bank deposit accounts were £3,458 million.

The cartel's influence also extends to the accepting houses. Although the accepting houses do not hold themselves bound to follow the cartel agreement on time-deposit interest rates, they have normally accepted the cartel rate as the standard rate for their ordinary customers.[34] On the other hand, by agreement with the clearing banks, they are not bound by the seven days' rule on deposit accounts: they can offer rates for

---

[30] As noted above, this discussion applies only to the time-deposit market for United Kingdom residents other than banks or financial institutions.

[31] Dollar holders can also go to the Euro-dollar market. In June, 1966, some major American banks began to offer negotiable certificates of deposit in London for U. S. dollars. Cf. *The Wall Street Journal*, June 10, 1966, p. 5.

[32] Cf. "The Overseas and Foreign Banks in London," Bank of England, *Quarterly Bulletin*, September, 1961, p 20. The Scottish and Northern Ireland banks also accept the cartel rate for their London offices.

[33] As noted above, there are no public figures on the breakdown between current account and deposit account of foreign and overseas banks.

[34] Cf. Sir Edward Reid, Radcliffe Hearings, p. 391; and Radcliffe Report, p. 69.

money at any period, even on call; and they pay more than the cartel on foreign-owned deposits.[35] In recent years, the rivalry between accepting houses and clearing banks has increased and has even extended into the provinces. The accepting houses were formerly inclined to limit their deposits to the large, more profitable balances in excess of £250,000; but some are now willing to consider business deposits as low as £20,000.[36] They have also begun to use their greater rate flexibility to offer more favorable rates to United Kingdom residents as well as to overseas residents.[37] It remains to be seen whether the accepting houses' challenge can significantly alter the clearing bank dominance of domestic time deposits. At the end of 1965, the total[38] accepting houses' deposits (held by United Kingdom residents other than United Kingdom banks) were £442 million.

The discount houses also offer large depositors an alternative to a commercial-bank deposit account, but the discount houses are not (and are not likely to become) an important part of this market. First, the discount houses' deposits (held by United Kingdom residents other than banks) are only a very small fraction of the clearing bank deposit accounts. Second, the discount houses are not in a position to emerge as significant competitors of the clearing banks for seven-day money because of their heavy dependence on clearing bank funds—at the end of 1965, for example, banks and accepting houses supplied all but £145 million of the discount houses' total borrowed funds of £1,381 million, and the clearing banks alone provided £849 million.

A large depositor can also place his funds with a large finance house[39] either on a fixed basis (usually three or six months) or, more commonly, on a basis of three or six months' notice. The interest rate on fixed-term deposits is fixed, but the rate on deposits at notice tends to fluctu-

---

[35] Cf. "Inflows and Outflows of Foreign Funds," Bank of England, *Quarterly Bulletin*, June, 1962, p. 98.

[36] Cf. *Economist*, June 6, 1964, p. 1133.

[37] In mid-1964, for example, the cartel rate was 3 percent on deposits at seven days' notice, but some accepting houses were offering about 4½ percent on balances maintained from a day to a month, and 4¾ percent for balances maintained for six months. Significantly, the deposit appeal to the smaller firms has encountered some resistance because the small firms are "afraid to jeopardise their relations with their local clearing bank branch" *(idem)*.

[38] There are also no public figures on the breakdown between current accounts and deposit accounts in the accepting houses.

[39] Instead of advertising for funds (as the smaller companies do), the large finance houses get their funds by contacts with business men, and through banks and brokers who also deal in the market for local-authority short-term borrowing. Cf. "Sources of Funds of Hire Purchase Companies," Bank of England, *Quarterly Bulletin*, December, 1962, p. 257.

ate with Bank Rate. The minimum deposit size at large finance houses might be £5,000 or more, and "anything up to £100,000 might be regarded as normal and taken at market rates."[40] Large depositors can sometimes negotiate somewhat higher rates for large amounts.[41] Although large depositors can secure higher rates on finance house deposits than on clearing bank deposits,[42] the finance house deposits, which are usually at three or six months' notice, are not perfect substitutes for clearing bank deposits, which require only seven days' notice. Moreover, most large finance houses have come under the ownership or control of the major banks,[43] and there is a real question whether or to what extent they have remained independent of their parent or associated banks in their rate policy.[44] As will be shown later, however, the finance houses have been growing more rapidly than the clearing banks[45]—by December, 1965, the deposits of the members of the Finance Houses Association had reached £654 million, whereas clearing bank deposit accounts were £3,458 million.

Finally, the national and local governments issue various short-dated securities which can substitute to a degree for commercial-bank deposit accounts in the portfolios of large savers. The most important are tax reserve certificates, treasury bills, and local-authority paper. The tax reserve certificate was introduced at the end of 1941 to minimize the effect of government spending on the money supply and to return to the government as quickly as possible funds accruing in the hands of the public.[46] It has been retained as an advantageous form of gov-

[40] *Idem.*

[41] Cf. Bank of England, *Quarterly Bulletin*, March, 1965, p. 89, note d. The managing director of a finance house gave the Radcliffe Committee a striking description of the bargaining power of a large depositer: "In my own case we may have an industrial concern which has 100,000 or 150,000 on deposit with us asking us to take another 50,000 or 100,000. We do not really want it, but we are frightened that if we do not take it they will go to another company, so we take it. I have been in the position of having money on deposit at the bank at 5 percent, and paying as much as 7 or 7½ percent for it to keep the good will of the depositor" (Percy Livsey, Radcliffe Hearings, p. 356).

[42] The rate is sometimes much higher—e.g., in August 1966, when the clearing bank deposit rate was 5 percent, the finance houses were offering 8–8⅛ percent for new deposits on a three months' fixed basis.

[43] Cf. *Banker*, January, 1966, p. 25; cf. also *Banker*, July, 1967, p. 584.

[44] The *Economist* has stated flatly that ". . . since the banks' participation, they [finance houses] can no longer be considered as rivals" (*Economist*, April 2, 1960, p. 76).

[45] For a discussion of the rapid increase in the deposits of the banks' hire-purchase affiliates, cf. "How the Banks Compete for Deposits," *Banker*, July, 1967, pp. 584–586.

[46] Cf. "Tax Reserve Certificates," Bank of England, *Quarterly Bulletin*, September, 1962, pp. 176–185.

ernment borrowing. The certificates—they are available on tap—are purchased by private individuals and partners in unincorporated business mainly to pay surtax, and by companies (including a few public corporations) to pay income tax and profits tax. The interest rate on these securities is set by the Treasury rather than the market, and it has ranged from a low of three-quarters percent (in 1946 and for a few years thereafter) to a high of 3½ percent.[47] In setting certificate rates, the Treasury takes account of the rates on treasury bills, other short-dated government securities, and deposits at banks, building societies, local authorities, or hire-purchase finance companies; as the Bank of England has stated, though, "There is . . . no strictly comparable security to act as a guide."[48] In February, 1966, the rate was 3½ percent, and the clearing bank deposit rate was 4 percent;[49] but since the interest on tax reserve certificates was tax-free, the gross effective rate was roughly twice the nominal rate even for a taxpayer with a small surtax liability, and could have been very much greater for those with higher incomes. On the other hand, by contrast with a commercial-bank deposit account, the tax certificate is fixed for up to two years; and though it can be redeemed in cash after it has been held for two months, the holder earns no interest at all. In February, 1966, the volume of these securities was only £197 million.[50]

The three months' treasury bill is another possible outlet for the short-term investable funds of large savers.[51] This security, which is issued in denominations ranging from £5,000 to £100,000, can be purchased at the Treasury's weekly tender in amounts of not less than £50,000.[52] The Treasury allocates the bills on the basis of the bids; but since the bids (other than the syndicated bid of the discount houses) are rarely sufficient to cover the total issue, the treasury bill rate at the weekly tender cannot normally exceed the collusive rate offered by the discount houses. Before 1951, business firms were not much interested in treasury bills, because bill rates were not much higher than

---

[47] Cf. *idem*, p. 184. For changes through February, 1966, cf. Bank of England, *Annual Report for 1966*.

[48] "Tax Reserve Certificates," Bank of England, *Quarterly Bulletin*, September, 1962, p. 180. In the opinion of the Bank of England, "The best guide to the right rate for the certificates is the inflow of subscriptions."

[49] Cf. Bank of England, *Annual Report*, 1966, p. 14.

[50] Cf. *ibid.*, p. 18. The Bank of England estimated that there were between 30,000 and 40,000 holders of tax reserve certificates in 1961. Cf. *Quarterly Bulletin*, September, 1962, p. 179.

[51] For a further discussion, cf. "The Treasury Bill," Bank of England, *Quarterly Bulletin*, September, 1964, pp. 186–193.

[52] However, banks will supply customers with individual bills of £5,000. Cf. *Economist*, August 19, 1961, p. 735.

clearing bank deposit rates. Their interest grew after 1951 and especially after 1955,[53] but they are still not a major element in the bill
market. At the end of March, 1964, the market held £2,595 million
of treasury bills: overseas central monetary institutions and international organizations, £1,086 million; domestic banks, £678 million;
discount houses, £363 million; other holders, £310 million; accepting
houses and overseas banks, £108 million; and other identified overseas holdings, £150 million. Since the "other holders" were mostly industrial and commercial companies, the volume of treasury bills held
by United Kingdom residents other than banks continues to be far
smaller than the deposit accounts at the clearing banks.

The higher rates on the short-term debt of local authorities are a
major reason why treasury bills have not become a more important
outlet for the short-term investable funds of business firms and other
large savers. Before 1955, local authorities used to secure their funds in
the form of loans from the Public Works Loan Board; after 1955, they
were virtually barred from access to PWLB funds, and they began to
solicit funds directly on the short-term open market. In soliciting deposits, they were clearly aiming for large savers—£5,000 appears to be
a minimum deposit, and the larger city councils do not accept deposits
for less than £25,000, or even £50,000.[54] The local-authority deposits
have been very popular because of their favorable yield and almost
zero risk[55]—for example, in mid–1964, when the clearing bank deposit
rate was 3 percent on seven-day money, the local-authority rate was 5
percent on a deposit for a minimum of three months and seven days'
notice thereafter. With short-term deposits (end of 1963) of £1,349 million,[56] the local authorities had become a very large element in the
market for short-term funds; indeed, they may have succeeded too
well. The extent of their short-term borrowing caused official concern
and, effective April, 1964, the government proposed to limit the amount
of temporary borrowing by local authorities by making the Public
Works Loan Board once again a major source of capital finance for the

---

[53] As a result of the strong demand for bills by industrial and commercial
companies, the discount houses' allotment of bills fell as low as 14 percent of
the bills offered at the tender of February 8, 1963. Cf. Bank of England,
Quarterly Bulletin, June, 1963, p. 87.

[54] Cf. *London Times* (airmail edition), January 2, 1965. According to a
different source, most local authorities do not accept deposits at seven days'
notice for less than £20,000. Cf. G. I. Lipscombe in *Journal of Institute of
Bankers*, October, 1963, p. 354.

[55] The credit-worthiness of the local authorities is "virtually as high as that
of the central Government." Cf. Radcliffe Report, p. 221.

[56] Cf. "Local Authority Borrowing," *Journal of Institute of Bankers*, August,
1964, pp. 254–255.

local authorities.[57] It was expected, however, that the transition would be very gradual.[58]

Time Deposits for Small Depositors

Traditionally the clearing banks have not been much interested in the deposit-account business of small depositors. As the Radcliffe Report explained, ". . . The clearing banks have broadly, as a matter of *deliberate and concerted policy*, stood aside while small savings have fed the development of building societies, savings banks, and other specialized financial intermediaries."[59] Although three of the Big Five banks have more recently exhibited a somewhat greater interest in the small saver (by offering savings accounts in a more popular form),[60] it remains to be seen whether this betokens a significant change in the clearing banks' attitude toward small savers.

At present, the building societies and, to a much lesser extent, the hire-purchase companies provide the most important nongovernmental substitutes for a commercial-bank deposit account at seven days' notice. At the end of 1965, there were about 650 building societies with more than £5 billion deposits, and 16 hire-purchase companies (members of the Finance Houses Association) with approximately £600 million deposits. Although there are no figures on the size-distribution of deposits in both institutions, it is clear (as shown earlier) that the building societies definitely prefer small depositors over large depositors, and that the large hire-purchase companies are primarily interested in medium-size and large savers.

The national government provides the small saver with a number of possible substitutes for a commercial-bank deposit account (Table 53). In addition to the deposit facilities of the Post Office Savings Bank and the trustee savings banks which have already been discussed, the national government offers various securities which are relevant in this context. The most important are National Savings Certificates, which

---

[57] Cf. *idem*.

[58] At the end of 1965, the local authorities had short-term deposits of £1,696 million. Banks and other financial institutions supplied £730 million, and non-financial institutions (industrial and commercial companies and others) supplied somewhat less than £1 billion. Cf. Great Britain, Central Statistical Office, *Financial Statistics*.

[59] Radcliffe Report, p. 44 (my italics).

[60] According to one writer, those savings accounts are ". . . basically the 'home safe' account introduced by all the banks in the thirties, now re-named and made more attractive by the right of withdrawal up to £10 at any branch (or, in one bank, open credit facilities at any branch up to any amount)" (*Banker*, June, 1963, p. 403).

have been available since 1916. The return on these certificates, which is earned in the form of capital appreciation over time, is not taxed. Although they are issued with several years' maturity (and sometimes with indefinite maturity, unless the Treasury gives a contrary notice), they can substitute for bank deposit accounts, because they can be cashed on application with only a slight sacrifice of interest. The amounts which any individual can hold have been limited, on the grounds that they are intended to appeal to small savers and carry a higher return than a marketable security of comparable life. National Development Bonds are another possibility. In 1964, they replaced Defence Bonds, which had been issued since November, 1939, and sold in units of £5.[61] Like Savings Certificates, they can also be cashed readily and with little sacrifice of interest; unlike Savings Certificates, the interest is taxable. The Premium Savings Bond, another possible outlet for small savers, was issued for the first time in November, 1956. These bonds can be cashed on demand. The total amount which an individual is permitted to hold is limited. The most distinctive feature of these bonds is that they do not earn interest—instead, the holders are included in a drawing for a tax-free cash prize. At the end of 1965, the volume of funds placed in this total group of government savings facilities amounted to more than £8 billion (Table 53). This was 87 percent of the amount of total gross deposits in the London clearing banks, and more than twice as large as the clearing banks' deposit accounts.

It is clear from the foregoing that small savers have a choice among a large number of substitutes for a commercial-bank deposit account;

TABLE 53
Selected Government Savings Facilities,
December, 1965
(£ 000,000)

National savings certificates		
Principal	1,970	
Accrued interest (estimated)	629	2,599
Defence bonds and National Development bonds		1,206
Premium savings bonds		530
Post Office Savings Bank		1,822
Trustee savings banks		
Ordinary departments	1,034	
Special investment departments	996	2,030
Total		8,187

SOURCE: Great Britain, Central Statistical Office, *Monthly Digest.*

---

[61] Cf. Central Office of Information, *British Financial Institutions* (London, July, 1966), p. 46.

but the total number of nominal alternatives is not a good guide to the market structure of the small-saver markets. Consider the nongovernment alternatives. First, suppliers who are located entirely in one particular local area are often not effective alternatives for small depositors in other areas. Second, even if all clearing banks became more interested in providing deposit-account facilities for small depositors, they would not constitute full-fledged alternatives because they submit to the regulation of the cartel in the matter of interest rates on deposit accounts.[62] Third, though the number of building societies is large, their rate policy is not independent. As noted above, their resources are heavily concentrated in a comparatively small number of institutions, and although each society is free to determine its own rate policy, they generally follow the rate structure recommended by the Council of the Building Societies Association. Fourth, the hire-purchase companies are not primarily oriented toward small depositors; if they were, their market-structure significance would have to be evaluated in light of the fact that they are highly concentrated and that many of the large companies have been taken over by the clearing banks.

Consider next the government alternatives. Although it is undeniable that the national government supplies important and effective substitutes for the savings deposit facilities which the private sector offers to the small saver, two considerations are overriding in an assessment of the market-structure significance of those substitutes. First, although it offers a number of different facilities, the government is a single supplier and pursues a coordinated policy in setting the terms on its different securities and deposit facilities. Second, in setting those terms, the government does not follow an independent policy as far as the private sector is concerned[63]—apparently from a conviction that competition in interest rates between the National Savings Services and the building societies, insurance companies, and co-operative and friendly societies is "hardly desirable and can work to the prejudice of the interests of the community as a whole."[64]

---

[62] On the other hand, as the cartel acts monolithically on the deposit rate and offers a common rate to all depositors, a small depositor in a one-bank (branch) provincial town secures the same terms from one bank as the large London depositor is offered by eleven clearing banks.

[63] This was made quite clear in evidence presented to the Radcliffe Committee. For example, cf. the description of the "cordial relations" between the National Savings Committee and the clearing banks, in Radcliffe Memoranda, I, 202.

[64] Memorandum submitted by the Post Office Department, in Radcliffe Memoranda, I, 209. Cf. also the following excerpt from the testimony of the Director of Savings:

QUESTION: . . . But if you do not regard the interest rate as competitive, I do not quite see where one gets to. Is there very much left, except a

COMPETITION IN THE DEPOSIT-ACCOUNT MARKET

Extent of Rate Flexibility

The clearing bank cartel has been particularly effective in restraining the competition of its member banks in the time-deposit market. As the Radcliffe Report stated: "Because the clearing banks are few in number and have sufficient identity of interests, it has been easy for them to hold to a concerted policy in this matter and, however actively they have competed with each other in other directions, they have abstained from competition in the terms offered for deposits."[65] As noted earlier, they pay a uniform rate of interest to all depositors for deposits at seven days' notice. As this rate is tied to the discount rate of the Bank of England, the flexibility of the cartel's deposit rates is determined largely by Bank Rate movements.

Bank Rate changed nineteen times (including six times in 1932) between April 21, 1927, and June 30, 1932. It remained unchanged at 2 percent (except for three changes between August 24 and October 26, 1939, upon the outbreak of the Second World War) until November 7, 1951, when it was raised to 2½ percent. The latter date marked the revival of a flexible monetary policy in England, and between the end of 1951 and mid–1966, Bank Rate was changed an average of twice a year. For a few years after 1951, the clearing bank deposit rate changed with Bank Rate but by different margins (Fig. 7). On January 27, 1955,

---

comparison of the services which one or other renders?

ANSWER: The building societies, particularly, are very touchy upon an increase in the interest rates in the small savings services. They regard any larger opportunities in small savings as something which, to some extent, takes money which might go to them . . .

QUESTION: Might you not say that competition on interest rates was desirable?

ANSWER: . . . I feel that interest rate competition between the various very estimable social savings services which are run in this country is rather bad for the community as a whole, because if there is going to be an upward surge of interest rates because of competition, then the general taxpayer, who often is a man who is not in a position to save, has got to find the interest.

* * *

ANSWER: . . . The line of policy should be to offer as low an interest rate as will attract as much money as possible, and to keep out of the picture any sense of competition in interest rates with other avenues of savings, building societies, etc., so as to have all of them encouraging the public generally to indulge in the function of saving to the maximum potential of each individual person (G. D. Frazer, Director of Savings, Post Office Savings Department, Radcliffe Hearings, pp. 456–457).

[65] Radcliffe Report, p. 44.

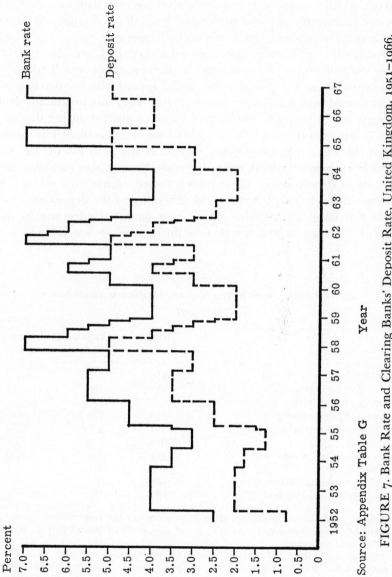

Source: Appendix Table G

FIGURE 7. Bank Rate and Clearing Banks' Deposit Rate, United Kingdom, 1951–1966.

when Bank Rate went to 3½ percent, the clearing banks raised the deposit rate to 1½ percent (and reduced the notice period from 21 to 7 days), and this two-percentage-point spread has been maintained to the present. Between 1955 and mid–1966, Bank Rate changed 25 times and ranged from a low of 3½ to a high of 7 percent.

Because the bank cartel has employed a very rigid formula to determine the interest rate on time deposits, the spread between Bank Rate and deposit rate has changed very little. Indeed, the two-percentage-point spread which has been in effect since 1955 was first established in 1920, and it probably would have been maintained during the '30's and '40's as well if Bank Rate had not fallen to 2 percent.[66] The stability of the formula is noteworthy because it has persisted in the face of wide variations in bank operating costs, bank profits, and the effectiveness of deposit competition from a variety of nonbank sources. It will be shown below that this rigid adherence to the deposit-rate formula has adversely affected the clearing banks' relative size in the English financial structure, especially during the postwar period.

TABLE 54

Interest Rates on Selected Savings Media for Small Savers
(percent)

	August 1956	August 1961	August 1966
Clearing banks	3½	5	5
Post Office savings banks[a]	2½	2½	2½
Trustee savings banks			
Ordinary department[a]	2½	2½	2½
Special investment department	3½ (or more)	4 – 4½	5¼
National savings certificates[a][b]	4¼	4¾₁₆	4½
Defence bonds	4½	5	
Building societies[c] (shares)	3.08	3¾	4
Hire-purchase companies	d	d	d

a First £15 of interest is exempt from income-tax but not from surtax.
b Held for more than seven years in 1956 and 1961, and more than five years in 1966.
c Tax paid by societies.
d Not available in official sources for small finance companies.
SOURCES: Radcliffe Memoranda, I, 205; *Annual Abstract*, 1964, p. 316; *Economist*, August 19, 1961, p. 735; Bank of England, *Quarterly Bulletin*; Central Statistical Office, *Financial Statistics*.

---

[66] Cf. Thomas Balogh, *Studies in Financial Organization* (Cambridge, 1947), p. 90. Deposit rate (London) was one-half percent before the Second World War (*idem*).

Extent of Rate Competition

Table 54 shows the interest rates that small savers could have received on savings media that compete with a commercial-bank deposit account. The relative attractiveness (in terms of interest rates)[67] of the different alternatives has varied because of different policies about adjusting rates to changes in the general level of interest rates. In the clearing banks, the deposit rate has changed automatically with Bank Rate. By contrast, the Ordinary Departments of the Post Office Savings Bank and trustee savings banks have maintained a flat rate of 2½ percent regardless of the rate on competing outlets, and their relative attractiveness has accordingly moved inversely with the general level of interest rates. The rate on building-society shares has been less rigid than the Post Office rate but more sluggish than the clearing bank rate, in line with the building societies' policy of maintaining stable interest rates and avoiding frequent changes for investors (and borrowers).[68] The interest rates on National Savings Certificates and on Defence Bonds also have not been closely related to Bank Rate—in part, the government has not wanted to be saddled with high rates if the securities (with maturities of seven or ten years) happened to be issued at a time when Bank Rate happened to be high;[69] and as noted earlier, the government has taken the view that interest-rate competition between the National Savings Service and building societies (or similar outlets for savings) is not desirable and can adversely affect the interests of the community as a whole. Finally, only a few of the small finance houses[70] quote a rate of interest tied to Bank Rate.[71]

The interest rates which large savers could have earned on investments that compete with commercial-bank deposit accounts are shown

---

[67] The relative attractiveness cannot be determined solely from the nominal rates, because the interest is tax-free on some of the savings media, and a tax-free rate of (say) 3½ percent is equivalent (even at the lowest tax bracket) to more than 5 percent of taxable interest.

[68] In a memorandum to the Radcliffe Committee, the Building Societies Association explained their rate policy as follows: "Building society rates do not follow every movement of the Bank Rate and, *per contra*, they vary at times when there has been no recent change in the Bank Rate. Where, however, a change in the Bank Rate is a symptom or a forerunner of changes in the general level of rates, societies are bound to be affected, though the effect is often slow to come about and not always the same as the change in Bank Rate" (Radcliffe Memoranda, II, 20).

[69] Cf. Memorandum by Post Office Savings Department in *ibid.*, I, 209.

[70] Large finance houses follow a different rate policy; but in view of the large minimum deposits they require, it is clearly the smaller finance houses that are relevant as alternatives for small savers.

[71] See "Sources of Funds of Hire Purchase Finance Companies, 1958–1962," Bank of England, *Quarterly Bulletin*, December, 1962, p. 257.

in Table 55. The clearing banks came under increasing pressure from some of these competing alternatives during the early years of the 1950's. Before 1954, the clearing bank deposit rate was not much below the treasury bill rate, and there was not much shifting from time deposits to treasury bills. After the treasury bill rate again became flexible in 1951, but especially after 1955, treasury bills became a serious competitive alternative to time deposits for the surplus funds of large depositors (including commercial companies, shipping companies, and oil companies).[72] The result was a shift of funds which put pressure

TABLE 55

Interest Rates on Selected Savings Media for Large Savers

	Notice period	Rate (percent)		
		February 1958	June 1964	August 1966
Banks:				
Clearing banks	7 days	5	3	5
Foreign and overseas banks	7 days	5	3	5
Accepting houses	1 day to 1 month	5	4½	
	6 months		4¾	
Other financial institutions:				
Discount houses	7 days	5¼	3¼	5¼
Hire-purchase companies	3 months	8	5–5⅛	8–8⅛
National and local governments:				
Treasury bills		6.02	4.44	6.70
Tax reserve certificates[a]		3½	2¾	4¾
Local authorities	Minimum of 3 months, and 7 days thereafter	7[b]	5	7½

a Interest was tax-free for the first two periods shown. On the last date, company tax-reserve certificate was subject to corporate tax at 40 percent.

b Rate for end of 1957.

SOURCES: Radcliffe Hearings, pp. 259, 356, 391; *Annual Abstract of Statistics*, No. 102, 1965; Bank of England, *Quarterly Bulletins*; Bank of England, *Report for the Year ended 28th February, 1965*; *Economist*, June 6, 1964, p. 1133, and June 30, 1962, p. 1332; and *Financial Statistics*.

---

72 See Wilfred King, "The Market's Changing Role," in Institute of Bankers, *The London Discount Market Today* (London, 1962), p. 11.

upon the liquidity of the clearing banks. In the past, the clearing Banks had responded to this pressure (and offered higher deposit rates than the cartel allowed) by accepting money fixed at three or six months and using the longer maturity as an excuse to pay a higher rate.[73] In 1955, however, the loss of deposits to treasury bills did not generate enough pressure to cause the banks to revert to the prewar practice of paying higher rates on longer maturities.[74] The pressures in later years also did not break the cartel agreement[75]—at least, there is no mention of overt violations in the banking literature—but they led to a certain amount of circumvention, because the banks offered certain large depositors higher rates than the cartel allowed by operating through a bank-owned or bank-controlled hire-purchase company.[76]

Given the presence of alternative suppliers for both large and small savers, the clearing banks' policy not to compete flexibly for deposits has had a pronounced effect on their growth. In absolute terms, clearing bank deposits grew during most of the postwar years—from £6,333 million in 1951 to £9,454 million in 1965 (Table 56); but in relative terms, the clearing banks as a group have declined. In 1951, the ratio of clearing banks gross deposits to Gross National Product was 49 percent, but only 30.6 percent in 1965. The clearing banks also declined sharply, relative to other financial institutions. Between 1951 and 1965, the clearing bank deposits increased only 49 percent (Table 57)—the only financial groups that grew less were the Scottish banks (even more heavily cartelized) and the two government savings banks. During this period, some of the other banking institutions enjoyed a phenomenal growth—for example, the American banks in London (almost 1,400 percent), the accepting houses (more than 600 percent), and the finance houses (more than 1,600 percent). Although the clearing banks indirectly shared in the spectacular growth of the finance houses, this does

---

[73] Cf. A. W. Tuke, Radcliffe Hearings, p. 292; and Economist, Banking Supplement, June 25, 1955, p. 2. This was clearly a device to circumvent the cartel, because there was no particular advantage to the banks in having the money fixed for the longer period. Cf. Tuke, idem.

[74] Throughout this period, the clearing banks considered that they were underlent as compared with the prewar period. Cf. Radcliffe Memoranda, II, 54.

[75] In 1960, however, a leading banker publicly examined the desirability of changing the deposit agreement; although he decided in the negative, the fact that he had raised the question led to speculation that "one or more of the other large banks must have been showing signs of finding the existing deposit-rate agreement too constrictive, as some of the smaller institutions are known to have done for some time." Cf. Economist, April 2, 1960, p. 76.

[76] Barclays, Midland, and Glyn Mills have been specifically mentioned in this connection. Cf. Economist, January 9, 1965, p. 141.

TABLE 56
Clearing Bank Deposits, 1951–1965

End of year	£ (million)	Percent of GNP
1951	6,333	49.0
1952	6,460	46.2
1953	6,694	44.8
1954	6,941	43.6
1955	6,612	39.0
1956	6,656	36.5
1957	6,929	35.5
1958	7,199	35.3
1959	7,667	35.9
1960	7,831	34.4
1961	7,928	30.7
1962	8,231	30.9
1963	8,337	30.9
1964	8,996	31.1
1965	9,454	30.6

SOURCES: Bank of England, *Quarterly Bulletin*; and Central Statistical Office, *Annual Abstract of Statistics*.

TABLE 57
Growth of Deposits, Selected Financial Groups, 1951–1965

Financial group (ranked by growth)	December 1951 (£ million)	December 1965 (£ million)	Growth (£ million)	as percent of 1951 deposits
1. Hire-purchase companies	38[a]	654	616	1,621
2. American banks in London	96	1,432	1,336	1,391
3. Trustee savings banks (special investment)	116	996	880	759
4. Accepting houses	136	1,030	894	657
5. Other foreign banks	75	523	448	597
6. Building societies	1,265	5,159	3,894	308
7. British overseas banks	542	1,677	1,135	209
8. Discount houses	46	111	65	141
9. Northern Irish	123	206	83	67
10. London clearing banks	6,333	9,454	3,121	49
11. Scottish banks	754	962	208	28
12. Trustee savings banks (ordinary)	817	1,034	217	26
13. Post Office Savings	1,926	1,822	−104	−5

a Figure for December 31, 1954—the earliest date for which an estimate is possible. Cf. Bank of England, *Quarterly Bulletin*, December, 1962, p. 256.

SOURCES: Radcliffe Memoranda, II, 200 and 204–219; Seymour J. Price, *Building Societies, their Origin and History* (London, 1958), p. 541; Central Statistical Office, *Annual Abstract for 1952*, Vol. 89, p. 285; cf. also sources cited in Tables 43 and 44.

not significantly alter their poor growth rate, because the finance houses' deposits are comparatively small—only the other foreign banks, Northern Irish banks, and discount houses have smaller deposits. In short, while savers' preferences for alternative outlets have undoubtedly changed during this period, the extent of the erosion of the clearing banks' position suggests that the cartel's rate policy is an important reason for their relative decline.

XVII

Competitive Regulations and Short-Term Business Loan Markets

SUPPLIERS OF SHORT-TERM BUSINESS CREDIT

There are about 140 financial institutions in England—clearing banks, foreign and overseas banks, accepting houses (members of the Accepting Houses Association), and discount houses (members of the London Discount Market Association)—which supply short-term business credit.[1] Most is extended in the form of advances (overdrafts and loans), but some is extended in the form of bill finance. The following examination of the market structure faced by different groups of borrowers (of short-term business credit) will proceed by the method of successive approximations in which the market-structure influence of each group of major suppliers is considered in turn.

Suppliers of Advances

The clearing banks are decidedly the most important institutional supplier of advances in England—at the end of 1965, they made 73.2 percent of the total advances made to United Kingdom residents (Table 58).[2] Moreover, in striking contrast to their attitude toward small depositors, the clearing banks welcome the business of small borrowers. As one banker told the Radcliffe Committee: "The small man is, after

---

[1] The hire-purchase companies are not included with this group because most of their business loans are made for medium-term financing, especially for the purchase of commercial vehicles, tractors, and earth-moving equipment. On June 30, 1962, a Board of Trade survey, covering 440 companies (with the overwhelming bulk of hire-purchase company resources), showed that hire-purchase companies held only £114 million of "other advances and loans," a miscellaneous category that included loans for house purchase as well as loans to business firms. Cf. "Assets and Liabilities of Hire-Purchase Finance Companies," *Board of Trade Journal*, October 19, 1962, pp. 785–786.

[2] Table 58 shows advances made for all purposes, but the overwhelming part is for short-term business credit.

TABLE 58

Major Suppliers (to United Kingdom Residents) of Advances, Acceptances, and Discounted Bills, December, 1965

(£ millions)

	Advances							Accept-ances	Discounted bills[b]
	Govern-ment	Local author-ities	Public corpor-ations	Financial institu-tions	Com-panies	Others	Total		
Clearing banks[a]	6	93	82	213	2,555	1,513	4,462	21	356
Accepting houses and overseas banks	—	565	1	174	766	106	1,612	461	101
Discount houses	—	5	—	5	4	9	23	—	333
Totals	6	663	83	392	3,325	1,628	6,097	482	790

[a] In order to show the same breakdown for the clearing banks as for the other suppliers in this table, it was necessary to derive the figure for the clearing banks as a percentage of the figure shown for "domestic banks." At the end of 1965 clearing banks total advances were £4,569 million and total advances for domestic banks were £5,392 million. The clearing bank advances in the table are based on multiplying the figure for domestic banks by $\frac{4,569}{5,392}$ or 84.7 percent. A similar procedure was used to derive the figures for clearing bank acceptances.

[b] Drawn on U.K. residents. Does not include U.K. treasury bills or "others."

SOURCE: Bank of England, *Quarterly Bulletin.*

all, the basis of our business, and we do everything we can to cultivate him."[3] This is borne out by the statistics which show that the clearing banks made more than 33 percent of their advances to borrowers with accounts of less than £10,000 (Table 59).

Small business borrowers are normally confined to the clearing banks which are in their local or nearby areas; large business borrowers are more mobile and, regardless of their location in England, could have access to any of the eleven clearing banks. In England, however, this mobility distinction by borrower size has different market-structure implications than in many countries with lesser banking concentration. First, because of interlocking ownership links, the number of separately-owned bank alternatives available to large borrowers is not eleven but eight. Second, the market-structure differences between large and small borrowers have been narrowed by the prevalence of nationwide branch banking under the control of a few giant banks. The clearing banks have blanketed England (and Wales) with more than 11,000 branches. The smaller clearing banks are not well represented in all parts of the country,[4] but most or all of the Big Five have offices in or near all but the smallest towns; and in some towns, the presence of a smaller clearing bank compensates for the absence of one of the Big Five. In short, for small borrowers who are located in London and other major cities, the nominal number of clearing bank alternatives is much the same as for large borrowers; for the small borrowers who are located outside of major metropolitan areas, it probably averages five in all but the

TABLE 59

London Clearing Banks' Advances, by Size of Account, June, 1958

Size of account	Percent of borrowers	Percent of advances outstanding
Less than £10,000	98.073	33.2
£10,000 – £99,999	1.747	22.9
£100,000 – £999,999	0.165	23.0
£1,000,000 and over	0.015	20.8

SOURCE: Great Britain, Committee on the Working of the Monetary System, *Principal Memoranda of Evidence* (London, 1960), II, 217.

[3] D. J. Robarts, Great Britain, Committee on the Working of the Monetary System, *Minutes of Evidence* (London, 1960), p. 285 (cited as Radcliffe Hearings).

[4] As shown earlier, District Bank and Martins Bank are comparatively sparsely represented in the south; Coutts and Glyn Mills are concentrated in London; Williams Deacon's is mostly in the Lancashire area; and National Bank has offices only in the important English cities.

smallest areas. Thus, the nominal number of separately-owned clearing bank alternatives for most borrowers in England ranges between five and eight. Third, as the intense concentration of resources among the clearing banks has led to agreements and understandings on loan-rate policy, there is little or no independent price action among the clearing banks. In this sense, the number of independent alternatives among the clearing banks approaches one for small and large borrowers alike.

In sum, in contrast to countries with lesser banking concentration, the more mobile large borrower would not face a much different market structure than the less mobile small borrower: if the clearing banks were the only suppliers of short-term business credit, both large and small borrowers would be confronted by essentially one cartelized supplier with respect to price; and both large and small borrowers would face a highly concentrated market with respect to the nonprice matters that the cartel does not regulate. In short, a combination of a highly concentrated banking system, a dense network of nationwide branches, and interbank agreements and understandings would put most borrowers in a similar market with an oligopolistic or even quasi-monopolistic structure.

In the method of successive approximations, the next question to consider is whether the existence of non-clearing-bank suppliers of advances has significantly altered the market structure that would exist if clearing banks were the only suppliers. The most important suppliers of advances that can substitute for clearing bank advances are the accepting houses and the foreign and overseas banks. At the end of 1965, their advances to United Kingdom residents[5] (£1,612 million) were 36 percent as large as the clearing bank advances, but the market-structure implications of this figure are less than might be supposed. First, the 36 percent figure exaggerates the importance of the accepting houses and foreign and overseas banks as suppliers to *private* United Kingdom residents. Whereas the clearing banks extended advances of £4,068 million to "companies" and "others" (borrowers primarily in the non-financial private sector), the accepting houses and foreign and overseas banks extended advances of only £872 million to these groups. Thus, their advances to the nonfinancial private sector were only 21.4 percent as large as the clearing bank advances to the same group. Second, the credit facilities of these institutions are not equally available to all domestic borrowers. Most foreign and overseas banks' advances—by far the major part of the combined total shown

---

[5] In the accepting houses and foreign and overseas banks, advances to overseas residents accounted for £2,163 million, or 57 percent of their total advances; in the clearing banks, advances to overseas residents were very small (perhaps £110 million).

for accepting houses and foreign and overseas banks—are extended to customers in connection with overseas trade financing.[6] As for the accepting houses, they tended (at least in the past) to extend their credit to customers of long standing for whom they provided a variety of specialized banking services. In addition, they historically concentrated their attention on large customers. As noted earlier, this has begun to change,[7] but it is too early to be sure how the present effort will develop. Finally, the accepting houses and foreign and overseas banks are not fully independent alternatives, because they generally adhere to the clearing bank cartel agreements on sterling advances.[8]

In a discussion of non-clearing-bank alternatives, it should also be mentioned that at least some large borrowers may be able to expand their alternatives by recourse to a foreign currency loan. This is potentially an important alternative for eligible borrowers. Since the clearing banks do not deal in this market, they have no cartel agreement on foreign currency loans. Moreover, London is an international financial center—it also holds a dominating position in Euro-dollar loans, the most important foreign currency loan sector—and an unusually large number of the possible foreign suppliers of foreign currency loans have London offices. The market-structure implications of this alternative have been limited, however, because no company in the United Kingdom (other than an authorized dealer) can borrow foreign currencies except with the permission of the authorities[9]—and the United Kingdom authorities have been less liberal in granting such authorizations than most other European countries.[10]

Suppliers of Bill Finance

Finally, it is necessary to inquire whether the existence of suppliers of bill finance has significantly altered the market position of the clearing banks as suppliers of advances. This depends on the extent of sub-

---

[6] Cf. Great Britain, Committee on the Working of the Monetary System, *Report* (London, 1959), p. 72 (cited as Radcliffe Report).

[7] In their search for new deposits and new outlets for credit (especially acceptances), some have opened branches in the provinces. Cf. "Merchant Bankers on the Road," *Economist*, June 6, 1964, p. 1333.

[8] Cf. Radcliffe Report, pp. 69 and 72.

[9] Under the United Kingdom Exchange Control Act of 1947, "except with the permission of the Treasury, no person, other than an authorized dealer, shall, in the United Kingdom, and no person resident in the United Kingdom, other than an authorized dealer, shall, outside the United Kingdom, buy or borrow any gold or foreign currency from, or sell or lend any gold or foreign currency to, any person other than an authorized dealer" (Ch. 14, pt. I, par. 1 [1]). Cited in Oscar L. Altman, "Recent Developments in Foreign Markets for Dollars and Other Currencies," in Joint Economic Committee, *Factors Affecting the United States Balance of Payments* (Washington, 1962), p. 507.

[10] *Idem.*

stitutability between a commercial bill and a bank advance, and on the importance (and other market-structure characteristics) of the suppliers of bill finance.

The substitutability between bill finance—in this study, bill finance refers to bank bills only—and a bank advance depends in part on the technical characteristics of bill finance.[11] In the opinion of experts, acceptance credit is not a perfect substitute because it is far less flexible and often less convenient than a bank advance. In this connection the accepting houses have stated that acceptance credits are suitable for transactions of a presumedly self-liquidating type but not suitable to provide for changes in working capital that are not related to particular transactions.[12]

The substitutability of a commercial bill for a bank advance also depends on its comparative cost. The cost of bill finance is composed of the acceptance commission and the discount rate. The acceptance commission is the smaller part—it is supposed to reimburse the acceptor for his work in scrutinizing documents and for his risk if the customer defaults when the bill matures—and does not vary with Bank Rate nor with changes in money rates generally.[13] The more important cost is the discount rate at which the accepted bill can be sold on the market—the most favorable discount rate (the prime or fine rate)[14] is reserved for

---

[11] Bill finance includes different categories of commercial bills. Commercial bills are divided according to their acceptors: bank bills (when the acceptor is a bank or accepting house) and trade bills (when the acceptor is a business firm). Trade bills are sold mostly to other business firms because banks are not willing to hold large quantities of trade bills. Since banks generally do not consider trade bills to be acceptable security for call money, the discount houses are also unwilling to buy large amounts. Bank bills are held almost entirely by banks (including accepting and discount houses).

Commercial bills are further divided into sight bills (payable on presentation to the drawee) and usance bills (payable at a later date). A usance bill must be "accepted" by the drawee. A prime bank bill is a bill drawn on and accepted by a United Kingdom bank or accepting house with an unquestioned financial standing. Bills are also divided according to whether they are self-liquidating, or not (finance bills). For a further discussion of these matters, cf. "Commercial Bills," Bank of England, *Quarterly Bulletin*, December, 1961, pp. 26–31.

[12] Cf. Great Britain, Committee on the Working of the Monetary System, *Principal Memoranda of Evidence* (London, 1960), II, 6 (cited as Radcliffe Memoranda). Most of the acceptance business of the accepting houses covers the movement of raw materials. *Ibid.*, p. 5.

[13] *Ibid.*, p. 4.

[14] This rate is close to but somewhat above the rate on United Kingdom treasury bills "because the standing of even the most highly regarded names on a bill does not match that of H.M. government, and because compared with Treasury Bills, commercial bills are relatively expensive to check and record." Bank of England, "Commercial Bills," p. 27.

prime bank bills (which are bought mostly by the discount houses). At the end of 1961, for example, the discount rate on prime bank bills (3 months) was 5⅝ percent per annum, and the acceptance commission was about 1¼ percent; hence, the full cost of bill finance was slightly less than 7 percent. On the same date, the cartel advances rate for most customers was 7 percent—Bank Rate (6 percent) plus 1 percent. Since the discount rate on prime bank bills varies between one-eighth percent and seven-eighths percent below Bank Rate, the full cost of bill finance is sometimes above and at other times below the rate on bank overdrafts.[15] These differences cause some business to be shifted back and forth between bill finance and overdrafts.[16]

In sum, there is evidence of sufficient substitutability between advances and bill finance to proceed to the final question: How does the existence of bill finance affect the market structure of the advances market as set forth in the earlier approximations? It is convenient to divide this question into the effects from the operations of those engaged in the accepting business, and the effects from those engaged in the discounting business.

The earlier tentative conclusion about the dominating position of the clearing banks (and, therefore, of the Big Five) in the short-term business-credit market does not have to be modified greatly because of the existence of an acceptance market. First, the acceptance facilities of the accepting houses have not been open to all borrowers on an equal basis. Historically, the accepting houses have concentrated their attention on large customers, and in spite of recent modifications of this policy, most of their business probably continues to be with large customers. To this extent, the acceptance facilities available at the accepting houses do not significantly moderate the concentration faced by small borrowers. Second, although the accepting business is conducted almost exclusively by the accepting houses and foreign and overseas banks, the total volume of their acceptance business with United King-

---

[15] *Ibid.*, p. 28.

[16] This does not mean that borrowers always respond to a change in cost. The Accepting Houses Committee has stressed that "The relative cost is an important factor but by no means the only one in deciding which method is used." Trade that is "normally financed by acceptance credits . . . tends within limits to continue to be so financed, even though temporarily the cost of so doing may compare unfavorably with the cost of other methods of finance available" (Radcliffe Memoranda, II, 5). In a similar view, the Bank of England has stated that "Because they are a convenient means of finance, companies are sometimes more concerned to keep acceptance facilities in use in order to guard against their reduction than to save by borrowing elsewhere at slightly cheaper rates" ("Sources of Funds of Hire-Purchase Finance Companies, 1958–62," Bank of England, *Quarterly Bulletin*, December, 1962, p. 259).

dom residents is only ten percent of the clearing bank advances (Table 58).[17]

There is also very little need to modify the earlier tentative conclusion (about clearing bank dominance of the short-term business-credit market) because of bill discounts. First, about 45 percent of the volume of United Kingdom (other than treasury) bills were discounted by the clearing banks (Table 58).[18] Second, the clearing banks are also important indirect suppliers to the discount market. At the end of 1965, the discount houses accounted for 42 percent of the total volume of United Kingdom (other than treasury) bills discounted; but since they depend heavily on the clearing banks to supply them with funds, they are careful "not [to] do anything to upset the banks."[19] Hence, they cannot be fully independent operators in the discount market.[20] As the

---

[17] There is some ambiguity about these figures because the bulk of accepting house acceptances comes onto the market, whereas the banks retain a large proportion of the bills which they accept under confirmed credits. The latter are not really acceptances, but more like security for advances, although they could be sold on the market if the bank wished. The point is, however, that the banks do not follow a uniform practice about carrying these acceptances on their balance sheets. Cf. Bank of England, "Commercial Bills," pp. 28 and 30.

[18] A certain amount of double-counting of bills discounted and acceptances cannot be avoided with the published figures, but the basic conclusions in the text are not affected.

[19] Sir Antony Macnaghten, representing the London Discount Market Association, in Radcliffe Hearings, p. 261.

[20] The fundamental weakness of the discount houses' position is evident in the following excerpts from the Radcliffe Committee Hearings:

QUESTION (to a witness for the London Clearing Banks): Do you think that [accommodation through the bill market] has spread as a result of the Government's policy of restricting bank advances?

ANSWER: It was spreading at one time, but *we frowned upon it and it contracted a bit.*

(Testimony of A. W. Tuke, Radcliffe Hearings, p. 268, my italics).

QUESTION (to another witness for the London Clearing Banks): A lot of the money which would be financing those bills in the money market would in fact be raised on loans from the banks; therefore, you say you frowned upon that. *Could you discourage your money being used in competition against you,* if you were refusing the finance because of a restriction that was being imposed?

ANSWER: *Yes; our sanction, if we choose to exercise it, is not to lend money on those bills.*

(Testimony of D. J. Robarts, Radcliffe Hearings, p. 269, my italics.)

This witness explained that, in being selective about the bills they accepted as collateral, the banks were not thinking of competition with their overdraft business but simply following an established principle to take certain bills but not others.

Radcliffe Committee noted, "The feeling on the part of the discount houses that they live partly by the goodwill of the banks militates . . . against any extended efforts to rebuild (against the historical trend) the commercial bill business."[21] Finally, the amount of the funds for discounted bills which the clearing banks did *not* supply, directly or indirectly, to the discount market was equal to only 2.3 percent of clearing bank advances (Table 58).

To summarize, in spite of the presence of other suppliers in the market for short-term business credit, the clearing banks (and, therefore, the Big Five) hold a strongly dominant position in this field. Large borrowers are in a somewhat more favorable position than small borrowers, because they have access to a somewhat greater number of financial institutions, and because they have greater resources for self-financing; but both large and small borrowers must seek their short-term financing in markets which are highly concentrated. Moreover, the high degree of market concentration in those markets can be traced directly to the high degree of banking concentration.

LOAN RATES UNDER THE CARTEL

Level of Loan Rates

English banking literature contains a wide assortment of views about the general level of loan rates at English banks. According to one view, loan rates are too high: "In Great Britain the faults of the commercial banking system have been over-caution and excessive margins to cover costs and risks."[22] According to a different view, loan rates are too low: ". . . Bank credit in Britain is much cheaper than in most other countries, and . . . rates charged at the margin are certainly much below the equilibrium rate. . . ."[23] Moreover, "By making finance artificially cheap the banks also make it artificially scarce; a sub-market price always carries with it some rationing of the product."[24] According to a third view, the truth lies between the two extremes: "All bank lending is not too cheap; the trouble is that the range of rates charged is too narrow. The blue-chip borrowers do not get their credit rates lower than they would pay elsewhere; small firms that are appreciably less credit-worthy, but paying only one-half or one percent more for their credit, clearly do."[25]

---

[21] Radcliffe Report, p. 59.

[22] G. D. H. Cole, *Money, Trade, and Investment* (London, 1954), p. 245.

[23] "Challenge from the Bank," *Banker*, June, 1963, p. 385.

[24] "Has Banking a Future?" *Economist*, January 26, 1963, p. 332.

[25] Lord Bilsland, chairman, Bank of Scotland, in *Economist*, April 13, 1963, p. 177.

On the basis of the available evidence, none of these views—all essentially impressionistic—can be accepted or rejected with certainty. In the first view, the conclusion that loan rates must be too high does not necessarily follow from the premise (even if correct) that banks charge excessive margins to cover costs and risks. In an economy where loan and deposit rates are both fixed by agreement, margins could be too high (by competitive standards) while loan rates, or some of them, are actually too low if, for example, borrower rates are subsidized by unduly low savers' rates. Given the low level of bank deposit rates as compared with other outlets for savers, this is not an implausible hypothesis, but it is difficult to test because there is no competitive standard in Britain to serve as a bench mark.

In the second view, loan rates are too low. Proponents of this view have argued correctly that artificially low rates must lead to an artificial scarcity of credit, but they have not provided the empirical evidence of artificial scarcity. Indeed, on one occasion the scarce funds hypothesis was being put forth at the same time that the chief officer of a major bank was declaring that the resources of the banks were not unduly pressed.[26] Also in connection with the second view, it is difficult to test the belief that English loan rates are low in comparison with rates in other countries. The difficulty stems in part from insufficient loan-rate information for the different countries, but other difficulties would remain even if better loan-rate figures were available. For example, except perhaps for blue-chip borrowers, it would be difficult to identify comparable borrower groups in different countries. This difficulty is compounded by the fact that some borrowers who would have to go outside of the banking system in England would be accommodated within the banking system in other countries. It would be difficult, however, to compare the effective rates in different countries even if the comparisons were restricted to prime borrowers. This is due partly to institutional differences (e.g., the English overdraft versus the American loan or discount) but even more to the fact that a bank loan is often a complex arrangement with many dimensions. Hence, to make a meaningful comparison of loan rates in different countries, it would be necessary to analyze banker-customer relationships in each country to determine how much of the total relationship is covered by the explicit loan rate. Finally, even if British loan rates were below those in other countries, it would not necessarily prove that the banks in Britain

---

[26] Cf. *Economist*, January 26, 1963, p. 353. According to Lord Monckton, there was a gap to be filled in 1958 when the restrictions on bank lending were removed, and the banks quickly responded. However, with the lending restrictions removed, ". . . the scope for expansion under current economic conditions is less obvious" (*idem*).

had made finance artificially cheap, because loan rate differences might be due to other reasons. These include the basic determinants of the general level of interest rates in each country as well as any special factors that affect the loan market in particular (such as government policy to control deposit rates in order to make possible a low level of loan rates).

In the third view, blue-chip borrowers do *not* (though small firms do) get their credit too cheaply. However, on almost the same date that one banker was expressing this view, other bankers were complaining that ". . . overdrafts available to blue-chip companies at a half per cent over Bank Rate with a minimum of 3½ percent, are a standing invitation to them to remain permanently in debt at their banks, even to the extent of using their liquid funds for profitable money market investment themselves, rather than reducing their non-costly indebtedness."[27]

In 1966, the Department of Economic Affairs reported that banks' published profits and dividends to shareholders "have in most cases increased substantially over recent years,"[28] and this charge prompted the government (on June 22, 1966) to constitute the National Board for Prices and Incomes as a Royal Commission to look into bank charges and profits. The Royal Commission (here called the Jones Committee) concluded that bank profits have been excessive in the sense that they accrued in part from a high average level of Bank Rate. The high average level of Bank Rate affected loan rates more than deposit costs because of the cartel agreements which prohibit interest payments on demand deposits but tie loan rates to Bank Rate. Although the Jones Committee recommended that the banks abandon both their loan and their deposit rate agreements, it accepted those cartel agreements as given in making its evaluation of the reasonableness of bank profits. Thus, the committee's conclusion that the high profits were not due to unnecessarily high loan rates was not based on a separate inquiry into the level of loan rates but on the committee's decision not to question the cartel's rate agreement in arriving at a judgment on bank profits.[29]

It is worth mentioning in passing that the Jones Committee received

---

27 This was reported as the view of "a number of head office managers today." Cf. "The New Official Request," *Economist*, June 29, 1963, p. 1367.

28 The (published) profits of the five major banks increased as follows in 1965 over 1964: Barclays, 65 percent; Midland, 65 percent; National Provincial, 61 percent; Westminster, 66 percent; Lloyds, 20 percent. Cf. *San Francisco Chronicle*, June 24, 1966.

29 Cf. National Board for Prices and Incomes, *Bank Charges* (London, May, 1967), pp. 19, 23, 59 (cited as Jones Report).

information about the true profits and reserves of the banks; but since this information was provided on a strictly confidential basis, the committee could not include it in the Jones Report, which was limited to showing indices based on aggregate figures. The reason for secrecy is that the published figures on bank profits are not the true profit figures. Under Parts I and III of the Companies Act of 1948, the banks may conceal their true profits in a number of ways. First, the banks may publish profit figures after deducting reserves and provisions out of revenue but without showing how much was deducted for these purposes. Second, they do not have to distinguish between reserves and provisions nor to show transfers to and from such accounts. Third, banks do not have to show the market value of their investments, which need only be described as "at or under cost." Fourth, they do not have to disclose the method adopted to value fixed assets or show separately amounts allowed for depreciation. Finally, the banks may publish a profit figure without having to reveal how much taxes they paid.[30]

The government has authorized these special exemptions to preserve public confidence in the soundness and stability of the banks. Because of changes in the value of bank investments and in bad-debt losses, bank earnings fluctuate widely from year to year. The government has accepted the argument that, to preserve public confidence and prevent bank runs, the banks ought not to disclose the full extent of these changes.[31] Although no one outside of the banks (except the banks' own auditors and the officials of the Inland Revenue) knows the true profits of the clearing banks,[32] informed observers believe that the banks' published profits conceal a substantial amount of true profits which have been allotted to formidable inner reserves.[33]

---

[30] Cf. Great Britain, Board of Trade, Company Law Committee, Minutes of Evidence on December 16, 1960, p. 592 (cited as Jenkins Committee Hearings).

[31] Ibid., pp. 593–595. However, the Jones Committee has recommended full disclosure of bank profits. Cf. Jones Report, p. 58.

[32] This includes the stockholders! When National Provincial Bank and District Bank were merged in 1962, the shareholders had to accept the directors' word about the stock exchange ratio because the stockholders did not have enough information about profits to form an independent judgment. See Economist, August 18, 1962, pp. 29–31.

[33] According to one estimate, the inner reserves are at least equal to the published capital and reserves. (Cf. W. Manning Dacey, The British Banking Mechanism, 4th rev. ed. [London, 1962], p. 91.) For another estimate (by the securities firm of Phillips and Drew), see Economist, Banking Supplement, June 18, 1966, p. xxxiv. For a discussion (in terms of index numbers) of the banks' profits, dividends, and reserves, cf. Jones Report, Chapter 3.

Opponents of the law have argued that, unless the banks' true profits are known, "the customer cannot tell if he has been charged too much for the service he receives."[34] The clearing banks reject the view that their ability to conceal profits can be dangerous to the customer because ". . . he has that facility which we know among ourselves as the facility of crossing the street. He can always go and see what the charges are in the next bank, and the fact of competition between us means that we are under discipline about our charges in the way which we know to be perfectly real. He is not very likely to be done down."[35]

A borrower who "crosses the street" may learn whether the charges in one bank are out of line with those in another bank, but he will not learn whether the general level of bank charges is out of line. Moreover, profit figures, even when fully and accurately reported, cannot answer this more fundamental question. Profits that are too high do not necessarily prove that bank charges are too high (by the standards of a reasonably competitive loan market) because, in a country where deposit rates are also controlled, high profits could be due to noncompetitive deposit rates. Alternatively, profits that are not excessive do not necessarily prove that bank charges are not excessive[36] (by the standards of a reasonably competitive loan market), because excessive customer charges could be absorbed by high costs due, say, to inefficiency.[37]

Structure of Loan Rates

As shown earlier, the clearing banks have adhered to a common policy on loan rates. Until the overhaul of the rate agreements in 1964–1965, all advances were made within a rate spread of one and a half percentage points, or one-half to one percent if private borrowers alone are considered. At present, the spread is somewhat wider—nationalized industries pay Bank Rate, prime customers pay one-half percent above Bank Rate, and all others pay 1½ or 2 percent more than Bank Rate[38]

---

[34] Jenkins Committee Hearings, p. 297.

[35] Testimony of Sir Oliver Franks, Jenkins Committee Hearings, p. 597.

[36] See Edward H. Chamberlin, *The Theory of Monopolistic Competition*, 8th ed. (Cambridge, 1962), pp. 195–196.

[37] The banks reject the possibility that their power to conceal reserves and profits could be used to conceal inefficiency in the use of the company's assets because ". . . the banks are in fairly violent competition with each other and if a particular bank was not making reasonably efficient use of its assets, I think that this would fairly soon over the years be disclosed in the performance of one bank in relation to the others . . ." (Sir Oliver Franks, Jenkins Committee Hearings, pp. 595–596). This argument is pertinent to the question of the comparative efficiency of individual banks, but it does not get at the comparative efficiency of the banks as a group (as compared, say, with a different market structure of banking).

[38] It has been alleged that "Customers who complain have managed to beat

—and all advances are made within a rate spread of two percentage points, or 1½ percent if private borrowers alone are considered. Critics contend that this spread between prime and marginal borrowers is too narrow, and they cite it as evidence that the banks have failed to differentiate sufficiently between various risks. In fact, however, even under the narrower spread that existed before the changes of 1964–1965, bankers may have been taking more account of risk differences than appeared from the narrow spread.

First, the narrow spread may be due in part to a failure to take full account of cost differences rather than a failure to allow for risk differences. Although loan costs per dollar of loan are higher on small than on large loans, bankers almost invariably explain the spread of borrower rates in terms of risk differences (viz., advances covered by Treasury guarantee, advances where there is "virtually no element of risk," and advances to the "run of customers") but not in terms of cost differences. In noting the bankers' failure to adjust loan rates to allow for individual differences in loan costs, Sayers has observed that "In England the same kind of borrower pays the same kind of rate on his loan, whether he is in London or in a petty market town in the North, and the rate he pays is not much higher than that charged to the big customers. *Costs are spread over the whole country.*"[39] If cost differences are handled to a significant extent by averaging, the differences in the loan-rate structure may make more adequate allowance for the differences in risk than has usually been assumed.[40]

Second, bankers may take more account of risk differences than appears from the narrow spread, since part of the reason for the narrow spread is that English bankers have followed a policy of sharply restricting the risks they are willing to undertake. Consider the following excerpt from the Radcliffe Hearings:

QUESTION: (to a clearing bank representative): You do not, as some lenders might, offer one man a loan on more speculative terms at a high rate of interest, and another man a more gilt-edge loan at a much lower rate of interest, as would happen in the long-term market?

---

their charges down; quieter souls have paid more" (*Economist*, June 25, 1966, p. 1446).

[39] R. S. Sayers, *Modern Banking* 6th ed. (Oxford, 1964), p. 270 (my italics). Sayers contrasted the English practice with the situation in the predominantly unit banking system of the U.S.A. where "costs tend to stick where they fall, and the small country bank lending to the small borrower is apt to charge much more than a great city bank charges to a big customer whom it is afraid of losing to a rival bank."

[40] In the view of one prominent banker, "I don't know that a small advance based on judgment of character carries a heavier risk than lending money in bigger packets to trading concerns" (John Thomson, chairman, Barclays Bank, in *Economist*, September 4, 1965, p. 899).

ANSWER: The spread is not as big, certainly.

***

QUESTION: Would you say that there are some clients to whom you refuse credit, but to whom you might be willing to give credit if you were charging them, let us say, twice the rate of interest which you normally charge?
ANSWER: That is not the way we conduct our affairs. A man is either credit-worthy or not credit-worthy; if he is credit-worthy he gets his accommodation . . . on the terms I have stated.

QUESTION: You do not hedge your judgment [about credit-worthiness of an applicant for advances] by charging a rate of interest that may reflect your hesitations?
ANSWER: Only within the limitations I have said, and they are pretty clearly defined.[41]

In short, if the range of borrower rates is narrow, the range of lender risks is also narrow.[42]

Third, the actual spread may sometimes be wider than it has appeared to be, because bankers occasionally "shade" the rate for large accounts. In the 1930's, large customers were supposed to be charged one-half percent over Bank Rate with a 4½ percent minimum; but it was reported that "In the period of very cheap money, cases were known where strong customers exacted even more favourable conditions by threatening to move their accounts to other banks or to avail themselves of different methods of finance."[43] In a similar vein, another writer has stated that "though in theory the banks used to have a system of uniform loan rates, this was often departed from in the case of really large loans . . ."[44] The Radcliffe Committee (in its Report of August, 1959) also observed that "a bank will on occasion trim its rate to keep or attract a particularly valuable customer."[45]

Finally, whatever may have been true about the spread of rates in the past may not hold for the future. The possibility of higher advances rates was under discussion in 1963 (after Lord Cromer had urged the banks to become more competitive in their deposit rates), but bankers' hopes for higher advances rates broke against government opposition to higher rates. This led the banks to cast about for other ways to raise their advances rates without having to change the general interbank

[41] Robarts, Radcliffe Hearings, p. 277. This is also the view of the Jones Committee. Cf. Jones Report, p. 36.

[42] The policy of restricting credit risks has been ascribed to a deep-seated banker conservatism. According to the Economist, "The banks tend to regard anything higher than 1½ percent over Bank Rate . . . as rather close to usury" (Economist, January 26, 1963, p. 332).

[43] Thomas Balogh, Studies in Financial Organization (Cambridge, 1947), p. 75.

[44] G. D. H. Cole, Money, Trade, and Investment, p. 209.

[45] Radcliffe Report, p. 47.

agreement on loan rates which fixed the prime rate at one-half percent above Bank Rate. Of particular relevance in the present context was their action in quietly raising the existing spread from a nominal one-half to one percent over Bank Rate to one-half to two percent over Bank Rate and then redistributing their borrowers within this wider range of rates.[46]

Flexibility of Loan Rates

In England, the flexibility of rates on bank loans (call loans as well as ordinary advances) depends almost entirely on the flexibility of Bank Rate. Between 1951 and 1965, the call rate fluctuated from a low of three-quarters percent to a high of 5⅜ percent, but the margin between Bank Rate and the clearing banks' call-loan rate remained virtually constant (Fig. 8). Toward the end of 1951, Bank Rate was 2½ percent and the minimum call-money rate (with treasury bill collateral) was three-quarters percent, or a margin of one and three-quarters percentage points. The margin was increased to two percentage points in March, 1952, when Bank Rate was raised to 4 percent. This lasted only until September, 1953, when Bank Rate was reduced to 3½ percent and the margin was changed back to one and three-quarters percentage points.[47] The call-loan-rate formula was changed only one other time, on November 20, 1958, when the margin was changed to one and five-eighths instead of one and three-quarters percentage points below Bank Rate. With this one exception, the formula for determining minimum call-loan rate has been as inflexible as the formula for determining deposit rate.[48]

The flexibility of the clearing banks' advances rates also depends on the flexibility of Bank Rate. As there is no official series on advances

---

[46] They also introduced commitment fees for the granting of overdrafts, and raised the minimum rates for prime borrowers, as a prelude to a general raising of minimum loan rates. In raising minimum loan rates, they were looking to the future because the new minimum rates were not applicable under the levels of Bank Rate which prevailed in 1964. For a fuller discussion of these changes, cf. "Levering Up Bank Lending Charges," *Banker*, September, 1964, pp. 551–554.

[47] In September, 1953, the clearing banks also introduced a three-tier system for call-money rates, according to the form of the collateral. The three-tier system was dropped after January 27, 1955.

[48] The call-loan rate has been closely tied to the clearing bank deposit rate. From 1951 through 1954, the minimum call rate (with treasury bill collateral) was the same as the deposit rate. On January 27, 1955, the deposit rate was set at 2 percent below Bank Rate and it has not been changed again. Therefore, the call rate was equal to deposit rate plus one-quarter percent from 1955 until November, 1958, and equal to deposit rate plus three-eighths percent thereafter.

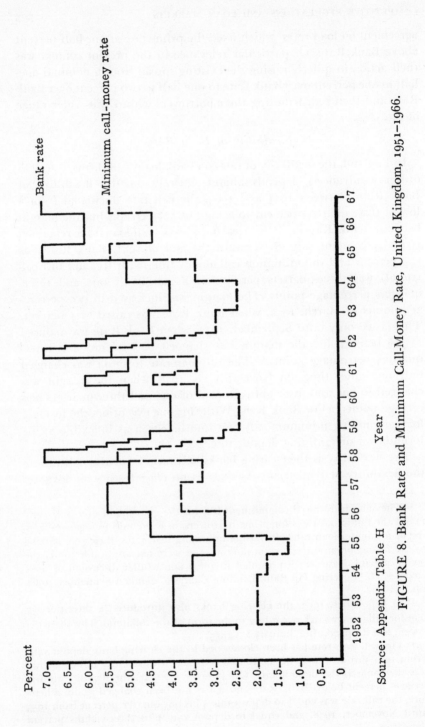

Percent

FIGURE 8. Bank Rate and Minimum Call-Money Rate, United Kingdom, 1951–1966.

Source: Appendix Table H   Year

rates (as there is on call-loan rates), it is not possible to demonstrate this point in detail. It is, however, a reasonable inference from the earlier discussion of the clearing bank agreements on advances rates; and this was also the conclusion of the Radcliffe Committee, which stated that "Apart from the automatic variations according to Bank Rate, changes in overdraft rates are very unusual."[49]

Although the general level of advances rates is linked with Bank Rate, all advances rates are not equally flexible (or inflexible), because the clearing bank agreements stipulate different minimum rates for different categories of borrowers. Accordingly, when Bank Rate is relatively low, a change in Bank Rate will not have an equal impact on all borrowers. For example, when Bank Rate was raised from 2½ to 4 percent on March 11, 1952, the large-borrower rate was increased by the full rise in Bank Rate of one and a half percentage points. At that time, there was no minimum rate for those borrowers, and many had been paying 3 percent (i.e., one-half percent over Bank Rate). Hence, when Bank Rate was raised to 4 percent, they were required to pay 4½ (and even 5) percent. By contrast, even before the increase in Bank Rate, the general run of business borrowers had been paying 4½ percent under the minimum-rate rule. Hence, when Bank Rate went to 4 percent, their advances rate was raised by only one-half percent (in accordance with the formula of Bank Rate plus one percent for this category of borrowers).[50] Similarly, when Bank Rate was cut from 4 to 3½ percent on September 17, 1953, the rate on large-borrower advances was also cut by one-half percent, but there was no change in the advances rate for those borrowers who were already paying their minimum of 5 percent.[51] Again, on November 20, 1958, when Bank Rate was cut from 4½ to 4 percent, it was reported that the lower Bank Rate would lead to lower overdraft rates although "some borrowers will receive less than a one-half percent reduction or no reduction at all . . . because minimum overdraft rates . . . are now effective in some cases."[52]

COMPETITION IN THE LOAN MARKETS

Clearing Banks and Rate Rivalry

The market for short-term business credit in England is an oligopolistic market, dominated by the London clearing banks and by the Big

---

49 Radcliffe Report, p. 47. In this connection, the Report also referred to the "considerable rigidity in overdraft rates."

50 See *Financial Times*, March 14, 1952, p. 1.

51 See "Bank Rate and the Public," *Financial Times*, September 19, 1953.

52 *London Times*, November 21, 1958, p. 12.

Five in particular. Except for occasional "shading" for a particularly valuable customer,[53] the clearing banks do not engage in overt rate competition with each other in the loan market.[54] This is clearly true in the borrower categories for which the cartel sets actual loan rates, and it is probably largely true also in the nonprime category for which actual rates are not specified. In failing to stipulate an actual rate, it is hardly likely that the cartel intended to admit more rate competition into the nonprime than the prime loan market; it is plausible to suppose that the different treatment is due to the difficulty (and perhaps impossibility) of achieving complete standardization of loan characteristics of the heterogeneous borrowers in the nonprime category. Significantly, although the cartel does not prescribe an actual rate for nonprime borrowers, the clearing banks have been able to achieve a consensus about the appropriate rate to charge most borrowers in this group—namely, Bank Rate plus $1\frac{1}{2}$ or 2 percent.

As noted earlier, the cartel has established minimum rates for all borrower categories. In the case of the nationalized industries or the "blue-chip" borrowers, these are clearly not limit rates that become effective by the play of competition. On the contrary, the minimum rate is a device for stipulating the actual rate at certain low levels of Bank Rate, and the cartel does not intend that the minimum rate might become an actual rate under any other conditions. The cartel probably takes a similar position with respect to the minimum rate which is stipulated for the nonprime-borrower category. At present, for example, the minimum for this category is the "blue-chip" rate (or, more precisely, something slightly above the "blue-chip" rate). In fact, however, the effective rate for the general run of nonprime borrowers is not at this minimum level and would not be expected to reach it unless Bank Rate fell to low levels. In short, the clearing banks have managed to avoid loan-rate competition by adhering to a formula in which, except for periods when Bank Rate is low and minimum rates become effective, Bank Rate is the pivotal rate in determining the struc-

---

[53] There is nothing in the banking literature to suggest that shading loan rates for large borrowers has ever reached the point of seriously jeopardizing the cartel's loan-rate agreements. It is pertinent to note in this connection that, as shown earlier, the large borrower's margin of competitive superiority over the small borrower is less pronounced in England than in countries with lesser banking concentration.

[54] A combination of an easy monetary policy and a sharp decline in the demand for advances during the '30's did, however, have an eroding effect on the prevailing minimum overdraft rate. (R. S. Sayers, "The Concept of Liquidity in English Banking," in Associazione Bancaria Italiana, First International Credit Conference, *Papers and Proceedings* [Rome, 1953], II, 231.)

ture, general level, and flexibility of advance rates for the different categories of borrowers.

In spite of its durability, the Bank Rate formula for determining advances rates is not necessarily an ideal formula for maximizing cartel profits. The profit-maximizing rate structure depends upon the banks' demand, risks, and costs, but the formula-determined loan rates may not be optimal on all these counts. It is unlikely, for example, that the demand for bank advances always changes at the same time and in a consistent manner with changes in Bank Rate; and even if the changes did happen to coincide, the formula-determined rate structure would be optimal only for very restrictive assumptions about the changes in the elasticity of demand in the different groups of borrowers.[55] Similarly, it is unlikely that the formula makes an optimal adjustment to changes in bank costs. By tying loan rates to Bank Rate,[56] the formula does take account of changes in one important bank cost which is also tied to Bank Rate (deposit account interest), but the interest cost on deposit accounts is not the only bank cost—at the end of 1965, deposit accounts were only 36.6 percent of total gross deposits of the clearing banks—and the change in Bank Rate is not a reliable clue to the change, if any, in the banks' operating costs.

From the cartel's point of view, the fact that the loan-rate formula does not necessarily maximize profits does not disqualify it as a useful pricing tool and may even increase its attractiveness. First, many statements in the banking literature suggest that the clearing banks are not motivated solely by profit considerations. Thus, the Radcliffe Committee observed that, although the first duty of the clearing banks is to conduct their business in the interests of their owners, "this commercial

---

[55] Bankers apparently believe that customers are not too sensitive to rate, and this belief is an important reason why they do not try to deter or encourage the demand for overdrafts by means of rate changes that are not related to Bank Rate changes. See Radcliffe Report, p. 47. For a summary of the evidence on the interest elasticity of demand for advances, see *ibid.*, pp. 158 and 159. Even if the overall demand for advances is as highly interest inelastic as bankers believe, a shift in the demand function for advances could change the profit-maximizing advances rate—and this optimal rate would not necessarily be the same as the formula-determined rate based on a rigid link to Bank Rate.

[56] One banker told the Radcliffe Committee that "We first of all put up our loan rate. Our loan rate depends on Bank Rate; when that goes up we can afford to pay more; and if the loan rate and the Bank Rate go down, we must pay less" (A. W. Tuke, Radcliffe Hearings, p. 289). He also agreed with a questioner that what the banks can do with the money governs the movement of what banks pay for money (*idem*). Another banker (testifying at the same session) gave an opposite description of the relationship between loan and deposit rates: "the [deposit] rate must control our lending rate, because, with overheads as they are, we have to have a given margin" (D. J. Robarts, *idem*).

interest has often been tempered by regard for a wider public interest."[57] Second, the loan-rate formula serves a useful role in terms of the bank image it projects. Since the banks' powerful market position (including both their high concentration and their freedom to collude on anticompetitive agreements) is dependent upon government policy, the clearing banks are vulnerable to political retaliation (including nationalization) if the public should believe that the banks were "abusing" their enormous market power. As one banker put it, "I think we would be criticised if we just put up our charges because of any kind of monopoly screw we could put on the borrower."[58] In this kind of environment, the loan-rate formula is a useful device, for it moderates, (or at least does not exacerbate) the political risk. At the same time, by achieving at least a partial adjustment of bank prices to changing conditions of demand and cost, it has enabled the clearing banks to earn a satisfactory and at times a very comfortable level of profits.[59]

Competitive Impact of the Open Market

Commercial bankers in England regard lending as their primary business, and except for the regular money that the clearing banks supply to the discount houses, the funds placed on the open market are generally surplus funds which are not being used for customer advances.[60] The open market is thus a channel for mobilizing the surplus funds of the banking system. In countries where the banking system is not highly concentrated, the open market can serve as an important competitive influence in the market for short-term business credit, or at least in the submarket of large borrowers for whom bill finance through the open market is a substitute for a bank advance. In Eng-

---

[57] Radcliffe Report, p. 43. In a similar statement, G. D. H. Cole has remarked that the joint-stock commercial banks ". . . did not . . . go all out to make as much profit as they could, regardless of consequences . . . Their very profitableness rendered them immune from the need to be guided exclusively by considerations of profit: like the Bank of England, they were run, not so much to make profits for themselves as to guarantee, within their rights, that the conditions of profit-making should be secured for others" (Cole, *Money, Trade, and Investment*, pp. 239–240).

[58] John Thomson, in *Economist*, September 4, 1965, p. 900.

[59] According to Cole (in a book written in 1954), the clearing banks have been able to earn enough profits, in good and bad times alike, to pay as much as they wanted to pay in regular dividends. (Cole, p. 240.) More recently, as noted above, the high level of bank profits led to an official investigation by the Jones Committee. Cf. Jones Report.

[60] As one banker told the Radcliffe Committee, "Our real business is advances, and we really invest the money that we cannot or do not want to lend" (Robarts, Radcliffe Heairngs, p. 280).

land, where the banking system is highly concentrated, the competitive impact of the commercial-bill market has been very limited.

First, the commercial-bill market has virtually no effect on over-draft rates. Under the clearing banks' loan-rate formula, an excess supply of funds in the customer loan market does not per se bring about a reduction in customer loan rates—but it might lead to "shading" for a few very large borrowers. Similarly, the loan-rate formula does not call for an automatic reduction in overdraft rates if a transfer of the surplus funds to the open market should depress bill rates. Under the loan-rate formula, the cartel will normally change advances rates only in response to a change in Bank Rate. Second, the cartel's failure to respond to the rate competition from the commercial-bill market appears to have only a very limited effect on the volume of bank advances. There was some discussion in the Radcliffe Hearings about borrower shifts between acceptance credit and bank credit in response to changes in their relative cost,[61] but there was no statistical evidence on the amounts involved. Although some shifting undoubtedly occurs, it is not very significant from the point of view of the clearing banks. This is a reasonable inference from the comparative size of clearing-bank advances and the total volume of acceptance financing to United Kingdom private residents. In addition, according to a suggestive bit of indirect evidence (from the Radcliffe Hearings), the shifts, for *all* reasons, from bank advances to acceptances had *never* been large enough to strain the acceptance-granting capacity of the seventeen (in 1958) members of the Accepting Houses Association![62]

There are two major reasons why the clearing banks can ignore to a considerable extent the competitive pressures that emanate from the commercial-bill market. One reason is that the imperfect substitutability between bank advances and acceptance credit limits the amount of pressure on the banks. As already noted, the facilities of the open market are not available to all bank borrowers but only to a selected subset; hence, the potential amount that could be shifted away from the banks is limited. Moreover, since acceptances and bank advances are not perfect substitutes for all purposes, the relative cost, while important, is not the only consideration in choosing between them.

Another major reason why the clearing banks have been able to resist the competitive pressures from the bill market is related to their enormous size. This has two aspects. First, the clearing banks are overwhelmingly the dominant suppliers of bank advances; and it behooves

---

[61] See Radcliffe Hearings, p. 392. Presumably this was the basis for the reference in the Radcliffe Report to the "quite powerful competitive elements in the credit market." See Radcliffe Report, pp. 68–69.

[62] Sir Edward Reid, Radcliffe Hearings, p. 392.

borrowers, even very large borrowers, to maintain good working relations with the clearing banks. This does not mean that borrowers can never shift to the open market in response to a relative decline in the cost of bill finance,[63] but it probably does mean that, in contemplating a shift, borrowers will calculate the cost in terms of their long-run relations with the clearing banks. A borrower who left his bank whenever a less costly alternative was available would probably rank lower in his banker's esteem than a borrower who did not, and probably would receive less favorable attention in a tight period. Second, the clearing banks are also large in terms of the bill market. Although more than one hundred banks and accepting houses supply funds to the open market, the overwhelming amount is supplied, directly or indirectly, by the clearing banks. As noted earlier, the clearing banks can use this power to limit the volume of financing through the open market—for example, when the bill market began to expand as a result of the government's policy of restricting bank advances, the clearing banks "frowned" upon the expansion, and the market contracted a bit.[64] The importance of the clearing banks as suppliers to the bill market also means that, if they choose to use their market power, they can limit the degree of rate pressure that can be generated by the bill market.

Competition in Credit Availability and Service

It is often stated that, in lieu of rate competition, the clearing banks compete in terms of credit availability and service. By competition in terms of credit availability, bankers mean their willingness to exercise independent judgment about credit-worthiness.[65] There is conflicting

---

[63] The difference between the overdraft rate and the effective bill rate (discount rate plus commission for acceptance) is not always as large as it appears. In part, this is because bill finance is extended for a stated sum and a fixed period, whereas an overdraft can be varied at any time. For example, this was one reason why bankers thought that, in spite of the seeming disparity between the two rates, there would not be a great shift away from overdrafts to bill finance after Bank Rate was reduced on September 17, 1953. See *Financial Times*, September 30, 1953, p. 4. In addition, wider discount rates are usually quoted on bill finance to business firms that seek to raise funds for operations that are not strictly self-liquidating. See *idem*.

[64] It is also pertinent to note that, as the chairman of Barclays Bank put it: "We are all pretty close in the City. There are interlocking directorships between discount houses and clearing banks." (Thomson, in *Economist*, September 4, 1965, p. 897.)

[65] Judgments about credit-worthiness can differ substantially, so that one banker will say "yes" and another banker not only will say "no," but will say "no" very emphatically to the same request. Cf. Robarts, Radcliffe Hearings, p. 227.

evidence on the extent of this competition. Bankers claim that borrowers who have been refused a loan by one bank (for reasons other than the government-requested loan squeeze)[66] can go across the street and try their luck with another bank, and that is is common for them to do so.[67] In a flatly contradictory statement, however, some businessmen (including a former banker) have reported that no bank will accept an application for an advance if the head office of another clearing bank has turned it down *for any reason whatever*.[68] This does not mean that it is impossible to go to another bank, but "The gentle art of switching bank accounts is to get the timing right."[69]

English banking literature is replete with references to the intensity of service competition, and bankers stress their claim that "The dissatisfied customer can always go to the bank across the road." In spite of such statements, the banks are not eager to deal with a borrower who "crosses the road" to bargain for more service as a condition of shifting his account. The clearing banks are tightly organized and conscious of their interdependence, and they are not disposed to permit their customers to play one bank against another in this kind of disguised rate competition. Competition in service (aside from competition in terms of branches) seems to mean primarily competition in the quality (i.e., "in the minute attentions which to go make up a good business")[70] rather than the terms of service—that is, the kind or amount of service provided for a given (explicit or implicit) price.[71]

---

[66] After the war, the Chancellor of the Exchequer had requested the banks to limit the volume of advances in order to support the government's monetary and economic policy. In conformity with this request, the banks agreed that they would not try to lure an account from a rival bank by offering a customer an advance which his regular bank had denied on credit restriction grounds. In general, whenever the banks are under special pressure, borrowing accounts will not be transferred from one bank to another without agreement at head-office level. Cf. *Banker*, July, 1965, p. 462.

[67] See A. D. Chesterfield, Radcliffe Hearings, p. 267. Sir Oliver Franks made a similar statement to Lloyds Bank shareholders in January, 1956, cited in Radcliffe Memoranda, II, 59.

[68] Cf. *Economist*, June 6, 1964, p. 1122.

[69] *Idem.* It was reported in this connection that a businessman had cancelled a loan application (which his branch manager had refused to sanction) to preclude its being forwarded to head office where a possible refusal might have blocked him from getting a loan from another bank.

[70] Robarts, Radcliffe Hearings, p. 267.

[71] Wilson has observed that bank competition is "mainly in the quality of service offered and in seeking new business" (J. S. G. Wilson, "Recent Changes in Commercial Banking Business," *Journal of Institute of Bankers*, December, 1964, p. 512). In a similar vein, the vice-chairman of Barclays Bank has stated (with reference to the banks' close relationships with customers) that "It is in this that competition between the banks is most keen and it is in

With or without keen competition in service, a certain amount of shifting of borrowers among banks is inevitable. In general, however, all but the largest firms in England typically use only one bank,[72] and bank–customer relationships tend to be very stable—it would usually be considered newsworthy if a large firm changed its bank. Bank relationships are generally stable because banker and borrower can usually achieve a mutually satisfactory relation over a period of time, and once achieved, it behooves banker and borrower not to disturb it. Banker–customer relations are comparatively informal and often close. As one banker explained, the bank manager who considers a loan application is in the position of a "confidential adviser who is anxious to understand the individual customer's financial problems and to help him as far as he can."[73] That kind of relationship cannot be easily transferred to a new banker. Moreover, the borrower knows that banking services are not likely to be available on better terms from any other bank. Hence, he is motivated to work out any grievance with his present banker. The banker, too, has an interest in preserving a customer relationship. He knows that it may be difficult but not impossible for the borrower to transfer to another bank; and the loss of a customer, especially a large one, hurts a bank's prestige and its image. This could be serious, because a bank which got the reputation of being unwilling or unable to hold its customers would be at a competitive disadvantage in appealing to new customers who seek their first banking connection.

---

quality of service that collectively they can best meet the challenge of Trustee Savings Banks, Post Office Giro and other competitors for deposits." Cf. Harold Darvill, "Bank Developments in the United Kingdom," *Stock Exchange Gazette,* June 17, 1966, p. 19.

[72] *Idem.*

[73] Westminster Bank, "Bank Liquidity—Control of Inflation," in Associazione Bancaria Italiana, First International Credit Conference, *Papers and Proceedings,* II, 244.

XVIII

Competitive Regulations and Monetary Controls

MONETARY CONTROLS AND THE CARTEL

The Bank of England

The Bank of England, the primary agency for the conduct of monetary policy, has been legally subject to the authority of the government since the passage of the Bank of England Act in 1946; but the 1946 legislation merely gave de jure recognition to a de facto situation. Although the government's relations with the Bank were not always smooth, the government's primacy had not been challenged for a long time. In 1925, the Bank of England (under Governor Montagu Norman) raised Bank Rate against the protest of the Chancellor (Winston Churchill); but in the following year, Governor Norman publicly acknowledged the government's full authority over the Bank of England: "I look upon the Bank as having the unique right to offer advice and to press such advice even to the point of 'nagging' but always of course *subject to the supreme authority of Government*."[1] Under the economic pressures of the '30's, the government increased its direction of economic affairs, and its influence over the Bank continued to grow. On October 7, 1936, Governor Norman once again publicly acknowledged the government's authority and pledged the Bank's cooperation: "I assure the Ministers that . . . they will at all times find us as willing . . . to do what they direct, as though we were under legal compulsion."[2] In 1946, the Bank of England Act nationalized the central bank and explicitly placed the Bank under government control. Under Section 4 (paragraph 1) of that act, "The Treasury may from time to time give such directions to the Bank

---

[1] Cited in Sir Cecil Ellerton, "Relations Between the Bank of England and the Commercial Banks of the United Kingdom," *Relations Between the Central Banks and Commercial Banks* (Frankfort on Main, 1957), pp. 107–108 (italics from source).

[2] Cited by A. M. Allen, "Great Britain," in A. M. Allen, *et al.*, *Commercial Banking Legislation and Control* (London, 1938), pp. 248–249.

as, after consultation with the Governor of the Bank, they think necessary in the public interest."[3] The government has not issued such directions and may never have to do so. As Hugh Dalton (who was Chancellor when the act was passed) has remarked: "It will only be necessary to
hint at the existence of this power."[4]

The Bank of England Act of 1946 also empowered the government
to control the privately owned commercial banks.[5] Some have questioned whether the government's powers to control the commercial
banks could be enforced in a crisis, because the powers are "ill-defined
and unbacked by penalties."[6] On the other hand, there exist important
counterweights to any legal inadequacies in the legislation: the long
tradition of cooperation between the monetary authorities and the
commercial banks,[7] and the probability that any defiance of government authority would raise the issue of nationalization once again.[8]

The Bank of England implements its monetary policy primarily
through the commercial banks. As earlier chapters have shown, the
English commercial banks are highly concentrated and committed to
anticompetitive practices. The Bank of England actively encouraged
some of the anticompetitive restraints (like the cartel agreement to fix
the call-loan rate) but, for the most part, it has not *officially* approved
or disapproved the restraints on competition. However, since the Bank
is fully aware of what is going on and can take whatever action it deems
necessary (under the Bank of England Act of 1946), its failure to act is
tantamount to tacit approval of the existing anticompetitive practices.
As the balance of this chapter will show, the Bank of England has done
more than give tacit approval to the anticompetitive restraints; it has
integrated the cartel and its agreements into the mechanism for conducting monetary policy. The manner in which the cartel and the
monetary-control mechanism have been linked together will be discussed for each of three major areas of central-bank concern: the allocation of bank credit, the supply of bank credit, and the pattern of short-
term interest rates.

---

[3] "Bank of England Act, 1946," in Hans Aufricht, *Central Banking Legislation* (Washington, 1961), p. 186.
[4] Cited by Thomas Balogh, "The Apotheosis of the Dilettante," in *The
Establishment*, Hugh Thomas, ed. (London, 1962 ed.), p. 103, n. 1.
[5] Cf. sec. 4 (par. 3) in Aufricht, p. 187.
[6] Cf. Balogh, *op. cit.*
[7] In April 29, 1937, Reginald McKenna (chairman, Midland Bank) acknowledged (in a speech to the British Bankers Association) the de facto authority
of the Treasury and the Bank of England over the clearing banks and declared that ". . . we bow willingly to their authority." Cited in Allen, p. 249.
[8] See G. D. H. Cole, *Money, Trade, and Investment* (London, 1954), p. 247.

Allocation of Bank Credit

Moral suasion, especially in the form of official "requests," is an important monetary control in England. The authorities prefer to make "requests" even though they have the authority to issue "commands." As noted above, the Bank Act of 1946 authorized the Bank of England to issue "directions" to the commercial banks, and the governor of the Bank of England has given public assurance that, if it were necessary in the public interest, the Bank would use its legal authority over the banks.[9] At the same time, however, the governor expressed a strong preference for mutual consultation with the clearing banks with a view toward determining what the public interest requires and how it can best be secured. The authorities prefer the method of informal cooperation because it is traditional in Britain, but also for the more practical reason that it puts the clearing banks and the authorities "on the same side of the fence."[10]

Moral suasion is effective in England for a number of reasons. First, the bankers as well as the monetary authorities prefer informal methods to formal controls or legislation. Second, the bankers are under no uncertainty about the true nature of the "requests." As one banker observed, "these three words [directives, suggestions, or recommendations] in practice amount to the same thing but more sensitive people prefer one word to another."[11] As a result, bankers listen very carefully to the governor's words, and as another banker said: "He might give us a hint and we should not be likely to ignore it."[12] Third, England has a highly concentrated banking system, and the banks are organized into a tight cartel. The governor of the Bank of England once remarked that "If I want to talk to the representatives of the British Banks, or indeed of the whole financial community, we can usually get together in one room in about half-an-hour."[13] Moreover, because the banks are few in number, it is easy for them to recognize their common interest

---

[9] See extract from speech by governor of Bank of England, at Ipswich, October 11, 1957, reprinted in Great Britain, Committee on the Working of the Monetary System, *Principal Memoranda of Evidence* (London, 1960), I, 51 (cited as Radcliffe Memoranda).

[10] Cf. also Bank of England memorandum in Radcliffe Memoranda, I, 39.

[11] Cf. Ellerton (n. 1 above), p. 115. In a similar view, another banker has stated that "However informal the relationship, I don't think we ever forget there being an iron hand inside the glove" (John Thomson, in *Economist*, September 4, 1965, p. 898).

[12] A. W. Tuke, Great Britain, Committee on the Working of the Monetary System, *Minutes of Evidence* (London, 1960), p. 280 (cited as Radcliffe Hearings).

[13] Radcliffe Memoranda, I, 52.

and to appreciate the impact that each can have upon a proposed policy. In short, given the preference for informal methods, the monetary authorities have found it desirable and expedient to incorporate the cartel into the informal apparatus for implementing monetary policy. From the point of view of the Bank of England, the high level of bank concentration and the cartel organization are highly useful features of the British banking system.

The monetary authorities have utilized moral suasion in the form of "requests" to regulate the use (as well as the volume) of bank credit. The "requests"—to favor certain application for bank credit and to deny others—originated during the Second World War and were aimed at denying credit for speculation in securities and commodity inventories and directing it to the war effort instead. The system of requests continued to be used after the war. In the immediate postwar period, particular emphasis was placed on credits to assist the export industries. In 1951, the government instructed the banks (by a request from the Chancellor of the Exchequer) to give priority to projects for defense, promotion of exports, savings of imports, relief of basic deficiencies (especially raw materials), and more economical use of resources. The banks were also asked not to lend for the production of "inessential" goods, especially those for the home market and which used metals.[14] Toward the end of 1964, the Bank of England asked the banks to be more "selective" in approving credit—that is, to give preference to exporters and manufacturers and to curtail lending for property development, installment buying, and other personal and professional uses.[15]

Requests have usually been formulated as broad guides with a good deal of detail left to the interpretation and judgment of the banks. In some cases, the guides provided contradictory indications—for example, in its domestic aspect, the entertainment industry was rated as a less essential enterprise and received a low priority; but as a potential earner or saver of foreign exchange, it qualified for the highest priority.[16] In other cases, the guides led to "endless argumentation about the definition of necessity,"[17] and there was a long-run tendency for the banks to interpret the requests less narrowly. This led one critic to conclude that "Except temporarily in periods of economic crisis, the

---

[14] See Treasury memorandum in Radcliffe Memoranda, I, 103.

[15] See *Wall Street Journal*, December 10, 1964.

[16] See E. J. N. Warburton, "Bank Lending under Directives," in Associazione Bancaria Italiana, First International Credit Conference, *Papers and Proceedings* (Rome, 1953), pp. 193–194. According to Warburton, "such examples could readily be multiplied." (Warburton was presumably describing the situation in the '40's.)

[17] *Idem.*

main effect of the requests was probably to provide a local bank manager with an even more impersonal excuse than 'head office' for refusing
an advance which he had no intention of making."[18] Finally, the use
of moral suasion sometimes had unintended and undesired side effects
which undermined the effectiveness of monetary control in other ways.[19]

In spite of these difficulties and limitations, successive chancellors of
the exchequer have acknowledged their satisfaction with the results
obtained by the system of requests.[20] Perhaps the best evidence that the
authorities find the system satisfactory is that they continue to use it.
In sum, moral suasion is an important instrument to control the use
(and, as the next section will show, the volume) of bank credit; and the
importance of this control instrument in England owes much to the
fact that banking is highly concentrated and that the banks are organized into a cartel.

Supply of Bank Credit

Long before the monetary authorities became interested in the banks'
liquidity ratio for its credit-control aspects, bankers used to look to this
ratio as a guide to the adequacy of bank liquidity. In 1885, George
Rae (chairman of the North and South Wales Bank) had proposed that
a bank ought to maintain liquid reserves equal to one-third of its liabilities to the public.[21] By 1931, the London clearing banks had still
not agreed in principle on an acceptable liquidity ratio; in practice,
they tended to hold about one-third of their total assets (and, therefore,
somewhat more than one-third of total deposit liabilities) in cash and
highly liquid short-term assets. By 1939, the 30 percent liquidity ratio
had gained considerable acceptance among bankers; by the end of 1946,
the London clearing banks had agreed that each bank would maintain
its *cash* ratio equal to 8 percent of its total deposit liabilities.

Although there are no statutory reserve requirements in England,
the authorities can use the informal arrangements that have evolved in
terms of the liquidity ratio as a monetary control. In 1951, the governor

---

[18] A. C. L. Day, *Outline of Monetary Economics* (Oxford, 1960), p. 191.
(Day's evaluation was made in the context of his discussion of the '40's.)

[19] For example, when the authorities requested the banks to restrict advances to hire purchase companies, the latter (deprived of their normal source
of funds) began to solicit deposits directly from the public, which has contributed to the relative decline of the commercial banks. This development
has concerned the monetary authorities because of its implications for the
effectiveness of central-bank control.

[20] See Warburton, p. 198, and Westminster Bank, p. 263, in ABI, *Papers
and Proceedings* (n. 16 above).

[21] "Bank Liquidity in the United Kingdom," Bank of England, *Quarterly
Bulletin*, December, 1962, p. 249.

of the Bank of England notified the clearing banks that a liquidity ratio of 28 to 32 percent of deposit liabilities would be considered normal, and that the banks ought never to permit the ratio to fall below 25 percent. In 1957, he raised the minimum to 30 percent. Despite some banker opinion that this was excessive in terms of normal banking procedure, the 30 percent ratio was maintained until early in 1963, when it was reduced to 29 percent, and then, in September, to 28 percent. The major liquid assets covered by the 28 percent liquidity ratio are cash (vault cash and bank deposits at the Bank of England), call loans to the discount market, commercial bills, and treasury bills.

Unlike the compulsory cash reserve required in some countries, the 8 percent cash ratio maintained by English banks has not played a key role in the central bank's attempts to influence the supply of bank credit, because the Bank of England (as lender of last resort) has been ready to supply needed funds. By tradition, it did not supply funds directly to the banks but only to the discount houses. This is a technicality, however. If the commercial banks needed cash, they could demand repayment of their call loans to the discount houses; and since the Bank of England would never refuse to lend to a recognized discount house (as long as it provides satisfactory security and accepts the Bank's price—normally Bank Rate), the banks could be perfectly confident that the discount houses would always be able to supply needed cash. During the 1930's, the central bank began to buy treasury bills directly from the banks. The practice expanded during the '40's and has continued to the present, but in contrast with the period 1940–1951, the Bank reserves the right to refuse to deal directly with the banks. However, as the clearing banks can resist, directly or indirectly, any pressure on their cash ratio, the monetary authorities have looked to the banks' liquid-asset ratio to influence the volume of bank deposits.

For several years after 1951, the liquidity ratio was above 30 percent (Table 60).[22] By the end of 1957, when the ratio had reached 38.4 percent, there was much concern that the central bank would be unable, if it became necessary, to carry out an effective restrictive monetary policy. This led the Radcliffe Committee to consider various schemes to increase the central bank's control over the banks.[23] Even before the committee had published its report, the Bank of England had an-

---

[22] In this table, the total liquid assets include coin, notes, balances (other than "special deposits") at Bank of England, money at call and short notice, and discounted bills. In other words, this is the clearing banks' conventional measure of liquidity. For a further discussion, cf. "Bank Liquidity in the United Kingdom," Bank of England, *Quarterly Bulletin*, December, 1962, especially pp. 251–252.

[23] For a good discussion of some of these plans, cf. Bank of England memorandum, Radcliffe Memoranda, I, 38–42.

nounced a standby scheme to control bank liquidity by means of a "special deposit" requirement.[24] This was a plan to raise the effective liquidity ratio, because the special deposits (which had to be placed with the Bank of England) could not be counted as part of the cash or other liquid assets which made up the 30 percent liquidity ratio. Since this scheme immobilized part of the bank's resources, the central bank proposed to pay interest on the special deposits (at the multiple of one-sixteenth percent nearest to the average treasury-bill rate at the preceding week's weekly tender).[25]

The system of special deposits, provided for in July, 1958, was not put into effect until April 28, 1960. Bank advances had risen steeply during the five weeks ending on April 20, a period in which little or no seasonal rise was expected,[26] and it was decided that further restrictive measures were required to supplement the rise in interest rates which had oc-

TABLE 60

Total Liquid Assets and Special Deposits,
London Clearing Banks, 1951–1966

| End of year | Total liquid assets[a] | | Special deposits (£ millions) |
	£ (millions)	Percent of gross deposits	
1951	2,100	33.2	—
1952	2,327	36.0	—
1953	2,460	36.7	—
1954	2,382	34.3	—
1955	2,471	37.4	—
1956	2,492	37.4	—
1957	2,664	38.4	—
1958	2,493	34.6	—
1959	2,543	34.2	—
1960	2,399	31.9	143
1961	2,666	35.3	221
1962	2,684	34.0	38
1963	2,723	32.7	—
1964	2,754	30.6	—
1965	3,039	32.1	91
1966	3,126	32.9	188

a Total liquid assets includes coin, notes and balances with Bank of England (excluding special deposits), money at call and short notice, and bills discounted.
Source: Bank of England, *Quarterly Bulletins.*

[24] See Bank of England, *Annual Report, 1959*, p. 4.
[25] See "Procedure of Special Deposits," Bank of England, *Quarterly Bulletin*, December, 1960, p. 18.
[26] For a fuller discussion of the considerations which led to this action, see *ibid.*, pp. 3–4.

curred earlier in the year. Accordingly, the Bank of England called for special deposits equal to one percent of gross deposits.[27] Special-deposit requirements remained continuously in effect until the end of 1962 and reached a maximum of £229 million in February, 1962.[28]

There were no special deposits required throughout 1963 or 1964— as noted earlier, the authorities wanted to facilitate bank advances in 1963, and reduced the required liquidity ratio to 28 percent—but on April 29, 1965, the Bank of England responded to a "disquietingly large" increase in bank advances by again calling on the clearing banks for special deposits of one percent (in two stages: one-half by May 19, and the rest by June 16). At the same time, the governor wrote to the chairman of the Committee of London Clearing Bankers to emphasize that, since the authorities wanted the call for special deposits to be fully reflected in bank lending policies, the banks were to avoid as much as possible countering the effect by selling investments.[29]

Until about the mid-1960's, it had been widely accepted that the authorities could generate pressure on the banks' liquidity ratio by taking actions which served to increase the amount of government securities held by the nonbanking public by more than any increase in government borrowing.[30] Budgetary policy was an important means of securing that result. The authorities could also put pressure on the banks' liquidity ratio by inducing the public to hold more treasury bills to replace maturing bills held by banks (or discount houses). Other things being equal, this shift required a relative rise in bill yields. The Bank of England could bring about the higher yields by means of open-market operations to force the market more heavily into the Bank; but since the relative rise in treasury bill yields was more important (in terms of the shift) than the absolute rise, the authorities also had to be concerned about the movements in other short-term rates.

---

[27] *Ibid.*, p. 4. On that date, the special deposits of the London clearing banks amounted to £70 millions. See Bank of England, *Annual Report, 1961*, p. 10.

[28] By comparison, on the same date, their total liquid assets (not including special deposits—i.e., the liquid assets included in their conventional liquidity ratio) amounted to £2,465 million.

In general, the full effect of the special deposits on the banks' liquidity ratio cannot be fully observed from the year-end data shown in Table 60. At the end of 1959, for example, the banks' liquidity ratio was 34.2 percent, but it had fallen to 30.8 percent by the end of June, 1960. It fluctuated between a low of 30.4 and a high of 33.1 percent during most of 1961 but rose dramatically in the last quarter and reached 35.3 percent by the end of 1961. For a negative evaluation of the effectiveness of the special deposits during this period, cf. W. Manning Dacey, *The British Banking Mechanism*, 4th rev. ed. (London, 1962), pp. 196–199.

[29] Bank of England, *Quarterly Bulletin*, June, 1965, pp. 110–111.

[30] For a discussion of these matters, cf. "Bank Liquidity in the United Kingdom," Bank of England, *Quarterly Bulletin*, December, 1962, pp. 253–254.

In this connection, the cartel agreement on the deposit rate was able to serve the ends of monetary policy. When the authorities tightened credit (or simply did not counteract a trend toward tighter credit) without raising Bank Rate, the treasury bill rate would rise, and because of the cartel deposit agreement, this rise would widen the differential with the deposit rate. When monetary policy again became flexible in 1951, the differential between the treasury bill rate and the deposit rate widened, and this induced the public to hold more treasury bills.[31] In 1955, there was a particularly large increase in the differential (Fig. 9), and this was associated with a large shift (especially by large corporations) from bank deposits to treasury bills. In subsequent years, the differential between the two yields has been wider, but it has moved through a much narrower range. Even more important, as far as nonbank buyers of treasury bills are concerned, there have been more attractive short-term outlets elsewhere. For example, in September, 1965, when the treasury bill yield was about $5\frac{1}{4}$ percent, a three-month deposit with a local authority was about $6\frac{1}{2}$ percent and certain finance houses were paying up to 7 percent.[32] In spite of these more attractive rates on other short-term outlets, however, the discount houses have sometimes had stiff competition from other bidders at the tender—on occasions, they have been allotted 10 percent or less of the bills they applied for; and for six continuous weeks during 1965, they received less than one-third of their applications.[33]

In recent years, the commercial bill has occupied a more important place in the clearing banks' liquidity ratio. At one point (April, 1965), the volume of commercial bills (United Kingdom and others) even exceeded (by some £49 million) the volume of treasury bills held by the clearing banks.[34] The resurgence of the commercial bill has raised questions (which it was thought the Radcliffe Committee had settled) about the mechanism for controlling the supply of bank deposits through control of the banks' liquidity ratio.[35] In the context of the

---

[31] The authorities welcomed the shift ". . . because it has the same effect as an open market operation and reduces the liquid resources of the clearing banks" (Ellerton [n. 1 above], p. 109).

[32] Cf. "The U.K. and U.S. Treasury Bill Markets," Bank of England, *Quarterly Bulletin*, December, 1965, p. 331. Such differentials have been an important factor in holding down the demand for treasury bills by industrial and commercial companies, especially in recent years. Cf. *ibid.*, p. 337; but cf. also *Quarterly Bulletin*, June, 1963, p. 87.

[33] Cf. "U.K. and U.S. Treasury Bill Markets," p. 335.

[34] Cf. Bank of England, *Quarterly Bulletin*.

[35] For a discussion of some of the issues that have been raised, see "Whatever Happened to Credit Control?" *Economist*, Banking Supplement, June 19, 1965, pp. vii–x; and R. L. Crouch, "Inadequacy of 'New Orthodox' Methods of Monetary Control," *Economic Journal*, December, 1964, pp. 916–934.

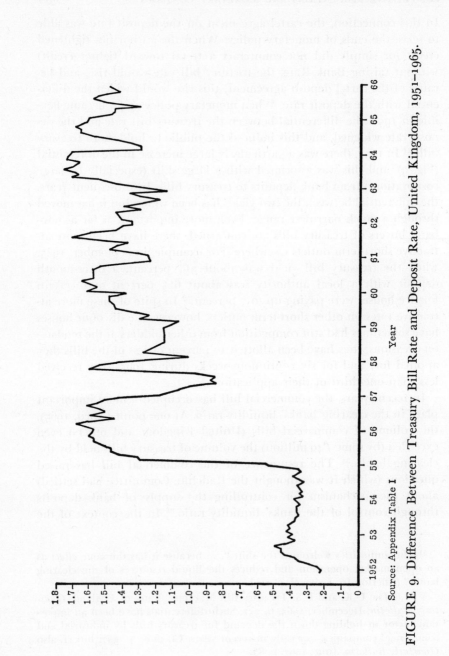

Source: Appendix Table I

FIGURE 9. Difference Between Treasury Bill Rate and Deposit Rate, United Kingdom, 1951–1965.

present study, the point to stress is that these developments have increased the importance of the cartel as an instrument of credit control, because they have led the authorities to place increased emphasis upon the use of "requests" to control the volume of credit. Thus, in May, 1965, the Bank of England asked the banks to keep loans for domestic purposes from rising more than 5 percent during the twelve months ending in March, 1966; on February 1, 1966, the banks were asked not to exceed until further review the levels set for March, 1966.[36] Under present conditions, such "requests" have become a major means of regulating the amount of bank lending.

Pattern of Short-term Interest Rates

It has sometimes been said that "Bank rate is the only rate which the Bank of England fixes specifically; it does not attempt to fix the deposit rate or the overdraft rate of the commercial banks."[37] It should be added, however, that the existence of cartel agreements and understandings also makes it unnecessary for the Bank to set those other rates. Table 61 shows the relation between Bank Rate and those short-term interest rates that are most directly affected by changes in Bank Rate. On the date shown in the table, Bank Rate happened to be 7 percent. Under the cartel's various rate agreements, the deposit rate automatically became 5 percent, the minimum call-money rate $5\frac{3}{8}$ percent, and the advances rate 7 to 9 percent.

The rates on prime bank bills and treasury bills are also related to Bank Rate. In Table 61, the two bill rates are wedged between Bank Rate as an upper bound and the minimum call-money rate (determined by Bank Rate) as a lower bound. This has been a stable and dependable feature of the short-term rate structure (Fig. 10). Bank Rate is an upper bound because, if the two bill rates rose above Bank

TABLE 61

*Bank Rate and the Structure of Short-term Interest Rates,
August, 1966*

	Rate (percent)
Advances	7–9
Trade bills (3 months)	8–8½
Bank Rate	7
Prime–bank bills (3 months)	$6\frac{15}{16}$
Treasury bills	$6\,{}^{7}/_{10}$
Call money (minimum rate)	5⅜
Deposit rate	5

SOURCES: Bank of England, *Quarterly Bulletin*, except for advances. The latter is based on the information about advances discussed in Chapter XV.

[36] Cf. Bank of England, *Quarterly Bulletin*, March 1966, p. 3.
[37] Ellerton (n. 1 above), p. 113.

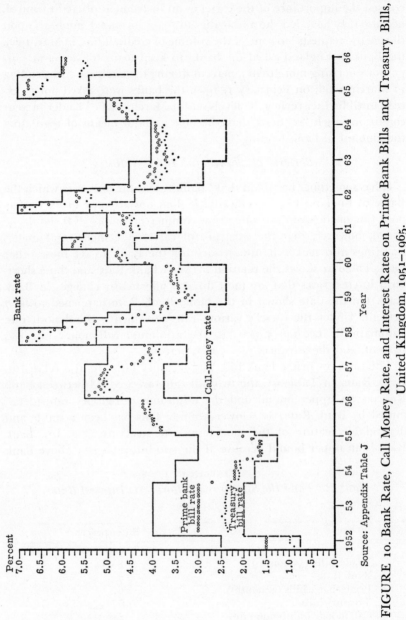

FIGURE 10. Bank Rate, Call Money Rate, and Interest Rates on Prime Bank Bills and Treasury Bills, United Kingdom, 1951–1965.

Source: Appendix Table J

Rate, the discount houses would be able to borrow at Bank Rate
(no longer penal) and relend to the market at a profit. The call-
money minimum rate is a lower bound because the discount houses,
which are an important part of the market, cannot afford to buy the
bills at rates below the minimum call-loan rate at which such a large
part of their own funds must be secured.

The Bank of England can do more than set the upper and lower
bounds for the two bill rates: it can largely determine their level
within those bounds. In part, this is because the Bank has the power
not only to set the terms on which it will lend to the market but also
to influence the amount which the market will be obliged to borrow
at those terms. The Bank can control the amount of borrowing by
using open-market operations to impair the banks' cash ratio, compel
them to call their loans to the discount market, and thereby force the
discount houses into the Bank.[38] The Bank can then deal with them
on whatever terms it wishes to set. The Bank has often dealt through
the "back door" at prevailing market rates (in direct dealings with
banks as well as with the discount houses), but it can close that "back
door" any time it wishes. The only lending commitment which the
Bank feels obliged to honor is the commitment to lend to the market
without limit *at a price*—and the *minimum* price is Bank Rate, a
penal rate.[39] In short, by a combination of setting Bank Rate and of
purchasing and selling treasury bills (through the "front door" or
the "back door," as the situation may require), the Bank has been able
to set the level of bill rates pretty much where it wished within the
upper and lower bounds.

The treasury bill rate was close to its lower bound from 1951 to
1954, and (with some exceptions) close to the upper bound during
most of the rest of the period shown in Figure 10; but except when

---

[38] To this extent, the 8 percent cash ratio still has a role to play, for the
degree of pressure on the cash ratio influences the treasury bill rate. See Bank
of England, *Quarterly Bulletin*, December, 1962, p. 251.

[39] See Sir Antony Macnaghten, Radcliffe Hearings, p. 258.
On January 3, 1963, the Bank of England announced that it would in the
future reserve the right to lend to the market on occasion at a rate above (instead of at) Bank Rate. (See Bank of England, *Quarterly Bulletin*, March, 1963,
p. 4.) This was a reversion to an earlier practice which began during the nineteenth century and which the Bank continued to employ for many years before
the Second World War. (After 1926, the margin was nearly always one-half
percent.) The main purpose of the new arrangement seems to have been to
permit the authorities to vary market rates with an eye to the position of
sterling on the foreign exchanges without at the same time necessarily affecting
bank overdraft rates. The new technique was used for the first time on March
19, 1963, when the Bank made advances to the discount market at 4½ percent
at a time when Bank Rate was 4 percent. The immediate effect was a sharp
lowering of the discount market bid at the next tender on March 22. See Bank
of England, *Quarterly Bulletin*, June, 1963, p. 87.

Bank Rate changed, both the treasury bill and the prime bank bill rates have typically moved within quite narrow limits—mostly a one-half percent range, and frequently much less. The Treasury places great emphasis on stable market rates. As the biggest borrower in the market, the government wants an orderly market, meaning that "the short-term rate of interest should not fluctuate wildly from day to day or week to week but should be reasonably stable."[40] It believes, moreover, that the market requires assistance to absorb the variations in the government's requirements without extreme fluctuations in the bill rates.[41] Accordingly, the authorities have acquiesced in certain noncompetitive arrangements involving the discount houses and the clearing banks.

To increase the market's ability to absorb varying volumes of treasury bills without wide variations in bill rates, the authorities have supported the arrangement whereby the discount houses informally undertake to cover the weekly tender. To assist the discount houses in carrying out this undertaking, the authorities have gone along with the noncompetitive syndicated bid of the discount houses and the arrangement whereby the clearing banks refrain from competing with the discount houses at the weekly tender. Although the discount houses do not have a monopoly at the tender, they have usually dominated it, and the rate at which they tender normally becomes the basis of the rates for treasury bill dealing until the next tender.[42] Moreover, to be in a position to make even a noncompetitive bid at a reasonably stable price (in relation to Bank Rate) for widely varying amounts of treasury bills, the discount houses have required assurance that they could secure their own funds at a reasonably stable cost. Since the discount houses borrow most of their funds from the clearing banks,[43] the authorities have supported the cartel agreement on the call-loan rate for "regular" money. To offer a reasonably stable rate on "regular" money, the clearing banks in turn have wanted assurance that they could secure at least part of their own funds at a stable cost, and the authorities have provided that assurance by permitting the clearing banks to collude on the deposit rate.

[40] Great Britain, Committee on the Working of the Monetary System, *Report* (London, 1959), p. 115 (cited as Radcliffe Report). The government is also concerned that "extreme variations in bill rates would be damaging to the bond markets and so to the Government's funding policy" (*ibid.*, p. 216).

[41] *Idem.*

[42] Cf. London Discount Market memorandum, Radcliffe Memoranda, I, 11, and "The U.K. and U.S. Treasury Bill Markets," Bank of England, *Quarterly Bulletin*, December, 1965, p. 335.

[43] The clearing banks supplied about half of the funds borrowed by the discount houses during most of the '50's. The proportion has been even higher in the '60's. At the end of 1965, for example, they supplied £849 million of the £1,381 million borrowed by the discount market.

The Radcliffe Committee looked into this system of anticompetitive arrangements and concluded (without necessarily accepting all of the official views on the matter) that "there is no case for deliberately disrupting it."[44] They based this conclusion in part on their judgment that the present system works satisfactorily for the authorities without, as far as they could observe, providing unreasonably high profits for market institutions.[45] At the time of the Radcliffe Report, there was ample reason to believe that the authorities were satisfied with the present arrangements;[46] more recently, the Jones Committee has recommended the abolition of the deposit-rate cartel and has also questioned the arrangements with the discount market.[47]

TOWARD A NEW POLICY ON BANK COMPETITION?

When the Radcliffe Committee accepted the present restrictive practices in the treasury bill market, it acknowledged that it was also implicitly accepting certain restrictive practices in the banking system; and it was willing to accept them because "As far as the banks are concerned, we have observed a sufficient spirit of competition between them, in their dealings with their ordinary customers, to justify acquiescence in the agreements that dominate the bill market."[48] In the past few years, the banks' competitive spirit has been increasingly questioned. As noted earlier, the gross deposits of the clearing banks have been declining as a percentage of Gross National Product during the postwar years. For many years, this decline caused no particular concern among bankers or nonbankers, and some even regarded it "as a healthy correction of overliquidity in the years of war and inflation. . . "[49] As the "correction" continued, doubts began to be expressed about its "healthy" character. This concern was heightened (in 1962) by the

---

[44] Radcliffe Report, p. 218.

[45] *Idem.* It should be added, however, that the Radcliffe Committee did not inquire into the total profit position of the clearing banks. (Cf. Radcliffe Report, p. 60.) That would have been necessary in looking for any evidence of monopoly profits from the collusive discount house operations, because the clearing banks keep a close watch on discount house profits and are quick to squeeze the discount houses if any excess profits show up.

[46] For a discussion of the Bank of England's views about whether treasury bill rates would be higher or lower under an alternative system, cf. Radcliffe Memoranda, I, 11–12.

[47] The Jones Committee speculated that the net effect of the collusive arrangements between the clearing banks and the discount houses may be to keep the treasury bill rate higher than it otherwise need be. However, on the grounds that these matters were beyond its terms of reference, the committee made no formal recommendations in this area. Cf. National Board for Prices and Incomes, *Bank Charges* (London, May, 1967), p. 39 (cited as Jones Report).

[48] Radcliffe Report, p. 218.

[49] "Banker to Europe?" *Economist*, June 30, 1962, p. 1328.

prospect of Britain's entry into the Common Market, for many considered the financial services available through the well-developed financial machinery of the City of London to be one of the most hopeful
areas in which England might compete after joining the Common
Market.[50]

With England poised on "the eve of the great adventure," the *Economist* offered a glowing description of the opportunities which were
in store for the City: "It is possible to see a great future for the City
of London in the common market. London has not so much the best
as the only really well-organised of Europe's money and capital markets.
With proper guidance it is possible that Lombard Street might even
perform for Europe what in the nineteenth century it did for England. . . ."[51]

Few, if any, doubted that English bankers could find ready takers
on the European continent for English bank loans at lower interest
rates and perhaps even at rates that were relatively high by London
standards. The problem was rather how to finance the lending. Clearly,
one possibility was for British exports to rise sufficiently to provide the
necessary surplus, but many believed that a more hopeful possibility
was for the banks to finance an increase in foreign lending by attracting funds from abroad. The critical question was whether the clearing
banks could be persuaded to become more competitive. The American
banks in London and the accepting houses had demonstrated that it
was possible to attract foreign deposits to London by offering competitive deposit rates; but in spite of their relative decline, the clearing
banks continued to remain shackled by the cartel agreement to hold
deposit rates at the uncompetitive level of two percent below Bank
Rate for foreign and domestic depositors alike.

The clearing bankers have based this noncompetitive deposit-rate
policy on a number of considerations. First, when the question was
raised at the Radcliffe Hearings, the clearing bank representatives explained that the banks had ample liquidity. In view of the bank lending restrictions (which had been in effect since the war), they were
not eager to secure more deposits by paying more if they were just
going to turn around and invest them in securities.[52] At that time, the
clearing banks' loan-to-deposit ratio (one measure of bank liquidity)
was about 30 percent (Table 62), and it had been even lower for sev-

[50] The discussion in the text is limited to the machinery for short-term financing, but similarly optimistic expectations were held for the City's long-term capital facilities. For a discussion of the latter, see Lord Cromer's speech to the
bankers and merchants of the City of London, October 3, 1962, in Bank of
England, *Quarterly Bulletin*, December, 1962, pp. 263–266.

[51] "Banker to Europe?" *Economist*, June 30, 1962, p. 1331.

[52] See D. J. Robarts, Radcliffe Hearings, p. 289.

eral years before 1958—the excess liquidity position of the banks extended back to the cheap-money era in the '30's. In 1960, the ratio had risen to almost 43 percent, but the bankers were still not concerned about their liquidity or prepared to compete actively for deposits.[53] In 1963, when the loan-to-deposit ratio had climbed to 47.5 percent, a prominent banker went on record with the view that "at this particular stage the resources of the banks are adequate for lending of the kind they have so far considered appropriate to their function . . ."[54] In 1964, the loan-to-deposit ratio reached a then postwar high of 50.4 percent, and it was reported that many bankers did become worried;[55] but the ratio fell in 1965, doubtless reflecting the loan-control measures taken by the Bank of England during that year.

A second reason why the clearing banks have not competed more ac-

TABLE 62

Clearing Banks Advances, 1951–1966

Year (end of year)	£ millions	Percent of gross deposits
1951	1,860	29.4
1952	1,665	25.8
1953	1,611	24.1
1954	1,783	25.7
1955	1,747	26.4
1956	1,832	27.5
1957	1,777	25.7
1958	2,126	29.5
1959	2,818	36.8
1960	3,229	42.9
1961	3,209	42.5
1962	3,506	44.4
1963	3,961	47.5
1964	4,538	50.4
1965	4,569	48.3
1966	4,492	47.3

SOURCE: Bank of England, *Quarterly Bulletin.*

[53] As one leading banker put it, the bankers hate to lose business (even when not especially profitable), but "if they [depositors] prefer to put their surplus funds into a Building Society or a Trustee Savings Bank, or into Treasury Bills when big money is involved, I do not think we should go out of our way to persuade them otherwise; certainly not when money is very plentiful" (A. W. Tuke, "The Chairman's Speech at Newcastle," *Barclay's Bank Review,* May, 1960, p. 24).

[54] Lord Monckton (Midland Bank), "Lord Monckton Reports on Banking in a Changing World," *Economist,* January 26, 1963, p. 353.

[55] *Ibid.,* February 1, 1964, p. 425. At the end of 1964, the clearing banks' loan-to-deposit ratio ranged from a low of 47.8 percent (National Provincial) to a high of 57 percent (District Bank). *London Times,* January 1, 1965.

tively for time deposits is their feeling that it is partly self-defeating, because the higher rates will induce some depositors to shift funds from current accounts (which do not earn interest) to deposit accounts (which do).[56] To this extent, it is argued, a higher-rate policy would not increase the total volume of bank deposits; it would simply shift competition away from the current-account market to the deposit-account market. The banks do not wish to encourage the shift because, as noted earlier, they consider that they are in a stronger position to compete in the current-account market where they can offer a variety of services (including checking and loan services) in connection with demand deposits. They also resist the shift because it would increase cost significantly but would not lead to higher deposits nor to higher-yielding assets. With respect to the latter, one banker explained that "We treat all our money alike; it goes into the common pot; and the fact that we had some fixed for a longer term . . . would not influence us in any way. Therefore it would not do us any good."[57]

A third reason for not competing is that the bankers have not been unduly concerned about the loss of deposits to local authorities or to such nonbanking institutions as hire-purchase companies and building societies. In the bankers' view, the funds thus shifted are not permanently lost to the banking system: the funds received by the local authorities pass into the bank accounts of contractors and suppliers; and the funds received by hire-purchase companies and building societies enlarge the demands for goods and services, and the bank accounts of those who provide them.[58] In short, since the deposits will in any case return to the banks, an offer of higher rates to keep them from leaving in the first place will simply raise bank costs without affecting the volume of bank deposits.[59] On the other hand, if an offer of higher rates could prevent funds from going into treasury bills or trustee savings banks, it would "increase the amount of funds immediately available for loans in the Banking System."[60] Since those rates have at times been significantly higher than the clearing banks' deposit rate, the bankers doubt whether the higher costs would be worthwhile. Moreover, many bankers believed that if the banks succeeded in getting more deposits at the expense of the Treasury, the authorities would simply take countermeasures, because "the overall amount of money is determined by

---

[56] See Robarts, Radcliffe Hearings, p. 289.

[57] A. W. Tuke, Radcliffe Hearings, pp. 292–293; for a similar view, cf. Radcliffe Report, p. 44.

[58] See Monckton, p. 353. However, he also noted that his analysis is incomplete, and that nonbanks have been lending in lieu of banks.

[59] For a different view (i.e., that the size of the banking system depends in part on the growth of nonbanks), see John G. Gurley and Edward S. Shaw, *Money in a Theory of Finance* (Washington, 1960).

[60] Tuke, in *Barclays Bank Review*, May, 1960, p. 24.

Government policy and nothing the banks do will increase or diminish it."[61]

A fourth consideration that has inhibited banks from competing more vigorously for time deposits is their feeling that they would not be successful. This is partly because they believe that the great majority of depositors are insensitive to rate differences among alternative savings outlets.[62] Bankers also doubt that a more aggressive bank posture could prevent the loss of deposits, because higher bank rates would lead to an increase in rivals' rates, and given the nature of the rivals' earning assets, the banks' competitors can afford the higher rates better than the banks. Again, the result would be higher costs but not more deposits. Moreover, the higher costs could force the bankers to raise at least some of their lending rates. Bankers would regret this necessity because they "take pride in the low level of their lending rates, and regard them as a vital service to the British economy."[63] In addition, higher loan rates would be "blunting an edge where the banks are keen competitors with other lenders . . ."[64]

Finally, bankers generally have also opposed the suggestion that they might compete for deposits by a selective (and discriminatory) approach within the banks. Many nonbankers who urge more bank competition for deposits agree with the banks that they ought not to pay interest on current accounts—that would be both prohibitive and unnecessary—but do not agree that all deposit accounts should be paid the same rate of interest. Instead, they have urged the banks "to compete only at the margin, for funds which genuinely are interest-sensitive and accordingly are being placed in growing volume outside the clearing banks . . ."[65] The reaction of at least some bankers has been that "We could not be sure of success in restricting higher rates to particular categories of depositors . . ."[66] Part of the difficulty arises from the banker–customer relation—if bankers tried to use a longer maturity or a minimum amount as a basis for paying higher rates, they would be hard put (in view of the personal and relatively informal relations between bankers and customers) to deny the higher rates to customers who just failed to meet those standards. Similarly, the banks have refused the suggestion that they adopt American-style certificates of deposit in minimum denominations of £50,000 or £100,000 as a means of preventing "the dreaded spillover" of higher rates onto all bank deposits. Apparently they think it would raise their costs without increasing their deposits;[67]

---

[61] D. A. Stirling (Westminster Bank), cited in *Banker*, February, 1964, p. 78.
[62] For example, cf. Tuke, Radcliffe Hearings, p. 289.
[63] *Economist*, January 26, 1963, p. 332.
[64] Monckton, *ibid.*, p. 353.
[65] *Economist*, January 26, 1963, p. 331.
[66] Monckton, *ibid.*, p. 353.
[67] Cf. John Thomson, in *Economist*, September 4, 1965, p. 898.

in any case, they probably believe they have the necessary flexibility by operating through the finance houses which they own or control.[68]

The general feeling among many bankers that they could not be successful in preventing the loss of deposits—and need not be too disturbed by it[69]—was challenged by an unexpected source (the governor of the Bank of England), in an unexpected form (a public speech), and on an unexpected occasion (the four-hundredth-anniversary dinner of Martins Bank). The governor devoted only two paragraphs of his speech (on April 25, 1963) to the question of bank competition, but the brevity of his remarks does not obscure their significance, for—as the *Economist* observed—"In the course of a few sentences . . . Lord Cromer subtly and decisively threw the weight of the Bank of England on the side of competition and innovation; and in doing so he turned the scales in the whole issue."[70] Because of their importance, Lord Cromer's comments on bank competition are reproduced in full:

It is becoming almost commonplace to observe that deposit banking now faces competition more intense and from more directions than perhaps ever before. In essence the competition as such should be beneficial as it gives the customer a wider range of choice to suit his particular needs. It would seem that existing and potential bank depositors—be they corporate or individual—are increasingly finding their needs met outside their bank account. One result of this is that bank deposits are not rising at the rate that might be anticipated from the growth of the economy through the years, and are not rising at a rate commensurate with the possible, and I hope likely, requirements of expanding industry. It is too facile to argue that because some deposits are being placed with other deposit-taking institutions who are bank customers themselves that this does not matter. And it is too facile to expect the authorities to ease the problem by creating additional liquidity expressly for this purpose, for indeed a situation could arise in which the limiting factor on banking activity is not purely and simply liquidity requirements but the fact that your overall resources may inhibit your fulfillment of what the national economy demands. There is, of course, I know, competition amongst banks and, in the matter of service, I am frequently informed the competition is intense. But the question this leaves in my mind is whether the competition is really for existing bank customers or whether it is in the sphere of seeking new depositors which, from my point of view, seems infinitely more important.

After 400 years I think perhaps we are entitled to question practices of more recent origin, be they, say, twenty years old or two hundred years old. Is the considerable rigidity in interest rates which has grown up in the banking world in the last twenty years or so an encouragement to the growth

---

[68] Cf. "Levering up Bank Lending Charges," *Banker*, September, 1964, p. 554. Cf. also *Economist*, January 9, 1965, p. 141.

[69] For example, cf. Tuke's statement to his fellow bankers: "I do not think that this need disturb us unduly and, even if we tried to stem the tide, I doubt if we should succeed" (*Barclays Bank Review*, May, 1960, p. 24).

[70] "The New Official Request," *Economist*, June 29, 1963, p. 1365.

of bank deposits? Are the traditional hours within which bank customers are expected to transact their business in step with demands of potential bank customers in the year of grace 1963? In brief, for time runs out, I would pose the question whether we as bankers, and speaking as a banker myself, are doing all that can be done to ensure that the banks serve the needs of the twentieth century community as well as they have served the needs of past centuries.

The governor's remarks were widely discussed and variously interpreted. According to one interpretation, the governor was concerned that the relative decline of the clearing banks could impede the higher economic growth rates on which the government has set its sights. In this view, the banks' failure to hold their deposit position would also threaten their position as lenders, and the credit facilities provided by their more rapidly growing rivals "are not regarded generally as an effective substitute for the flexible overdraft facilities traditionally provided by the big deposit banks, at least so far as the needs of industry are concerned."[71] The relative decline of the clearing banks could concern the monetary authorities for a second reason. The major instruments of monetary control bear upon the clearing banks with particular force. To that extent, the effectiveness of the controls is blunted as the clearing banks become a less important part of the financial structure.

Although Lord Cromer clearly rejected the clearing bankers' basic argument that bank competition for deposits is either self-defeating or unnecessary, he apparently did not mean to propose unrestricted interbank competition for deposits.[72] The official opposition to unrestricted deposit-rate competition apparently was based on two major considerations. First, the government feared that such competition would significantly raise bank costs and force the clearing banks to raise their lending rates.[73] This fear was much in evidence in the events which followed Lord Cromer's speech when it was reported as "all but certain that a major move by the banks to compete for deposits will be made, and quite likely that it will be made this summer."[74] However, in the

---

[71] "Challenge from the Bank," *Banker*, June, 1963, p. 382. For a similar interpretation, see "The New Official Request," p. 1368: "The burden of the governor's message was that present financial intermediaries are not an adequate substitute."

[72] This view was generally shared by his supporters in the push for more bank competition. For example, the *Economist* stated that "No one is contemplating any all-out drive for higher deposits at any costs . . ." (June 29, 1963, p. 1367). Similarly, the *Banker* declared that "there is little or no support for a return to pre-war practice, which left the banks free to pay whatever they chose for funds at more than seven days' notice . . ." (June, 1963, p. 385).

[73] For example, Col. Marshall Brooks (District Bank) was certain that bank overdraft rates would have risen sharply if deposit rates had been raised in response to Lord Cromer's speech. Cf. "More Competition in Banking," *Banker*, February, 1965, p. 80.

[74] Cf. *Economist*, June 29, 1963, p. 1365.

autumn, when the banks appeared to be on the verge of beginning to compete for deposits, it was reported that they had been "frustrated by the Treasury, which indicated that the Government would not like to see the banks offset the higher costs of competing for deposits by charging more for loans."[75] A second reason for the official position was that the deposit-rate cartel is part of a complex and interdependent set of arrangements that determines the structure and level of short-term interest rates. If the banks abandoned their deposit-rate agreement, they would threaten their present call-loan arrangements with the discount houses, and eventually they would begin to tender directly for treasury bills.[76] This would force the discount houses to withdraw their guarantee for treasury bill tenders, and bill rates would doubtless exhibit greater instability than the authorities have been prepared to accept.

Events have moved swiftly since Lord Cromer made his pathbreaking challenge to the banks, and his proposals for reform of the bank cartel are mild compared with those made a few years later by the Jones Committee. In its report of May, 1967, the Jones Committee made a number of revolutionary proposals in support of its view that "the financial system should be so organized that it adapts flexibly to the evolution of the requirements upon it of borrowers and lenders, that it meets these requirements adequately and equitably so that individual groups of borrowers and lenders are not arbitrarily disadvantaged, and that all the possible economies in administration and other costs are realized."[77]

In the committee's opinion, these desirable characteristics of a financial system could be advanced by increasing the competition in banking. To this end, the committee recommended the abandonment of the deposit-rate cartel, and the dissolution of the collective agreement on advances rates (except for export loans). As noted earlier, it also questioned the cartel agreements in the discount market but did not pursue this matter, which was beyond the committee's terms of reference.

At a minimum, the recommendations of the Jones Committee are evidence of a dramatic evolution in official thinking about bank competition. Whether the recommendations of the Jones Committee, if adopted, would actually result in significantly greater competition (as the committee clearly expects)[78] is another matter. As noted elsewhere in this study, a removal of artificial restraints on competition cannot assure competitive results in markets that are concentrated.

---

[75] "Why Bankers Come to London," *Economist*, May 16, 1964, p. 739. For another view of this episode, cf. "How the Banks Compete for Deposits," *Banker*, July, 1967, p. 583.

[76] See Radcliffe Report, p. 217.

[77] Cf. Jones Report, p. 27.

[78] For example, cf. *ibid.*, p. 39.

Part Four
International Comparisons

XIX

The Regulation of Bank Competition: Alternative Policies and Market Effects

In each country included in this study, the authorities have influenced the nature and extent of bank competition, indirectly by their controls on bank concentration and directly by their controls on the conditions of bank competition; but each country has followed a different set of regulatory policies. It has been the purpose of this volume to study the different kinds, forms, and combinations of the controls that regulate bank competition in these countries, and to show how alternative combinations affect banking market structures, market performance, and the efficacy of monetary policy.

Although this final chapter is not a summary of this study, it does pull together some of the earlier material by means of a point-by-point cross country comparison of different policies to regulate bank competition and their effects on banking markets. This comparative survey serves to highlight the range of policies that can be employed to regulate bank competition, and at the same time it provides a basis for important generalizations about the underlying relationships that determine the market impact of alternative sets of regulatory restraints on bank competition.

REGULATION OF BANKING CONCENTRATION

Policies on Bank Concentration

Each country studied has pursued a different policy with respect to bank concentration. Bank concentration was regulated first in England, but it was already well advanced when the government started to control it. The authorization of limited-liability banking in 1858 inaugurated a period, which lasted until 1918, during which neither legal nor political barriers impeded the growth of bank concentration. There was an enormous amount of merger activity during those years, and by the end of the period, the banking population of England had been reduced to a tenth of its size at the beginning of the period. Until the closing years of that period, the mergers which were expanding the branch networks of the survivors had mostly eliminated smaller banks. Toward the end of the period, mergers began to eliminate large banks which already possessed large branch networks. This change in the merger pattern aroused fears that a money trust was in the making, and the Colwyn Committee, which was appointed in 1918, recommended that no further mergers be allowed without the prior approval of the government. By 1918, however, the Big Five were already dominant banks, with a combined total of about 80 percent of all commercial bank deposits and branches. In part as a result of continued merger activity, bank concentration continued to increase. In short, the concentration policy in England has led to an exceptionally high level of bank concentration.

In Italy, the second country to regulate bank concentration, the original policy and the circumstances in which it was carried out were quite different from the English situation: in England, the government intervened to arrest the increase in bank concentration; in Italy, the government intervened to foster further concentration. The policy of increasing concentration began with the Banking Law of 1926 and was reinforced by the Banking Law of 1936. In 1926, there were almost 4,000 banks in Italy and almost 12,000 branches; by the end of 1945, the bank population had been reduced to 1,432, and the number of branches to 6,889. The postwar governments pursued a different policy on concentration—they authorized a large expansion in the number of branches; and instead of expanding large banks (public law and national interest banks), they fostered an expansion of the banking offices of smaller banks (savings, people's cooperative, and ordinary credit banks). In trying to avoid excessive bank concentration, the Italian authorities have been concerned about the effect not only on bank competition but also upon the government's economic development program. To stimulate economic development (especially in less developed and rural areas) without encouraging a growth in industrial concentration, the government has deemed it necessary, because of the high positive correlation between size of bank and size of borower in Italy, to foster a banking structure with a wide and balanced representation of bank sizes. Under this concentration policy, there are almost 1,300 banks and more than 10,000 branches; and the half-dozen largest banks hold approximately one-third of bank deposits.

In France, the last country to regulate bank concentration, public policy has led to a level of bank concentration between the English and Italian levels. The Vichy regime inaugurated government control of bank concentration with the Banking Act of 1941. At that time (according to a bank census of 1942), there were 356 banks (*banques inscrites*)—but six large banks (*établissements de crédit*) held almost 56 percent of total bank resources, and 22 other banks (half affiliated with the Crédit Industriel et Commercial) exercised important influence in their respective regions. The large banks, which had mostly been organized in the second half of the nineteenth century, had achieved their dominant positions by being highly aggressive, competitive, and innovative; overwhelmingly, they had grown by adding branches *de novo* rather than by acquiring branches.

After the war, the Conseil National du Crédit (CNC) (acting under the Banking Act of 1945) regulated the number of banks and branches by controlling mergers, entry, and closings. At the outset, the CNC announced a policy of increasing bank concentration in order to rationalize the banking structure and to reduce bank costs (by eliminating "unnecessary" banking facilities, and making wider use of mechanization and other modern techniques). In later years, the CNC did not express any clear-cut statements about its concentration policy; but its general views can be inferred from the fact that, under CNC administration of the banking structure, the number of banks fell from 444 (in 1946) to 329 (in 1965), while the number of branches increased from 3,549 to 4,340. By 1965, the three largest banks held 48.7 percent and the half dozen largest banks held 67.4 percent of total banking resources.

For a number of years the CNC appeared to be satisfied that this size-distribution of banks was an acceptable compromise between excessive concentration (which might impair a desired level of competition) and an excessive number of small banks (which might sacrifice the economies expected from large-scale banking). In 1966, however, the authorities took a major step to increase bank concentration by merging the Banque Nationale pour le Commerce et l'Industrie (BNCI) and the Comptoir National d'Escompte de Paris (CNEP) into the Banque Nationale de Paris (BNP), now the largest bank in France. This merger was expected to improve bank efficiency by eliminating wasteful duplication of branches and services, and also, by creating a "Common-Market-sized bank," to serve better the needs of large firms (which are expected to multiply under the stimulus of the Common Market economy). After this last merger, the three largest banks held 56.5 percent, and the six largest banks held almost 70 percent of the total resources of the banques inscrites. It remains to be seen whether the removal (in 1967) of branch entry restrictions for existing banks will lead to a significant change in bank concentration.

Effects on Market Structure

In each country, the policies on bank concentration have had different effects on banking market structures. In part, of course, this is because the different policies have led to widely different levels of banking concentration. Since bank concentration does not, however, translate directly into market concentration, the effects on market concentration have been quite different in different banking markets. In each country, the market-structure effects of a given level of bank concentration have also been influenced by the mobility of the banks, the nature and extent of nonbank alternatives, and certain restrictions on bank competition. Insofar as these have been different in each country, the market-structure effects from bank concentration would also have been different even if the levels of bank concentration had been identical in all countries.

(*1*) *Level of bank concentration.* Although bank concentration differs in the three countries, it is not possible to describe those differences with precision. Due to ambiguities in the definition of a bank, any measurement of banking (as distinct from banking market) concentration contains an inherent element of arbitrariness. These ambiguities (along with other reasons) made it difficult to trace the early historical growth of English banking concentration—some enterprises were unambiguously banks, but others (like some merchant banks) were hard to classify, because they conducted a substantial commercial banking business along with other activities. Similarly, in France, there was no legal definition of a bank before 1941; and the estimates of French bank specialists for the period before 1941 differ widely about the number of banks and branches.

Although those early sources of confusion have been removed, the definition of a bank continues to be ambiguous, and the ambiguities make it difficult to compare the levels of banking concentration in different countries. These difficulties cannot be overcome by calculating banking concentration in terms of the legal characteristics of a bank, because the banks in each country are a heterogeneous collection in terms of their legal characteristics. In Italy, the *banche* is one basic grouping of banks, but it includes a heterogeneous assortment of institutions (public law banks, national interest banks, ordinary credit banks, and people's cooperative banks) operating under different legal forms; it is distinct from another important bank grouping, the *aziende di credito* (banche plus the savings banks). In France, the *banques inscrites* is the basic grouping; this, too, includes a wide assortment of banks with different legal characteristics, and it excludes a number of other banks (e.g., popular banks, agricultural banks, savings banks, and many others). In England, the London clearing banks (or perhaps the domestic banks, a conglomerate of London clearing banks, Scottish banks, and northern Irish banks) is the basic bank group, but it does not include such other legally distinctive bank categories as accepting

THE REGULATION OF BANK COMPETITION

houses or savings banks (both Post Office and trustee savings banks).

If bank concentration is calculated on an economic basis, a different set of problems must be faced. On an economic basis, a bank is any financial institution (whether or not it is legally a bank) which performs a banking function. In this study, main interest has centered on the banking functions of supplying short-term deposits and short-term business credit, but this framework does not provide an unambiguous economic definition of a bank. For example, exactly how long-term might a short-term deposit be? In Italy (after the 1963 reform), a deposit with an eighteen-month maturity has generally been the dividing line for short- and longer-term financial institutions; in France (before the 1966 banking reform), it was two years or less; and in England, the only distinction at the clearing banks is between a current account (which is paid on demand) and a deposit account (which requires seven days' notice). As *any* dividing line between short-term and non-short-term is inherently arbitrary, it is as troublesome to determine the maximum maturity of short-term business credit as of short-term deposits.

As a practical matter, it is usually necessary to settle for a definition of short-term which accords with the definitions which the authorities in each country use to compile official statistics; but this does not settle the matter for purposes of calculating banking concentration. Even though "short-term" may have an accepted meaning in each country, there is no "pure" short-term institution in each country. In addition, even predominantly short-term institutions do not deal to the same extent in both of the short-term banking functions. In Italy, for example, the banks of national interest and the savings banks engage in short-term loan and deposit operations in quite different proportions. The problems are perhaps least acute where predominantly short-term institutions differ solely by their different combinations of short-term operations. On the other hand, there are some banks, like the French *banques d'affaires* (especially before 1966) that deal in both short-term deposit and loan operations but also carry on a very substantial medium- and long-term business. Other institutions, like the French *chèques postaux*, engage in one of the short-term banking activities (selected as the criterion for defining a bank) but not in both; and some institutions which deal in only one of the short-term operations also operate (and in different proportions) in the medium- or long-term sectors as well.

If banking concentration is to be calculated on an economic basis, which of these institutions should be included as "banks"? If they all should be included, what part of the resources of the different hybrid institutions ought to be excluded from the concentration calculation? And if that last question could be answered to full satisfaction, how likely is it that the official statistics (on which the concentration computations must be based) will be available in the necessary detail for each investigator to make his preferred calculations?

The conventional figures for bank concentration (including those published by official sources), are calculated on a single base, and this obscures their arbitrary character. Thus, it is conventional to calculate English bank concentration in terms of the Big Five as a percentage of the London clearing banks, French banking concentration in terms of the nationalized *établissements de crédit* as a percentage of the banques inscrites, and Italian bank concentration in terms of the public law and national interest banks as a percentage of the aziende di credito. In this study, bank concentration was calculated on alternative bases. This procedure exposes the inherent arbitrariness of any bank concentration figure and underscores the fact that all such figures must be used and interpreted with great care. If their limitations are not ignored, however, bank concentration figures can be useful in conveying a general impression of the banking structure in a country and of broad differences among different countries. As shown above, the difficulties of measuring the exact levels of bank concentration do not obscure the fact that bank concentration is different in the three countries—highest in England, least in Italy, and in-between in France.

(2) Multiplicity of banking markets. Even if bank concentration figures were not plagued (or not as much) by the difficulties associated with the definition of a bank, it would be invalid to use them (as they often are used) as a rough index of competition in the banking system. Bank concentration is not related to banking market structures in any single, direct relation; and a given level of bank concentration can have quite different effects in different banking markets. In this study, there are three broad markets of primary interest—short-term business credit, demand deposits (for transactions purposes), and short-term time deposits—but this is only a first approximation breakdown in which a banking market has been defined in terms of a banking product or service (which in turn has allowed for substitutability characteristics as perceived by prospective users). Each market can be further subdivided in line with the market segmentation that is caused by immobilities of banks, bank customers, or both. As customer immobilities[1] in each of the three broad markets tend to cluster in terms of customer size, the basic division of submarkets—in this study, mostly limited to "large" and "small" customers—is determined by these "inherent" immobilities.[2]

---

[1] It is convenient to classify the submarkets in terms of customer immobilities and to allow later for the market effects of bank immobilities.

[2] These are not the only sources of customer immobilities. Others (discussed later) are based on law (like the territorial competence regulation in Italy) or on custom (like the *chef de file* and *crédit consortial* arrangements in France).

It follows from the above that any market concentration effect from bank concentration must be sought in the submarkets. For a given financial service (say, short-term business credit), the extent of concentration in the banking structure (appropriately defined) establishes the lower bound of market concentration for the most mobile bank customer (who cannot tap foreign sources); but the upper bound of market concentration, faced by the least favorably situated and least mobile bank customers, may be only remotely connected, if at all, to the overall level of bank concentration. Customers with limited mobility who are located in small local areas with few banks may not be significantly affected even by sharp increases in the overall level of banking concentration; but customers with similarly limited mobility could be adversely affected if they are located in large metropolitan centers, because the larger number of independent alternatives which those areas could support may not materialize (or survive) if there is high concentration of banking.

Even the largest and most powerful bank customers are vulnerable to the market effects of high bank concentration. In England, where banking concentration is very high, large bank customers do not enjoy the same differential advantage over smaller customers as do the large borrowers in countries with lesser bank concentration. Both the largest and the smallest borrowers (in the short-term business loan market) in England must operate in highly oligopolistic markets in which effective concentration is further intensified by interbank agreements on rates and other conditions.[3] In short, a high level of bank concentration is usually reflected in a high level of market concentration in the large-borrower submarket.

It should be noted that an increase in bank concentration as conventionally measured (i.e., within a given country) may not in the long run raise the level of market concentration in the large-borrower submarket if the higher bank concentration is associated with a geographical expansion in banking markets. The BNP merger, which raised the immediate level of bank and market concentration in France, may turn out to be a case in point. At least for the most mobile bank customers, the progressive economic integration of the Common Market countries may increase the number of possible bank suppliers; other things being equal, this could counter the effects of the BNP merger to increase concentration. Of course, in the circumstances posited, concentration in the long-run would have been even lower without the BNP merger.

(3) Mobility of banks. The mobility of banks refers to their ability

---

[3] On the other hand, in France and Italy, where bank concentration is much lower than in England, various regulations and conventions (discussed later) raise the effective concentration in the large-borrower market significantly above the levels that would prevail, based on bank concentration only.

and willingness to operate in different banking markets (including submarkets). Bank mobility can often substitute for customer mobility. Thus, for any given level of banking concentration, the extent of market concentration in banking submarkets (except perhaps for the largest bank customers) could be affected by different bank mobility. In the countries studied, the major differences in bank mobility have been related to differences in legal restrictions on mobility, composition (by kind of bank) of the banking structure, geographical distribution of banks, and size-structure of the banking system.

In the countries studied, there are three major differences in the legal restrictions on bank mobility. One difference relates to the restriction on geographical mobility in terms of branch entry, which is regulated in Italy but not in England or in France (since January, 1967). A second legal restriction, also on geographical mobility, concerns a bank's zone of activity. This restriction is enforced in Italy; it is a dead letter in France; and it does not exist in England. A third form of legal restriction concerns limits on the maturity of deposits or loans. This set of restrictions is strongest in Italy; it has recently been eliminated in France; and it has never existed in England.

Other differences in bank mobility are due to differences in the banks' willingness to operate in different banking markets, and these differences, in turn, are partly related to the differences in the kinds of banks in each country. In Italy, for example, the presence of banks of national interest has meant that an important segment of the banking system has not played a full part in the operation of small-customer markets. Virtually from their founding, these banks have been important suppliers of business credit to large business, and they still prefer to operate in the large-customer market. By contrast, the presence of the savings banks has been important for small customers in Italy. True to their historic origins, they have retained a strong interest in small savers and small borrowers. In England, the accepting houses have generally not been available to small customers, although this traditional attitude of the accepting houses may be changing. In France, the Paris deposit banks have had little effect on the market structure of the small-depositor and small-borrower markets in Paris, because those banks have largely adhered to the *haute banque* tradition of dealing with a small number of large, long-time customers; and the large établissements de crédit also have generally tended to ignore small customers. These self-imposed restrictions on mobility can have the same market effects as legal restrictions on mobility.

The composition of the banking structures in these countries also differs in terms of the extent of public or private ownership of the banks. In Italy, a substantial segment of the banking system, comprising the largest banks in the country, is owned outright by the government or (as in the case of the public law banks, other than the government-owned Banca Nazionale del Lavoro) is under de facto public ownership. Similarly, in France, the three banking giants (*établissements de crédit nationalisées*) are nationalized banks. Only England has retained exclusively private ownership of its commercial banks. These differences might have been reflected in mobility differences, but as far as one can tell, government ownership in these countries has not significantly, if at all, influenced the choices of government-owned banks with respect to mobility in different banking markets.

The mobility of banks in different countries is also affected by the geographical distribution of banks and banking offices. Because of "inherent" mobility limitations of small customers, a bank cannot serve a small customer unless it has an office in the small customer's local area. In England, where the banking system is dominated by giant branch banks, the Big Five in particular can reach small customers in any part of the country, for they have blanketed the entire country with branches. As a result of the wide geographical distribution of clearing bank offices, even small borrowers outside of major cities (except perhaps in the most isolated areas) generally have access, either in their local or in nearby areas, to not less than five alternative bank sources. Nationwide branch banking in France or Italy is much less important than in England; both France and Italy also have important regional banks and (especially in Italy) a fair number of local banks. The particular geographical distribution of the regional and local banks in those countries influences the pattern of local and regional concentration in different areas; but the nationwide branch banks also contribute to regional and local differences, because they are typically not uniformly represented in all local areas. In short, because of differences in the geographical distribution of banks and banking offices, a given level of overall bank concentration is consistent with different patterns of concentration in local and regional banking markets.

Finally, bank mobility in each country is different because of different size-structures of the banking systems and also the different associations between bank size and banker preferences. In England, there are only a handful of commercial banks, dominated by a few giant banks; both France and Italy have a much larger number and much wider size-distribution of banks. In England, the clearing banks have shown a keen interest in the loan business of small customers but little interest in their deposit business; in both France and Italy, there is a strong tendency for small banks to deal with small customers and for large banks to concentrate on large customers.[4]

---

[4] This strong association between size of bank and size of customer doubtless reflects customer preferences, but there is clear evidence that banker preferences are also involved.

The implications of the immobilities associated with a particular size-distribution of banks are generally more serious for loan than for deposit markets, because there are more nonbank alternatives for the latter than for the former. Since the immobilities associated with size of bank can have a major effect not only on the terms but perhaps even more on the availability of bank credit for smaller customers, the Italian authorities have consciously manipulated the size-structure of the banking system to influence the allocation of bank credit.

The particular association between size of bank and size of borrower can also influence the market effects of bank mergers. For example, the BNP merger in France increased market concentration materially in the large-borrower market, but owing to the comparative neglect of the small-borrower market by large banks, the elimination of the BNCI and CNEP was less important in small-borrower markets. On the other hand, it also follows that a change in banker attitudes and preferences about dealing with small borrowers could reduce market concentration in small-borrower markets in France and Italy even if bank concentration did not change, or even perhaps if it increased. During the postwar period, large banks in France did exhibit a greater interest in small borrowers, because of the difficulties of prying loose the large customers of other banks, a growing recognition of the profitability of lending to small customers, and as a form of risk diversification. In Italy, too, there has been a tendency for large banks to deal with a wide range in size of borrowers, owing in part to government pressure to favor the growth and development of small and medium-size business firms.

(4) Nature and extent of nonbank alternatives. The market-structure significance of any given level of banking concentration must also be appraised with reference to nonbank substitutes. There are differences in the nature and importance of substitutes in different banking markets in the same country and in similar banking markets in different countries.

In all of the countries studied, there are no important nonbank substitutes in the large-demand-deposit market. While cash has a limited role to play, the large-demand-depositor market in each country is overwhelmingly the private preserve of the banks—in England, of the commercial and (to a much lesser degree) the merchant banks; in France, of the deposit and (to a lesser degree) the investment banks; and in Italy, essentially of the public law and the national interest banks.

In all of these countries, the banks are far less dominant in the small than in the large-transactions-deposit market, because the large banks have little interest in small accounts, and even more because cash is an important (and often a preferred) alternative for small depositors. In addition, there is a postal giro in Italy (though it's not too important) and in France; in England, the trustee savings banks have recently entered the checking field, and a postal giro is scheduled to go into operation in 1968 or 1969. In short, while they are not uniformly important, noncommercial bank alternatives for small demand-deposit accounts do exist in all three countries.

In each country, the banks hold a strong position in the markets for short-term business credit. Large borrowers can secure a limited degree of substitutes for short-term bank credit in the form of trade credit, access to the capital markets, internal financing, and (in some cases) access to foreign suppliers. Except for trade credit, these nonbank alternatives either do not exist or are not important for the typical small borrower.[5] Even in England, with its highly developed financial system, banks hold a dominant position in the field of short-term business loans. Indeed, owing to the exceptionally high level of bank concentration in England, the clearing banks also dominate (directly and indirectly) the commercial-bill market. Thus, although the commercial-bill market in England performs an important role as a repository for the temporarily surplus funds from the bank customer loan market, it cannot (in England) be considered a fully independent alternative for short-term business credit from commercial banks.

In all of these countries, the banks must compete with nonbank substitutes in the markets for time (including savings) deposits. It is important to stress, however, that the existence of even excellent substitutes does not necessarily imply a corresponding enhancement in the competitive structure of the deposit markets. One reason is that the substitutes may not be independent of the banks—for example, in England, the large depositors can turn to the finance houses, but since those institutions have been largely taken over by the banks, they are not fully independent alternatives. The competitive significance of a nonbank substitute can also be undermined if it depends on a single supplier (e.g., some of the government-supplied substitutes), or on a highly concentrated group of suppliers that tend to follow a uniform policy (e.g., the finance houses or the building societies in England). The market significance of many government-supplied substitutes is also conditioned by the fact that the government may regulate the degree of market rivalry with bank-supplied alternatives—for example, in Italy, the Post Office provides an important outlet for small savings, but the government carefully regulates the rates on postal accounts to direct the flow of savings between banks and Post Office in the manner desired by the government; in France, the authorities maintain a close correspondence between the rates (which are now identical) offered by the

---

[5] In Italy, however, they have access to a limited amount of government credit at a preferential rate.

caisses d'épargne and the banks; and in England, the government offers a number of forms of National Savings for small savers, but it has been government policy to avoid undue rate competition with the clearing banks, on the grounds that it would be bad for the taxpayer (who would have to pay for higher rates with higher taxes) as well as for the clearing banks. In sum, although the market significance of banking concentration must be evaluated in light of the existence of substitutes, the market effect of the substitutes must in turn be evaluated in terms of the independence of their suppliers, the nature and extent of concentration among the suppliers, and the market policy of the suppliers.

(5) *Competitive restrictions.* Finally, the market-structure effects of the bank-concentration policies have been affected in some cases by the existence of certain competitive restrictions. A restriction on the geographical zone of operation is a prime example. Even when it is imposed impartially on all banks and bank borrowers, the restriction per se could have a significantly different impact in different borrower markets, due to "inherent" differences in borrower mobility. Thus, it would not affect small borrowers whose natural mobility does not extend beyond their assigned zone of activity, but it could impair the mobility of medium-size and large borrowers and, *ceteris paribus*, increase the concentration of the loan markets in which they operate.[6]

There is no territorial competence restriction in England. Indeed, because of the existence in England of a powerful oligopoly of banks with nationwide branch bank systems, a territorial competence restriction per se would have no significant effect on market concentration. As far as bank alternatives are concerned, both large and small borrowers face a markedly similar level of market concentration. In short, the effect which a territorial competence restriction could achieve, *ceteris paribus*, in a less highly concentrated banking system can be achieved in England without such controls and solely by high bank concentration.

In France, bank concentration is not so high as in England, and the territorial competence restriction is not enforced, as it is in Italy, but market concentration in the large-borrower market has been increased by competitive restrictions in the form of the traditional practices which have grown around the syndicated credits (which are common for large loans). When the syndicated credit is in the form of a *crédit global*, the large borrower can deal independently with each of his banks and thus benefit from any lack of banking concentration; but when the credit

---

6 In Italy, as noted earlier, the existence of large branch banks with offices in major cities has tended to counter the concentration-increasing effects of territorial competence in the large-borrower market.

is in the form of a *crédit consortial* proper and arranged by a *chef de file*, the large borrower must deal with a single bank which represents them all, and this raises the effective market concentration virtually to the monopoly level.

DIRECT CONTROLS ON THE CONDITIONS OF COMPETITION

Differences in the Control Apparatus

The nature and structure of the direct-control apparatus is different in the three countries. The Italian control apparatus still retains strong traces of the control system that was established by the Banking Law of 1936. That legislation declared the collection of savings and the granting of credit to be functions of public interest, and empowered an inspectorate for the defense of savings and the regulation of credit (together with the Committee of Ministers) to set limits on deposit and loan rates, terms and conditions for savings and current accounts, commissions for bank services, and other terms and conditions of the banking business. The inspectorate delegated these powers to the Associazione Bancaria Italiana (ABI) and made membership in the cartel compulsory. After the Fascist government fell, the control apparatus was restructured, but the Interministerial Committee for Credit and Savings continued the prewar practice of delegating its competitive-control powers to the reconstituted ABI. In short, while leaving no doubt about the real locus of decision-making authority in the matter of competitive controls, the authorities have given the bankers a substantial role in setting the curbs on bank competition. In this connection, the governor of the Bank of Italy has stated that he prefers to restrain deposit and loan rates by agreements among banks rather than by government-imposed controls; but as he also noted, the authorities rely on the judgment of bankers who are in close contact with the market because they "do not consider themselves, at present, to be possessed of sufficient knowledge to replace the market by their own rules." When the cartel reaches agreement on a set of competitive curbs, the authorities give it powerful support, but they do not issue the Interbank Agreement as a formal government edict.

The French apparatus to control bank competition looks superficially much like the Italian. During the Vichy period, the government "organized" the banks under government control, and delegated power over the *conditions de banque* to the Association Professionnelle des Banques (APB), a compulsory bank cartel. When the control apparatus was swept away in 1945, the formal structure of the new control apparatus was modeled in key respects along the lines of the earlier structure; but the structural resemblances masked a real shift in the locus of effective power. In the postwar period, membership in the APB continued to be compulsory, and the APB continued to serve as an intermediary between the authorities and the banks. In the earlier structure, however, the bankers had exercised real power, and the government merely held a veto power; in the postwar structure, the banks have lost all but the appearance of self-regulation, and even the appearance has not always been maintained. In Italy, the ABI works out the details of the Interbank Agreement which is then validated (unofficially) by the authorities; in France, the authorities make the decisions about the conditions de banque and then issue instructions to the APB for transmission to the banks. While the APB can express its views to the authorities before a directive becomes effective, this is essentially a face-saving arrangement to give the banks a sense of participation in setting the conditions de banque.

In striking contrast to the French and Italian banks, with their elaborate machinery and detailed regulations to curb bank competition, the English banks manage to restrain competition with a minimum of formal organization or detailed agreements. The Committee of London Clearing Bankers is convened monthly, and in sessions which are informal and intimate, matters of common interest are discussed and common policy is determined. The members of the cartel do not publicize many of their agreements. As far as the public knows, the only formal agreements concern the rates and terms on deposits (both current accounts and deposit accounts) and the formal agreement on the call rate to the discount houses; the agreements on loan rates appear to be less formal than those on deposit rates. The government does not officially take part in the clearing bank agreements; but since the government has broad authority over the banks (under the Bank of England Act of 1946) and is fully informed about any agreements and discussions, its failure to raise any objections to the cartel's actions must be interpreted as tacit approval.

In spite of their informality and the absence of an elaborate superstructure of detailed cartel agreements, the English banks have been more successful than their continental counterparts in restraining bank competition. In Italy and France, where the cartel has great disciplinary powers to enforce anticompetitive regulations, cartel violations have on occasion been very serious; in England, where the cartel has no formal machinery or authority to impose sanctions for violations, cartel violations have never been a problem. The Committee of London Clearing Bankers has great moral authority and depends for the enforcement of its decisions upon the close and intimate cooperation of a small number of people, who are in frequent contact with each other, and whose sense

of solidarity is reinforced by the "old boy network." The solidarity of
the English bank cartel is based not only on sentiments of loyalty and
cooperation but also on the powerful sense of interdependence which
is inescapable in a highly concentrated banking oligopoly. The recognition of this interdependence is perhaps the most powerful influence that
keeps them in lockstep.[7]

Measures to Curb Bank Competition

In each country studied, bank competition has been curbed by a different set of restrictive measures. The major competitive restraints (examined in this study) are the restrictions imposed on loan or deposit
maturities, on deposit and loan rates, on commissions for bank services,
on zone of activity, on the "aggressiveness" of bank rivalry, and on such
other matters as banking hours.

In Italy, the authorities are empowered under the Banking Act of
1936 to regulate banks with respect to *all* of the foregoing. The restriction on loan and deposit maturities (in the aziende di credito, and the
medium- and long-term savings and credit institutions) are imposed not
to restrict competition but to match the maturities of the banks' credit
and deposit operations. Notwithstanding the intent, one effect of these
restrictions (insofar as they are observed) is to compartmentalize the
markets for credits and for deposits of different maturities. In this way,
and to this extent, the maturity restrictions affect market structures as
well as the allocation of resources.

The other restrictions (listed above) are unambiguously intended as
competitive restrictions. Price competition for loans is restricted by a
set of minimum loan rates, which are broken down according to whether
the loan is secured or unsecured, the kind of collateral, the form of the
loan (i.e., overdraft, bill discount, etc.), and other such matters. Price
competition for short-term deposits is restricted by a set of maximum
deposit rates, which are broken down by size of deposit, size of bank,
maturity of deposit, and so forth. The agreements on deposit and loan
rates are spelled out in great detail, but since they are not published
in full detail, customers cannot take full advantage of the limits as a

---

[7] A critic once wryly observed (to the author in an interview) that the characteristic reaction of an English clearing banker to anything new which comes
up is: (1) Has it come up before? (2) What did we do then? and (3) What are
the other banks doing? In a similar vein, another critic has stated that "In
Britain the bankers' biggest problem is, perhaps, themselves in committee.
Individually, most of the bankers have come to realize the problems that their
banks face . . . but unfortunately none of them is often willing to make a first
isolated move in tackling these problems; with rare but blissful exceptions
everything must first be agreed collectively" (*Economist*, November 24, 1962,
p. 804).

bargaining device in dealing with bankers. Price competition is eliminated, not just restricted, for a number of bank services on which the Interbank Agreement sets the commissions.

The Italian authorities also seek to curb competition by the zone-of-activity law, which restricts each bank and even each branch to a particular area. While this restriction may (as proponents have claimed) protect some banks against the perils of operating in distant and unfamiliar places, a major purpose of the original law was "to combat one of the most insidious and troublesome forms of banking competition." In keeping with the anticompetitive intent of the restriction, the authorities have given great weight to the possible injury to a local bank in determining whether to grant an exception for an outside bank to enter a local area. In mid-1966, the authorities decided that they would continue to enforce a territorial competence restriction but on a more liberal basis.

Finally, the Italian authorities have sought to curb nonprice as well as price competition. For example, to dampen the aggressiveness of bank rivalry, they have forbidden banks to offer an unsolicited line of credit to another bank's customer as an inducement to lure him away from that bank. In a similar vein, they have specifically enjoined the banks from soliciting deposits outside of their zones of activity—it will be recalled that the territorial competence restriction does not prevent a bank from accepting but only from soliciting deposits outside of its zone of activity. The authorities have also sought to limit nonprice competition by strictly regulating banking hours.

Before the French banking reforms of 1966 removed some of the competitive restrictions on French banking, there were more similarities than at present in the formal structure of French and Italian competitive controls. Both countries restricted price competition by means of prescribed commissions on a number of bank services, by maximum deposit rates, and by minimum loan rates—but even before the French banking reforms of 1966, there had been fewer competitive restrictions in France than in Italy. Under the French Banking Law of 1945, the deposit banks could not accept deposits with more than two years' maturity, but they were not restricted by law on the maturity of their loans. Similarly, while French law provides for a "zone of activity" restriction, it is not enforced, and French banks have always been free to conduct their banking operations in any part of the country. Finally, the French authorities, unlike their Italian counterparts, have not (as far as the public record shows) issued any instructions to curb the "aggressiveness" of bank rivalry. By removing the restrictions on deposit maturities in deposit banks and investment banks, and abolishing the minimum loan rate, the 1966 French banking reforms have widened the gap between both the formal structure and the spirit of the French and Italian competitive control systems.

The restrictions on bank competition in England differ from those in both Italy and France. In England, there are no legal restrictions on the banks' loan or deposit maturities, or on their zone of activity; but the banks have agreed not to accept time deposits except on the basis of seven days' notice. There are strong curbs on price competition in English banking, but the restraints take different forms than in the other countries. Instead of stipulating limit rates, as in Italy and France, the cartel prescribes a number of actual rates. In the case of deposits, the cartel prescribes a zero rate for current accounts and (with minor exceptions) a single rate for all deposit accounts (on the basis of seven days' notice, but without other distinctions, such as size of deposit, location of bank). In the case of loans, the cartel prescribes actual rates for some borrower categories (nationalized firms, prime borrowers, and certain others), and achieves a consensus (expressed in terms of a stated margin above Bank Rate) on the rate to be paid by the average non-prime borrower. The cartel also prescribes a minimum rate for each category of borrower, but this is just a way of stipulating the actual rates which come into force at certain levels of Bank Rate—that is, the minimum rates in English banking are not limit rates which depend on the state of competition to be made effective.

Market Effects of the Rate Controls

Although all of the countries in this study have used rate controls, the market effects have been different, partly because of differences in the form of the rate controls, the level of the regulated rates, and the flexibility of the prescribed rates.

(1) Form of the rate control. The differences in the form of the rate controls—limit rates in Italy and France, and actual rates in England—can have important consequences on market behavior. Under the limit-rate form of control, market forces have been free (within the prescribed limits) to operate on the rates as well as on the volume of loans and deposits; under the actual-rate form of control, market forces could operate only on the volume of deposits or loans.

The form of the control could have an additional important effect in the loan markets. In the nonprime loan market, the use of an actual-rate form could impair the bankers' freedom to assume a wide range of borrower risks and to charge rates commensurate with the added costs or risks; the limit-rate form could not have that effect. In France and Italy, the limit-rate form is explicitly intended to apply only to prime credit risks, and the authorities have often stated that they expect the bankers to charge nonprime risks more than the limit rate in order to cover the added costs and risks. In England, the cartel does not formally prescribe an actual rate for the nonprime borrower category, but its members appear to operate under a consensus about the rate to be charged to the typical nonprime borrower. Although English bankers have stated that they are not interested in extending their risk limits by charging higher loan rates, it seems likely that the consensus on the nonprime rate, which (insofar as it is effective) has the same effect as a prescribed actual rate, also tends to inhibit them from taking on borrower risks which cannot be compressed within the agreed rate structure.

The different effects that might be expected from different forms of rate controls have not materialized in some markets because the formal differences in the two kinds of rate controls have sometimes been muted by other influences. The rate on bank deposits in France is one example. The French government officially sets only a ceiling rate on bank deposits; as it also provides a number of substitutes for bank deposits and sets the actual rates on the substitutes, it has exercised a powerful influence on the actual rates on bank deposits as well. It has used this power (both before and after the reforms of 1965–1966) so that the ceiling rates have been tantamount to actual rates. The rate on prime loans in France (before 1966) is another example. The minimum loan rates set by the French authorities became the actual rates for prime borrowers. This was due not (as in the deposit market) to pressure from government-provided substitutes for bank loans but to the implicit pressure of the government's authority over the banks and its expressed desires on the matter of loan rates. As a result, although French bankers operated under a system of limit rates, they had no more leeway in setting prime rates than the bankers in England who operated under the actual prime rate set by the cartel.

(2) *Level of the regulated rates.* The market impact of the rate controls in the three countries has also been different because each country has followed a different policy with respect to the level of the prescribed loan rate. In this context, the pertinent differences have less to do with the absolute levels of the prescribed rates than with the relation of the prescribed rates to those that would have prevailed in the absence of rate controls. Consider the differences in the prime loan markets of the three countries. In Italy, market concentration in the prime loan market is comparatively low, and the minimum loan rate is probably generally higher than the rate that would have prevailed in the absence of the present rate controls. The bankers (with the authority and approval of the government) set the present minimum loan rate, and their purpose is to prevent rates from falling as low as they would without the controls. In France (before 1966), minimum loan rates for prime borrowers were probably generally below the levels that would have been reached

without the rate controls. The minimum loan rate was set by the CNC, not by the bankers (APB), and the CNC did not hesitate to reduce the minimum loan rate (which became the actual rate for prime borrowers) against the vigorous opposition of the bankers. Market concentration in the prime loan market in France is high enough so that, in the absence of government-prescribed minimum loan rates, the banks would probably have been able (by a tacit accord) to maintain rates above the levels set by the authorities. In England, the cartel's prime loan rates are probably much the same as they would be if the cartel were illegal. At present, the cartel sets the loan rates at the level which seems appropriate to the banks, and the government tacitly supports the overt collusion among the bankers. In the absence of the cartel, the clearing banks would not be able to rely on overt collusion in setting the loan rates; but as they are few in number and extremely powerful in loan markets, they would probably arrive by an oligopoly rationale at a consensus which is much the same as the one they now achieve by overt collusion. In Italy, by contrast, bank concentration is much lower than in England, and it would be less efficient or reliable for the bankers to depend upon an oligopoly rationale in lieu of explicit agreements.

In the preceding description of the differences in the three countries between the rates prescribed under rate controls and the rates that would have prevailed in the absence of rate controls, the existing deposit controls were taken as given. It is important to stress this point, because the deposit rates prescribed in the three countries have been deliberately held at a low level in the interests of borrowers. Thus, in England, the government (in 1963) opposed any moves toward the greater bank competition for deposits that had been urged by Lord Cromer, lest higher deposit rates lead to higher loan rates. In France, the authorities have repeatedly declared that the reduction of loan rates is one of their main and enduring objectives—the abolition of the minimum loan rate in 1966 represented a change of method rather than a change of view. Significantly, many deposit rates continue to be controlled in France, and a major reason is to prevent excessive deposit rates, which would be counter to the efforts to reduce loan rates.[8] In Italy, too, the authorities have been concerned to restrain deposit rates in the interests of lower loan rates, and the governor of the central bank has stated that the ultimate goal for the country should be to regulate deposit rates but not loan rates.[9]

---

[8] Cf. CNC, *Rapport annuel*, 1965, p. 123.

[9] Cf. Governor Carli in Camera dei deputati, *Commissione d'inchiesta sui limiti posti alla concorrenza nel campo economico*, seduta del 22 novembre 1962, interrogatorio del Dottor Guido Carli, p. 19. Cf. also Bank of Italy, *Annual Report for 1966*, p. 138.

(3) Flexibility of the regulated rates. The market effects of the rate
controls have also differed in the three countries because of differences
in the flexibility of the prescribed rates on loans and deposits—that is,
in the frequency and extent of change in the prescribed rates, especially
in response to changes in the demand and supply for funds. The greatest
overall flexibility has probably been achieved in England: prescribed
rates change on a formula basis in response to changes in Bank Rates,
and since Bank Rate has been used actively as an instrument of monetary policy, the prescribed rates have changed fairly often. In Italy, by
contrast, there is no formula flexibility, and any rate flexibility is due
to special action by the ABI—changes are considered during the annual
review of the Interbank Agreement, or sooner in unusual circumstances.
In practice, maximum deposit rates have been quite inflexible; minimum loan rates have been somewhat more flexible, for they are usually
adjusted when Bank Rate changes, but this does not yield much flexibility because Bank Rate does not change very often. French rates
have exhibited an intermediate degree of flexibility. In France, as in
Italy, the controlled deposit rates have not been tied to Bank Rate
and have been comparatively inflexible. On the other hand, by contrast
with Italy, the minimum loan rate (before 1966) was tied to Bank Rate,
which was actively manipulated as an instrument of monetary policy.
However, the French minimum loan rate did not fluctuate as much or
as often as Bank Rate, because the French authorities took steps (in
1959 and again in 1963) to loosen the link between loan rates and
Bank Rate.

The different rigidity of the prescribed rates has been one of the
factors responsible for the different experience in the three countries
with respect to violations of the rate controls. Thus, rate violations
were most severe with respect to deposit rates in Italy and France (where
rates were comparatively rigid), only moderately troublesome with respect to loan rates in Italy and France (where loan rates were less rigid
than deposit rates), and probably nonexistent on either loan or deposit
rates in England (where rates were relatively flexible). Although de facto
rate flexibility achieved by violations has compensated in part for the
differential flexibility of the controlled rates, it has been severely discriminatory, and mostly benefited large customers.[10] This discriminatory treatment is inherent in rate violations—it would not be eliminated
even if the bargaining powers of large and small customers were identical—because it is more difficult to maintain secrecy about illegal terms

---

[10] Insofar as the banks in England have achieved deposit-rate flexibility by
circumventing the cartel and operating through the finance houses, the result
has also been discriminatory. Cf. National Board for Prices and Incomes, *Bank
Charges* (London, May, 1967), pp. 30–31.

for small customers, who are far more numerous than large customers, and who do not carry on enough other business with banks to provide concealment for illegal rate terms.

COMPETITIVE CONTROLS AS ADJUNCTS TO MONETARY CONTROLS

One of the most striking aspects of the competitive controls has been the change in the purposes served by those controls in all of the countries studied. In each country, the restraints on rate competition were originally imposed by private banks to shelter the banks and their depositors against the rigors of uncontrolled competition; in each country, they have evolved into major instruments of public policy. In Italy, the rate controls originated in 1919 in the collusive arrangements of a private bank cartel which wanted to prevent "detrimental competition." Under Fascism, competition was regulated in the interests of general economic stability, and also because the authorities preferred administrative to market "discipline" of the banks. Although the Italian authorities have at all times been concerned with the safety of deposits, they have in recent years supported the cartel primarily as an instrument of monetary and economic policy.

In France, the restraints on the conditions of bank competition originated in 1925 with a private entente which was sponsored by the large banks to restrain the troublesome competition from the small and medium-size banks. The interbank agreements on deposit and loan rates and on certain commissions were carried over to the '30's, ostensibly to safeguard depositors, even though there was no general collapse of banks in France during those years. Under the Banking Law of 1941, the Vichy regime continued the competitive restraints as a means of giving the government control over the banks. The postwar government also imposed strict controls on bank competition, but the protection of depositors, while continuing to be an important concern of the state, was no longer a major consideration. The more important reasons for the postwar competitive restraints have been related to the government's desire to use the banking system to foster its program for economic growth and development.

In England, the restraints on the conditions of bank competition originated with some private bank ententes in the fourth quarter of the nineteenth century. Although the interbank agreements to regulate rate competition have remained in private hands, they have received the support (usually tacit) of the government, which makes use of the agreements as instruments of monetary control. Indeed, one of the firmest cartel agreements, the minimum rate on call loans to the discount market, was actually instigated by the government after the First World War.

In addition to the change in the purposes of the rate controls, there has also been a change in the purposes served by the controls on bank structure. At one time, as shown earlier in this chapter, merger and entry controls were imposed to regulate the intensity of bank competition; over the years, however, bank structure has often played an important role as an instrument of monetary control. At present, official views about an appropriate or desirable level of bank concentration go beyond the question of competitive effects to consider the wider goals that banking structure has come to serve.

Major Monetary Control Uses of Competitive Controls

At one time or another during the postwar years, the authorities in all of the countries studied have used competitive controls as major instruments of monetary policy. The experience in the three countries has been quite varied, because each country has adapted its own set of competitive controls to its own circumstances and in its own way. In some cases, the competitive controls have become virtually permanent features of the monetary control apparatus; in other cases, they have been used as monetary controls for shorter periods, to meet a particular set of circumstances, or until a change in the underlying circumstances had rendered them less effective.

In spite of the great diversity in the specific applications of the competitive controls as monetary controls, it is possible to group them according to four major uses: First, the controls on bank structure have been used as a powerful tool to influence the allocation of bank credit. In Italy, for example, the authorities have taken note of the strong association in that country between size of bank and size of bank customer, and they have used the controls on bank structure to promote a "balanced" size-distribution of banks, which would ensure that smaller and medium-size business firms would not be forced out of business for lack of bank credit. In England, the authorities have made use of the high concentration in the banking structure to influence the allocation of credit by means of "requests" made to the banks by the governor of the Bank of England. A similar system has been used in the other countries as well; in England, owing to the exceptionally high level of bank concentration, moral suasion has been a particularly effective and flexible device which has operated with a minimum of red-tape to influence not only the allocation but also the total supply of bank credit.

Second, the rate controls have been used to influence the total supply of bank credit. In England, for example, the authorities were able during one period to employ the deposit-rate agreement to influence the supply of bank credit, because they could put pressure on the banks' liquidity by widening the spread between treasury bill rates and deposit rates and thereby inducing the public to shift from bank deposits to treasury bills. The cartel's deposit-rate agreement was a key element in the mechanism, because it permitted the authorities to raise the market rate on bills (other than by a change in Bank Rate) with the assurance that the deposit rates would not also rise and frustrate their attempt to widen the spread. In France, the rate controls were adapted to the control of bank credit in a quite different way. In 1959 and in a later reform in 1963, the French authorities introduced a new rate T to increase the effectiveness of Bank Rate changes in influencing the volume of bank borrowing at the central bank. Since the essence of the reform— a loosening of the link between changes in Bank Rate and changes in loan rates—depended on the existence of the minimum-loan-rate regulation, the latter became an integral part of a major policy device to regulate the supply of bank credit.

Third, the authorities in the three countries have relied heavily on rate controls to improve their control over the banks' rates on loans and deposits. In England, the authorities have been able to exercise significant control by means of changes in Bank Rate, since the cartel's rate agreements tie both loan and deposit rates to Bank Rate. In France and Italy, however, deposit rates have not been tied to Bank Rate. Although loan rates are tied to Bank Rate, changes in Bank Rate have been a less effective device than in England for controlling loan rates— in France (before 1966), the authorities deliberately loosened the link between Bank Rate and loan rate; in Italy, the authorities make very sparing use of Bank Rate changes. Nevertheless, the authorities in France have been able to exercise great control over bank rates because they directly administer the rate-control mechanism; the authorities in Italy exercise control indirectly by making their views on bank rates known to the cartel which prepares the rate agreements. It is interesting to note that the limit-form of rate control was retained in France and Italy even after rate controls had become important as monetary controls. The limit-rate form, which can be fully effective when the primary purpose of the control is to limit competition in the interest of bank solvency or profit, may be less satisfactory when the primary purpose is monetary control, because it cannot per se always provide precision in controlling market rates.

Fourth, the monetary authorities have made use of rate controls, especially on deposit rates, to gain greater control over the interest rates and supply of funds to the money and capital markets. In England, for example, the authorities have depended on the cartel rate agreements to strengthen their control over market rates (especially on prime bank

bills and treasury bills) and to make it possible to finance the Treasury's
needs without extreme instability in treasury bill rates. In Italy, too,
the authorities have utilized the deposit-rate controls to influence conditions on the capital market, especially in 1961 and 1962, when the
favorable capital market situation that was essential to a continuation
of the Italian "economic miracle" had seriously deteriorated. The
deposit-rate controls were directly involved because the banks' failure
to observe the deposit-rate ceilings was an important factor that diverted
funds away from the capital market and caused an unwelcome rise in
long-term rates. To restore the favorable capital-market situation and
to regain a greater degree of freedom for the central bank to control
the supply of liquidity to the economy, the authorities emphasized adherence to the deposit-rate controls as a key part of their monetary
controls.

Rate Controls and Market Structure

As shown earlier, the authorities in the three countries have supported the rate controls to protect bank solvency, but more important,
to gain greater control over market rates for purposes of monetary
control, economic control, and market control (e.g., to establish a low
level of rates in a market where a high level of concentration has
undermined market competition). The experience of these countries
suggests, however, that governments which make intensive use of rate
controls to regulate market rates cannot on that account afford to ignore
considerations of market structure,[11] but for different reasons in the
case of standardized or nonstandardized services.

The degree of standardization of different bank services is an important determinant of the degree of control over market rates which
can be achieved solely by means of rate controls and irrespective of
market structure. On the most standardized bank services, the authorities could set the actual rates and could be confident, given a sufficient
enforcement apparatus, that the actual rates would become the effective
market rates without any assistance from market structure. Thus, in
France (before 1966), the authorities prescribed the actual commissions
to be charged on a number of standardized bank services, and this gave
them direct control over price independently of the market structure
in the markets for those services. Deposits, especially when divided into
subgroups, are also susceptible to a high degree of standardization. Since
it is possible to prescribe actual rates for standardized services, it is also

---

[11] The term "market structure" (instead of "the state of market competition")
has been used in this context, because in policy discussions, market structure
and rate regulation are often treated as trade-off variables (e.g., in proposals to
allow a higher level of market concentration and to rely on rate controls, if
necessary, to counter any adverse rate effects).

possible to control the banks' deposit rates by means of rate controls and without reference to the state of competition in the deposit markets.

Although market structure can be ignored in setting the effective market rate for standardized services, it may not be possible to ignore it on other grounds. In England, for example, competition from non-bank substitutes has caused a relative decline in the volume of clearing bank deposits, and this has troubled the monetary authorities who fear that it may impair the banks' ability to finance the credit needs of business firms. Although the authorities have traditionally acquiesced and on occasion even insisted on low deposit rates in order to maintain low loan rates for borrowers, they have in recent years been paying more attention to the neglected fact that low deposit rates can have a dual impact on borrowers. This consideration (along with other causes for official concern about the relative decline of the banks) led Lord Cromer and later the Jones Committee to make strong public statements urging the banks to compete more aggressively for deposits. Similarly, in France, where the CNC has followed a low-rate policy on deposits throughout its existence, the authorities have become concerned by the banks' failure to mobilize the public's savings as effectively as will be necessary if banks are to play the key role assigned to them under the Fifth Economic Plan. One result of the new view of the authorities is reflected in some of the reforms of 1965–1966 (such as removing the restrictions on deposit maturities in deposit and investment banks) which were designed to introduce more competition into deposit markets.

On the least standardized bank services, rate controls per se are a less effective instrument for achieving complete control over effective market rates. In the case of the short-term business loan, the most important example of a comparatively nonstandardized bank service, it is very difficult and perhaps impossible to have a system of rate controls with actual rates prescribed for literally all borrowers. Thus, in England, the only country in this study that uses actual rates in its system of loan-rate controls, the actual rates are prescribed for some borrowers but not for all. The English cartel's present structure of rates is based on three main groupings of borrowers (aside from certain special cases): nationalized industries, prime commercial and industrial borrowers, and all others. Actual rates are prescribed only for the first two categories— significantly, those are the categories in which the borrowers can most readily be classified by objective criteria; they are not prescribed for the third category in which there is the greatest degree of borrower heterogeneity. In the absence of a prescribed actual rate, each nonprime borrower must negotiate the rate question separately with his banker, and the degree of competition in the nonprime loan markets can have a decisive influence on the outcome.

If the loan-rate controls are in the form of limit rates, market forces can play an important part in determining whether or to what extent the limit rates will become effective market rates. The experience in France (before 1966) and Italy is suggestive in this connection. In both countries, the only rate controls imposed on short-term business loans have been in the form of limit rates for prime credit risks; since the market pressures have been different, the authorities have been confronted with quite different problems in relying on limit rates to influence effective market rates. In Italy, where the minimum loan rate has probably been generally higher than the rate that would have prevailed in the absence of rate controls, the authorities have been concerned not that market pressures would be too weak to bring prime rates down to the limit rate but rather that they would be too strong and push the prime rate below the limit rate. On a number of occasions, they have resorted to exhortations, threats, and other forms of administrative pressure on the banks in an attempt to counter the excessive pressure from the underlying market forces. In France, the prescribed limit rates were probably often below the rates that would have prevailed without the rate controls; though the authorities clearly intended the limit rate to be the effective rate for prime borrowers, it is doubtful whether they could have relied on the pressure of existing market competition to drive the prime rate down to the prescribed minimum levels. That the authorities were apparently completely successful in establishing the limit rate as the effective rate for prime borrowers was due to political more than to economic pressures: given the vast powers of the French authorities, it did not behoove the bankers to ignore the official wishes. It is important to stress, however, that this implicit administrative pressure was not a uniformly reliable means for implementing the government's views on loan rates for all borrowers. It was fully reliable in the case of the prime credit risks (or at least for those who could be unambiguously identified as such), but less reliable for the nonprime borrowers. Indeed, the open-ended nature of the government's policy on rates for nonprime borrowers (viz., that they should pay more than prime borrowers but only enough more to cover their higher costs and risks) was a tacit acknowledgement of the practical difficulties of trying to achieve for a large number of heterogeneous borrowers the same measure of control over effective rates that it was possible to achieve for the prime credit risks. Under the circumstances, the implementation of the government's policy on rates for nonprime borrowers was critically dependent on the existence of sufficient competition in the market to bring about the desired results.

In France and Italy, market structure has also had an important influence in determining whether the rate controls could be used to set effective market rates for deposits. In spite of the fact that deposits are susceptible to a high degree of standardization, the controls on deposit rates in both countries have generally been stated in the form of limit rather than actual rates. In both cases, however, market pressures in the deposit markets have made the limit-rate form almost as efficient as the actual-rate form as a device for setting the effective market rates. In both countries, the governments have exerted much of the market pressure in their capacity as major suppliers of substitutes for the banks' deposit facilities. By selecting the terms for the substitutes, the authorities have been able to exert a powerful influence on the rates which the banks must offer to be competitive.

As the preceding discussion has shown, the market structure of banking markets can be an important element in the success or failure of rate controls as an instrument to determine effective market rates. In this context, an optimal market structure is one that provides the required degree of competition to implement a given rate policy. As the experience of Italy and France suggests, a market structure which produces too much competition can be as frustrating to the goal of achieving a particular rate level as one that produces too little competition. The practical problem of selecting an optimal market structure is complicated by the fact that market behavior is not perfectly related to market structure. In addition, banks are multiproduct firms, and the banking structure that could ensure the desired amount of competitive pressure in one market (say, a deposit market in which there are also nonbank suppliers) might not be optimal to ensure the desired amount of competitive pressure in some other market (say, a loan market in which banks are virtually the sole suppliers).

INTERRELATION OF THE RULES ON BANK COMPETITION

The preceding discussion has shown that, contrary to a widely held misconception, governments which regulate intensively about the conditions of bank competition in order to implement a particular rate policy, whether for purposes of monetary control or for market control, cannot on that account afford to ignore whether banking market structures are competitive or monopolistic. In addition, of course, market structure considerations cannot be ignored because they also affect the market's capacity to perform a number of key functions: protecting customers against adverse discrimination, promoting efficiency in the internal operations of banks, stimulating the development of new and improved services for customers, and promoting an optimal allocation of resources among the competing demands for bank funds.

During most of the years covered by this study, bank competition has been curbed in all of the countries studied. In recent years, the authorities in those countries have been reducing the emphasis on administrative regulation of bank competition in favor of greater reliance on market regulation. In Italy, the authorities have taken steps to liberalize the territorial competence restrictions,[12] and the governor of the Bank of Italy has publicly considered the possibility of abrogating the minimum-loan-rate regulation. In France, the authorities have made a significant retreat from their former policy of regulating intensively about the conditions of bank competition, and they have also removed some of the barriers that had compartmentalized deposit markets. In England, a governor of the Bank of England urged the bank cartel to relax its curbs on competition in the deposit market, and the Jones Committee has recommended similar reforms in the banks' loan markets as well as in their deposit markets.

In connection with the drive to promote more bank competition by the actions or proposals to dismantle some of the competitive curbs on the conditions of bank competition, little (if any) attention has been given to the possible role of market structure in implementing the reforms of the direct controls on bank competition. This omission could be serious, because many of the banking markets affected by the reforms are highly concentrated; as noted earlier, an assurance of competitive market behavior requires more than a release of artificial restraints on the conditions of bank competition.

As stated at the outset of this study, bank competition can be affected by the government's rules about the conditions of bank competition and rules about banking structure. In most countries, the rules were evolved over a long period and in response to a wide array of historical pressures and circumstances, and each element or change in the regulatory structure tends to be evaluated solely or primarily on its own terms. This study has shown, however, that the possible market effects of alternative systems of regulating bank competition will depend not only upon the particular kinds and forms of the controls but also upon the complex interrelation of the rules on banking structure and those on the conditions of bank competition. To be effective, public policy (whatever its goals) will have to be based on a clear recognition and understanding of this fundamental interrelation.

---

[12] Cf. Bank of Italy, *Annual Report for 1966*, p. 134.

Statistical Appendix

APPENDIX TABLE A

Minimum Spread Between Loan and Deposit Rates,
As Set by Interbank Agreements, Italy, 1947–1965
(percent)

Maximum deposit rates			Minimum overdraft rate[a] (crediti in conto corrente)	Difference between overdraft rate and rate on	
Year	c/c liberi	depositi vincolati (3 months)		c/c liberi	depositi vincolati (3 months)
1947	.50	1.50	8.00	7.50	6.50
			9.50 (Sept.)	9.00 (Sept.)	8.00 (Sept.)
1948	.50	1.50	9.50	9.00	8.00
1949	.50	1.50	9.50	9.00	8.00
			8.50 (April)	8.00 (April)	7.00 (April)
1950	.50	1.50	8.50	8.00	7.00
			7.50 (April)	7.00 (April)	6.00 (April)
1951	.50	1.50	7.50	7.00	6.00
1952	.50	1.50	7.50	7.00	6.00
1953	.50	1.50	7.50	7.00	6.00
1954	.50	1.50	7.50	7.00	6.00
		2.50 (Feb.)	7.50	7.00	5.00 (Feb.)
1955	.50	2.50	7.50	7.00	5.00
1956	.50	2.50	7.50	7.00	5.00
1957	.50	2.50	7.50	7.00	5.00
1958	.50	2.50	7.50	7.00	5.00
			7.00 (June)	6.50 (June)	4.50 (June)
1959	.50	2.25 (Jan.)	7.00	6.50	4.75 (Jan.)
1960	.50	2.25	7.00	6.50	4.75
1961	.50	2.25	7.00	6.50	4.75
1962	.50	2.25	7.00	6.50	4.75
1963	.50	2.25	7.00	6.50	4.75
1964	.50	2.25	7.00	6.50	4.75
1965	.50	2.25	7.00	6.50	4.75

[a] Does not include the commission on overdrafts.
SOURCE: Banca d'Italia, *Bollettino.*

APPENDIX TABLE B

Changes in Bank Rate and Cartel Minimum Rates on Loans, Italy, 1944–1965
(percent)

Date	Bank Rate	Discounted commercial paper (sconto di effeti fino a 4 mesi)	Overdrafts[a] (crediti in conto corrente)
Sept. 11, 1944	4.00	5.50	
June 1, 1945			8.00
Sept. 6, 1947	5.50	7.00	9.50
April 9, 1949	4.50	6.00	8.50
April 6, 1950	4.00		
April 15, 1950		5.25	7.50
January 1, 1957		5.50	
June 7, 1958	3.50	5.00	7.00

a Plus .125% commission per quarter-year on maximum amount outstanding.
SOURCE: Banca d'Italia, *Bollettino*.

APPENDIX TABLE C

Changes in Bank Rate and Cartel Maximum Rates on Deposits, Italy, 1947–1965
(percent)

Date	Bank Rate	"Free" current accounts (c/c liberi)		Savings deposit accounts (depositi a risparmio)			
		Under 5 million lire	5 to 500 million lire	"Free" (liberi)	"Tied" (vincolati)		
					3 months	6 months	12 months
Sept. 6, 1947	5.50	.50a		1.00a	1.50a	2.00a	2.00a
April 9, 1949	4.50						
April 6, 1950	4.00						
February 1, 1954			2.50	1.25	2.50	3.25	4.00
June 7, 1958	3.50						
January 1, 1959			2.25		2.25	3.00	3.75
January 1, 1960			2.00				

a These rates were in effect throughout 1947. The *Bollettino* does not indicate the first date on which they became effective.
SOURCE: Banca d'Italia, *Bollettino*.

APPENDIX TABLE D
Measures of Bank Liquidity, Italy, 1955–1965
(percent)

End of year	Loans / Deposits	Liquidity[a] / Deposits
1955	74.3	8.4
1956	76.8	6.9
1957	75.8	7.2
1958	69.0	12.1
1959	67.7	12.5
1960	71.3	8.1
1961	71.7	6.3
1962	74.4	5.5
1963	79.8	4.8
1964	75.3	5.8
1965	68.5	6.1

a "Liquidity" includes credit margin with Bank of Italy, free treasury-bill holdings, and "others" (cash; deposits with Bank of Italy; deposits with Treasury, etc.; stock-piling bills; and convertible foreign currencies). For the composition of "others," cf. Bank of Italy, *Annual Report*, 1961, p. 57.

Source: Banca d'Italia, *Bollettino*.

APPENDIX TABLE E

Changes in Bank Rate and CNC Maximum Deposit Rates, France, 1947–1965
(percent)

Effective date	Bank Rate	Sight deposits[a]	Fixed deposits[b] 6 months–1 year	1 year–2 years
February 15, 1945			1⅝	2[c]
January 9,1947	1¾ and 2¼			
October 9, 1947	2½ and 3			
November 27, 1947		½	2	2½[c]
September 4, 1948	3½ and 4			
September 30, 1948	3			
April 5, 1950		½	2¾	"Free"
June 8, 1950	2½			
October 11, 1951	3			
November 8, 1951	4			
September 17, 1953	3½			
February 4, 1954	3¼			
December 2, 1954	3			
October 25, 1956		½	2¾	3
April 11, 1957	4	½		
August 12, 1957	5			
May 9, 1958		½	2¾	3⅛
October 16, 1958	4½			
February 5, 1959	4¼			
April 23, 1959	4			
October 6, 1960	3½			
January 1, 1961		½	2⅝	2⅞
May 3, 1962		½	2¼	2⅝
April 10, 1963		½	2	2⅜
November 14, 1963	4			
April 8, 1965	3½			
January 1, 1966		½	2¾	$3^1/_3$

a First category, Paris banks. This category was discontinued after January 1, 1966.

b Smallest size category of deposits in Paris banks. The size of the smallest deposit category did not change over time. This category was discontinued after January 1, 1966.

c Rate on deposits held for between 1½ and 2 years.

SOURCES: J. S. G. Wilson, *French Banking Structure and Credit Policy* (London, 1957), p. 66; and CNC, *Rapport annuel* and *Annexes au rapport annuel*.

APPENDIX TABLE F

Changes in Bank Rate and CNC Minimum Loan Rates, France, 1945–1965
(percent)

Date	Bank Rate	Effets commerciaux	Découverts
January 20, 1945	1.625		
September 18, 1946			4.25
January 9, 1947	1.75 and 2.25^a		
February 8, 1947			5.75
July 18, 1947			6.25
October 9, 1947	2.50 and 3.00^a	3.10	
October 15, 1947			6.75
January 15, 1948			6.75
September 4, 1948	3.50 and 4.00^a	4.10	
September 30, 1948	3.00	3.60	
End of 1949			6.35
June 8, 1950	2.50	3.10	
July 29, 1950			6.10
October 11, 1951	3.00	3.60	
October 25, 1951			6.35
November 8, 1951	4.00	4.60	
November 9, 1951			6.85
September 17, 1953	3.50	4.10	
February 4, 1954	3.25	3.85	
October 25, 1954			6.60
December 2, 1954	3.00	3.60	
April 11, 1957	4.00	4.60	7.60
August 12, 1957	5.00	5.60	
December 2, 1957			8.60
October 16, 1958	4.50	5.10	8.10
February 5, 1959	4.25	4.75	7.85
April 23, 1959	4.00	4.50	7.60
December 17, 1959		4.40	6.60
October 16, 1960	3.50	3.90	6.10
November 14, 1963	4.00		
November 21, 1963		4.15	6.35
January 28, 1965		4.00	6.20
April 8, 1965	3.50		
April 30, 1965		3.75	5.95

^a For explanation of two Bank Rates, cf. P. C. Dupont, *Le Contrôle des banques et la direction du crédit en France* (Paris, 1952). Rates include the compulsory *commission d'endos*. All minimum loan rates were abolished as of April 1, 1966.

SOURCES: Wilson (see Table E), p. 80; and CNC, *Rapport annuel* and *Annexes au rapport annuel*.

APPENDIX TABLE G

Changes in Bank Rate and Clearing Bank Deposit Rate, United Kingdom, 1951–1966
(percent)

Date	Bank Rate	Deposit Rate
November 8, 1951	2½	¾
March 12, 1952	4	2
September 17, 1953	3½	1¾
May 13, 1954	3	1¼
January 27, 1955	3½	1½
February 24, 1955	4½	2½
February 16, 1956	5½	3½
February 7, 1957	5	3
September 19, 1957	7	5
March 20, 1958	6	4
May 22, 1958	5½	3½
June 19, 1958	5	3
August 14, 1958	4½	2½
November 20, 1958	4	2
January 21, 1960	5	3
June 23, 1960	6	4
October 27, 1960	5½	3½
December 8, 1960	5	3
July 26, 1961	7	5
October 5, 1961	6½	4½
November 2, 1961	6	4
March 8, 1962	5½	3½
March 22, 1962	5	3
April 26, 1962	4½	2½
January 3, 1963	4	2
February 27, 1964	5	3
November 23, 1964	7	5
June 3, 1965	6	4
July 14, 1966	7	5

SOURCE: Bank of England, *Annual Report* and *Quarterly Bulletin*.

APPENDIX TABLE H

Changes in Bank Rate and Minimum Call-money Rate,
United Kingdom, 1951–1966
(percent)

Date	Bank Rate	Minimum Call-money Rate
November 8, 1951	2½	¾
March 12, 1952	4	2
September 17, 1953	3½	1¾
May 13, 1954	3	1¼
January 27, 1955	3½	1¾
February 24, 1955	4½	2¾
February 16, 1956	5½	3¾
February 7, 1957	5	3¼
September 19, 1957	7	5¼
March 20, 1958	6	4¼
May 22, 1958	5½	3¾
June 19, 1958	5	3¼
August 14, 1958	4½	2¾
November 20, 1958	4	2⅜
January 21, 1960	5	3⅜
June 23, 1960	6	4⅜
October 27, 1960	5½	3⅞
December 8, 1960	5	3⅜
July 26, 1961	7	5⅜
October 5, 1961	6½	4⅞
November 2, 1961	6	4⅜
March 8, 1962	5½	3⅞
March 22, 1962	5	3⅜
April 26, 1962	4½	2⅞
January 3, 1963	4	2⅜
February 27, 1964	5	3⅜
November 23, 1964	7	5⅜
June 3, 1965	6	4⅜
July 14, 1966	7	5⅜

SOURCES: Bank of England, *Annual Report* and *Quarterly Bulletin.*

APPENDIX TABLE I

Difference Between Treasury Bill Rate and Deposit Rate, United Kingdom, 1951–1965

(percent)

Month	1951	1952	1953	1954	1955	1956	1957	1958	1959	1960	1961	1962	1963	1964	1965
January		0.22	0.39	0.37	**	1.57	1.19	1.27	1.12	**	1.25	1.35	**	1.72	1.60
February		0.24	0.42	0.32	**	**	**	1.02	1.09	1.55	1.31	1.41	1.45	**	1.48
March		**	0.40	0.35	1.30	1.68	1.07	**	1.30	1.59	1.48	**	1.55	1.30	1.45
April		0.35	0.41	0.34	1.31	1.61	1.01	1.28	1.25	1.65	1.45	**	1.71	1.30	1.45
May		0.37	0.38	**	1.42	1.45	0.84	**	1.33	1.58	1.38	1.44	1.67	1.35	1.31
June		0.43	0.37	0.36	1.47	1.59	0.87	**	1.45	**	1.50	1.30	1.69	1.44	**
July		0.46	0.35	0.32	1.47	1.51	0.85	1.15	1.46	1.58	**	1.40	1.77	1.57	1.59
August		0.46	0.36	0.35	1.50	1.53	0.97	**	1.48	1.58	1.71	1.29	1.71	1.65	1.56
September		0.49	**	0.38	1.57	1.61	**	1.15	1.48	1.53	1.60	1.19	1.69	1.65	1.51
October		0.43	0.36	0.34	1.57	1.54	1.60	1.15	1.43	**	**	1.21	1.67	1.69	1.42
November	**	0.38	0.35	0.35	1.60	1.51	1.54	**	1.39	1.24	**	1.27	1.75	**	1.45
December	0.23	0.41	0.36	0.53	1.58	1.44	1.43	1.16	1.61	**	1.35	1.14	1.74	1.62	1.48

** Months in which Bank Rate (and, therefore, also Deposit Rate) changed.

SOURCES: Bank of England, *Quarterly Bulletin*; and *Federal Reserve Bulletin*.

APPENDIX TABLE J

Interest Rates on Prime Bank Bills and Treasury Bills, United Kingdom, 1951-1965

(percent)

A. Interest rates on prime bank bills

Month	1951	1952	1953	1954	1955	1956	1957	1958	1959	1960	1961	1962	1963	1964	1965
January		1.50	3.00	2.19	2.02	4.22	4.85	6.51	3.28	4.14	4.45	5.65	3.69	3.91	6.84
February		1.50	3.00	2.15	2.58	4.77	4.44	6.17	3.23	4.69	4.48	5.65	3.63	4.00	6.74
March		2.48	3.00	2.16	3.81	5.34	4.25	5.98	3.41	4.74	4.61	5.13	3.70	4.53	6.74
April		3.00	3.00	2.17	3.83	5.27	4.18	5.47	3.40	4.80	4.63	4.50	3.88	4.53	6.78
May		3.00	3.00	1.89	3.94	5.14	4.04	5.24	3.43	4.76	4.55	4.14	3.88	4.56	6.73
June		3.00	3.00	1.66	3.99	5.20	4.08	4.65	3.54	5.04	4.64	3.98	3.84	4.64	6.04
July		3.00	3.00	1.60	4.00	5.10	4.06	4.31	3.57	5.76	4.72	4.09	3.87	4.73	5.97
August		3.00	3.00	1.62	4.06	5.08	4.17	3.98	3.60	5.75	6.91	4.02	3.85	4.84	5.97
September		3.00	2.67	1.64	4.15	5.18	5.40	3.82	3.59	5.71	6.84	3.93	3.88	4.84	5.97
October	1.50	3.00	2.19	1.62	4.16	5.14	6.81	3.80	3.58	5.62	6.31	3.92	3.86	4.88	5.92
November	1.50	3.00	2.19	1.62	4.21	5.08	6.78	3.67	3.55	4.98	5.67	4.03	3.91	5.42	5.91
December	1.50	3.00	2.19	1.78	4.22	5.07	6.67	3.34	3.72	4.64	5.61	3.86	3.91	6.84	5.91

B. Interest rates on United Kingdom treasury bills

Month	1951	1952	1953	1954	1955	1956	1957	1958	1959	1960	1961	1962	1963	1964	1965
January		0.97	2.39	2.12	2.05	4.07	4.69	6.27	3.12	4.07	4.25	5.35	3.51	3.72	6.60
February		0.99	2.42	2.07	2.68	4.69	4.30	6.02	3.09	4.55	4.31	5.41	3.45	3.91	6.48
March		2.01	2.40	2.10	3.80	5.18	4.07	5.78	3.30	4.59	4.48	4.86	3.55	4.30	6.45
April		2.35	2.41	2.09	3.81	5.11	4.01	5.28	3.25	4.65	4.45	4.26	3.71	4.30	6.45
May		2.37	2.38	1.79	3.92	4.95	3.84	5.02	3.33	4.58	4.38	3.94	3.67	4.35	6.31
June		2.43	2.37	1.61	3.97	5.09	3.87	4.44	3.45	4.88	4.50	3.80	3.69	4.44	5.59
July		2.46	2.35	1.57	3.97	5.01	3.85	4.15	3.46	5.58	5.10	3.90	3.77	4.57	5.59
August		2.46	2.36	1.60	4.00	5.03	3.97	3.81	3.48	5.58	6.71	3.79	3.71	4.65	5.56
September		2.49	2.27	1.63	4.07	5.11	5.42	3.65	3.48	5.53	6.60	3.69	3.69	4.65	5.51
October	0.51	2.43	2.11	1.59	4.07	5.04	6.60	3.65	3.43	5.36	5.94	3.71	3.67	4.69	5.42
November	0.84	2.38	2.10	1.60	4.10	5.01	6.54	3.46	3.39	4.74	5.41	3.77	3.75	5.18	5.45
December	0.98	2.41	2.11	1.78	4.08	4.94	6.43	3.16	3.61	4.44	5.35	3.64	3.74	6.62	5.48

SOURCES: Bank of England, *Quarterly Bulletin*; and *Federal Reserve Bulletin*.

Index

Accepting houses. *See* Merchant banks

Agricultural banks, France: discussed, 106–107; branch expansion, 119–120; coordination of deposit rates and terms, 145; and compulsory reserve requirements, 206

Albery, Michael, 249n

Alhadeff, David A., 20n, 58n, 124n

Allen, A. M., 236n, 313n

Altman, Oscar L., 31n, 181n, 292n

Anderson, A. P., 220n

Armstrong, W., 256n

Associazione Bancaria Italiana (ABI): and allocation of branch permits, 13–15; supported by authorities, 27; and regulation of bank competition, 29–30; and bankers' associations in other countries, 349–351

Association Professionnelle des Banques (APB): and allocation of branch permits, 117n; replaced private bank cartels, 135–137; under the 1941 banking law, 137; under the 1945 banking law, 139–140; and enforcement of competitive controls, 153–154; and bankers' associations in other countries, 349–351

Aufricht, Hans, 234n, 314n

Aymard, Philippe, 108n, 126, 140n, 155n, 184n, 192n, 196n, 202n, 206n

Aziende di credito, 7, 35, 340

Baffi, Paolo, 47n, 79n, 87n, 93n

Bain, Joe, 49n

Balogh, Thomas, 242n, 249n, 253n, 261n, 264n, 282n, 302n, 314n

Bambridge, Anthony, 270n

Banca (or banche), 11, 340

Bank credit, allocation of: influence of bank structure, 20–21, 82, 84; and moral suasion, 57, 81, 208, 210, 315–317; and state-owned companies, 81–82; and rediscount policy, 83, 208; and prior approval requirement, 208–209; and direct government intervention, 208–210; comparative controls on, 358

Bank credit, volume of: and rediscount mechanism, 76–77, 80, 201–204; and compulsory reserve requirements, 78–79, 204–206; and open market operations, 79, 207–208; and foreign exchange operations, 80; and moral suasion, 80, 323; and branch permits, 80; and rediscount ceilings (plafonds), 202–203; and plancher requirement, 204–206; and coefficient de tresorerie, 205–206; and general ceiling on bank lending, 206–207, 323; and minimum loan rate regulation, 203–204, 213; and banks' liquidity ratios, 317–318, 320–321; and special deposits, 319–320; comparative controls on, 358–359

Banking hours, 35, 268

Banking laws, England: Banking Act of 1826, 233; Banking Act of 1833, 233–234; Bank Charter Act of 1844, 234–235; Joint Stock Bank Act of 1844, 235; Banking Act of 1857, 235; Banking Act of 1858, 236; Companies Act of 1862, 236; Companies Act of 1879, 236; Bank of England Act of 1946, 313–314

Banking laws, France: Banking Law of 1941, 117–118, 136–138, 160;

379